S0-AVC-784

Anne Edwards

Road to Tara

The Life of Margaret Mitchell
Author of *Gone With the Wind*

"A meticulous biography . . . a sensitive portrait."
—*The Washington Post Book World*

"Sure-fire. . . . A rich narrative peopled with vivid characters full of drama. . . . It's hard to imagine this biography could be better done. . . . It is candid but sympathetic. One is quickly 'hooked.' *Road to Tara* is hard to put down." —*The Wall Street Journal*

"Ornery, loving, scared, proud . . . if that description reminds you more than a little of a fictional character named Scarlett O'Hara—well, read the book."
—*The Atlanta Journal and Constitution*

"A rousing good story." —*Richmond Times-Dispatch*

"A fascinating, page-flipping book that sheds new light on Miss Mitchell and the characters she created. . . . An exciting biography. . . . Keepers of the Mitchell flame will be pea-green with envy because they did not write it." —*The Chattanooga Times*

Books by Anne Edwards

Biography

Sonya: The Life of Countess Tolstoy
Vivien Leigh
Judy Garland
Road to Tara: The Life of Margaret Mitchell
A Remarkable Woman: A Biography of Katharine Hepburn

Novels

The Survivors
Miklos Alexandrovich Is Missing
Shadow of a Lion
Haunted Summer
The Hesitant Heart
Child of Night

Autobiography

The Inn and Us (with Stephen Citron)

QUANTITY SALES

Most Dell Books are available at special quantity discounts when purchased in bulk by corporations, organizations, and special-interest groups. Custom imprinting or excerpting can also be done to fit special needs. For details write: Dell Publishing Co., Inc., 1 Dag Hammarskjold Plaza, New York, NY 10017, Attn.: Special Sales Dept., or phone: (212) 605-3319.

INDIVIDUAL SALES

Are there any Dell Books you want but cannot find in your local stores? If so, you can order them directly from us. You can get any Dell book in print. Simply include the book's title, author, and ISBN number, if you have it, along with a check or money order (no cash can be accepted) for the full retail price plus 75¢ per copy to cover shipping and handling. Mail to: Dell Readers Service, Dept. FM, P.O. Box 1000, Pine Brook, NJ 07058.

Road to Tara

Anne Edwards

LAUREL

A LAUREL BOOK
Published by
Dell Publishing Co., Inc.
1 Dag Hammarskjold Plaza
New York, New York 10017

Copyright © 1983 by Anne Edwards

All rights reserved. No part of this book may be reproduced or transmit-
ted in any form or by any means, electronic or mechanical, including
photocopying, and recording, or by any information storage and retrieval
system, except as may be expressly permitted by the 1976 Copyright Act
or in writing by the publisher. For information address: Ticknor & Fields,
New Haven, Connecticut.

Laurel ® TM 674623, Dell Publishing Co., Inc.

ISBN: 0-440-37438-3

Reprinted by arrangement with Ticknor & Fields

Printed in the United States of America

May 1986

10 9 8 7 6 5 4 3 2 1

WFH

Contents

To S.C.

Preface

I DID NOT KNOW Margaret Mitchell personally, but, after a decade of involvement in her life and the writing of her one great novel, *Gone With the Wind*, I believe I know her better now than most of her friends did. My immersion in her work was not a quick, baptismal thing, but a step-by-step process led on by a curious set of circumstances that seem in retrospect to have been guided by fate.

Ten years ago, I began a biography of the English actress Vivien Leigh, who, among other great film performances, had portrayed Scarlett O'Hara, the heroine of *Gone With the Wind*. For the purposes of my research, I visited Atlanta, Georgia. Miss Leigh had attended the premiere of *Gone With the Wind* there in December, 1939, and I wanted to recreate with first-hand authority the excitement of that occasion. To do this, I had to evoke a clear picture of the city as it was at that time and, since perhaps no city in the United States has grown and prospered and changed as overwhelmingly in the intervening years as has Atlanta, this meant interviewing a large number of residents who had been involved in the premiere activities.

I learned quickly that *Gone With the Wind*, both the book and the film, had a special place in the hearts and lives of the people of Atlanta, as did their fellow Atlantan Margaret Mitchell, the author of this publishing phenomenon. It did not seem to me that even Thomas Wolfe was as closely aligned with his hometown of Asheville, North Carolina, which he fictionalized in *Look Homeward, Angel,* as Margaret Mitchell was with Atlanta. I made some fine friends during my short stay in the city. Upon my return home, I wrote asking them questions — not further inquiries about Vivien Leigh and the premiere of *Gone With the Wind,* but about Margaret Mitchell, who, although I did not realize it, had already captivated me with the aura of mystery, defiance, and drama that surrounded her extraordinary life and her tragic and dramatic early death.

One morning, when I was waiting for the galleys of my biography of Vivien Leigh, I received a call from my agent. He informed me that Richard Zanuck and David Brown, the producers of such films as *The Sting* and *Jaws,* had acquired the sequel rights to *Gone With the Wind* and were looking for a writer to develop the story. Would I be interested? Since I had just seen the film several times to evaluate Miss Leigh's performance in it for my book, the story and characters were fresh in my mind. I agreed to talk with David Brown in New York. A few days later, I was on a plane to California to speak with Richard Zanuck, and, by that weekend, I had been engaged to write "The Continuation of Gone With the Wind" — later to be called "Tara" — as a book which, if approved, would then be adapted for a screenplay.

That summer, my husband and I spent ten weeks traveling through the South. Then I settled in Atlanta for a time. I worked in the same libraries, and in one case with the same librarian, that Margaret Mitchell had over forty years earlier. Almost everywhere I went in search of my material, I encountered men and women who had met Miss Mitchell in the course of their work, or who had a story they had heard about the writing of *Gone With the Wind* or about Margaret Mitchell and her husband, John Marsh. By the time I left Atlanta, I knew the names of most of Miss Mitchell's close circle of family and friends and had met a number of them. I did not know it then, but my work on the life of Margaret Mitchell had already begun.

"Tara: The Continuation of Gone With the Wind" was completed and was approved by Richard Zanuck and David Brown in the fall of 1978. James Goldman was assigned to write the screenplay. Unfortunately, at this writing, the film has not yet come to fruition. I went on to write the biography of Sonya, Countess Tolstoy. It was not until the winter of 1979, when I returned to Atlanta to visit my newfound friends, that I began actual work on this book.

The destruction by fire of all of Margaret Mitchell's *Gone With the Wind* papers, unpublished manuscripts, and personal letters had been so well publicized that I feared an in-depth biography might be difficult. Margaret Mitchell, however, was a compulsive letter writer. She replied to something in the neighborhood of twenty thousand letters from admirers of her book (she did not like to use the word *fan*), and commented on, clarified, and argued points at length with her correspondents. It is impossible to calculate the extent of her personal correspondence, but with her good friends she did not let much time elapse between the receipt of a letter and her reply. From the time of the publication of *Gone With the Wind*, most of these letters were typed with a carbon. It was these carbons, as well as the letters that she received from her friends, that Margaret Mitchell's secretary and a janitor in her apartment house burned at the insistence of Margaret Mitchell's husband, John Marsh, and Stephens Mitchell, her brother. Letters were then written to Margaret's correspondents telling them that she had requested that all her papers be destroyed, and asking that they be kind enough to comply. This instruction was not included in her will, however, which was handwritten by her just nine months before her death.

Over the years, enough of Peggy Mitchell's personal papers had been shown to me to indicate that friends had not destroyed her letters. To her good friend Edwin Granberry, professor of English at Rollins College, she had written a warning not to destroy her letters, that they were her bequest to him. She was aware that they would one day be quite valuable. Yet, money had little to do with her friends' decisions not to sell or destroy Peggy's correspondence. These letters kept her alive to them. She wrote to her friends as she talked to them. And when Margaret Mitchell engaged anyone in conversation, she was a real spellbinder.

To those who knew Peggy Mitchell personally and shared their memories with me so that I could write this biography, I am deeply indebted. Never have I encountered such patience and careful recall as I did in the close friends of Peggy Mitchell. Almost everyone I contacted shared impressions and anecdotes. Some lent me their entire correspondence with Peggy. Others gave me photographs and memorabilia. Several key people in her life freely gave hundreds of painstaking interview hours and devoted additional time searching through their own personal archives and helping me ferret out the facts necessary for a truthful portrait.

In the course of the writing of the book, an extraordinary discovery was made: Macmillan's files on *Gone With the Wind*, previously thought to be lost, turned up in the riverside warehouse of the New York Public Library in four cardboard boxes, the contents yet to be inventoried. Inside were over a hundred manila envelopes filled with the editorial and publishing history of *Gone With the Wind*. There were all of John Marsh's editorial comments and Peggy Mitchell's changes in the manuscript, all of Macmillan's letters to the author of *Gone With the Wind*, along with contracts, interoffice memos, travel diaries, foreign rights agreements, correspondence, and publicity records. Not only had the collection never been catalogued, it had never been put into acetate containers, so telegrams, newspaper clippings and anything on yellow copy paper had almost turned to dust. But a valuable cache of letters and contracts and memos remained.

Of the many people who helped me to bring this intimate study of Margaret Mitchell to fruition, eight have contributed more bountifully than others: Frances Marsh Zane and C. Rollin Zane, Augusta Dearborn Edwards, Peggy Mitchell's lifelong friend; Richard Harwell, editor of *Margaret Mitchell's* Gone With the Wind *Letters, 1936–1949*; Andrew Sparks, of the *Atlanta Journal and Constitution*; Olive Ann Sparks; and Franklin Garrett, historian and former president of the Atlanta Historical Society. I am especially grateful to Frances Marsh Zane for her permission to include some of John Marsh's personal letters and photographs in this book, and to Stephens Mitchell for the right to quote from letters in the Margaret Mitchell Archives, University of Georgia.

I owe special thanks to George Walsh of Macmillan, who was responsible for helping me locate and preserve the Macmillan papers in the New York Public Library; to Jeremiah Kaplan, executive vice-president of Macmillan; to John Stinson, Rare Books and Manuscripts, New York Public Library; to J. Larry Gulley, Rare Books and Manuscripts, University of Georgia; and to Raleigh Bryans and Yolande Gwin of the *Atlanta Journal and Constitution*.

I am also indebted to many other people who have contributed meaningfully to this book: the Reverend D. L. Blacksheet (Mt. Pleasant Baptist Church, Atlanta), Professor Harold Blodgett, Philip Bolton, Miss Billie Bozone (Librarian, Smith College), Chris Bready, Mary Ellen Brooks, Katharine Brown, Russell A. Browne (Librarian, Dalton Jr. College), Erskine Caldwell, John K. Cameron, Mrs. Colquitt Carter, Mary Civille (the *Atlanta Constitution*), D. Louise Cook, Bill Corley, Malcolm Cowley, Scott M. Cutlep (Dean, University of Georgia), the late Frank Daniel, Howard Dietz, Lucinda Dietz, Thomas F. Dietz, P. K. Dixon, Mrs. Margaret Gaydos, David Hammond, Diane Haskell (Newbury Library), Larry Hughes (Publicity Director, Macmillan), Diane C. Hunter (Director of Library Services, *Atlanta Journal and Constitution*), Herbert Johnson (Director of Libraries, Emory University), Dorothy Kasica (Alumnae Association, Smith College), Maureen J. Kelly (Harvard Alumni Records Office), Senator Edward M. Kennedy, Helen Lane, Estelle Lantzy (Jonesboro Library, Clayton County), Sue Lindsley, Dr. Edwin Lochridge, Jr., Mrs. Helen Turman Markey, Mrs. Lethea Turman Lochridge, Linda Mathews (Special Collections, Emory University), Mrs. Colyne Cooper Miller, Fred B. Moore, Kathleen Morehouse, Fanny Neville-Rolse (Sotheby Parke Bernet), David M. Pelham, Deborah Perry (Atlanta Public Library), Miriam E. Phelps (Research Librarian, *Publishers Weekly*), Anne A. Salter (Assistant Archivist, Atlanta Historical Society), Mrs. Janice Sikes (Special Collections, Atlanta Public Library), Mrs. Patsy Slappey, M. M. "Mugsy" Smith, Jeff Stafford (Special Collections, University of Georgia), Marguerite Steedman, Mrs. Carlotta Tait, James Taylor (Rare Books and Manuscripts, University of Georgia), Lloyd Terrell, Mary B. Trott (Archivist, Smith College), Samuel Y. Tupper, Jr., Mrs. Marshall J. Wellborn, Robert Willingham (Special Collections, University of Georgia), Patsy Wiggans (Archivist, Atlanta Historical Society), Herschel Williams, Ms. Margie Williams (Librarian, Margaret Mitchell Library, Fayetteville, Georgia), J. Travis Wolfe, Mrs. Yates-Edwards (Atlanta Public Library), Maurice C. York (Curator, East Carolina Manuscript Collection, J. Y. Joyner Library), Lydia Zelaya (Macmillan), Edwin A. Zelnicker, Jr., and to the following who granted me permission to reprint letters, excerpts, and photographs: Macmillan, Inc., the University of Georgia, the Atlanta Historical Society, William Morrow & Company, Inc., the *Atlanta Journal and Constitution,* Sue Lindsley, Edwin Granberry, Richard Harwell, and the late Finis Farr.

I extend my deepest thanks to my publisher, Chester Kerr, and to my agent, Mitchell Douglas, and for the fine editorial help of Mary Cable, the superb copy-editing of Katrina Kenison, the early research assistance of Rosalie Berman, and the typing skills of Barbara Mitchell and Barbara Howland.

My greatest appreciation goes to my husband, Stephen Citron. His contribution at each stage of this biography is inestimable. He took time from his own demanding career in music to travel with me to Atlanta and many other American cities where I had to conduct interviews and seek research material, and he participated in both of these trying tasks. He read my various drafts with fresh comments each time, and he encouraged and supported me through the entire period of the writing of this book. *Road to Tara* is dedicated with love and gratitude to him.

Was Tara still standing? Or was it gone with the wind which had swept through Georgia? She laid the whip on the tired horse's back and tried to urge him on while the waggling wheels rocked them drunkenly from side to side.

— *Gone With the Wind*

Peggy Mitchell Marsh

Chapter One

As HE STEPPED off the train from Charleston into Atlanta's bustling depot, Harold Latham entertained doubts about the success of his trip. It was an unseasonably warm morning for April, and he stood blinking his owlish, bespectacled eyes in the dazzle of the hot sun. A large man with a peaked face and a stomach that protruded above his belt, the vice-president and editor in chief of the Macmillan Company still had a certain jauntiness about him. He wore a stiff-brimmed Panama at a rakish angle on his graying hair, and he carried a mono-grammed leather briefcase. He was annoyed that no representative from the local Macmillan office was there to meet him but he knew it was his own fault; he had taken an earlier train than his itinerary called for. To his further irritation, when he arrived by taxi at the Georgian Terrace Hotel on Peachtree Street, his suite was not yet ready.

To fill the time, Latham went for a walk. He was disappointed by what he saw. Atlanta had none of the old Southern charm of the other cities he had visited on this trip. Indeed, it looked much like any Northern city of around five hundred thousand inhabitants. Most of the buildings and homes he strolled past struck him as the worst examples of Victorian architecture. Peachtree Street, one of the more elegant boulevards, had no peach trees and had little more than its width and sporadic patches of green curbside planting to recommend it, although

3

there were large, old magnolia trees with dark, glossy green leaves in front of a few houses, serving as reminders that this was the deep South. Latham could not recall much of Atlanta's history, but he knew that the city had been nearly razed to the ground by Sherman's army in 1864, and that it had always been a railway terminus.

In fact, Atlanta had been called Terminus in the 1840s. Later it was known as an "over-seers' city" because a great part of its cosmopolitan population was made up of citizens sent South by national concerns to found bases for their Southern operations. Most of Atlanta's old families had made their money in real estate, by investing in their home product, Coca-Cola, or by taking advantage of the city's geographical position, which made it a communications and distribution center. It was a city that was constantly outgrowing itself, changing too rapidly to fit any conventional mold.

Latham had come South from New York to scout for manuscripts. It was 1935, and times were hard for most of the nation, but not for the publishing industry, which had nearly tripled its volume of sales since 1929. Books offered escape at an affordable price and, to fill the demand for them, publishers had been sending acquisitions editors to England to sign up British authors for American publication. Latham had been doing this for five years. Then, in 1934, to the industry's surprise, *Lamb in His Bosom,* a first novel by a Southern woman, Caroline Miller, had not only been a best-seller, but had won the Pulitzer Prize. Excited by the idea that Mrs. Miller's book might be the precursor of a trend, Latham went to Macmillan's president, George Brett, and told him that he would like to head South in his search for new writers.

In a young country scant on tradition and with few sagas of its own, tales of the vanquished South and its "lost cause" filled a hungry need for romance. For fifty years Southern writers had been creating a legend of the past in which, as one historian put it, "the great houses became greater, the lovely women lovelier, the chivalrous men more chivalrous, the happy darkies happier." But now, since the Crash, some of the new Southern novelists had begun to deal with their homeland in an iconoclastic, sometimes grotesque manner. Erskine Caldwell, for example, in *Tobacco Road*, made the illiterate Jeeter Lester family repulsive in their squalor. Latham did not think much of Caldwell's books, but their overwhelming success suggested to him that the book-buying public was fascinated by the South.

By the time Latham reached Atlanta, his hopes for discovering another Erskine Caldwell or Caroline Miller had dimmed. He had been to Richmond, Charlotte, and Charleston and he had not found one publishable manuscript. It was too late to turn to England for books to fill Macmillan's 1936 spring list; the competitive New York houses would already have signed up any worthwhile author. Once in his hotel rooms, Latham got on the telephone to his Atlanta office. To his disappointment, he learned that his representatives had no promising material to show him. Plans had been made, however, for him to meet as many young writers as he could during his forty-eight-hour stay.

In desperation, Latham rang Lois Dwight Cole, an editor in Macmillan's New York office who had formerly been their Atlanta representative. It had been two years since she had been in Atlanta, but he asked her if she recalled any promising writers in the city.

"Peggy Mitchell Marsh," Lois replied with some reluctance. "She has a manuscript she has been working on for years. She's told me it's about the Civil War and Reconstruction, but I haven't read it. No one has, except her husband, John Marsh."

Lois warned Latham that Peggy was a rare writer — one who did not seek publication — and that she might not welcome his inquiries. The previous year, Lois herself had written to Peggy asking her to submit her manuscript to Macmillan. Peggy had not only refused but had asked Lois not to discuss the book with anyone, as she had no intention of ever publishing it. Now Lois felt uneasy about betraying this confidence, but she had always had a hunch about her friend's novel. "If Peggy writes like she talks," Lois told Latham, "the book is bound to be spellbinding."

The best way to reach Mrs. Marsh, Lois suggested, would be through her old friend and fellow newspaperwoman, Medora Field Perkerson. Ten years ago, she explained, Peggy Marsh had been the star feature writer on the *Atlanta Journal Magazine*, and she and Medora Perkerson, wife of the magazine's editor in chief, had been colleagues there. Latham's spirits began to rise. By coincidence, Angus Perkerson was to host a luncheon in his honor that day. Latham lost no time in calling Mrs. Perkerson at her newspaper office, and he was extremely forthright about the reason behind his request that Mrs. Marsh be invited to join them for lunch.

"Peggy won't like it, but I'll try to arrange it," Medora said.

❧

Atlanta, along with most of the country, was deep in the Depression doldrums, but the dogwood in nearby Druid Hills was in extravagant white bloom and Peggy Mitchell Marsh was in high spirits after the luncheon. Pointing out landmarks along the way and chatting nonstop, she drove Harold Latham and Medora Perkerson out to see the unfinished monuments of the sixty-foot equestrian figures of three Confederate heroes that were to be carved high up into the side of Stone Mountain. Conversation about Confederate heroes was exactly the fuel that fired Peggy's enthusiasm.

This was Latham's first trip South, and most of the women he had met had seemed like hothouse flowers. But his small, vivacious guide — with her bobbed auburn hair, wide sailor-blue eyes, and a few bold freckles across the bridge of her impertinent nose — was of sturdier stuff. There was a strong contradiction in her appearance that was fascinating. She was certainly beautiful, and brimming with energy, but she had a way of looking rooted to the earth whenever she did stand still. It might have been the orthopedic shoes she wore, though Latham thought otherwise, for he had not even noticed them until rather late in the day. On first meeting Peggy Marsh, Latham had thought she must be no more than twenty years old, at least fifteen years younger than he now reckoned. Her size contributed to this false impression — she was under five feet tall — but there was also the youthful hairstyle held back with a demure bow, and the unguardedness of her expression. An aging bachelor, and a bit defensive about his unmarried state, Latham was always uncomfortable with women who played the femme fatale, and, at first, Peggy's natural flirtatiousness had caught him off guard. But her worldly sense of humor and ribald conversation were even more surprising.

Actually, Peggy was quite proud of her rebellious streak, and liked to think of herself as "a product of the Jazz Age, one of those short-haired, hard-boiled young women who preachers said would go to Hell or be hanged before they were thirty." However, she was now thirty-five and she had not gone to hell at all. In fact, she still captivated most people she met with her good humor, salty tongue, and feminine charm. That was the enigma of Peggy Mitchell Marsh; she was a curious mixture of emancipated woman and Southern belle. Within an hour, Latham had fallen completely under her spell.

Peggy drove her dented green Chevrolet at a slow, deliberate pace along the back roads that she knew so well. Chance, she thought, had her playing guide in the environs of a city that she considered as much a kin as any of her own family. Medora had rung her up only a few hours earlier to say that Angus had been called away at the last moment and could not host a luncheon the *Journal* was giving for Mr. Harold Latham of the Macmillan publishing company, and would Peggy be an absolute angel and step in and act as cohostess. Peggy, never able to refuse a friend in distress, agreed. Now, as she spoke entertainingly about the history of the giant stone sculpture, she was glad she had come along.

Peggy Mitchell Marsh had had no idea of Latham's motives until he confessed during the course of the luncheon that he had heard she had written a novel and that he would like to see it. "I have no novel," she had replied.

They had gone on to discuss well-known authors and their books, and had found that they had similar literary tastes. When Latham offered her a small commission if she would scout books in the Atlanta area for Macmillan, she had agreed.

Latham was not discouraged when she denied having written a novel herself, for the way she had avoided looking him straight in the eye as she said it had made him certain that she was lying. And he sensed that, for all her loquaciousness, Mrs. Marsh was not a woman who could easily tell a lie. He also found himself in agreement with Lois Cole; this fiery little woman was one of the best tale benders he had ever heard. She spoke with smooth, precise diction in a lilting Southern voice, talking rapidly and with much skill. Peggy Mitchell Marsh, he decided, enjoyed being a raconteur. She was downright funny, a woman who possessed a rare sense of humor, and, as she recounted the story of how, during her newspaper days, she had been tied into a boatswain's chair and suspended from a sixth-floor window so that she might share the sensations of the sculptor who had carved a head on the side of Stone Mountain, he was more anxious than ever to have a look at her manuscript.

"No sooner had I got the feel of solid floor under my feet," she told him, "but the photographer told me the slide in his camera had jammed and that he would have to reshoot. Well, I turned and faced him and stared right up into his eyes. 'If the fate of the whole Confederacy rested on my being hung six stories from the ground again,' I declared, 'Sherman would have to make another march to the sea!' "

When they were back in the car, Latham brought up the subject of her novel again, taking the chance of losing her good will. "I hate to press," he began, "but Lois Cole did say that you *indeed* had written a novel, and I would like very much to see the manuscript."

She glanced over at him, frowning, before starting the car. "I have to admit I have been working on a novel, but it's too early to talk about it."

"Well, can you at least tell me what it's about?"

"The South," she said.

"Like *Tobacco Road*? Any degenerates in it?" he prodded.

"No, but there are some pretty stubborn characters who refuse to accept defeat."

"Why haven't you submitted your book to anyone?" Latham asked.

"It's not ready, for one thing, and, for another, I don't think it will sell because it's about a woman who is in love with another woman's husband and they do nothing about it, and because there are only four Goddamns and one dirty word in it."

"Oh? Which one is that?" he said, smiling.

"Never mind."

"Well, I would like to see your manuscript anyway."

"As I told Lois, if I ever do finish the novel, I'll let Macmillan see it first."

❦

The next day was a perfect April morning, the sun soft and buttery, the scent of spring in the air. Peggy, having promised Mr. Latham and Medora that she would scrounge up all the young authors she knew and bring them that afternoon to a Georgia Writers' Club tea, spent the morning on the telephone. By the afternoon, as she wrote later, she had "jackassed" various and sundry hopefuls into the car "and gotten them to the tea where they could meet a live publisher in the flesh."

At the tea, Latham broached the subject of her book for the third time.

"Please don't talk about this. I really have no manuscript to show you," she insisted.

"Look here," he replied, "this is the strangest build-up I have ever encountered. You say you have no manuscript ready to show, yet you have all your friends rooting for you."

She glanced away and quickly changed the subject.

Twilight was drawing on when Peggy piled her charges into her car to drive them home. One of them asked when she planned to finish her book and why, as long as she was now scouting books for Macmillan, she hadn't given her own manuscript to Mr. Latham.

In the four years that she had written for the *Atlanta Journal*, Peggy had established a reputation as the magazine's star reporter. Even now, ten years after she had left the paper, she was still considered something of a celebrity and literary authority, and budding authors often sought her counsel. Now, a young woman who had lately been hounding Peggy for advice on a book she was writing cried out from the back seat, "Why, are *you* writing a book, Peggy? How strange you've never said anything about it! Why *didn't* you give it to Mr. Latham?"

"Because it's so lousy I'm ashamed of it," she replied.

"Well, I daresay, really! I wouldn't take you for the type who would write a successful novel!" the girl exclaimed.

Fury rose inside Peggy Mitchell's small-breasted chest. What did this child know about her life and what type she was, or about what she had been or experienced or suffered? She was certain that, if confronted with the truth, the girl would be too shocked to believe it. The irony of this turned Peggy's anger into indignant laughter. She laughed so hard that her foot hit the brake. The car stopped short.

"See!" the girl said, when the sudden jolt catapulted her forward. "That confirms my opinion. You lack the seriousness necessary to be a novelist."

The words made Peggy so mad that as soon as she had left her passengers at their destinations she tore home. She had been working sporadically on a novel since 1926, and the more than two thousand pages of it were stuffed into soiled manila envelopes stored wherever she had found space for them in her apartment. It was shortly after 6:00 P.M.; Latham had said he was leaving late that night. She rushed around the apartment without bothering to restore order. Some of the envelopes were stacked under a bath sheet on her sewing-table desk, the rest were in more curious hiding places. She had to squirm under the bed to drag out the sections dealing with the Reconstruction, and then balance herself on a tall stool to reach the top of the pot and pan closet for the antebellum chapters.

Once she had assembled what she thought was the entire manuscript, she recalled that there was no first chapter, or rather, that there were sixty first chapters, and that they were all terrible. So she sat down at her typewriter and rewrote the one she thought the best, starting it, however, on page three since she was too flustered to produce a whole new opening. She attached a note stating that she would write a two-page opening later. So many connecting links were missing between sections that she thought of the contents of the envelopes as "excerpts," and she wrote several other covering notes to help avoid confusion in the reading.

Not until Peggy was in the lobby of Harold Latham's hotel did she realize what she looked like — "hatless, hair flying, dust and dirt all over my face and arms, and worse luck, my hastily rolled up stockings coming down about my ankles," she later recalled. She had left the envelopes out in the car, but when she rang Latham in his room and he agreed to come downstairs, she ran back to fetch them, returning with her arm load just as he stepped out of the elevator. She was barely through the door when she began dropping envelopes, and by the time Latham reached her side there were already three bellboys picking them up behind her. Latham, fighting to keep a straight face, greeted her as though there was nothing at all odd in her appearance.

Finally, she made her way to a sofa and sat down, piling the envelopes beside her. Latham later said he would never forget the sight of that "tiny woman sitting on a divan, with the biggest manuscript beside her that I had ever seen, towering in two stacks almost to her shoulders."

"Well, can this be your book, Mrs. Marsh?" Latham inquired.

Peggy bounced to her feet, scooped up what envelopes she could hold in her arms, and handed them to Latham. "If you really want it you may take it, but it is incomplete and unrevised," she warned.

Latham lost no time in taking possession of the unwieldy manuscript. He was already packed and now had to buy a "please-don't-rain" cardboard suitcase from a bellboy. Peggy helped him stuff the envelopes inside it. Across the top of one was scrawled, "The Road to Tara."

"Tara?" Latham asked.

Tara, she explained, was her heroine's home. "The book is about what made some of our people able to come through a war, a reconstruction, and a complete wrecking of the social and economic system. They used to call that quality 'gumption.' "

"It's a Civil War novel then?" Latham asked.

"No," she replied, "It's about the people in the South during those times who had gumption and the people who didn't."

Peggy left Latham there in the lobby of the elegant Georgian Terrace Hotel, trying to lock the great mound of parcels inside his new case. The editor was already doubting his first hunch about Peggy Mitchell Marsh and her novel. From the stacks of envelopes and the weight of the makeshift valise, it was obvious that the book was of epic length, and fears of having "discovered" nothing more than a long, boring history of the Civil War set in. It was not until he had boarded his train for New Orleans and had opened the first envelope that he realized that this was also the worst-looking manuscript he had ever been given in his long career in publishing. After all his efforts to wrangle a look at it, he now considered not bothering to read the jumbled mess at all. When he arrived in New York he could simply return it with a note asking the author to submit a more organized manuscript. As it was, chapters were out of order and sometimes two or three versions of the same chapter were included in one envelope; whole pages were rendered incomprehensible by balloons and arrows and hen-scratch markings; inserts were placed on the backs of pages and not noted on the front. But Latham's curiosity — and his desperation — got the better of him.

He settled back in the plush green Pullman chair and began to read. And, like all future readers of this book, whose numbers were to be in the millions, Harold Latham was hooked.

Margaret Munnerlyn Mitchell

Chapter Two

ATLANTA WAS ONLY fifty-five years old when Margaret Munnerlyn Mitchell was born on Tuesday, November 8, 1900, the day William McKinley was reelected president. The city was an upstart when one considered that Savannah and Augusta had long since celebrated their centennials and that nearby Athens would soon have one. Margaret's ancestors had arrived in Georgia at different times. Her mother's family had immigrated to Charleston around 1685, after the Huguenot troubles in France, and had moved to Georgia after the Revolutionary War. Her father's people had come to North Carolina from Scotland with the Hector MacDonald Colony after the failure of the Stuart Uprising, and had moved to Georgia before the Revolutionary War. The two families' histories and the growth of Georgia as a state formed the basis of many of Margaret's nursery tales. But even at the age of three or four, it was stories about the history of Atlanta that she liked best.

Margaret was born in the home of her widowed maternal grandmother, Annie Fitzgerald Stephens, at 296 Cain Street. The house had miraculously escaped destruction on the night of November 15, 1864, when General William Tecumseh Sherman and the Union Army set fire to Atlanta before Sherman began his devastating March to the Sea. Grandmother Stephens would sit on the front porch with baby Margaret on her lap and point out where a line of Confederate entrench-

15

ments had passed through the back yard. Then she would describe to her that terrible night when "vast sheets of flame devoured the city and everywhere you looked, a strange indescribable glare lighted the sky." And how, by morning, every house of importance, the railroad depot, and the business section were in ashes.

Annie Stephens shared her home with her daughter, Maybelle, her son-in-law, Eugene Muse Mitchell, and her two grandchildren, Stephens Alexander and Margaret. Annie had moved to Atlanta in 1863, as a wartime bride, from the Fitzgerald plantation in nearby Jonesboro, in Clayton County. Her father, Philip Fitzgerald, who had come from Tipperary County, Ireland, as a young man, owned 2,375 acres and thirty-five slaves; and his good wife, Eleanor McGhan Fitzgerald, saw to it that every one of them was instructed and baptized in the Catholic faith. The Fitzgeralds, ardent believers, had endured much prejudice on behalf of their religion in Protestant Clayton County, but Philip gained a reputation for toughness and outspokenness, and was elected a senator in the state legislature.

Annie thought of her adopted city as home. She liked its youth and brashness, and felt she had a solid place in its beginnings. After the fire, there had begun a great exodus from Atlanta, as terrified families fled to Macon, their possessions piled high in open wagons. The bodies of thousands of soldiers were buried in shallow graves; rotting carcasses of horses and mules killed during the combat littered the recent battlefields around the city, which was itself a rubble heap.

Of Atlanta's more than four thousand buildings, only about four hundred still stood, and most of these had been damaged. Dogs that fleeing families had left behind lived amid the rubble and formed wolflike packs at night, baying in unison. Lean and hungry, they became increasingly vicious as the winter went on. But the many horrors did not discourage Annie and James Stephens, who remained to help raise Atlanta out of the ashes at the same time that they raised six daughters.

By the time Margaret was born, her Grandfather Stephens, a wholesale grocer and real-estate speculator, had been dead four years and Grandmother Stephens was fifty-six. Thirty-eight years after the burning of Atlanta, she still considered as newcomers those families who had moved to Atlanta after the fire, and she had no use for anyone who had run off to another city. A strong, civic-minded woman, she could, according to her granddaughter, "go to the mayor and city council and reduce them to jelly by a few well-chosen words concerning male shilly-shallying and inefficiency." With the help of some of her equally tough female contemporaries, Annie Fitzgerald Stephens managed to push through legislation even without the clout of a vote. Her daughter, Maybelle, was a firebrand in her own right, and by the time Margaret was two it had become obvious that her mother and grandmother could not live under one roof.

The Mitchell family moved to a small house owned by Grandmother Stephens around the corner, at 177 Jackson Street. A year later, Eugene Mitchell, whose law practice was prospering, bought a twelve-room, two-story Victorian house on a large lot just a few doors down, at 187 Jackson Street. This rambling, drafty house, set back among giant oaks and with a great sweep of lawn in front, was in an historic section of Atlanta, and on its northernmost boundaries one could still see the trenches from which the Confederates had fought the Battle of Atlanta. No longer the elite section of town, it was, however, old guard; the majority of the houses were still owned by the families who had built them.

Traditionally, most girls in the Stephens family were convent-educated. Margaret's mother had been packed off to an old Royalist Convent in Canada where, as Maybelle told her daughter, they "taught things as they were in the good old sixteenth century." Maybelle was a tiny woman with fly-away red hair, sharp blue eyes, and chiseled features. If her carriage had not been so proud and her figure so neat, she might have appeared to be dwarfed, for she stood no more than four feet, nine inches. Despite her diminutive size, the role of "the little woman" was not for her. Indeed, Maybelle was the mainspring of the Mitchell family, her mother's equal, and the president of one of Atlanta's most militant groups of suffragettes. At meetings, often held in the living room of the Mitchell house, she would stand on a stool in order to be seen and, in a style of oratory that had its roots in preachers' fiery sermons on hell and damnation, she would shout about the inequities forced upon women. Meanwhile, her wide-eyed children would watch surreptitiously from the top of the stairs.

The first time Margaret was permitted to stay up later than six o'clock was on the tremendous occasion of a suffragette rally that had as its guest speaker Carrie Chapman Catt, president of the National American Woman Suffrage Association. Mrs. Catt was world-famous, and Maybelle would not have considered missing her appearance in Atlanta. So, when the Mitchells' nursery girl took sick an hour before the rally, Maybelle tied a "Votes for Women" banner around Margaret's chubby middle, hissed a blood-curdling threat guaranteed to make her behave, and took her along to the meeting. From her spot on the platform between the silver pitcher and the water glasses, Margaret watched, entranced, as Maybelle made an impassioned speech.

Eugene Mitchell viewed his wife with awed respect. Only five feet, five inches himself, he did not find his short stature an obstacle in achieving most of his life's goals; his own limited vision had cut down the size and shape of them. He was in partnership with his brother, Gordon, in a successful law firm specializing in real estate and patents, an expertise not looked upon with great admiration by Maybelle, who had learned early that short people could become just as influential as tall ones — they just had to exert twice the energy.

Eugene Mitchell did not share his wife's Catholic faith, but, despite their religious differences, their marriage was solid, held together by mutual dependence. Maybelle seemed to possess the strength, the intuitive wisdom that he did not. Drawn to Maybelle because of her vigor and staunch purpose, reliant upon her drive, Eugene tacitly accepted her dedication to the Roman Catholic church and the suffrage movement. Husband and wife did, however, share a great loyalty to their family, Atlanta, and the South. A scholarly man, Eugene Mitchell found solace in reading and was an expert on the history of his city. He was also a clever businessman and used his legal knowledge to its fullest advantage in real-estate transactions and to protect his small financial investments. Perhaps Maybelle would have preferred to live more adventurously, but her husband was not a man to take chances.

Once the Mitchells had moved to Jackson Street, Margaret's life was more strictly ruled than it had been at her Grandmother Stephens's. Her mother's unyielding nature was difficult for the child to understand; nothing Margaret did appeared to please Maybelle, who was quick with the hairbrush whenever she thought her daughter was acting spoiled or ill-mannered. Stephens was a fair-haired, pug-nosed boy, short for his age. Margaret, five years younger, had to fight for his attention and admiration. This usually meant attempting feats even Stephens and his friends were too timid to try. During Margaret's childhood, there was no tree too tall to climb, no space too minuscule to squeeze through if she was called upon to try.

She loved her father dearly but, in those days, saw little of him. He was a soft-spoken man with dark, alert eyes and a mustache that he could twist about at the ends and that bristled against her cheek when he kissed her good-night. On weekends he was preoccupied with his books. He was then president of the Young Men's Library Association, and from 1900 to 1905 he served on the board of trustees of the newly built and funded Carnegie Library, devoting most of his free time to collecting and purchasing volumes on Georgia and Atlanta for the library's reference department.

The population of turn-of-the-century Atlanta had trebled in a little over two decades to nearly ninety thousand. Since it had been almost entirely rebuilt in the 1870s, the city appeared newer than most Southern towns. Jackson Hill, the section where the Mitchells lived, looked across open pastures where livestock grazed, to the business district with its tall, recently built bank and insurance buildings.

There was a large vacant lot halfway down Jackson Street, where the Mitchells pastured a Jersey cow. Tuberculosis had been a scourge in the Mitchell family for generations, and Maybelle supported a new theory that the rich cream off the milk of this breed of cow would prevent the white plague. Stephens's pony, a Texas mustang, was also let loose to roam in this field. Maybelle had given him the animal for his eighth birthday, declaring that every man ought to learn to ride a horse by the time he was eight.

Margaret greatly envied her brother's new acquisition but, as she was only three, her parents refused to allow her even to be seated on the back of such a spirited animal. She had strict orders to stay on the veranda while Stephens and his young friends rode the mustang up and down the road in front of the house. One windy day she stood watching them for hours, until she became chilled through. To warm herself, she ran inside and stood over an open heating grate. Unknown to the household, a fire had started in the basement, and now a sudden draft sent flames up from beneath her, setting her skirts afire. Margaret's terrified screams brought Maybelle running from a nearby room. Shouting for help, she scurried for blankets to wrap about the hysterical child in order to smother the flames. The servants doused the fire with buckets of water while Maybelle carried her bundled daughter out to the buggy and set off for the hospital — all in a matter of minutes. Maybelle's quick thinking was no doubt responsible for the fact that, though Margaret suffered serious burns on her legs, she was left with few scars.

For weeks the little girl was bedridden, tended by Maybelle and entertained by Grandmother Stephens with stories of her own childhood. When she was allowed up, bandages still swathed her legs, and Maybelle dressed her in Stephens's old pants to conceal them. Later, after the bandages were removed, Maybelle insisted on keeping her in boys' clothes to avoid the occurrence of another such accident. This boys' attire was a source of great embarrassment to Margaret. Neighbors called her "Jimmy," after a fancied resemblance to a character in a contemporary comic strip, and she was taunted by the other children on the block. The trousers set her apart from the neighborhood girls but, at the same time, they made her company more acceptable to her brother and his peers. Now Stephens even allowed her to feed the animals with him, the Mitchells' menagerie having increased lately to include several ducks, two small alligators, a collie, and a number of cats. There were, Margaret learned, great advantages to illness and to being "different"; it was a lesson that she would never forget.

April 26 was then a major holiday commemorating Atlanta's Confederate dead. The first time Maybelle took Margaret to the parade that marked the occasion, she was four years old and tiny for her age. She stood beside Stephens on tiptoe, craning to see, asking questions and being told she must be very quiet or she would have to leave. Instinctively, she knew this was not like any other parade.

Georgians had come from every corner of the state, and the town swarmed with people. "It was like an ancient tribal gathering," Stephens recalls. "Everyone, from old men on canes down to the perambulators, was there lining Peachtree Street." It was a somber crowd, and faces were strained with checked emotion. There were no balloons, shouts, or cheers, as at other parades. First came a band playing Confederate songs; then the artillery and artillerymen sitting on the caissons, their arms crossed; then the infantry and cavalry. As they marched by, people would shout, "Hello, Bill!" and "Hello, Joe!" But when the band stopped playing, a sudden hush swept through the spectators. No one moved as marchers held high a great mass of blood-red flags emblazoned with white stars. Shuffling along behind was a long line of old men, survivors of the great war. These were Atlanta's soldiers, the men who had fought *their* cause, and tears flowed down many cheeks. It was 1904, forty years after the Battle of Atlanta, but the town was still Confederate at heart, and the people who stood crying at the sight of the soldiers who had come home were mourning the loss of their nation.

After the parade, Maybelle took the children to the post office to see the U.S. flag, the only one in town and so different from the flag of the Confederacy. Maybelle stood there with them in solemn silence, her head bowed, her grip so taut that her nails cut into the children's palms. This was conquered territory and they were a conquered people, and the children could feel it. Never would they get it out of their bones.

Like her mother and her Grandmother Stephens, Margaret felt a strong bond with Atlanta. From her cradle days she had heard her parents talking so often about the fighting and hard times of the Civil War that she assumed that they had been through it all themselves. It was not until years later that she learned the war had not ended shortly before her birth.

Indeed, the early years of Margaret's life were heavily influenced by a war fought four decades earlier. She was taught the names of battles along with the alphabet, and Maybelle's lullabies were doleful Civil War songs. Maybelle was completely tone deaf, but her voice rose and fell in mournful cadences, and the small child clutched her pillow to her in fear as she stared up at her mother's tear-stained face in the dimly lit room. And after Maybelle left, turning out the gas lamp as she went, Margaret would lie awake in the darkness, unable to sleep as the images in her mother's songs seemed to materialize in the shadows.

> Into a ward of whitewashed walls
> Where the dead and dying lay —
> Wounded with bayonets, shells and balls —
> Somebody's darling was borne one day . . .

At the age of five, Margaret knew all the stanzas of this song by heart, along with a half dozen similarly depressing ones sung by her mother as lullabies. Her education concerning the harrowing days of the Civil War did not end there, however. Sunday afternoons, arrayed in her best clothes (usually a dress made by Grandmother Stephens), she was taken to call on elderly relatives, and if she sat quietly and listened to the Battle of Gettysburg and the Valley Campaign without interrupting, her reward was an invitation from an obliging veteran to put her two thumbs into the two dents in his skull where a minié ball had gone in and out.

Often, as she later recalled, she would be "scooped up into a lap, told that [she] didn't look like a soul on either side of the family, and then forgotten for the rest of the afternoon while the gathering spiritedly refought the Civil War." An impressionable, sensitive child reared to believe children should be seen and not heard, she bore the discomfort of these afternoons in respectful silence as she sat "on bony knees, fat, slick taffeta laps, and soft, flowered muslin laps," not daring to wriggle for fear "of getting the flat side of a hairbrush where it would do the most good."

"Cavalry knees," she said, "were the worst knees of all. Cavalry knees had the tendency to trot and bounce and bob in the midst of reminiscences and kept me from going to sleep."

During these Sunday excursions she heard about battle wounds and the primitive way they were treated, how ladies nursed in hospitals, the way gangrene smelled, what measures were taken when the blockade got too tight for drugs and food and clothing had to be brought in from abroad. She heard about the burning and looting of Atlanta and the way the refugees from the town had crowded the roads and the trains to Macon. And how her Grandfather Mitchell had walked nearly fifty miles after the Battle of Sharpsburg with two bullet wounds in his skull. She heard about Reconstruction, too. In fact, she heard all there was to hear about the Civil War except that the Confederates had lost it.

None of these happenings were discussed as having occurred forty years earlier, or even as particularly remarkable events; they were just a part of her family's lives. Gradually they became part of Margaret's life as well, so much a part that she grew to feel she must have experienced some of the most vivid of them.

Each old-timer repeated how "terribly important little Atlanta was to the Confederacy." Margaret felt great pride in this knowledge and paid special attention to stories about *her* city. At five, she knew all the industries that had sprung up in Atlanta during the war and could rattle them off like the ABCs: "pistol factories, percussion-cap factories, tanneries and boot makers, saddle and harness factories, machine-manufacturing shops, iron-rolling mills where the armor plate for warships was turned out, iron rails for the railroad tracks, wagon shops, hat and cap factories." She appointed herself chief storyteller to her brother and his friends and would inform them how Atlanta, because of its safe position behind the lines, had been admirable for base-hospital purposes, and she would recount in grizzly detail the horrors of the wounded, sick, and maimed who passed through the city during the war. Such stories were as much a part of Margaret Munnerlyn Mitchell's childhood as *The Adventures of Huckleberry Finn* or *Rebecca of Sunnybrook Farm* were of other children's. At one Sunday gathering when she was four, she was asked to recite the poem "I'm a Good Old Rebel and That's What I Am." It never struck her as odd.

Young Atlanta had risen to the Confederacy's needs; it was a great and brave city. And, whereas Margaret never felt quite a true child of Maybelle's — whom she considered to be all the things she was not: blessed by God, adored by Eugene Mitchell, and revered by most people who crossed their threshold — she did consider her relationship with Atlanta, whose history had formed her earliest impressions, to be deep and binding.

Chapter Three

WHEN SHE WAS FIVE, Margaret's father bought her a small roan plains pony, which she lost no time in learning to master. She sat erect with pride in the saddle, riding with good hands and a long stirrup as she loped down the newly paved street that passed their front door. After a great deal of fuss and argument — her mother thought her too young — Eugene Mitchell set up jumping bars in the field, but the pony balked and, to her great disappointment, Margaret was ordered to abandon the sport.

Instead, every afternoon she would go riding with an old Confederate veteran whom she later called her "boon companion." The grizzled vet had long silver hair and a white goatee, wore a jimswinger coat, and won Margaret's heart by gallantly kissing her grubby childish hand. The two of them would head out to the country dirt roads, where they would invariably pick up another veteran or two and form a military line. The Confederates' families and Maybelle encouraged these afternoons in the mistaken belief that the child and the old-timers would keep each other out of mischief.

A day seldom passed when the old boys did not have a heated argument about the Civil War. As far as Margaret was concerned, these quarrelsome vets were ideal company. Proud to be considered one of the gang, she still wore Stephens's outgrown pants, tucked her pigtails under a boy's cap, and sat a horse like a midget sergeant major. No quarter was given because of her extreme youth. She was expected to keep up with the company as a rookie and to hold her tongue and, although she delighted in her friends' salty language, she remained an admiring though silent observer, fearful that any impropriety on her part could bring the outings to an end. Anyway, as she said afterwards, "It would have taken the lungs of the bull of Bashan to be heard above their tumult." Eyes wide, horrified and amused by turns, she listened closely to these quarrels encompassing a myriad of subjects, each old soldier bragging about his own regiment in the Confederate Army and spewing invective on all the others. Margaret cherished every minute of these excursions and was sad and resentful when she had to give them up in order to attend school.

Returning from her first day at North Boulevard School, Margaret told her mother that she hated arithmetic and did not want to go back. Maybelle's response was to bare her daughter's rear and give her a good whacking with a hairbrush. When she was done, she ordered Margaret into the Mitchells' stylish horse-drawn carriage, took the reins herself, and drove out toward Clayton County and the Fitzgerald farm at such a clip that Margaret gripped the seat in fear. Maybelle drove in silence as she followed the railroad tracks onto the Jonesboro road, where gnarled, ancient oaks now cast late-afternoon shadows. An unearthly stillness seemed to have settled over the countryside and, as the red sun slipped behind the hills, the tall pines that grew on their slopes became dark skeletal giants. Margaret, sensing the significance of this excursion, glanced at her mother in the shadowing red-rimmed twilight. Maybelle's eyes glinted with fierce emotion.

"Fine and wealthy people once lived in those houses," she told the child, slowing the horses and pointing at the shabby former plantation houses that they passed. "Now they are old ruins and some of them have been that way since Sherman marched through. Some fell to pieces when the families in them fell to pieces. See that one there?" she said as they passed a derelict farmstead. "The people who lived in that house were ruined with it."

She wheeled the trembling child around to look toward the

opposite side of the road and motioned to an old but well-tended dwelling. "Now, those folk stood as staunchly as their house did. You remember that, child — that the world those people lived in was a secure world, just like yours is now. But theirs exploded right from underneath them. Your world will do that to you one day, too, and God help you, child, if you don't have some weapon to meet that new world. *Education!*" Maybelle bellowed in a voice that cut the silence of the country twilight. "People — and especially women — might as well consider they are lost without an education, both classical and practical. For all you're going to be left with after your world upends will be what you do with your hands and what you have in your head. You will go back to school tomorrow," she ended harshly, "and you will conquer arithmetic."

And with that, she let go of her daughter, grasped the reins, and, turning around, cracked the buggy whip and started swiftly and silently on the long ride home.

❧

Many of Margaret's childhood summers were spent at "Rural Home," the Jonesboro farm of her spinster Fitzgerald aunts, Sis and Mamie. Margaret was especially fond of her Aunt Sis who, even in later middle age, was a beautiful woman with waving gray hair, large soft eyes, fair magnolia skin, and a winning silvery laugh. Best of all, she told her young niece stories about the Fitzgerald family history with great flair. Aunt Sis, as faithful a Catholic as the rest of the Fitzgeralds, would repeat over and over what prejudice there had been toward "our holy religion" from the earliest settlement in Georgia. And, of course, she also told stories of what had happened when Sherman's army had marched through Jonesboro, raiding so many of the homes; how the Fitzgerald house had been spared, but how the farm had been destroyed; and how Philip Fitzgerald, then a man of sixty-five years of age, took up "the remnants of his large property and began all over again with no slaves, no food, and only three of his daughters and an ailing wife at home to help with the work."

Aunt Sis was fond of explaining, "There was just two kinds of people, wheat people and buckwheat people. Take wheat —

when it's ripe and a strong wind comes along, it's laid flat on the ground and it never rises again. But buckwheat yields to the wind, is flattened, but when the wind passes, it rises up just as straight as ever. Wheat people can't stand a wind; buckwheat people can."

The Fitzgeralds had that instinct for survival that Maybelle so respected. They had survived the war and had become stronger people through their trial.

Margaret could sit at Aunt Sis's feet for hours listening to her recreate the terror of living in a town suddenly full of freed slaves, Yankee troops, and recently paroled Confederate soldiers. According to Aunt Sis, "Annie, visiting from Atlanta, had the spunk in the family" and had marched "straight through federal camp and the headquarters of General Wilson and requested a guard of Union soldiers to protect the Fitzgerald house — and got it."

Sepia photographs of the Fitzgerald family were lined up on the dark mahogany library table in the seldom-used front parlor, and there Margaret was introduced to all her Fitzgerald ancestors: her thick-set, Irish great-grandfather, Philip; her delicate, fair-haired great-grandmother, Eleanor McGhan; and Uncle James, Philip's brother, the fiery schoolteacher who had perhaps encountered more prejudice than any other Fitzgerald because he had brought his ardent Catholicism into his schoolroom. There were photographs of her mother as an appealing girl, looking younger than the years Aunt Sis ascribed to her as she told Margaret how Maybelle had spent summers at Rural Home, just as Margaret was doing, and how Philip Fitzgerald would take the frail girl, who had been "weakly as a child," up onto his horse with him, where she would sit in front of him "hangin' on for her own small life," her short skirts billowing scandalously in the wind as they rode about the county visiting disapproving neighbors.

The Fitzgerald farm was plain compared to the much grander neighboring plantations. There was Stately Oaks, owned by the McCords, on the Atlanta Public Road, where Union troops had camped on the grounds. The old Johnson House, with its eight imposing white columns in front, had been used during the war, both as a Confederate commissary and then as a hospital for wounded soldiers. Stories of the Warren House, which had been the headquarters of the Fifty-second Illinois Regiment, were retold in stiff, uncompromising tones. Sherman had spared the Warren place, and, after the war, old man Warren, suspected of Northern sympathies, had been labeled a Yankee and run out of town. The bullets in Warren's walls and the cannonballs in his yard did not allay local bitterness toward him, a bitterness that Aunt Sis still nurtured.

Margaret liked the Crawford House best. Six fluted Doric columns graced the broad porches and supported the long second-floor balcony. The house was the scene of lavish parties and barbecues and, there, it was not difficult for Margaret to transport herself back to the early days in Clayton County.

The young girl took refuge in these vivid imaginings; indeed, the past was the most satisfying thing in her life. Never happy in school, she made few friends. At home, she felt she did everything wrong; she doubted her mother's love and was fearful of losing her father's. So, she fantasized about living in the past, and made up little stories and plays in which she was the heroine in Yankee attacks — and many of the stories she made up were based on those told by Jonesboro survivors of the war.

Jonesboro had been a busy railroad junction in the 1860s, and when the Atlanta Campaign dragged on, prolonged by Hood's doggedness, Sherman had changed his strategy. He moved the bulk of his armies to the south, cut the Confederate supply lines, and then moved north again to Jonesboro to destroy the railroads before his final attack on Atlanta. Hood's orders to General Hardee — in charge of troops in Jonesboro on Wednesday morning, August 31, 1864 — were to "hold against the Union forces at all costs." By evening Jonesboro was battered, a smoking ruin. According to one account, dead were "heaped like so much cordwood in the pinewoods" for a quarter mile above the courthouse, near the railroad tracks, which were now a twisted mass of steel. When the battle was over, the Fitzgerald farm stood raped and silent, its fields stripped, its slaves and animals gone, the house emptied of most valuables. But Eleanor Fitzgerald's dark velvet drapes still hung defiantly at the windows, and her few small personal treasures, including her sacred gold cross, were buried under the pig house in an old tea caddy. This story was told to Margaret so often by her aunts that she was to remember the statistics of the dead and the exact details of the attack twenty years later with infallible accuracy.

Cotton had been the source of economic salvation in those days, and, at the Fitzgerald farm in the rolling foothills of north Georgia, cotton was still the main crop while Margaret was growing up. The red Georgia clay, "blood-colored after rains, brick dust in droughts," was generally considered "the best cotton land in the world." When Margaret was ten, she nurtured vague fantasies of living on a cotton plantation, and she decided to spend the summer of 1911 at Rural Home helping the Fitzgerald field hands pick cotton, a choice frowned upon even by her country kin. It was almost unendurable work, but she refused to quit, laboring beneath a blistering sun, her back aching, her hands bleeding. It was a summer that was to have a great impact upon her life. Although she stuck it out, at the end, she turned away forever from the land. And, from the blacks in the field, she learned for the first time — and to her shocked disbelief — that the South had not won the war.

By the time Margaret was ten, her coppery hair had turned to deep auburn; her eyes, to an indigo blue. But what gave her a unique beauty was the extreme liveliness of her expression. She talked incessantly and with vivacity. Her parents called her "Chatterbox" and found it fitting that the magazine she bought out of her small allowance each month was so named. Maybelle, with high hopes, replaced Margaret's pants with skirts and sent her to various dance classes, but these efforts on Maybelle's part did not erase Margaret's tomboy image — her walk was boyish, and with her capable, strong hands she could shinny up a tree as fast as any of her brother's friends. She loved the excitement of baseball and was accepted on the neighborhood all-boy baseball team as pitcher, a position she retained until she was fourteen years old. Mudball battles were another great sport. Dressed in the raggediest, skimpiest clothes possible, Margaret would be there on the ready, crouching behind the big girders on neighborhood building sites and passing mudballs to the larger boys in front.

At the northeast corner of the Mitchell land, looking down over the entire city of Atlanta, was a giant pine tree that must have survived the Civil *and* Revolutionary wars. Margaret and Stephens built a treetop platform in it, complete with an elevator with a basket carriage in which they would pull up the family's feline pets.

All this boyish behavior did not dislodge the feminine and romantic notions of the ten-year-old girl. On days when the weather kept her indoors, she would read for hours — not the books Maybelle wanted her to read, "the classics and perennials" as they were called, but fairy tales and Victorian novels that she would check out when her father took her with him to Carnegie Library. She wrote stories as well, using small squares of paper that she would pencil line herself and tie together with bright ends of yarn. One, entitled "The Knight and the Lady," was written in a wavering, lopsided script and with numerous misspellings. In it, good overcomes evil and the "beautiful lady" marries the "good knight" after he impales the "wild, rough knight."

These romantic tales were abandoned when Margaret began collecting book series such as the Rover Boys. Stephens told her that the plots were always the same and that the style was terrible, but she would answer in defense of the books that a good plot would stand retelling, and that the story, not style, was what mattered. And thus, ignoring his disdain, she began to write tales of bandits and frontiersmen, and heroines (usually named Margaret) threatened by imminent danger but bravely overcoming it. Penciled in a large, childish scrawl, these stories filled lined school tablets and were filed away in two rusty breadboxes that Maybelle had discarded.

A story entitled "The Little Pioneers," dated January 31, 1910 (she was nine), and written in a slightly steadier script than her previous literary efforts, ends:

In the night Margaret was awakened by shrieks and yells mingled with shouts of defiance from the garrison. Quickly slipping on he[r] clothes she hurried out only to start back at the scene which lay before her. Many men lay, either wounded or dead on the ground while the air was thick with smoke and shots whistled through the air. As the sun arose all could be plainly seen: the band of Apaches were, in the usual way, galloping around the fort, and firing. Every little while one, bolder than the rest, would clamber over the stockage, only to be shot or beaten back by the brave defenders whose rank were steadily thinning out.

She left her readers to wonder what happened to poor Margaret, but her story-telling talents were already apparent.

To her brother's and her male cousins' terrified delight, Margaret also spun spooky ghost tales. And she wrote short skits, which were performed in the Mitchells' parlor in full costume and in which Margaret almost always cast herself as the hero. The often violent plots of these plays and tales did not sit well with the Mitchells, who were, in most respects, an old-fashioned family despite Maybelle's emancipated views on women's rights. Among the books that were forbidden in the Mitchell house as immoral were *Tom Jones* and *Don Juan*. However, Maybelle believed that a girl was not well educated unless she had read the classics, providing they were the ones that, according to Stephens, "contained depravities of a more orthodox type, like the seduction of Little Emily in *David Copperfield*." Margaret managed to read the novels of Sir Walter Scott and Charles Dickens by the time she was twelve, but only in exchange for bribes of five, ten, and fifteen cents from her father. And she preferred having "the hide beat off of" her to reading Tolstoy, Thackeray, or Jane Austen.

Most of the spankings Margaret endured were for infractions of one of her parents' own personal beliefs rather than for the mischievous things for which young children are usually chastened, and, generally, it was her mother who was the disciplinarian.

One time when Maybelle was away and Eugene Mitchell was left in charge of the children, Margaret dramatized Thomas Dixon's book *The Traitor*, which, together with his *The Clansman*, was later adapted into the film *The Birth of a Nation*. Eugene was at his office when Margaret directed her drama, playing the lead part of Steve because none of the little boys in the neighborhood would condescend to play any part that involved kissing a girl. The production took place in the Mitchell sitting room, and the young clansmen performed in their fathers' shirts with the shirttails cut off at the knees. Margaret wrote Mr. Dixon years later:

> I had my troubles with the clansmen as, after Act 2, they went on strike, demanding a ten cent wage instead of a five cent one. Then, too, just as I was about to be hanged, two of the clansmen had to go to the bathroom, necessitating a dreadful stage wait which made the audience scream with delight, but which mortified me intensely. . . . On (my mother's) return, she and my father . . . gave me a long lecture on infringement of copy-rights. . . . For years afterward I expected Mr. Thomas Dixon to sue me for a million dollars.

Not only did Eugene scold her harshly, he also gave her quite a spanking, so that, as Margaret went on to explain, "I would never forget I must not take what wasn't mine," and that "plagiarism was exactly the same as stealing."

As a patent and real-estate lawyer, Eugene Mitchell's reputation had been built on protecting his clients' patent rights and deeds. Plagiarism was a new word to the small girl, but it was a word that she took seriously for the rest of her life. And, not only did one not plagiarize, one did not allow others to plagiarize one's own work.

Margaret's efforts as a playwright and author were not encouraged by her mother. To Maybelle, who had great respect for scientific achievement and who relaxed with problems in calculus and trigonometry while other women embroidered, Margaret's plays and stories were fancies that fed a lazy mind; she considered the time Margaret devoted to them a shameful waste. If a girl wanted to make something worthwhile of her life, she had to master math and Latin and science. Maybelle followed the career of Madame Curie with awe, and she never forgave herself for not going to college and realizing her own youthful dream of becoming a scientist. As for Margaret, she was well aware of her mother's hopes for her, and she was desperate to gain Maybelle's approval. So, despite the obvious pleasure she took in writing, whenever anyone asked her what she wanted to be when she grew up, Margaret always replied, "A doctor."

This admirable goal somewhat mitigated Maybelle's displeasure over Margaret's casual attitude toward the Catholic church. The girl never went to mass and said her prayers only when prodded. Maybelle attributed this lapse to Margaret's "scientific mind," and by the time her daughter was eleven Maybelle was discussing with her the grand future she would have as one of America's few woman physicians.

Still, there was a certain remoteness between mother and daughter. Margaret was of such a secretive nature that once, in a pique, Maybelle accused her of taking after an uncle of Eugene Mitchell's who would walk a mile out of his way rather than let a neighbor know in which direction he was going.

Jackson Hill, the neighborhood where the Mitchells' house stood, had always been a suburban development. It was a solid middle-class section, but it did not have the fame nor the éclat of Peachtree Street. By 1911, Eugene Mitchell was president of the Atlanta Bar Association and of the Board of Education, and a man of means. Nothing would do but to move his family to a more prestigious neighborhood. Maybelle, who wanted the best for her family, agreed, and he purchased a large lot in the center of one of Peachtree Street's loveliest blocks.

With the approaching change of residence, Eugene traded the children's ponies for a larger animal, a pedigreed horse that they named Bucephalus, after Alexander the Great's famous mount. Margaret was thrilled; horseback riding remained her favorite sport. It did not take her long to learn how to handle the huge black horse and, having done that, she could barely wait to see how fast he could gallop. Stephens now had little interest in riding but, during the first weeks of ownership, Margaret was out with Bucephalus for hours every day, racing him lickety-split up and down the hill, whooping and hollering as she tore at a great gallop past the house. She was still so small in stature that even riding as erectly as she did, she looked ridiculously tiny astride the giant of a horse.

One sunny day, while Stephens and her cousins stood admiringly on the curbside, Margaret let out a great whoop and, tearing past them, shouted, "Watch me turn him 'round!" She pulled Bucephalus into a sharp turnabout, but the horse lost his footing and careened to the ground with Margaret beneath him, screaming in terror. When the boys reached her, she was lying unconscious on her left side, her left leg oozing blood and badly crushed, and Bucephalus was running wild in the tall grass of the open field.

Chapter Four

DESPITE MARGARET'S desperate pleas, Bucephalus was sold during the months of her recuperation. She was further distressed by the edict that she must never again attempt to ride a horse. With Stephens in school most of the day and Maybelle engaged in her suffrage activities, Margaret was forced to entertain herself during the long convalescence that followed the leg surgery she had undergone. With her mother's prodding, she began in earnest to read the books in the family's extensive library.

Leathered volumes of Byron, Burns, Scott, Thackeray, Dickens, and Tolstoy shared shelves with the well-read Civil War books. Maybelle renewed her efforts on behalf of *War and Peace*, but the book defeated Margaret. "Tolstoy and most of the Russian writers were the damned dullest, most muddled headed, confused bunch," she later declared. But to Maybelle, or anyone else who asked if she had read *War and Peace*, she lied outright. In fact, in her adolescence, she would talk knowingly and at length about the book to Maybelle's visitors, having never read more than the opening chapter.

Though her leg injuries healed far more favorably than the doctor had expected, Margaret was left with a slight limp. Most athletic activities were curtailed, but she returned to her dancing lessons in order to strengthen the weakened muscles.

Eugene Mitchell promised the family a vacation in New York

35

that summer, while the construction of their new house was being completed, and Margaret looked forward to the trip with great enthusiasm.

The family left home in June, boarding a steamship out of Savannah. To her relief, Margaret was not seasick. She roamed the decks with her father during the day and in the evening waltzed with him in the ship's lounge to the new "Dream of Heaven Waltz." Her leg injury had not made her dancing awkward, and Maybelle finally had reason to believe that her daughter might turn into a lady after all.

New York, with its milling crowds and skyscrapers, was fascinating. Yet, Margaret felt overwhelmed, too. People found her Southern accent amusing, and absolute strangers would comment about it in restaurants and stores. The Mitchells visited Maybelle's sister, Edyth Ney Morris, in Greenwich, Connecticut, and took the day-long Hudson River boat trip to Albany and back. Then, to Margaret's disappointment, Stephens and her father remained in New York City while Margaret was dispatched with her mother to the Milk Cure, a health farm in New Jersey. She found it boring, but she returned to Atlanta in August, 1912, looking rosy-cheeked and robust, and she was able to join spiritedly in the move from Jackson Hill to the Mitchells' new house.

Though Peachtree Street was considered a fashionable address, the stretch of road that went past the house was still packed dirt, like most of Atlanta's streets. But the new house was grand enough to be called a mansion, and the first time Margaret set eyes upon the great, dignified white facade, so unlike the other houses on Peachtree Street, most of which were Victorian, she was stunned, and more than a bit uncomfortable. With two-story Doric columns in the front, it was a fine example of classical revival architecture, a style popular in the South long before the Civil War and revived at the turn of the century. A few of the ruined and deserted plantation houses in Clayton County were of the same design. The Mitchell's new neighbors considered the house gauche — it was one thing to live in a monumental Greek revival house that had been built in the first half of the nineteenth century, quite another to build a new one.

Her parents may have been paying their respects to the past with this imposing structure, but all Margaret knew was that the house looked strange and awkward on its small city lot; it did not seem to belong on Peachtree Street any more than she did. Nor was she pleased by the manicured landscaping in this section of town, although there were some wooded areas and a small park across the road. She sensed that life was going to be necessarily different on Peachtree Street, and change did not sit well with her.

The interior of the house was even more impressive than the outside. One entered into a large central hall with a sitting room to the left and a music room to the right and, when the walnut doors were flung back, the length of the three combined spaces stretched for seventy feet. This mansion, with its carved mantels and high ceilings and a grand staircase that demanded a queenly descent, was no place for the tomboy who had raced through the more comfortable old Victorian house on Jackson Street to the shuddering claps of slamming doors. A glance at the finely dressed and well-mannered neighborhood children told her that they might be very nice indeed, but that they would never understand a girl of eleven who, despite her mother's efforts, still enjoyed wearing pants and throwing mudballs.

Not only was Margaret in a new house, two trolley-car rides from her old neighborhood, but she was enrolled in a new school. Like the house, the Tenth Street School seemed enormous to the girl, and she made few friends. She was now a part of a more elite society than that of Jackson Hill, and she felt somehow stained by Maybelle's suffrage activities and her Catholicism. Margaret was not accepted by the young residents of Peachtree Street, who had been learning the social niceties of Southern society while she had been skidding into first, second, or third base. And, though she was a vivacious, pretty girl, she had a penchant for saying things that shocked her proper new friends. They thought she was funny and they laughed at her jokes, but they did not come to her home nor invite her to theirs. And Stephens, a good-looking young man of seventeen, was preparing for college and was in and out of love. He had always been at the center of his sister's life; now he treated her in a patronizing fashion. For Margaret, those first months on Peachtree Street were lonely and unhappy.

To maintain their new, higher standard of living, the Mitchells hired more servants than they had had on Jackson Hill. Now uniforms and formal address replaced the casual dress and attitude of the domestic help they had once employed, and, worse, the expense placed a strain on the whole household. Suddenly Margaret was aware of what the Mitchells *could not* afford. The heat was kept way down in winter because, as she was often reminded, her father was "not a millionaire"; guests were few, and far between; and any proposed purchase had to be discussed at length before it was agreed to. Even Maybelle's spirit seemed to wither with the move to Peachtree Street and, though she remained active in the women's movement, meetings were no longer held at the Mitchell house.

Margaret felt a stranger in her own home. Her great solace was in writing romances, mostly in play form. In the yard there was a circle of privet bushes that she called her "magic ring," and in good weather she would sit cross-legged in its center, filling lined tablets with tales of adventure set in exotic lands.

On the back page of one of these notebooks is the heading "Locations." Beneath it is a list of likely story backgrounds, including Africa, Alaska, China, Egypt, Hades, Mexico, Russia, Turkey, South America, and Paris. Listed as well are these themes: "Crook, Civil War, Smugglers, Shipwreck, Sepoy Rebellion, 'Society.'" A sense of the flavor of Margaret's writing at this time can be gleaned from the titles of some of her stories: "Phil Kelly: Detective," "A Darktown Tragedy," "The Cow Puncher," "In My Harem," and "The Fall of Roger Rover."

During the Easter holiday, her mother took Margaret on a buggy trip through the back country and over the dirt roads of Georgia, where Maybelle spoke to groups of farm women about women's rights. It was Maybelle's intention to awaken Margaret to what she must face as a woman, but Margaret was far more interested in the old foundations of some burned-out houses, and in the tales of how their owners had been forced to flee as Sherman torched his way to Savannah. Maybelle's fiery speeches to the back-country women did not ignite a sense of "sisterhood" in Margaret; in fact, Maybelle seemed to communicate with these strange women better than she did with her daughter. Margaret returned from this trip feeling troubled and even more an outsider in her mother's world.

❧

Not since the firing on Fort Sumter had the American people been so shocked as when, on August 4, 1914, the news came that war in Europe was a reality. Thirteen-year-old Margaret, having listened to grim tales of war all her life, understood its waste and devastation better than most educated Northern adults. Her parents and their friends discussed the war in Europe endlessly and were against isolation. The Mitchell and Stephens families were always proud to say that their ancestors had fought in the Revolutionary War, the War of 1812, and the Seminole, Mexican, and Civil wars. They had "fought for Georgia whenever they could get a chance and if there wasn't one, then they made it." They hadn't taken arms in the Spanish American War because they thought it "a piddling sort of war at best," but they were prepared to send their sons into battle again if they must.

Stephens stood ready to fight for his country and Maybelle stood proudly, though apprehensively, behind him. But the thought that her brother might be involved in the kind of bloody combat she was hearing discussed terrified Margaret, and, in the fall of 1914, she went off to her first day of school with a heavy heart.

Having completed grammar school with no special honors, Margaret now entered Washington Seminary, a private school for girls founded by two great-nieces of George Washington. Here, manners and proper female deportment were part of the curriculum. Margaret went unwillingly, but her only alternative seemed worse: a convent school like the one that Maybelle and all the Fitzgerald women had attended. Still, the atmosphere at Washington Seminary was oppressive enough, and Margaret's four years there were not happy ones.

There were girls in Margaret's class who admired her daring. She swam better than most and, despite all the dire warnings of her doctor, rode horseback with great style. She was the most tireless girl on hiking expeditions and could always think of some amusing activity. Her jokes, colorful language, and witty comments were often quoted. Nevertheless — perhaps because of her boyishness and her candor, or because of her somewhat bossy manner — few of the girls accepted her and she was not invited to join any of the school sororities. Her best friends were still the boys from her old neighborhood, with whom she could be herself, roughhouse, use slang, and discuss more vital subjects than those typical of "girl talk." In an unpublished memoir, Stephens looked back on this time and wrote that she "had not made a social success at her school, though she came of an old family who had sufficient means to provide her with the proper things for a girl entering on her social life in the city."

It was more than unpopularity that plagued Margaret at Washington Seminary. Stephens added that "she made enemies" and that this "led to much bitterness." He also claimed that these hard feelings followed his sister throughout her life, and that she "never forgot who were her enemies." A classmate who perhaps fell into that category asserts that, as a young woman, "Margaret was only happy if she could boss people around." The fact is, Margaret was something of a loner at school.

Washington Seminary was housed in an old mansion, white-columned and enormous, and the elegant rooms and grounds were scrupulously maintained. The original house was reserved for the boarding students, and behind it stood the more modern buildings. According to Atlanta women of Margaret's era and social level, "Nearly *everybody* went to Washington Seminary." The school was located only a few minutes from the Mitchell house, which meant that it was easy for girls who lived on Peachtree Street to stop by on their way home. No doubt sensing the problems her daughter was having socially, Maybelle encouraged after-school visits, but when classmates dropped by she would lecture them on women's rights, and this did not help her daughter's popularity.

Margaret's most sympathetic teacher, Mrs. Eva Paisley, taught English II and III in a long, narrow, damp classroom in the basement of Washington Seminary. Mrs. Paisley recognized Margaret's writing talent and made extensive notes in red ink in the margins of her theme papers: "Unity, Margaret," "Sentence balance," "Coherence," "Simplify!" To Margaret's embarrassment, Mrs. Paisley often read her themes before the class. "Listen to what you are saying," she instructed. "Good writing must also be good listening!"

Margaret confided little in her mother and never showed her the stories she wrote. No doubt she feared Maybelle's disapproval of her efforts, but, beyond that, she was a very private person. She kept a diary for several years and then, the year that she was in Mrs. Paisley's class, she decided to write a novel. For several months, she would hurry home from school and lock herself in her room to work on a book she called "The Big Four," about the adventures of four close friends in a girls' boarding school. Written painstakingly in longhand, it covered four hundred copybook pages and was divided into fourteen chapters. On the back inside cover she wrote: "There are authors and authors but a *true* writer is born and not made. Born writers make their characters real, living people, while the 'made writers' have merely stuffed figures who dance when the strings are pulled — that's how I know I'm a 'made' writer."

The plot of this first ingenuous effort was an extension of Margaret's own fantasies. In one episode, the fictitious Margaret saves a friend's family from ruin by destroying some incriminating papers; in another chapter, she fearlessly leads her classmates to safety during a disastrous fire. Margaret stuck with the novel to the end, but, on rereading the work, it seemed to her little more than a "string of plain old lies."

Having, in her mind, failed as a novelist, Margaret channeled all her creative energy into the school's dramatic club and soon became their star performer, leading playwright, and secretary. And, although her attempt at a novel had not been successful, she continued to write short stories, one of which appeared in the school's class book under the nickname she now adopted for herself — Peggy Mitchell.

"Peggy lay in the sand behind some mesquite bushes, hugging her father's rifle to her breast and watching Alvarado's men move about the house," began this tale of a young girl who survives the massacre of her entire family by a Mexican bandit and then confronts the desperado herself. "Out in the early sunlight hurried the bandit leader, tossing away a cigarette as he came and hastily buckling on his belt. With infinite care Peggy slid the gun up to the level of her eyes and found the man across the sights. Coldly, dispassionately, she viewed him, the chill steel of the gun giving her confidence. She must not miss now — she would not miss — and she did not."

Initially, this story was rejected by the class book's student editor, but Eva Paisley, who oversaw the publication, intervened, and the piece was included. A picture of the dramatic club taken in the fall of 1916 shows twenty-two members of the club, dressed in white middies and dark skirts, gathered about a Ford two-seater. The twenty-third member, Margaret, is perched on the roof.

On April 6, 1917, the United States declared war on Germany. The Allies' position could hardly have been worse than it was that spring. The casualties had been extraordinarily heavy; the naval situation was perilous after an appalling number of sinkings; and England had only about three weeks' worth of food for its armed forces. Stephens, who had graduated from the University of Georgia in 1915 and had then gone on to Harvard Law School for nearly two years, now returned home to become one of the first Atlantans to be conscripted. He was sent for his officer's training to nearby Fort McPherson, between Oakland City and East Point.

No sooner had the shock of war hit Atlanta than a catastrophe took place that was to bring back memories of the summer of 1864. On the morning of May 21, 1917, after a particularly dry month, a hot wind blew from the south. At 12:46 P.M., the fourth telephone alarm of the morning came into the fire department. There was a fire on the roof of an old Negro pesthouse, then being used as a storage depot for Grady Hospital. It did not sound serious and, as all the best equipment was already out, a fire truck without a proper hose was sent. By the time a second vehicle was dispatched, the fire was beyond control and sweeping a hot path northward into the white residential section of Jackson Hill, just up the road from where the

Mitchells had lived and near Grandmother Stephens's house. Fanned by the wind, flames swept across the open fields, moved along the crest of the hill, and then rushed downward, leaping from house to house so swiftly that residents did not have time to save much more than their children and the sick and elderly as they made a wild dash toward safety. In less than an hour, twenty blocks were ablaze, the sky was a "hideous red glow" and the acrid smell of smoke hung thick in the air.

Streets had now begun to fill with automobiles, trunks, and all manner of household goods and treasures, from shoe brushes to pianos. People ran screaming ahead of the fire, tripping and falling over the abandoned possessions scattered promiscuously on pavements and streets. An hour of sustained fear passed before Grandmother Stephens was found well and safe (having been downtown shopping at the time the fire broke out), although her house, which had survived Sherman and the burning of Atlanta, was razed to the ground.

Atlanta was in a state of dire emergency as the hot breeze continued to spread the flames. In a desperate effort to stop the conflagration, the fire department employed explosives to destroy houses that were in the flames' path, in order to create a burned-out belt around the fire. The deafening explosions created more pandemonium. The entire population was wild with terror as flames and black coils of pungent smoke shot up into the sky and houses halfway across the city shook from the blasts of TNT. But not even dynamiting could stop the flames. They leaped across trenches, spread out east and west, gutting whole streets. Then, suddenly, as the wind shifted, the fire spent the major part of its force.

A refuge center was set up at the municipal auditorium and Margaret rushed down to help. She was faced with lost children screaming for their parents amid mass confusion. Bits of people's lives — salvaged furniture and clothing — were heaped along one side of the huge auditorium. Household pets yipped and meowed. Minor injuries were being treated, while people with serious wounds were carried out on stretchers to be moved to the various hospitals outside the fire zone. It was a terrible, unforgettable sight that met the young girl's eyes. She wanted to help the injured, but someone suggested she tend to the children first. Dressed in her school middy, her hair in pigtails, she jumped up on a desk top and shouted, "Lost children here!" over and over again until a bedraggled, teary-eyed, youthful group formed around her. Then she called out each child's name as she lifted it onto the desk with her in an attempt to reunite families.

To her surprise, she herself was "reunited" with Stephens, who arrived with a group of soldiers from Fort McPherson to help in the emergency. It was late that night before the fire was under control. Losses were tremendous. The Mitchell family's old house was destroyed, along with eleven other houses owned by Grandmother Stephens (their rents having been her livelihood). The family suffered personal financial losses perhaps even more extensive than anyone else in the city; still, since none of their members had been injured, they considered themselves fortunate.

Fires smoldered in the devastated area for a week as houses that had collapsed into their cellars continued to burn. Hundreds of torches blazed where houses had stood, marking the breaks in gas lines. When the last flame was extinguished, three hundred acres of the city had been laid waste, nearly two thousand homes had been totally destroyed, and ten thousand people were homeless. But, miraculously, although there were numerous and serious injuries, only one person had died. It was many days before the dispossessed could be housed even temporarily, and hundreds slept in the parks and vacant lots.

Atlanta recovered swiftly from this tragedy, however. The country was at war and the townspeople had more important things to do than cry over what had been lost. Within a short time, there was not only Fort McPherson but Camp Gordon, too, on the outskirts of the city, and thousands of young soldiers who were being prepared for battle were now in their midst. In the summer of 1917, sixteen-year-old Margaret, like her family and the people of Atlanta, was filled with patriotic zeal. Most of the officers in the regiments of the two camps were university students or recent graduates. It did not take much on Margaret's part to persuade her parents that it was her social duty "to see that the soldiers had as nice a time as they could."

The Mitchell house was big enough and their staff large enough to accommodate quite a number of Stephens's friends on the weekends. Margaret was treated affectionately and was made the confidante in several of the romantic liaisons that grew out of the dances and parties. She returned to school in September with fantasies and yearnings of her own, but with fears for her brother's welfare and the lives of all the young men she had met that summer. The terrible war stories she had heard in her childhood returned to haunt her, and it was at this time that she began to suffer the nightmares and insomnia that were to plague her for the rest of her life. For the first time, she was aware of how young the old veterans she had once ridden with must have been when war shattered their lives and the lives of the women they had left behind.

Chapter Five

IN JUNE OF 1918, Margaret learned how to drive the Mitchells' black six-passenger Hanson, the only motorcar manufactured in Atlanta. Early on Saturday mornings, she would drive out to one of the camps, pile in as many young officers as the car would hold — that count went as high as nine if the men were slight of build — and bring them back to her house for the weekend. The former tomboy, good friend, and sister had suddenly emerged into one of those most beautiful of all flowers — the Southern belle. Loose hair drawn back with a ribbon replaced the braids; organdy and silk edged out the schoolgirl's cotton and serge. She was tiny — under five feet — weighed ninety-two pounds, and had a nineteen-inch waist. But her most endearing quality was her lively sense of humor; in addition to her feminine charms, she was extremely spirited, good fun, and knew how to be "one of the gang." According to Stephens, "There was no girl in Atlanta more popular with the officers."

On the veranda behind the white columns of the Mitchell house, with the scent of verbena clinging in the air, Margaret learned how to flirt. However, she confessed later to friends that she never let anyone kiss her. Maybelle had frequently warned her that the only answer for sexual curiosity was early marriage and Margaret was not ready for such a commitment.

To let someone kiss her meant, somehow, that she must become engaged. It was all very exciting and romantic. There were always rumors of the men having to leave at once for overseas, and, to help them forget the grim reality they would soon face, parties filled every moment of the weekends. Barbecues and picnics, as well as dances, were held at the Mitchell house, or at the Capital City Club roof garden or the gracious Piedmont Driving Club. Orchestras under the stars, paper lanterns casting dancing lights and shadows, great groups of young people intent on celebrating the last days of their youth — it was a striking scene. Stephens recalls that his mother "insisted that I spend whatever of my cadet's pay and officer's pay I had on having a good time, and she wanted Margaret to have a good time because she philosophised, 'You are seeing the end of an era and are able to see it under very attractive circumstances. Don't let the chance of seeing this go by you. . . . Things have a habit of disappearing during war, but what you have seen and what you have done are something that will always be with you.' "

Margaret heeded Maybelle's advice. At one of these parties she met a young officer, Lieutenant Clifford West Henry from New York, who was stationed at Camp Gordon. He was a Yankee, which made him quite exotic, and he had just graduated from Harvard that June. Clifford Henry was well-read and, to Margaret's delight, he could quote poetry and passages from Shakespeare. He was slim and fair, rather effete-looking. Some of Margaret's schoolmates thought he was ineffectual, not as strong a personality as Margaret, slightly effeminate. Margaret, however, was quite taken by the poetic lieutenant, "so sadly handsome in his officer's uniform." To his detractors she said he was "most sincere," and he vowed true affection for her.

Lieutenant Henry loved to dance as much as Margaret did, and as they floated in each other's arms across the smooth floors of the Capital City Club to the wispy strains of "Poor Butterfly," they were the center of attention. Besides being a graceful dancer, the attentive lieutenant was a good listener, and Margaret confided to him her plan to study medicine and specialize in psychiatry. (This last was a new idea, for she had just begun reading Freud.) Clifford Henry was entranced by

47

the soft Southern nights of Atlanta, the drives, the dances, the Mitchell house with its wide romantic terraces, the black guitar players strolling in the deep shadows of the oaks, and by Margaret — a burgeoning beauty with shining blue eyes, a perky urchin face, and a bevy of young officers always crowded around her. Clifford Henry put an end to that. He gave her a heavy, gold crested family ring. She was dazed and dazzled and very, very much in love, and so, it seemed, was the lieutenant.

In August, Clifford learned he was to be transferred and would soon go overseas. That night, on the veranda, he and Margaret became secretly engaged. By the end of the month, both Stephens and Clifford Henry were on troop ships headed for France.

Having graduated from Washington Seminary in June, Margaret was to go to Smith College, in Northampton, Massachusetts, in the fall. She had insisted upon an Eastern school as an alternative to the Southern colleges usually attended by Washington Seminary girls. Smith had been her final choice because of its excellent academic reputation, its record in women's rights — important to Maybelle — and its proximity to her Aunt Edyth. It was also near Clifford Henry's family in Connecticut. She planned to go from Smith on to medical school, and had told her few friends at Washington Seminary that her dream was to go to Vienna to study with Freud before taking up her own practice, presumably in Atlanta. Her desire to please Maybelle was apparent.

As she waited for her college life to begin, Margaret wrote Clifford long letters filled with her dreams for the future. Neither marriage nor their plans for a life together were ever discussed. Once the war was over, Clifford was to work toward his law degree and then go into his father's Connecticut real-estate business. How this was going to be reconciled with Margaret's intention of returning to Atlanta to become a disciple of Freud was discreetly not mentioned.

After a series of disastrous Allied losses in June and July, 1918, it had looked as though the Germans might win the war. Then came the brilliantly executed counterattack at the Second Battle of the Marne and, within three days, the tide of the war had turned. On August 10, General Pershing obtained Allied consent to a plan for an independent American Army; the Allies, meantime, had deeply penetrated German lines and there were rumors that peace negotiations might well be under way, for all chance of a German victory had vanished.

Their spirits brightened by this hope, Margaret and Maybelle boarded a train for New York two weeks before the start of Smith's fall term. For once, mother and daughter were in rapport, and the two of them had a grand time sightseeing, window-shopping, and selecting Margaret's college wardrobe.

One afternoon they took the train to Greenwich to visit Aunt Edyth and sat opposite a man who looked vaguely familiar to Margaret.

"I noticed that he was looking at us," she wrote in a letter to her father and Grandmother Stephens, continuing,

> Our Southern accent marks us anyway. But when I pulled off my glove and changed the heavy ring from one hand to the other, I caught his brown eyes and grinned for I knew who he was. He arose and came over to us —
>
> "You are Miss Mitchell, aren't you?" he questioned, smiling. And as if I had been meeting him every day for years, I replied —
>
> "You are Clifford's father." And it was!
>
> "I recognized the ring," he laughed. "Cliff was so fond of it."
>
> And then we all began to chatter. I liked him immensely and I believe Mother does too. He is a pleasant man, with a quiet sense of humor and he is more forceful than Clifford. He's no plain New Yorker but very cosmopolitan and well educated. He is intensely proud of his son, though he tries not to show it and he handed me some letters from him that he had in his pocket.

Mr. Henry invited them to meet Mrs. Henry for lunch at the Waldorf the next Wednesday, and to attend a matinee.

"Funny meeting, wasn't it," Margaret wrote her father. "Of course he had seen some awful snapshots of me but it must have been my accent and the ring that did the trick." She added, "If you get any letters from Cliff to me, *please* hustle them up here. P.S. Please save my letters. Just put them away somewhere."

Eugene Mitchell was concerned about the seriousness of his daughter's affection for Clifford Henry. Margaret was only a girl of seventeen, he reminded Maybelle in a letter. Perhaps they should not encourage her friendship with the Henrys, which could draw her deeper into a relationship she might regret and from which she would not know how to free herself.

Maybelle wrote him a placating letter on September 10:

Dear, you must have had no youth or forgotten it if you attach so much importance to the affections of seventeen years. The Henrys so far as I have seen are good people, well travelled, educated, how much or how little money I do not know, but respectable. The boy is over in Europe perchance for life. Why worry over what can't happen for four or five years and 99 to 100 will not happen at all. Can you remember how many girls Stephens has been in love with since he was seventeen? Youth has ways of its own for its own education. I will tell the Henrys when I see them that they must not say anything of Margaret to any one, so as to leave both their son and Margaret freedom to change their minds if they so desire. Margaret herself is not ignorant of the natural manner of seventeen to change its mind. So put *your* mind at rest about this affair, as there can come no harm of it.

Margaret was impressed neither with Connecticut nor her aunt's circle of friends, and she wrote to her father:

This is a barbarous country. I wouldn't live here if Rockerfellow [sic] himself proposed to me. I don't like the atmosphere or the people, they are cold and they hold on to their ratches in the first moments of your acquaintance. Then its money, money, *money* that counts and that doesn't appeal to me, who love[s] roughnecks for their own pennyless selves. I now see why the Yankee soldiers like the Southerners — it's because these girls are Amazons, huskies who "can take care of themselves" but they lack lightness — lightness of body and of repartee. There are no young men here as this is not an army town and I miss the gold shoulder bars. Darn these people with their patriotism! They screech it from the housetops and condemn you as a spy if you don't do likewise. The women spend their time racing around in uniforms of useless organizations (except of course the Red Cross) and they don't seem to do anything but rush without any definite object. I went to lunch at the Smiths' the other day (their father is Alfred Smith who is in Spain on a diplomatic mission) and they lived in the most beautiful house I have ever seen, set back amid acres of ground and so well kept that 8 men must work on it. At lunch we were served by two white maids and from the looks and size of the house it must have taken quite a number of servants to keep it up. I learned from "snooping around" that even the assistant scullery maid gets $45 a month. There are no older boys in the family, so the war doesn't touch them. The older girl sold me a 50¢ trinket for the Red Cross — Bah! Patriotism! Why the devil don't those people give up a servant, a car, a club — something that really counts and quit yelling patriotism and selling 50¢ things when they are supporting a useless retinue? Why the pay they give a useless maid per month would buy a Liberty Bond! It makes me sick but you can't say anything.

Perhaps I'll like the North — I'm going to try for I want to like the place I must live in for nine months, but it will be rather difficult. Perhaps Northampton is different from Greenwich. I hope so any way for I want to get to a place where the individual and not the millions count.

The luncheon at the Waldorf with the Henrys was a great success, and Margaret liked Mrs. Henry as much as she did Mr. Henry. Afterwards, the four of them took in a musical revue. Clifford was in all of their thoughts, and the families exchanged such comments as, "Cliff would have loved this show," and, "We'll do it again when Cliff comes home."

Early the following Sunday morning, Maybelle boarded the train with Margaret for Northampton. That fall's freshman class of 775 students was the largest in Smith's history, nearly double the enrollment of the other three classes. Due to this, several large, old rooming houses near the campus had been taken over to accommodate the overflow. Margaret was at Ten Henshaw Street under the guidance of a Mrs. Pearson, a proper New England lady upon whom Maybelle felt she could rely. Maybelle left late that afternoon, after helping her daughter get settled, and that night Margaret was without a member of her own immediate family for the first time in her life.

🙖

Smith was not the "crusty old place" Margaret had feared it might be. The girls were more spirited than those at Washington Seminary. Yet Margaret did not feel any more comfortable with her new classmates than she had with her former. Smith attracted the daughters of some of the most socially prominent and well-to-do families in the East. They were sophisticated, well-traveled, and well-read, and they played a game she did not know — bridge. French was used casually and as a sort of punctuation to the tony English the girls spoke, and their clothes were tremendously chic. Margaret's wardrobe, by comparison, was plain and conservative. She had never been out of the United States, and, though she could read a little French, as a conversational language it defeated her. There were few Southerners in her class, and she was teased about her accent, her short stature, and her naiveté.

A small, spartan room on the second floor of Ten Henshaw Street, with a fine view of Smith's handsome brick buildings and thickly wooded campus, became Margaret's home. For the first month, several girls in succession shared it with her before finding someone else to room with for the term. Margaret was feeling intensely the outsider until, at last, she made friends with a few of the girls: Ginny Morris, a tall, lively blond girl who was her final roommate; Sophie Henker, who liked horses almost as much as she did; Madeleine Baxter, who was called Red because of her glorious Titian hair (and who was also Margaret's roommate for a time); and Helen Atkinson, who planned to be a teacher.

A quick camaraderie developed between Margaret and the other girls in the house as soon as Ginny Morris moved into her room, for Ginny was outgoing, loved by all, and the catalyst in most activities. The girls viewed Margaret as a romantic if enigmatic figure because she was engaged to an officer overseas and received letters from him almost daily. She was known to her Smith friends as Peggy and, except in letters to Clifford and her parents, signed herself as such.

In discussions of world affairs, music, or art — about which she knew little and in which her housemates were well-versed — Margaret was reticent, but at other times she could be wickedly funny, and on her favorite subject, the Civil War, she could hold any audience. Her roommate, Ginny Morris, writes:

> The rest of us were awed by the bulk of her overseas mail and enslaved by her Irish sense of humor which was considerably broader than you'd expect to find in a frail flower of the south.

Moreover, we respected her scorn for campus rules and her smoking skill — when to be found with cigarettes was a shortcut to being expelled.

We were all movie fans, cutting classes to see the latest pictures starring Charlie Ray, Norma Talmadge or Wallace Reid. And one evening every week was put aside for play-going at the local stock company where the dangerously irresistible leading man was one William Powell. We liked him especially in a little dramatic bomb shell known as "Captain Jenks [sic] of the Norse Marines."

In the evenings, no one ever thought of studying. Instead there was usually S.R.O. in our room listening to Peggy talk. When topics took more serious turns you could pretty safely depend that Peggy would get around to the Civil War. . . . She could sling you off a well-rounded little tabloid description of the Second Battle of Bull Run with the same eager sparkle another girl might tell you about last night's bridge hand. She felt about Robert E. Lee pretty much as if he was the current film idol. Whenever she got mad enough to call me a "Damn Yankee" I knew our home life was threatened!

Early in October, just when life at Ten Hen (as the girls called the house) had begun to take on some order, an epidemic of Spanish influenza swept over New England, heading west. The disease was mysterious in origin and the medical profession was at a loss as to how to combat it. None of the available drugs for influenza seemed to have an effect on those afflicted by this new strain, and the mortality rate was alarmingly high. Schools across the country were closed by federal order. Smith and many other colleges were placed under quarantine and classes were suspended. The girls were not allowed to leave Northampton, visit other houses, nor gather for group activities or sports, although they were permitted to hike in small numbers in the woods bordering the school.

"These Yanks," Margaret wrote in a letter to her parents on October 5, "are strong on cross country 'Tramps' and as the fields and woods are beautiful now and in the open it's far safer, I intend to stay out a good deal."

Three weeks later, when the quarantine was lifted and the flu scare over, Clifford's letters, always a month late, ceased coming. The last one had been dated September 11 and postmarked Saint-Mihiel. It was Ginny who brought Peggy the news. Early on the morning of September 12, blanketed by heavy fog, the American-led army — ten American and three French divisions — had attacked the Germans who held that area. In two days the Germans had been routed, but at the cost of nearly eight thousand lives.

Margaret telephoned the Henrys, but they had not heard from Clifford either. The vigil began, but was to end quickly. The Henrys received a telegram informing them that their son had been severely injured in the battle at Saint-Mihiel, having bravely taken over for his disabled captain in what amounted to hand-to-hand combat. Fragments from a bomb dropped by a German plane had severed the lieutenant's leg and penetrated his stomach. He had been awarded the Croix de Guerre as he lay in his hospital bed, but, on the morning of October 16, he had died.

Margaret was deeply grieved over Clifford Henry's death. Stephens has claimed that Clifford Henry was the great love of his sister's life. Margaret did maintain contact with the Henrys for many years, but probably she had been more in love with a romantic fantasy than with Clifford Henry himself. She had admired his intellect, his golden good looks, his poetic nature, and his gentlemanliness, but it is doubtful that Margaret truly understood the young man she thought she loved. Clifford Henry's friends had recognized and accepted his homosexual tendencies, but Margaret had seemed completely oblivious to this side of her fiance's nature.

In this period of her life, Margaret suffered a great confusion as to her own sexuality — certainly not a unique occurrence in girls of seventeen. She enjoyed being desired and playing the vamp, but the idea of having sexual relations with a man terrified her. With Clifford Henry she had not had to concern herself about sex, for their relationship had been, as she liked to think, "on a higher level." She had never known anyone with such an extensive vocabulary or with a knowledge of the arts. In turn, he had greatly admired her vitality and the way she could tell a story about the past and make it live. Clifford Henry was exciting but safe, and his letters had made her the center of envy of her female friends. She did not, however, share the contents of these letters, for they were not passionate but were filled instead with the disillusions of a young soldier at war.

The busy regime at Smith kept Margaret from dwelling on her unhappiness. Although she continued to mourn for Clifford, she loosened up considerably with the twenty-five girls who shared the house at Ten Hen. Most of them were impressed by her large collection of photographs of U.S. fighting men, given to her by the young soldiers who had visited the Mitchell home during the past two summers.

Red Baxter, one of Margaret's closest friends in Ten Hen, remembers that "Peg" loved to recite poetry — a love she had acquired from Clifford Henry. One of the girls' favorite pasttimes was to ensconce themselves in the two tubs in the upstairs bathroom and then "try to stump each other with poetic recitations, keeping the hot water dripping and parboiling our skins to lobster red."

Another roommate, Doris James, recalls the time Calvin Coolidge, then governor of Massachusetts, came to visit Ten Hen's proprietors, Mr. and Mrs. Pearson. Northampton was the home of the Coolidge family and they and the Pearsons were old friends.

> One evening Peg and I went to the Pearsons' living room to ask about the chance of some of us going to the movies. . . . We found Mr. Pearson and Mr. Coolidge there and after Mr. P had muttered, "Governor this is Miss Mmmmmm, and this is Miss Mmmmmm," he went to find Mrs. Pearson and we were left alone with the great man.
>
> "This is a lovely evening," Peg said. (It was a particularly foul one.)
>
> Mr. Coolidge thought this over and finally replied, "You wear your rubbers tonight."
>
> "How are things in Boston?" Peg asked brazenly.
>
> After due reflection, from which we thought he would give out with something profound about the Commonwealth, he said, "Yes, if you're going out tonight, you want your rubbers."
>
> We waited then in painful silence for Mrs. Pearson and when at last she appeared, Mr. Coolidge greeted her with, "I told the girls they want their rubbers tonight."
>
> Before we were hardly out of earshot, Peg said, "I must remember those deathless words."

Margaret was doing well in only one subject, English composition. Yet this single achievement could not compensate for her lackluster performance in her other courses. Too, in her eyes, the English professor lacked Mrs. Paisley's keen literary sensibility. And when, after reading one of her assignments, he proclaimed her "a youthful genius" on the strength of what she thought was a "rotten theme," Margaret lost faith in the professor's evaluation of her work. Her low estimation of her abilities, her opinion that any praise was unwarranted, that for some reason she had not truly earned it, began to manifest itself at this time. From her recounting of the incident later, and the fact that she remembered it and referred to the professor's good words as fraudulent praise, one cannot help but sense Margaret's feelings of inferiority. It did not help that she was barely passing in her other classes. The rest of the girls, who seemed better prepared to cope with Smith's requirements, might not have had to study much to keep up their grades, but Margaret realized that if she intended to remain at the school, she would have to, and she applied herself quite diligently to the task in the months that followed the news of Clifford Henry's death.

She was to spend Christmas on the campus, along with many of the other students, because the trip to Atlanta would have been too time-consuming, and because her father was recuperating from a bout of the highly infectious Spanish influenza. At Ten Hen, only Ginny, of her closest friends, was not at Smith for the holidays. There were a great many Christmas activities and most of them involved a squadron of Air Force men who had returned to the States following the November 11 armistice and were now stationed not far from the campus, waiting to be discharged from the service.

In the days before Christmas, the telephone booth in the downstairs hallway of Ten Hen was the hub of life. A dance was being planned and the men were to come from the Air Force base. Every time the phone rang, there was a general stampede to answer it, then, as Margaret described the scene in a letter to Ginny, some of the girls would stand around the hall "painfully breathless" until the one in the booth came out announcing, "Thank God, it was only the poor fool wanting to know what kind of flowers to send!"

It snowed heavily on the Saturday of the dance. During the

afternoon, Margaret had to sing in the Glee Club, an onerous duty, for she carried a tune no better than Maybelle, and had been coerced into stepping in for an absent friend. Once back at Ten Hen, she was more an observer than a participant in the general hysteria that was all around her. Dresses from New York or Springfield, ordered weeks before, had not yet arrived. Shoes did not seem to fit. The damp weather was ruinous to the hair of the girls who were giving themselves marcels, and, as Margaret wryly observed, the rage of plucking eyebrows made "the air thick with screams and discarded lashes." And when the gowns did arrive, in the nick of time, the girls flitted around "trailing evening dresses and calling the world to witness that they looked like 'Hell on Wheels.' "

Margaret attended the dance with a young man named Al, a date with whom she was obviously displeased, for she wrote Ginny the next day that he was a "wreck" and that his long silences had been a welcome relief. She was arrayed, she added, "like a lily in the field," and she commented that the next morning she was so exhausted she looked "like the end of a misspent life."

❦

Stephens, who had acquitted himself quite nobly and without injury on the battlefield in France, returned to Atlanta shortly after the New Year to find his father recovered, but his mother severely ill with the flu. For nearly two weeks Maybelle stoically fought this illness. The news was kept from Margaret but, on January 22, her father was forced to write her that her mother's condition was serious. The following day, Maybelle, who had grown still weaker, dictated a letter to Stephens for her daughter, in the belief that she would not see her again.

January 23, 1919

Dear Margaret,

I have been thinking of you all day long. Yesterday you received a letter saying I am sick. I expect your father drew the situation with a strong hand and dark colors and I hope I am not as sick as he thought. I have pneumonia in one lung and were it not for flu complications, I would have more than a fair chance of recovery. But Mrs. Riley had pneumonia in both lungs and is now well and strong. We shall hope for the best but remember, dear, that if I go now it is the best time for me to go.

I should have liked a few more years of life, but if I had had those it may have been that I should have lived too long. Waste no sympathy on me. However little it seems to you I got out of life, I have held in my hands all that the world can give. I have had a happy childhood and married the man I wanted. I had children who loved me, as I have loved them, I have been able to give what will put them on the high road to mental, moral, and perhaps financial success, were I going to give them nothing else.

I expect to see you again, but if I do not I must warn you of one mistake a woman of your temperament might fall into. Give of yourself with both hands and overflowing heart, but give only the excess after you have lived your own life. This is badly put. What I mean is that your life and energies belong first to yourself, your husband and your children. Anything left over after you have served these, give and give generously, but be sure there is no stinting of attention at home. Your father loves you dearly, but do not let the thought of being with him keep you from marrying if you wish to do so. He has lived his life; live yours as best you can. Both of my children have loved me so much that there is no need to dwell on it. You have done all you can for me and have given me the greatest love that children can give to parents. Care for your father when he is old, as I cared for my mother. But never let his or anyone else's life interfere with your real life. Goodbye, darling, and if you see me no more it may be best that you remember me as I was in New York.

Your Loving Mother

The same day this letter was mailed, Margaret received a telegram telling her that her mother had fallen into a coma and that she should hurry home. That night, Ginny and Mrs. Pearson saw her to the station in the midst of a terrible snowstorm. During the long journey, she had a prescient feeling that her mother had died, and as she stepped off the train in Atlanta to be reunited with Stephens for the first time since he had gone off to France, his somber expression confirmed her fears that she had arrived too late.

She was able to cope with this news but, though Stephens warned her that their father was in complete despair, she was not prepared for the sight of the incoherent, grief-stricken man who greeted her in the downstairs hall, his usually kempt self in wild disorder — hair uncombed, beard unshaved, eyes red and glazed from crying, and dressed as though he had been awakened in the middle of the night and had simply put on whatever was near at hand. Worse than his appearance was the fact that he was talking wildly. "Your mother's not well," he kept repeating, and it was not until Maybelle's coffin had been lowered into the earth and he had broken down and wept in his children's arms that he accepted the reality of her death.

The funeral was a distressing affair, some of the Fitzgerald family having been so incensed at the disregard Margaret and Stephens paid to "proper Catholic rites" that they stalked out of the cemetery before the eulogy was spoken. Margaret did not concern herself with this family squabble, for she had far too much with which to cope.

Besides the household tasks, there were times during the next few weeks when her father would fall back into unreality, and she feared he might be losing his mind. It was with much relief that his children finally saw him begin to pull himself together. Even though he continued to wander aimlessly through the house, he made brief visits to his office. However, he spent most of his time at home in bed. One day he called Margaret into his room. "Go back to Smith," he told her. "I want your brother, now that he is out of the army, to stay with me. I think I will want you to come back, but do not miss the year you have begun."

These had been Maybelle's wishes, and Margaret felt committed to carrying them out. Yet, when she returned to Smith, nothing seemed quite the same. "I am beginning to miss Mother so much now," she wrote her father on February 17. "I only had her for eighteen years but you loved her for twenty-six years and I know how lonely you must be now. I wish I could make up just a little for her in the place in your heart."

Margaret was faced with a serious dilemma. With Maybelle dead, much of her motivation to study was gone. All her life she had fought for her mother's approval, and her being at Smith and planning to be a doctor was part of that pattern. Quitting school in favor of caring for the two Mitchell men began to have special appeal. For one thing, she would be, for the first time, the only woman in the lives of her father and brother, and, for another, the competition at school was beginning to overwhelm her. Midyear examinations found her just skimming through. She was a C student and had not shone in any area — academic, athletic, literary, or musical. Smith was a college of nearly two thousand young women, and Margaret had found that there were many more clever and talented girls than she. "If I can't be first, I'd rather be nothing," she wrote her brother.

But she did play the Southern belle. Her roommates report that she had replaced the U.S. Army photographs on her bureau with a collection of recently acquired male college students' pictures, all warmly inscribed. And whenever someone's date did not show up for a special occasion, Margaret could always be counted upon to produce an attractive substitute, usually from Amherst, Dartmouth, or Harvard. Sophie Henker, the classmate who shared Margaret's love of horseback riding, came from nearby Amherst, and Margaret visited at her home several weekends and became friends with some Amherst men. She had always been able to make male friends easily. Young men accepted her as one of the gang, a rare member of the opposite sex in whom they could confide. She was also the one girl at Ten Hen whom a young man dating one of Mrs. Pearson's other charges could trust as a willing conspirator when a window had to be left open for his date to sneak in through after curfew.

But her social success did not make up for the inferiority Margaret felt in the classroom, and she made the decision to return to Atlanta. She seems to have had no qualms about leaving Smith, and her final grades were even worse than she had expected — barely passing, except in English. In May Margaret boarded the train for home, fully aware that she was ending her formal education. Maybelle's lectures to her on the importance of an education had been pushed aside. On her deathbed, Maybelle had said that Margaret should think about herself first, and with this new decision, she felt that she was doing exactly that. It might seem she was being self-sacrificing in returning home to take care of her brother and father, but it was what she wanted to do. Being first did matter to her, desperately, and if she could not succeed at college, then she could at least be first in the hearts of her immediate family.

During her last week at Smith, Margaret had a date with an Amherst student from the Midwest, Billy Williams. They ended up sitting on the steps of the boathouse at Smith in a driving rain, both feeling a little forlorn, both conscious of their extreme youth. "When I get through here," she confided, "I'm going to find out if I can really write." Williams, who also had dreams of being a writer, looked at her with surprise. She had made the statement with unusual vehemence, yet he did not recall either Peggy Mitchell or any of her Smith friends mentioning that writing might be her life's ambition. He questioned her, but she refused to discuss the subject further. They walked back to Ten Hen in the teeming downpour, in silence.

"Queer girl," Williams thought, and then, remembering that she had endured the deaths of two loved ones that year, attributed her sudden reticence to her grief.

Peggy Mitchell
1919–1925

Chapter Six

SHE GOT OUT of the great black touring car that had once brought as many as nine young officers back to the house on Peachtree Street to dance and sing and weave fantasies. She was home. Bessie, the cook, must have been listening for the sound of the motor because now she stood squinting into the sun on the veranda, the front door open behind her. Charlie, the yard-man, his black face smiling in welcome, took the bags from the trunk of the car. A smallish black girl, her hair tied back with a white kerchief, stood in Bessie's tall shadow; this was Cammie, the fifteen-year-old housegirl. If it had not occurred to Peggy Mitchell before, it must have at that moment — she was now mistress of the house on Peachtree Street, and she was only three years older than the skittish Cammie.

Peggy started up the steps. The house seemed even more imposing than she remembered and, without the romance of officers with gold bars and lilting dance music coming through the windows, Peggy liked it less than ever.

Her girlhood had been left behind at Smith. With Maybelle dead, she was now the woman in charge of the Mitchell house-hold, and she saw things with new eyes. She was shocked to discover that they were not as rich as she had thought, and her first step was to fire most of the large staff of servants her mother had employed, keeping only Bessie, Cammie, Charlie, and a laundress, Carrie Holbrook, who came in two days a week. To Eugene Mitchell's amazement, his daughter extracted as much work from the diminished staff as Maybelle had from the full complement.

It was not long before Peggy Mitchell — her family refused to use the name, but the servants complied with her request to be addressed as "Miss Peggy" — realized that with her mother's death her father had lost the driving force in his life. What ambition he had had was gone. She would never replace her mother in his heart, and neither could she expect him to take over what she now saw had been her mother's role: head of the family. It had been Maybelle who had both set the scene and directed the action of their life drama.

Eugene Mitchell could not be called a man of daring or of foresight. Nor did he have the quality of endurance of his male ancestors. His father, Russell Crawford Mitchell, had walked with his skull split open for a hundred and fifty miles to safety during the Civil War, transporting an injured cousin with him, and had survived until 1905, raising twelve children and supporting them comfortably. Grandfather Mitchell had insisted that his rather dreamy, intelligent son Eugene should study law, and Russell Crawford Mitchell was not a man to challenge. He himself, as a young man, had practiced law in Florida after the war and had been disbarred for assaulting a state official. With his career in law at an end, he and his wife had returned to Atlanta, where he became successful in the lumber business. But early on, Grandfather Mitchell had decided that his sons would succeed in the profession in which he had failed.

Eugene had graduated from the University of Georgia with honors in 1885, qualifying for his law degree within a year. Never adventurous, he had settled into making a good living by drawing wills, examining land titles, and securing patents. He suffered a severe financial setback in the depression of 1893, just after marrying Maybelle, and she never completely forgave him for his lack of courage in facing that crisis. It did not destroy the bond they had, but it brought an undercurrent of dissatisfaction — at least on Maybelle's part — to their union. Stephens Mitchell says that the Panic of '93 took from his father "all daring and put in its place a desire to have a competence assured to him." Eugene had regained some of his losses by the time Margaret was born, but he was never to achieve more than middle-class prosperity.

Eugene Mitchell devoted his greatest energy to his love of Southern history and the world of books (although he often said no book worth reading had been written since the death of Queen Victoria), and to his positions on the board of the Carnegie Library and the board of education of Atlanta. To him, truth was paramount, and a contract, will, or title deed, inviolable. In midlife he was a bookish, dour man, meticulous in his work and somewhat aloof in his relationships with family and friends. Yet, underneath his rather cold exterior, there was a restlessness that hinted at deeper currents, and sometimes he displayed a flash of humor that gave evidence of a lighter side to his nature. With Maybelle's death, he had withdrawn into himself, and Peggy's return home did not assuage his grief. To her dismay, she was no more an integral part of her father's life now than she had been when her mother was alive.

No sooner had Peggy established a routine in the household and begun to settle into her new responsibilities than Grandmother Stephens, accompanied by her younger spinster sister, Aline, descended upon her, along with trunks of personal possessions and boxes upon boxes of currently fashionable feathered hats. Now a septuagenarian, Annie Fitzgerald Stephens was still as feisty as ever, and quite determined that Peggy should not throw away her life by becoming a household drudge to Eugene and Stephens Mitchell. She fought with her son-in-law over his "stealing a young woman's youth" and doggedly tried to convince her granddaughter to continue her education, and, when she failed at that, she began a campaign to "spruce the girl up."

Ties and middies and serge skirts began to mysteriously disappear from Peggy's wardrobe every laundry day. Grandmother Stephens then brought in a seamstress. Peggy protested all this waste and extravagance quite vociferously, and, within four months, her grandmother realized the two of them simply could not live in the same house. With Aunt Aline in tow, she haughtily departed to temporary quarters at the Georgian Terrace Hotel. But her efforts had not all been in vain; Peggy did, indeed, look different — her skirts had been raised; her hair, cut and becomingly coiffed; and not a middy blouse or long tie remained in her wardrobe. Yet, she chose to wear only the plainest of the clothes Grandmother Stephens had had made for her. There was more than mulishness attached to this.

The cost of food and other goods had risen astronomically since the war's end. Inflation had quadrupled prices in some instances and the American public, fearing where this would end, demanded that the government put a stop to such profiteering. When, by the spring of 1920, no change had been wrought, consumers went on a buyers' strike. For women, the vogue became last year's dress. Rent strikes opposing steep increases by landlords swept the nation, and the courts were often on the side of the tenants. Newspapers printed menus for feeding a family of five on fifty cents a day. Thrift, as well as old clothes, was in style, and Eugene Mitchell, who could not forget the vicissitudes of 1893, thoroughly approved of his daughter's stance. In fact, at her suggestion, he had a tailor "turn" a suit of clothes for him — a procedure that involved turning a suit inside out and redoing the buttonholes, pockets, and lapels so that an almost-new suit replaced the former shiny, worn one at about one-sixth the price of a custom-made model.

Left on her own once again to run her father's household, Peggy began to contemplate the life she had come home to, and the kind of future she could expect. Though her father encouraged her to go out with friends and to attend social events, her former friends in Atlanta now seemed cool to her.

It had not taken Grandmother Stephens's warnings for Eugene Mitchell to see what Peggy's lack of a social life and her devotion to her family could mean. Visions of a spinster daughter may well have been behind his insistence that Peggy make a formal entrance into Atlanta society, where she could meet young people her own age and, eventually, a well-off, socially acceptable young man whom she might wish to marry.

After much pressure from Stephens as well as her father, Peggy agreed to make her debut and, in January of 1920, after a tense wait, she was approved for membership in the elite Debutante Club for the winter season of 1920–21. According to Stephens, on the social and financial scale in white Atlanta, families had serial numbers from 1 to 200,000, and the Mitchells were somewhere near the halfway mark.

Considering her strong feelings about her Aunt Edyth and Greenwich "society," one cannot help but wonder why Peggy went along with this plan to launch her into local society and find her a husband.

There were, however, indications that she was rebelling unconsciously. One fair February day, a month after her acceptance to the Debutante Club, Peggy drove out to a stable near Stone Mountain, where she rented a large black horse reminiscent of Bucephalus. She rode the animal off the bridal path to a steep, narrow hill covered with low branches. At the top of the slope was a stone wall that separated the horse farm from the road. Instead of turning back at this point, Peggy decided to jump the wall, but her approach was short and the horse did not clear the top. Peggy was thrown and the horse came down on top of her. She lay there in pain and shock for nearly an hour before other riders happened along the same isolated path.

The leg that had undergone surgery years before was once again severely injured. This time, Peggy was to take seriously the doctor's warning that she must never do "a damn fool thing like that again," for her recovery was slow and painful. Grandmother Stephens came in every day to help, but this only created more tension in the house. It was the young black girl, Cammie, upon whom Peggy now came to rely for errands, and the girl seemed to enjoy the responsibility and freedom this gave her. Cammie could be exasperating, but she could be amusing, too, and she was wily and clever, two traits Peggy admired.

It was summer before she was on her feet again. To strengthen the muscles of her leg, she took a dance class offered by one of her former instructors. Even so, to her disgust, the doctor ordered her to wear heavy, low-heeled shoes.

By early July she had improved enough to accept a date to go on an overnight camping trip to Lake Burton with a young intern, Dr. Leslie Morris, several other couples, and a youthful chaperone. One of the girls she met on this trip, Augusta Dearborn, was to become a close friend. Augusta lived in Birmingham, but was in Atlanta visiting a married sister for the season. Peggy's ankle was still bandaged and the handsome Dr. Morris treated her protectively. Augusta was fairly certain he was in love with Peggy and thought Peggy was attracted to him. They did appear to have much in common: medicine, poetry, and an interest in Georgia's history. But Peggy was adamant that the life of a doctor's wife did not appeal to her.

Upon their return from this trip, Dr. Morris invited Peggy to attend a costume ball being given at the East Lake Country Club. Peggy accepted only at Augusta's insistence, for she was not yet comfortable in Atlanta society. She felt that the Mitchell and the Fitzgerald families, because of their dedication to the growth of Atlanta, had as much of which to be proud in their ancestry as did the city's arrogant and more wealthy social leaders; still, conflicting emotions of inferiority and contempt rose whenever she was in their company.

On the warm August night of the dance, Leslie Morris escorted Peggy into a ballroom full of masked dancers wearing colorful costumes of the past. Peggy had considered donning a boy's outfit, something to suggest Puck in *A Midsummer Night's Dream*, but she'd finally dressed as a small antebellum girl, complete with long curls, poke bonnet, and pantaloons. She was the only young woman in such unconventional costume; the others wore the flattering, coquettish gowns of earlier Southern belles. Even on the arm of the attractive Dr. Morris, who had dressed as a Confederate officer, Peggy was a comical sight on the dance floor.

Dominating the stag line that night was a young man named Berrien Kinnard Upshaw, a broad-shouldered University of Georgia football player with a reputation for wildness. "Red" Upshaw, at six feet two, towered over Peggy, and with his brick red hair, sloe green eyes, cleft chin, and bright pirate costume, he cut a dashing figure. Red Upshaw was amused and attracted by the rebellious quality he recognized in Peggy, and he admired the courage she displayed in not leaving the dance even though it was obvious that she was being ridiculed. The chaperones, from their posts in the gilt chairs that encircled the room, watched with arched brows and pursed lips as this oddly matched pair danced together, and they were quick to notice when the couple left early and in each other's company, leaving Leslie Morris behind.

Peggy was smitten by Red Upshaw from the start, and when

Augusta asked her to join a group at her sister's summer cottage on Saint Simons Island, Upshaw was included in the party. The girls strongly disagreed about Upshaw. Augusta found him "unpolished," not at all suitable, in her opinion, as a beau for Peggy. Red Upshaw was almost always irreverent. He called Augusta "Aggie," a name she hated; and Peggy, "Short-Leg Pete," or just "Short Legs." Peggy appeared to be furious at him for this, but there was an undeniable chemistry between the two of them, even as — to the discomfort of her hostess and the other guests — they teased each other unmercifully, seemingly always on the brink of violent argument.

There was a certain mystery surrounding Upshaw that intrigued Peggy; he had an aura of glamour that made him a topic of discussion among her peers and their families. It was known that he was the eldest son of a respectable old Georgia family now living in North Carolina, but there were also whisperings of scandal — although no one seemed to know any of the details — and Peggy rather enjoyed the small sensation and the family censure her friendship with him caused.

The twenties began much as they were to end, as a materialistic decade dominated by business and the getting of money. Idealism seemed to have been lost somewhere on a French battlefield. The young had fought a war and had returned home to find that they had helped save the world so that more automobiles, chewing gum, and face powder could be sold; their world was in upheaval, and the codes taught them as children now seemed irrelevant. The sale of liquor had been prohibited, and young men who had only recently carried army rifles now kept flasks filled with bootleg gin on the ready. Young women tapped their toes as they cranked up the Victrola. They read the fevered verses of Edna St. Vincent Millay and the shocking novels of James Branch Cabell, and they painted their nails, penciled their brows, and wore heavy perfumes when they were out to vamp a man. But the changes in women went much deeper than their made-up faces and brazen flirtations. They now had a say in politics, and they spoke up loud and clear. One year after Maybelle's death, women had finally won the right to vote, and this gave them a new place in society and a new freedom. It was not easy for either of the sexes to determine just how far this freedom should extend.

For all her later claims of being a true flapper of the twenties, Peggy Mitchell was slow in taking steps toward her own liberation and never truly won it. She sent up flares from time to time, flouted the old conventions of society, and acted the role of the new, daring woman when she could use the pose as a weapon to get back at those who had hurt or slighted her, or when it served to hide her true feelings. But the puritanical side of her character kept her from really letting go. In truth, she cared very much about what other people thought of her, especially those people whose love and admiration she so desperately needed.

She was unsure of what she should or should not do as a "new woman." She smoked, drank, read the most controversial books, and flirted outrageously. But she still thought that sex before marriage was unthinkable, and that although it was acceptable for a bachelor to have sexual needs, her own desires were cause for guilt. To add to her confusion, she had left the church for good following the angry scene at her mother's funeral. Never a devout Catholic, she now felt adrift without any religious support whatsoever. She had always felt a great ambivalence where the Catholic church was concerned, and had been torn between her parents' religious beliefs, for, though he was not a pious man, Eugene Mitchell had retained his Protestant faith. Grandmother Stephens's enforced evening prayers had been a great source of conflict when she had come to stay at Peachtree Street. Getting down on her knees in her own home was something that Peggy Mitchell simply could not and would not do. Now, with the appearance of Red Upshaw in her life, she needed explanations for some of the contradictory emotions she was experiencing. Never before had she met a man whose very masculinity made her unsure of herself. All the other men in her life — her father, Stephens, Clifford Henry, the young soldiers preparing to go off to war — had needed mothering, had made her feel just a bit superior. But not Red Upshaw. He laughed at what he called her "pretensions," and was never taken in by her self-righteous poses. Indeed, he liked her best when she was being distinctly *un*lady-like, and he shared her pleasure in risqué stories and was not critical when she smoked or took a drink.

Peggy had cut herself off from Grandmother Stephens and she could not turn to the church for answers, so she turned instead to her father and Stephens. Fearing Red Upshaw's improper influence on Peggy, they urged her to continue with her plans to make her debut. She hated the idea more than ever, and might have held out but for the fact that Upshaw quit college, where his grades had been impressive, to bootleg liquor. This caused a rift between them, not because Peggy disapproved of his covert activities but because she thought he was throwing away a brilliant future.

For a year Peggy had been advocating austerity in the family's wardrobe. Now, as if in sudden revolt, she did a turnabout and, as the fall season approached, she spent hours pouring over the current fashions in magazines like *Vogue* and reading the social columns in the *Atlanta Journal* to see who wore what where. "When a girl is making a social career," she told Stephens, "clothes are a uniform to be worn like a soldier's." And she entered into the preparations with the fervor befitting a good officer.

The season began in October. With it came new friendships with young women of social standing in Atlanta. It was a chance for a fresh start, and it began quite well. Peggy became friends with two sisters, Helen and Lethea Turman, as well as with several other debutantes who thought she was "terribly amusing and great fun," and who particularly admired her physical prowess.

Peggy was growing increasingly secretive about her personal life, and no one outside the family knew how serious her leg injury had been — despite the doctor's orders, she was not wearing the prescribed shoes that she so loathed. The debs of her group considered her a tomboy and, because of Upshaw, they did not think much of her taste in men. But she made a concerted effort not to flirt with their escorts, and that ranked high with them. And, although the members of the Debutante Club did not have the verve and enthusiasm of Ginny Morris, they did satisfy Peggy's need for female companionship. "A woman who doesn't like women can't have much fun," she claimed, but, as the season progressed, she began to fall out of favor with one girl after another because of her outspoken criticisms of the way the events were run by the older society women who had been debutantes once and who now controlled the prestigious Junior League.

The season consisted of scores of lavish parties given by the debutantes' parents and close family members at their homes and at various country clubs. Eugene took over the role of host, but most of the parties he gave were planned by Peggy. who kept a cautious eye on their budget, for her father made no secret of the fact that his practice was failing seriously since the bottom had fallen out of the real-estate business. Peggy managed to trim household expenses to a minimum to help alleviate some of the pressures, but the situation made her short-tempered. Unfortunately, she vented her anger on the senior society women.

Many charity affairs, sponsored by various clubs, were given during the season, and the current debutantes were expected to appear. They were celebrities, Atlanta's own stars, and their pictures appeared in each Sunday's rotogravure in the *Atlanta Journal.* Most of the girls took classic, full-face portraits. Not Peggy. She was always caught doing a stunt. One photograph shows her in a trainman's hat driving a locomotive; another, in a policemen's uniform. She smoked in public and let it be known that she took a drink from time to time. None of these things set well with the old guard, but they endured their displeasure discreetly until plans were set forth for the Mi-carême Ball, the grandest charity affair of the season. It was Peggy's contention that if the debutantes were the main attraction, they should be the ones to decide what charity would be the beneficiary. Not only did she speak up on her own account, but she convinced two other girls to join her in her challenge, which she lost ungraciously.

The dance music that season consisted of "cheek-to-cheek" songs like "Whispering" and "The Japanese Sandman," but the current rage was "The Sheik of Araby," which had been inspired by a novel of desert passion, *The Sheik,* by E. M. Hill. Surely knowing what kind of criticism it would evoke, Peggy decided she would highlight this Mi-carême Ball with an exhibition Apache dance in costume, and she chose as her partner a Valentino-type young man, Al Weil, who was a student at Georgia Tech. Her father and Stephens tried to talk her out of this plan, first, because they were fearful of the consequence to her leg and, second, because they believed the dance and her costume were too suggestive and would incur much disfavor. Peggy refused to back down.

Dressed in black stockings, and a black satin slit-front skirt sashed with crimson, and with a pouting red lipsticked mouth to match, she swooped and slid across the dance floor with wild shrieks of simulated terror and passion and, probably — due to her weak leg — pain, as her partner tossed her about, bending her so far back over his arm that her head touched the floor. The athletic Mr. Weil had rehearsed the dance with Peggy for a week, and they put into it all the drama of a Paris hoodlum dancing with his slavish whore. The older women were shocked. Even Polly Peachtree, the gossip columnist for the *Atlanta Journal*, was embarrassed and commented that Peggy had offered "herself and all she was on the altar of charity." As far as Atlanta's society matrons were concerned. Peggy's Apache dance was the final straw. The fact that she was Annie Fitzgerald Stephens's granddaughter had gotten her into the Debutante Club, but this blatant display of sensuality had to be censured.

To make it into Atlanta's high society at that time, a debutante had to be accepted as a member of the Junior League. Invitations went out a few months after the end of the season, and usually all the members of the Debutante Club were invited to join. Peggy looked forward to receiving her invitation with great expectation. When none came, it was a great shock, and the wound went deep. She would never forget this cruel snub and her pain and humiliation. One day, she vowed, she would get back at the ladies of the Junior League.

Chapter Seven

PEGGY MITCHELL celebrated her twenty-first birthday on November 8, 1921, quietly with her family. Grandiose dreams of practicing medicine or going off to Vienna to study with Sigmund Freud had been buried along with Maybelle. The life of a society woman was now barred to her, and she remained adamant about not attending a local college for a teaching degree.

During the queer aftermath of the war, she had harbored the idea of writing and, her feelings for Clifford Henry still unresolved, she had discussed with close friends the possibility of writing about the death of a soldier in the war. But the idea was abandoned before she'd even begun, and the possibility of a literary career was never mentioned in the Mitchell house.

Contemporary literary stars awed Peggy, and she read two, sometimes three, of their books a week: Booth Tarkington's *Alice Adams, The Girls* by Edna Ferber, John Dos Passos's critically acclaimed *Three Soldiers* (which she did not like), and E. M. Hill's *The Sheik* (which she did). Her favorite novels that year were F. Scott Fitzgerald's *The Beautiful and the Damned* and James Branch Cabell's *Jurgen: A Comedy of Justice*. These two writers were what she called "stylists"; they seemed to her to be consummate literary artists, the kind of writer she could never even hope to become. Too, they wrote about women in a way that was daring for the time. Cabell's novel even managed to be sexy without being pornographic. She read H. G. Wells's *Outline of History,* and the modern poets — poetry was enjoying a tremendous vogue — like Edna St. Vincent Millay, yearning to meet these poets and authors in the same way that other girls yearned to meet the current matinee idols. She went so far as to write fan letters to F. Scott Fitzgerald and Stephen Vincent Benét, but they did not reply. This seems not to have offended her, but it did deepen her sense of inferiority; she decided that she was unworthy of their response.

There is little doubt that Peggy Mitchell harbored a desire to become a published author, for she gave such an exalted place in her admiration to the authors whose books she read. But the more good literature she read, the deeper she submerged her own creative drive. She had always had to balance her feelings of inferiority with her vanity. By calling attention to herself, by flouting convention, she had been able to feed her ego. The rejection by the Junior League had damaged her confidence so severely, however, that she had momentarily lost her initiative, although she had not shed her daring. She still "hooted at convention" as Augusta Dearborn phrases it, recalling the time they were both invited to attend a bridal shower for one of the previous season's debutantes. "And to the piles of lingerie in virginal white laid out for the guests to see, Peggy solemnly added her own contribution, a nightgown of violent purple!" Augusta was shocked, as was their hostess, at Peggy's act of defiance.

Peggy's friendship with Augusta was of a curious nature. She admired Augusta's gentle charm and artistic nature, her ability to communicate with old and young. But Peggy was never completely at ease with Augusta, and her friend's dogged loyalty was at times an irritation as well as a support that she could not do without.

The camaraderie that had once existed between Peggy and Stephens had disappeared with their new maturity. He was now a member of her father's law firm and was gone all day, and in the evenings he socialized with his own circle of friends. Stephens appeared to be as troubled as his father about his sister's future and felt she needed another woman in the house, someone like Grandmother Stephens, who could help her through this difficult stage. But Peggy would not hear of it, even though she was alone in the house most of the day, except for the household staff.

The Mitchell staff kept to the house as much as possible at this time, for, after a hiatus of fifty years, white-robed, masked figures were assembling for midnight conclaves under flaming crosses. The Ku Klux Klan, which had once been active in Atlanta, had suddenly sprung to life again, occupying respectable executive offices in a building just a few doors from the *Atlanta Journal*, and blacks all over the city were terrified.

Within a few months, the Ku Klux Klan had taken charge of Atlanta, its followers having been either elected or appointed to the major city jobs. Stephens Mitchell has said, "After the folks came back from World War I there was a pretty good difference in Atlanta. There was a growth of people that had a crude agricultural background, which supported [the Imperial Wizard, Colonel William B.] Simmons and his Ku Klux Klan." A former circuit rider of the Methodist Episcopal church, Simmons said in an interview with Angus Perkerson that, as a child, he had been fascinated by the stories "his old black mammy" used to tell him about the Ku Klux Klan of post–Civil War days, and that one night he had had a vision of white-robed Klansmen going past on horseback. He had gotten down on his knees then and sworn to form a new chapter of the "old fraternal order."

It sounded almost clubby the way Simmons explained it, but the rebirth of the Klan in Atlanta, which included two bona fide members of the original Klan of the Reconstruction period, created not only a wave of anti-black, anti-Jewish, and anti-alien demonstrations in that city, but throughout the South, and then swept upward to the Midwest and from there, across the nation. And Atlanta, as national headquarters, was the capital to an alarming six million Klansmen. Blacks in Atlanta were terrified, and rightly so, as the self-styled vigilantes set fire to their churches, farms, and small businesses. The city's blacks had been brought up on hair-raising Ku Klux Klan stories calculated "to bring terror into the heart of a small black child." Cammie, upon whom Peggy relied for most errands, now re-

78

fused to go anywhere near Klan headquarters or to venture out at all after seven o'clock at night.

In the elections of 1922 through 1926, the Klan concentrated its powers at the polls so effectively that it was able to elect in Georgia, as well as in other states, U. S. senators, congressmen, and state officials sympathetic to its cause.

Although she considered herself a conservative Democrat, Peggy had only a superficial interest in politics. She had always had a deep-rooted affection for what she called "our colored population," who had tilled the red clay of Georgia and had planted and picked the cotton that had brought the state its first prosperity. She felt the "white folk" of Atlanta should be responsible for the welfare of the Negroes and, though this was hardly a liberal viewpoint and smacked of old-plantation mentality, it was a long, scrappy way from the views of the reactionary state government.

Stephens claims he was most influenced at this time by automobiles, music, and dancing. But that was not the case with Peggy. She was affected by what she read and by history, and since her literary preferences leaned toward the fine, liberal writers, and because her roots were so deeply in Atlanta, she was considerably distressed by the racial situation that prevailed in her city.

In the spring of 1922, Peggy rekindled her friendship with Red Upshaw. They both joined the Peachtree Yacht Club, a drinking club that had nothing at all to do with boats. None of the club members criticized her drinking or smoking or her pranks or her love of the theatrical. On the contrary, they greatly admired her ability to hold her liquor and to enjoy a good joke. To amuse her new friends, she began to write short plays, nothing serious or revealing, aimed to display her cleverness and ribald sense of humor. Soon, her Yacht Club friends began coming to the Mitchell house to perform with her in these playlets. One typical offering was a take-off on Donald Ogden Stewart's *Parody of the Outline of History,* itself a satire on H. G. Wells's best-selling book of the previous year. Eugene Mitchell was furious, and reminded her of the licking he had given her when she had plagiarized Thomas Dixon's book *The Traitor.* The plays stopped but the pranks continued.

Once, she and a group of friends dressed outlandishly in loud clothes and red suspenders and boarded a train coming from New York at the stop before its destination. The "locals" were given quite a shock when this bizarre company stepped onto the platform at Atlanta's Terminal Station.

A rather meek, amiable man when Maybelle was alive, Eugene Mitchell was growing increasingly cantankerous. These were difficult times in the Mitchell home; the family continued to suffer financial setbacks, and Peggy's errant behavior only created more tension. Cammie had married and moved to Birmingham, and the household staff now consisted of the wiry young black woman, Bessie, who both cooked and cleaned; Carrie, the part-time laundress; and a yardman. To cut winter fuel bills the house was maintained at a frigid temperature.

Peggy's new, hard-drinking, wild friends helped compensate for her grim home life. She was going through a period of rebellion and, according to Augusta Dearborn (who, though not one of the Yacht Club crowd, remained a staunch ally), "Many a night she routed Stephens out of bed to get some man out of jail." Usually it was one of her Yacht Club pals who had not been able to hold his liquor.

Along with her derring-do, shorter skirts, and bobbed hair, Peggy's sexuality burgeoned forth. She was seen by the young men and women in her crowd as "exceptionally charming but a big flirt and tease," despite the fact that she was seeing a great deal of Red Upshaw.

Close friends from this time characterize Upshaw as "unstable," "a wild creature," "dashing," "sexy," and of "low morals"; others recall him as "masterful" and "brilliant." He was certainly a man of voracious sexual appetites. Several of his contemporaries state unequivocally that, drunk, Red Upshaw had to satisfy his sexual needs, and if he did not, or could not, he became violent. At these times, the age or sex of the nearest body did not matter. Yet, when sober, there was an aura of excitement about him, of sexual magnetism; he was not only handsome, he radiated what one acquaintance called a "razzle-dazzle" kind of charm. He had celebrated his twenty-first birthday on March 10, 1922, and, although he was five months

Peggy's junior, he seemed to her the most worldly man she had ever known.

Red came from Monroe, Georgia, the son of an insurance salesman, William F. Upshaw, and Annie Likhs Kinnard Upshaw. He claimed to have played a secret, dashing role in the war, something to do with espionage and being behind enemy lines. This was obviously fabricated, for he was only seventeen at the war's end, and, according to his school records, appears never to have been inducted into the service. He did attend the United States Naval Academy at Annapolis, where the records state he entered on June 26, 1919, resigned voluntarily on January 5, 1920, was readmitted in May, and resigned again on September 1, 1920. Two weeks later, he enrolled at the University of Georgia in Athens. Because his family now lived in Raleigh, North Carolina, he did not qualify as a Georgia resident and paid the full tuition. Later, he wrote in a distinctive, flowing hand on his University Alumni application that he had not been a loan-fund beneficiary nor had he earned his own tuition. Since he admitted openly that his parents had cut off his allowance after Annapolis, one might wonder where he got the money to live as he did — for Red Upshaw liked expensive clothes, drove a flashy car, and always had cash in his pocket. However, it was not exactly a secret at the Yacht Club that Upshaw was involved in bringing bootleg liquor down from the Georgia mountains, for he supplied the club with most of its contraband.

Eugene Mitchell did not approve of Upshaw or of any of Peggy's Yacht Club friends, and the atmosphere in the Peachtree house grew increasingly frigid. This did not appear to intimidate Peggy, for she continued to invite her friends home and gave frequent parties. One day Upshaw showed up at the Mitchell house with another young man, about five years older than he, with whom he had just rented an apartment in Atlanta.

Both Stephens and Mr. Mitchell claimed they liked John Marsh at this first meeting, despite the fact that he was Upshaw's friend and roommate. Peggy seems to have liked him as well, but certainly not in the same way that she did Red. However, Peggy had developed her art of coquetry to a point where she could have several men in love with her at the same time and still manage to keep them all at arm's length. In the spring of 1922, John wrote his younger sister, Frances:

My new Sweetie may be the reason why I haven't written to you lately. It is because I have spent about as much time with her as the law allows. I would like for you to meet her and to pass on her. I have a high respect for your opinion. However, I am not contemplating matrimony as much as I would enjoy it. We have made a solemn promise not to fall in love with each other. Peg has made a success at that sort of relationship and she has the largest collection of man friends, real friends, of any girl of twenty I have ever encountered. I suppose eventually like the others I will be secretly in love with her, covering up an apparently hopeless passion. Ah well. Ho hum. The friendship of a girl like Peg is worth having and I value it.

She is an ardent young revolutionary with a helluva lot of common sense as well. You'll like her, I am sure. If you don't, I promise to choke you on the spot with my bare hands.

A few weeks later, Peggy had become close enough friends with Marsh to invite Frances down from Lexington, where she was finishing her senior year at the University of Kentucky, for the Easter holiday.

Despite the cool reception given her by Mr. Mitchell, Frances Marsh had an enjoyable time in the "big cold house" on Peachtree Street. She took to Peggy immediately and was impressed by the way she ran the Mitchell household by herself. During Frances's visit the house was the scene of several parties. At one, Upshaw drew her into a corner and confided, "John thinks he is going to win Peggy but I'm pulling the big guns." Frances recalls, "I assumed that meant he was using all of his sex appeal — which he had a lot of!"

Peggy basked in the excitement of this competition for her affections, prompting John to comment that she should be shot for giving a lifelike imitation of a modern young woman whose blistering passions were only held in check by an iron control. Peggy herself admitted to Frances that her coquetry frequently succeeded so well that all thoughts of seduction were tabled and "rape became more to the point."

After Frances's visit, the two women continued their friendship by mail. Some years later Peggy was to write Frances,

"John never tried to rape me. In fact he was the only one of my gentleman friends who didn't have dishonorable designs upon me. It used to worry me an awful lot and I wept many tears for fear I was losing my sex appeal." And John later confessed that he desisted only because everyone else was doing it, and he blandly hoped to shine in contrast.

Always a flirt and a tease, Peggy now seemed to take a certain pleasure in pushing her beaus to the very edge of control — at which crucial moment she would suddenly become all righteous indignation. There was a kind of danger in this situation that titillated Peggy, and it appeared to be enough to satisfy her sexual needs. The game worked with men like John Marsh, who were staunch in their moral beliefs, but Red Upshaw was neither accustomed to being held off in this fashion by a woman nor would he accept such treatment complacently. His pursuit of Peggy intensified.

Marsh remained constant but unpersisting, and Peggy successfully played one man off against the other for several weeks. Two men could not have been more dissimilar than Red Upshaw and John Marsh. One wonders how they ever came together as roommates. Upshaw was always in search of new excitement — he drove his car too fast, drank too much, spent money recklessly, dared strangers who criticized his behavior to fight or back down, and appeared fearless. If he had plans for the future, they were the only thing he kept to himself. Once out of school he seldom picked up a book, although he had been a brilliant student.

John Marsh, on the other hand, was an extremely conservative and trustworthy man who seemed older than his twenty-seven years. He was not particularly attractive or memorable. Soft-spoken, almost as tall as Upshaw, but stoop-shouldered, he had the pallor of a man who had often been ill and who had never fully recovered. Glasses shielded his nondescript gray brown eyes. His sandy hair was already receding and flecked with gray. Peggy was the first woman — other than his sister and his mother, to whom he was devoted — with whom he had ever felt comfortable. There had been only one other girl in his life, Kitty Mitchell (no relation to Peggy), who had been in school with him at the University of Kentucky. He had thought they were secretly engaged but, during the war, in which he had served with a medical unit in England and France, she had met and married a wealthy Cuban businessman and gone to live in Havana. This had been quite a blow to Marsh, who had not seriously dated another woman in the intervening four years.

Marsh was employed as a copy editor for the Associated Press in Atlanta and had also worked on the staffs of the *Atlanta Journal,* the *Atlanta Georgian,* and the *Lexington Leader.* Before the war, he had taught English briefly in his hometown of Maysville, Kentucky. He and Peggy could talk about books and authors, and she shared with him short stories she had written. Marsh was convinced that she had potential as a writer, although Peggy was not inclined to share his enthusiasm for her talent. Marsh had, in fact, once had literary ambitions himself, but he had given them up soon after the start of his newspaper career. Being a sensible, practical man, he had assessed his talents and had come to the conclusion that he might at best be a good editor one day, but that he lacked the creativity required to write a novel. Yet, he recognized Peggy's ability, and he assured her that she could one day write "a fine American novel."

By June, both men claimed to be in love with Peggy and would even divide an evening with her, tossing a coin to determine who got her for the preferred latter half. But it was not long before the outcome became obvious. There had always been a restless, rather wild side to Peggy's personality; danger appealed to her as much as did thumbing her nose at convention. Upshaw's unpredictability excited her imagination, and his domineering personality made her feel tremendously feminine.

It was simple — Upshaw sent Peggy's sexual temperature soaring, Marsh did not. For a time, these divided evenings helped her to control her natural response to Upshaw's charms. At last, apparently remembering Maybelle's advice that the answer to sex was marriage, she accepted the proposal she more or less elicited from Upshaw with the age-old line, "Not unless we are married."

Peggy's engagement to Upshaw had the same effect on Atlanta society as her Apache dance had had — everyone was properly shocked and disapproving. For that matter, no one close to the couple accepted the news with enthusiasm. Marsh was crushed but, being a good sport — and an exemplary martyr — he agreed to be best man. Eugene Mitchell tried to talk his daughter out of the wedding until the last moment; Grandmother Stephens warned her that she was making a great mistake; and Stephens told her she had chosen the wrong man. At the same time, he argued with their father that Eugene's violent stand was giving Upshaw just the edge he needed. Peggy would marry Upshaw out of her own stubbornness if Eugene persisted. Of course, Eugene Mitchell did persist, and the wedding was set for Saturday, September 2, 1922. Since the bridegroom claimed no religion and Peggy did not want to be married in the Catholic church, the house on Peachtree Street was chosen for the event.

More was made of Marsh's position as best man than of the wedding news itself. Not only did the local gossip columnists record their shock and astonishment, but the story of the best man who had also been a serious suitor and lost out to the groom was carried in the *Lexington Leader* as a feature story. What the papers did not know was the extent to which John Marsh had carried his gallantry. He wrote his sister how devastated he was by Peggy's choice, but, with a touch of wry humor, he also told her that he was "helping Red to get a trousseau because he was getting ready to get married without even the proper clothes."

Peggy and her grandmother tried to patch up their differences to plan for the wedding, but Grandmother Stephens remained disapproving of the groom and of Peggy's plan to be married by an Episcopalian clergyman. The Mitchell house was the scene of many family arguments during the few weeks preceding the wedding, and both Peggy and her grandmother were reduced to tears more than once. But Annie Fitzgerald Stephens hadn't lost any of the grit that had helped her survive the Civil War and, twice, the burning of Atlanta. She brought in her dressmaker, arranged the menu, and ordered the flowers. There was an impasse when Peggy threatened to carry a bouquet of red roses, her favorite flower, but she finally backed down in favor of the traditional bridal white spray. Grandmother Stephens must have sighed with great relief — Maybelle's daughter would have a proper wedding, despite a "heathenish bridegroom and an Episcopalian minister." Peggy was even to have the traditional trousseau tea the day before the ceremony.

Grandmother Stephens did her job well. The house on Saturday evening, September 2, 1922, was a perfect wedding scene. An altar constructed of palms, ferns, Easter lilies, white roses, and lilies of the valley, and guarded on each side by six silver candelabra, had been placed in the center of the entrance hall, its back to the front door and facing the wide Colonial stairway with smilax entwined about the banister. The guests, who numbered about eighty-five, entered through the French doors leading from the veranda and were assembled in the two large reception rooms that flanked the hallway.

At exactly 8:30 P.M., there being no piano in the Mitchell home, a recording of the popular "Kashmiri Song," Peggy's selection, was placed on the phonograph that had been set on a table in the stairwell. As the wedding party appeared at the top landing, a thin, high baritone voice signaled the start of the bridal procession.

> Pale hands I loved beside the Shalimar
> Where are you now? Who lies beneath your spell?
> Whom do you lead on rapture's roadway far
> Before you agonise them in farewell
> Before you agonise them in farewell
> Pale hands I loved beside the Shalimar
> Where are you now? Where are you now?

It was a song of parting, and it rather surprised some of Peggy's guests, who were to recall it sixty years later as a bizarre choice.

The two flower girls, Peggy's young cousins, wore frothy lavender dresses and carried baskets filled with Ophelia roses and lilies of the valley. Following them, as the procession moved down the staircase, was Augusta Dearborn, the maid of honor, in an orchid, brocaded satin gown, carrying a bouquet of orchids and pink roses, and looking quite stunning. Stephens and another groomsman escorted two lavender-gowned bridesmaids.

All eyes were on the top of the stairs as Peggy appeared on the arm of a dour-faced Eugene Mitchell. Her low-waisted dress was trimmed in pearls and ended at her knees, and her forehead was banded, flapper-style, by pearls that held her lace-and-tulle veil in place. A long narrow train, trimmed with pearls and bordered with silk orange blossoms with seeded centers, was attached to the back of her dress, and in one arm she carried a lavish spray of white roses and lilies of the valley, decorated with long white streamers. If the "Kashmiri Song" had been a strange choice, her flapper bridal gown, with its long grafted train and the oversized coronet and veil, was disastrous. As the towering bridegroom and his tall best man met her at the foot of the stairs, she looked like nothing so much as a child playing dress-up.

Upshaw, handsome and elegant in a dark gray suit, a white rose in his lapel, stood erect and smiling, with Marsh, stoic and bland-faced, behind him. Peggy marched grandly and slowly to his side before the altar, stopping as the record ended. When the bride and groom knelt to exchange their vows, Grandmother Stephens lost her composure, sobbing so loudly that she was forced to retreat to the rear hall so as not to disrupt the service.

The bride and groom made a dramatic departure immediately after cutting the cake. Still in their wedding attire, Peggy's train nearly tripping her up as she tossed her bouquet to Augusta, they ran out into the night, jumped into Red's bright green automobile, and drove away with a screech of rubber on pavement. They did not go far, however, as arrangements had been made for them to spend the night at the bachelor apartment of Upshaw and Marsh. Early the next morning, they left for North Carolina, where they planned to stay at an inn in Asheville before going on to Raleigh to visit Upshaw's parents.

After the honeymoon, friends noticed an edge in Peggy and Red's attitude toward each other that seemed to indicate that it had not been the happiest of times. Later, Peggy conceded that she never should have discussed her romantic feelings for Clifford Henry during the trip, nor sent the Henrys a postcard.

The young couple were to live at the Peachtree Street house by decree of Eugene Mitchell, who said he did not want to see his daughter starving somewhere in a rented room — nor did he want to lose her services as housekeeper. An argument developed on this point almost upon their return. Although his finances were unstable at best, Upshaw wanted Peggy to leave Peachtree Street with him and take her chances on how he was to support her. She refused to do so until he found a position with a guaranteed weekly paycheck. Quarrels ensued, and Peggy wrote complaining letters to John Marsh, who had been transferred to the Washington office of the Associated Press right after the wedding, telling him of their disharmony. Marsh's return letters were always mediatory.

But John Marsh was not the only person to whom Peggy wrote of her woes. As October 16, 1922, the fourth anniversary of Clifford Henry's death, approached, she began a correspondence with Mr. and Mrs. Henry that was on a close, intimate level. It was at the time of her marriage to Red Upshaw, Stephens claims, that Peggy realized Clifford Henry had been her one true love. If true, this must have greatly affected her relationship with Upshaw. At this time, she often talked about Clifford Henry and their idealized romance to her close friends, and she discussed it in several letters to the Henrys. As for Upshaw, he was frequently and publicly drunk and was abusive to her at these times. Once, he physically assaulted her before guests.

In December, Peggy begged John Marsh to return to Atlanta to talk to Red about his drinking problem. Frances Marsh was visiting her brother in Washington at this time, and he discussed the situation with her. "I think he went back to Atlanta mostly because of his love for her," she says. "It was a steady love as far as he was concerned. Maybe for her, too. She realized that he would be what Red wasn't, you see. Red was a wild creature."

Marsh did, indeed, return to Atlanta and it would seem from his sister's words that he intended to woo Peggy away from Upshaw. It was not too difficult a task, for no sooner had he arrived than they telephoned to tell him they had decided to get a divorce and were on their way over to his hotel to speak to him. John calmed them down that night, but Peggy went home alone.

"They attempted the impossible," John wrote Frances, "and failed after an honest effort because it was impossible. Both of them have brilliant possibilities for the future if they leave each other alóne. It is most gratifying to me that our trio remained a trio and didn't turn into a triangle."

The morning following their discussion with John, Red appeared at the house, pale, hung-over, drained of all anger and emotion. He dispassionately told Peggy he was going to Asheville, North Carolina, where he had a chance of a good job, and that she could go ahead and get a divorce if she wanted because he was never coming back to Atlanta. There was an indifference in his attitude that was to disturb Peggy for years to come. Perhaps if he had made some small conciliatory gesture that morning, she might have been willing to try again. But he left the house on Peachtree Street without a backward glance. He drove off in his sporty green car and did, indeed, head for North Carolina. But he was to return.

Chapter Eight

PEGGY TURNED to John Marsh as soon as Red Upshaw was gone, enjoying with him a warm, almost platonic relationship that put no pressure on her. Marsh admired Peggy, not for her daredevil abilities (he had never been either physically agile or inclined to any sport other than swimming), but for the writing talent he believed she possessed and which he knew he did not. There were other reasons, of course. Marsh was kind, gentle, unobtrusive, always dependable, a man who could be relied upon to get a job done in an impeccable fashion. But he was not an exciting or venturesome person and, until Red Upshaw had come into his life, he had been pretty much of a loner. He was not antisocial, but he was of a reticent nature and did not make friends easily. Like Upshaw, Peggy was a glamorous figure, and she appealed to him for some of the same reasons that his old roommate had. Not only was she a firebrand, and daring where he was not, she also had a quick sense of humor and a unique look that made her the center of attention at most gatherings. In Peggy's company, Marsh had a sense of identity — a sense of importance and of being needed — that he did not have otherwise.

It did not take a great deal of convincing on Peggy's part to persuade John to remain in Atlanta, but he had to quit his job to do so, for the Atlanta office of the Associated Press now had no room for him. A position soon opened in the public-relations department of Georgia Power and Light, and, although the work was not creative, he wrote Frances that the pay was good and that he "wanted to get on with making the best living" he could.

Her marriage to Upshaw over except for the legalities, Peggy was once again faced with the problem of her own immediate future. Eugene Mitchell's financial position had not improved, and there would be no support coming from Upshaw. Either she had to be content to be her father's housekeeper or she had to find a job. She elected to do the latter, and John Marsh convinced her that she had enough education and talent to become a reporter.

Gathering together both her courage and some of her Smith English compositions, she went to the offices of the *Atlanta Journal*, in an old, five-story, red brick building that rose in grimy ruggedness above the railroad tracks on Forsyth Street. Peggy asked for an interview with city editor Harlee Branch and, after a two-hour wait, she was finally ushered to his desk in the paper-and-spittoon-cluttered city room and began her assault. Branch was a tough-talking old pro who did not much approve of women in newspaper offices and who was as proud of his all-male staff's ability to drink hard as he was of their ability to work hard. He later said he was impressed by Peggy Mitchell's earnestness and the way she had gone about asking for a job, and he claimed he would have given her one but for the fact that the only women reporters on the paper worked on the Sunday magazine and the society sections, and he did not feel the time had come for the *Journal* to hire "regular" women reporters.

Peggy went back to John with this news, and he wasted no time in contacting Medora Field Perkerson, whom he had known when he had worked as a copy editor for the *Atlanta Journal Magazine*, to tell her about Peggy. Medora was married to Angus Perkerson, the magazine's editor, and was herself the assistant editor. She suggested that the young woman call Angus for an appointment.

Perkerson was the dour Scotsman that his name suggested. Yet, he was a mild-mannered, gentle man, and those close to the Perkersons felt that he made few moves without Medora's approval. His wife had liked the idea of a former debutante working on the Sunday magazine, believing it might lead to some good society stories, and, as a woman staff writer was quitting to get married, Angus agreed to see Mrs. Upshaw. When Peggy — weighing less than ninety pounds and looking about sixteen in her boyish suit, a beret pulled down gamine-fashion over one eye — walked into his office, he was not at all sure Medora's first instincts had been sound. But the more Peggy talked, glibly exaggerating her experience, telling him of her brief — and, he was certain, nonexistent — newspaper job on the *Springfield Republican,* and "swearing she was a speed-demon on a Remington," the more he became convinced that his wife was right. Mrs. Upshaw would make a good newspaper reporter, for she knew how to talk her way into someone's confidence. By the time she left the office, Peggy had been hired as a cub reporter at twenty-five dollars a week, the lowest pay on the paper, and with the warning that she was only on trial.

The third-floor rear office in which the Sunday magazine was quartered was dark and gloomy. The entire staff worked in one large room with six battered desks, files jammed against the walls, and a telephone on the front reception desk that was constantly in service.

"She had something of the look of a little girl playing dress-up in 'grown-lady' clothes," Medora later recalled of Peggy's first day as a reporter. "She wore a tailored dark blue suit and a white shirtwaist, anchored to the skirt with a big safety pin, which was very much in evidence before the day was over. But she was too serious about her new job to give the safety pin anything more than absentminded attention."

Peggy was told to use the desk at the entrance to the office, the same one that served as the base for the telephone. Except for Medora's private extension, this was the only telephone for a staff of twelve, and people were constantly perched on the edge of Peggy's desk as they talked on the telephone. The desk and chair were both so high that her feet didn't touch the floor, but she had no complaints.

Her first assignment — "Atlanta Girl Sees Italian Revolution," December 31, 1922 — was an interview with a Mrs. Hines Gunsalas who had been to Europe on a three-month clothes-buying spree. Peggy had been assigned the interview in order to report the latest European fashions, but the lady just happened to mention that while she was in Rome the Mussolini coup had taken place. Peggy made a short mention of this at the end of the article, the name Mussolini being unknown to her. Angus Perkerson turned the item into the lead and heavily edited the article, making it a news rather than a fashion story. Peggy also came up against Perkerson's tough standards and unrestrained criticism. Not only did he rewrite the piece, he told Peggy in no uncertain terms what she had missed and what was badly written. This shook Peggy's confidence somewhat, but Perkerson thought she had potential and was positive that she would turn into a clever interviewer. Her second assignment was an interview with a local plant doctor — "Plant Wizard Does Miracles Here," January 7, 1923. "There's a man out Peachtree Street," Peggy's story began,

> who can give a strawberry plant a "shot in the arm" and make it feel so good that it doesn't give a whoop for freezing weather. He has a bunch of these immoderately bold plants with big, red, juicy strawberries on them, growing out in the open air, right now — not in a hothouse or under glass — but in the chill of the January weather. And winter-bearing strawberries are not the only strange things that this plant magician has produced. He has pried into Nature's innermost secrets, so that he is able to make ordinary plants and trees do extraordinary things.
>
> With a doctor's hypodermic needle, he injects a mysterious solution into a plant and makes it forget all the traditions of its ancestry . . .

She goes on to describe Iverson G. Hodgins, Atlanta's plant wizard, as

> . . . a small man with a kindly face, a white mustache and a shock of white Paderewski-like hair on which a battered derby was tilted. A shirt open at the collar, a sailor's pea jacket and a pair of muddy kneeless trousers completed his costume. But from the lips of the muddy little man issued faultless English and a bewildering flow of Latin names of his beloved plants.

Perkerson printed the entire article (approximately three thousand words), this time as she had written it, and gave it a full page with a photograph of the wizardly gentleman himself.

Peggy's by-line for this story read, "Margaret Mitchell Upshaw," her legal name. She was pleased to have a by-line, but, without John's prodding she might not have gone that Monday morning, as she did, into Perkerson's office to ask for a desk of her own and the title of feature writer. She got both, but it was several months before her salary was upped to the lordly amount of thirty dollars a week, still not on the level of the men in Sports and News. She was assigned another feature right away, and this time she wanted it understood that the by-line would read simply, "Peggy Mitchell." It did.

Her new desk was by the window. Railroad tracks ran directly below it and steam locomotives belched thick clouds of sooty black smoke that blocked the view in winter and made it difficult to breathe in the summer. Peggy quickly and aptly named the office "The Black Hole of Calcutta."

Peggy's desk and chair had both been designed for a large man, and the janitor was called in to saw off about three inches from the legs of both. Medora Field Perkerson's desk was directly to her right, and the women got on well from their first meeting. Medora was only a few years older than Peggy, a dark-haired, square-faced, capable-looking woman with many of Maybelle's most striking traits — an authoritarian manner, which some might have called bossiness, a tremendous talent for organization, a social conscience, and a quick grasp of issues. Seasoned reporters would shrink a bit when facing Medora across her desk, but she quickly became Peggy's protector — not that the young woman needed to be shielded for long, for she was able to give and take with the best of them in a short time.

Erskine Caldwell, who was a *Journal* reporter during Peggy's time, remembers her as being "stylish except for her high buttontop shoes with large, thick heels. She made a loud *thumping* sound when she walked." Peggy was well aware of this, and she wrote Frances, "I look like a hat rack because I have to wear high-laced shoes on account of my ankle, and no matter what I wear I look awful."

Caldwell also recalls, "She was perky and friendly enough to have been nicknamed 'Bubbles' or 'Smiley,' but the feature writers did not associate much with the news and sports writers (the latter being the most prestigious group on the paper). . . . Life on the *Journal* was exciting journalism. Competition was the afternoon *Georgian* and the two papers had plants facing each other across the street. Both papers raced to get editions on the street and tried to outdo each other with blazing headlines. Atlanta was a great railroad and hotel town in the twenties, and was perhaps the leading convention city of the South. There seemed to me a constant flow of well-known political, business, and sports personalities, ready and willing to make comments and give interviews. A real good newspaper town."

And William Howland, who was also on the staff then, adds, "As rugged as was the physical setup of the *Journal* in the twenties, perhaps even more rugged was the professional setup. Those were the days . . . of *Extra* editions, when newspapers strained every nerve and muscle to be on the street first with any big news; when the newsboys calling 'Extra! Extra!' were the public's first warning of sensational events."

Despite their grubbiness, the *Journal* offices had an undeniable *esprit de corps.* At lunchtime, the cafeteria on the ground floor, nicknamed by its clientele "The Roachery," was crowded with every level of employee, from top executives to pressmen in soiled overalls and sweaty shirts, all sitting at rickety tables or milling about the counter, shouting back and forth, telling jokes as they ate "the rugged fare." According to Howland, it was a rowdy, free-and-easy group and, though they complained about the low pay, they worked for the paper with "an enthusiasm money could never buy. They cursed the long hours and at the end of the long day, they had steam enough left over to work up elaborate practical jokes involving the connivance of every department of the paper."

Within a short time, Peggy was accepted as one of the team. She was seeing John Marsh on a steady basis, but it seemed a close friendship rather than a romance to those who knew them both. More and more, she grew to depend on him, not only showing him most of the stories she wrote before she handed them in, but often giving them to him for editing. One early story that survives in galley has his hand-written corrections and deletions on it, and the story was published exactly as he edited it. The title, "Atlanta Sub Debs Pass up Tutankhamen," is also written in his hand, over her by-line. The corrections are pedantic, and do not affect the style of the piece. Still, there is no question that Peggy benefited greatly from John's English-teaching, copy-editing background, for her work soon had a polished, professional flow to it.

Peggy worked a six-day, sixty-hour week, leaving the house at seven in the morning before Bessie arrived. She took the trolley that went right past her house, breakfasted at the Roachery, and was the first of the day staff to appear at the *Journal* offices. Within a few months, she had become the most prolific feature writer on the paper. According to the records that still exist, in her four years and four months on the magazine, Peggy wrote 139 by-lined features and 85 news stories, assisted in the writing of a personal-advice column and a film column, and wrote a chapter for one of the *Journal*'s weekly serials when parts of a manuscript were lost. She could be counted upon to do a good job on any assignment she was handed, to meet deadlines, and never to complain when she pulled night work or when a story did not earn a by-line. For that matter, few of her stories for Harlee Branch in News were signed, and, though Branch liked Peggy personally, he still gave the men on his staff first consideration.

Not only was Angus Perkerson a dour man, he was also a tyrannical taskmaster. If a word was not exactly right, he made the reporter go back to the dictionary for a better one. Facts had better be correct; references, noted; and spelling, accurate. Peggy adhered to his rules without complaint. Nor did she ever turn down a story or feel that any assignment was beneath her. And thanks to Marsh's editorial help, her writing seldom required copy-editing. She wrote her leads last and her final paragraphs first, a curious habit that she was to retain, not "due to any Chinese blood," she explained, "but to the fact that I am an effect to cause reasoner rather than a cause to effect one."

Her stories were typed on an old upright Underwood that lacked a back-space key, but that "had the sweetest running movement," she said, "of any typewriter I ever used." In truth, Peggy enjoyed her newspaper days as she never quite enjoyed anything before or after. Best of all, she liked interviewing Atlanta's elderly. "Most of the things I asked them," she was later to comment, "had nothing to do with the story I wrote eventually. I was interested in how people felt during the siege of Atlanta, where casualty lists were posted, what they ate during the blockade, did boys kiss girls before they married them and did nice ladies nurse in the hospitals." She had no idea why she asked such questions, except that she "just wanted to know those things." She always liked to hear people talk about the things they knew best, and it was the war and the hard days after that the old-timers recalled most vividly.

Politics and economics held little appeal for Peggy and she seldom covered these subjects. However, she did interview Vice-President Coolidge when, shortly before President Harding's death, the Coolidges came through Atlanta. She did not remind him of their meeting at Mrs. Pearson's, but she made note of his "taciturnity" and his "spindly legs," and took up a good amount of space discussing the Vice-President's penchant for window-shopping. Mrs. Coolidge commented that he often returned from these excursions with a purchase that he thought she might like, and that at these times — and although he *was* a frugal man — "he became the most extravagant of husbands."

In March, just ten weeks after she had started the job, Peggy interviewed Hudson Maxim. A controversial figure, Maxim was known as the world's greatest inventor of high explosives and smokeless powder. As such, his opinions often gave an insight into what was happening in the arms race between countries. Peggy started her article with a good lead:

Mrs. Maxim, tiny and sweet-faced, was holding Hudson Maxim's bare feet in her lap, drawing on his socks in their room at the Piedmont Hotel, where the interviewer entered somewhat abashed. . . . Hudson Maxim tugged at his white beard and smiled — a sturdy old man with a magnificent leonine head topped by a mass of unruly white curls, a personality as well as a celebrity.

But buried in the middle of the three-thousand word article is this amazing quote of Maxim's, which elicited no editorial comment from Peggy:

There will be another war with Germany . . . the biggest war the world will ever see . . . between the clear-thinking sane people of the world and insane rabid force. A war that will be fought with weapons never even thought about before, high explosives that will lift entire towns off the maps — bombing planes that will carry huge crews and worst of all the gas . . . the United States Government has at present a formula for poison gas that is the most destructive thing the world has ever known.

To say that Peggy Mitchell was a great newspaper reporter would be an overstatement, for she never had a strong point of view and seldom caught the social or political ramifications of her articles. But she did have a unique eye and an ear for stories that would hold a reader's interest, and she possessed a fine ability to describe what she saw and heard in a fresh way.

A persuasive interviewer, she could often garner information withheld from one of the gruffer newsmen. When she did land a good news lead in this fashion, Angus would pull the story and send it down to Harlee Branch in News. Perkerson recognized, as did Medora and their co-workers, that Peggy had a great instinct for a story and an eye for detail; she could take a report on the Traveler's Aid or the Atlanta Humane Society and turn it into a gripping well-researched piece that qualified as a front-page Sunday magazine article.

Whenever Marsh could, he accompanied her on assignments. His job was not as exciting as hers and he was beginning to live vicariously through Peggy, enjoying her adventures and achievements. He remained cautiously in the background, waiting in hotel lobbies while she did interviews in celebrities' rooms, or remaining in the car when an assignment took her to a subject's home, or jail cell, or hospital ward.

Her work, John, and the big house on Peachtree Street left Peggy little free time, and she saw less and less of her old friends at the Yacht Club. Her father and brother were delighted by this and felt Marsh was a steadying influence. To some extent this was true, but more important was the fact that Peggy had finally found something that she enjoyed doing — gathering facts for stories, meeting interesting and exciting people, traveling about the city.

Curiously, what she liked least about her job as a reporter was actually sitting down at her old Underwood and writing her stories. Medora noted, "Writing always came hard to Peggy. I could always tell when she was stuck, for she would get out her lipstick and make up her mouth."

One bright spring morning, for the sake of a good story, Peggy allowed herself to be strapped into a boatswain's chair — which she judged was "about as large as the palm of your hand" — and shoved out of a window on the top floor of a fifteen-story building that had been selected as an imitation Stone Mountain, the site for the carvings by sculptor Gutzon Borglum that would "bring into existence the world's most magnificent monument to the Southern Confederacy." The idea was for Peggy to simulate the experience Borglum and his assistants would have while carving the work hundreds of feet up in the air. She wrote:

In an enormous pair of size 40 overalls, which gave the effect of a deep sea diver's costume, and with a hammer and chisel to complete the workmanlike rig, I was strapped and swung far out of the window. A dizzy whirl — buildings, windows, a glimpse of the sky, anxious faces at the windows, all jumbled up for an instant of eternity, a feeling of nausea, then BUMP! completed the first swing in the air and I came against the side of the building with an awful wallop. The wall felt good. It was rough and it hit me with a jolt, but it was solid and secure. Before I could catch hold of it, however, Newton's third law of motion asserted itself — for every action there is an equal and opposite reaction — and pendulum-like we started to swing out over the great, wide world again.

"Hey!" shouted a distant voice. "Look down this way and smile!"

Smile! Ha! Smile! Imagine that at a time like this! Except that both hands were so busy holding on to the leather straps I would have laughed up my sleeve at him. I glanced down to give him the most cutting, scornful look in my repertoire and — What a sensation!

The realization of how high above the world I was hit me with a jolt. There was a sickening sensation in the pit of my stomach. I jumped. The seat of the swing slipped from under me for a terrible instant, I hung there spinning, with only the strap under my arms between me and the hard, hard street 200 feet below.

Fortunately I had been fastened in so tight that I could hardly breathe and the strap held. They lowered me down the side of the building and swung me around some more and after a while they decided that the cause of journalism had been sufficiently served and they consented to pull me back up to the window and the thing was over. But the feel of solid floor beneath my feet brought back the jolly old bluff and I managed to pull a weak sort of smile and announce — "Oh it wasn't so bad!"

Directly after the publication of this article, complete with photographs of Peggy in action, she went to Angus Perkerson and asked that she be given the opportunity to write some stories of higher literary value. Her idea was to do a four-part series dealing with women in Georgia's history. Perkerson was not keen on the idea but finally agreed, with the proviso that it be written when she had time to spare from other more "pertinent" stories ("Football Players Make the Best Husbands" and "How a Perfect Lady Refuses a Proposal").

For the first time, Peggy walked through the doors of Carnegie Library in quest of material on Georgia's history for a story. Something must have stirred within her as she went about her task in an organized and industrious way, for she reported to Medora that she had not enjoyed any previous assignment as she was enjoying this one. She selected four women to profile for the first article, "Georgia's Empress and Women Soldiers." The only one who fitted the ladylike stereotype of the Southern heroine was Rebecca Latimer Felton, the first woman to become a United States senator, although by appointment upon the death of her husband rather than by election. The others in Peggy's quartet were Lucy Mathilde ("Bill") Kenney, "large, masculine in appearance, a fine rifle shot and absolutely fearless, who enlisted as a man with her young husband in the first volunteers that went off to the Civil War from Georgia and became a 'hero' at the Battle of Sharpsburg but who did not reveal herself until her 'buddy' (and husband) was killed in the second battle of Manassas so that she could take his body home"; and Mary Musgrove, crowned empress of the Creek Nation and who "despite her years among the civilizing influences of the colony and her three successive white husbands remained an untamed savage until she died"; and "Cross-eyed" Nancy Hart, "who stood six feet tall, was broad and muscular in proportion, red-haired and cross-eyed. Her neighbors were often given to saying that her disposition was cross-grained, too."

During the Revolutionary War, Nancy Hart had killed one Tory and had single-handedly captured a marauding troop of Redcoats who had invaded her kitchen, and was quoted afterward as saying, "I wasn't goin' to have any Tories eatin' my pun'kin pie!"

The day after the article appeared, Angus Perkerson called Peggy into his office and showed her a stack of mail the paper had received protesting the contents of the story. She had been accused of everything from defaming Georgian womanhood to bastardizing history in order to sell newspapers. Terribly upset by these accusations, she asked Perkerson if she could write a piece on the authenticity of her research. He refused and, to her great disappointment, cancelled the rest of the series.

Criticism was difficult for Peggy to accept; it set her back and gave her a "writer's block" for several days thereafter. To shield her from these bouts of insecurity, Medora did not show Peggy any negative responses to her articles, as she was anxious to avoid the loss of a good reporter's services. Peggy's sensitivity to criticism, her inordinate need to write lengthy replies to her detractors, and her testiness when her work was attacked, were the reasons Medora and Angus Perkerson so seldom gave her stories with much depth. This kept peace in the feature department, but it also kept Peggy from any significant writing achievement.

Though it was nearly 5:00 P.M., a bold, yellow sun blazed in the summer sky as Peggy stepped off the trolley on July 10, 1923, and started across Peachtree Street. The glare was so strong that she was almost to the curb before she recognized the green sports car parked in front of her house. Red Upshaw, bronzed and trim, got out from behind the wheel and stood barring her path. She had been certain that if they were ever to meet again, she would feel nothing but fury. Reality was another matter. After a short exchange, she asked him to come into the house.

Only Bessie was at home; Stephens and her father were still at work. Peggy and Upshaw talked for a while in the living room about what they had been doing during their six months of separation, though Peggy did not mention that she was seeing John Marsh.

In a sworn deposition taken less than a month later, as evidence for her divorce, Peggy said that after about ten minutes she and Upshaw went from the living room upstairs to the bedroom they had shared. She did not mention that they had been separated for half a year, nor did she state whether or not she went upstairs with him of her own accord. Once in the privacy of their bedroom, she claimed, "Mr. Upshaw demanded his connubial rights after striking me with his fist upon my left arm about the elbow." The court representative then asked if she had given her husband cause for such violence. "I've been very kind and affectionate to my husband ever since our marriage and he has not had the least cause to complain of me," she answered. She refused his advances, she said, out of fear that he would treat her "in a cruel and inhumane manner." The counsel added that Upshaw had "jerked her against a bed, causing her to be bruised all over her body," as she successfully tried to fight him off.

"Is that the truth, Mrs. Upshaw?" the judge asked.

"Yes sir," Peggy replied, and then went on to explain that her shouts and screams had finally brought Bessie, who appeared in the doorway just as Red was leaving the bedroom, with Peggy crying hysterically as she ran after him, yelling at him to get out of the house. To Peggy's horror, he turned then and struck her a vicious final blow in the left eye.

Peggy was rushed to the hospital, and it was two weeks before she had sufficiently recovered from the effects of this beating to return home. Her hospitalization was kept secret even from close relatives, for the humiliation was almost more than she could bear. Her bruises and abrasions were still much in evidence when she was discharged, and at home the same veil of secrecy prevailed. Peggy had asked her brother to tell Medora that she had had to leave town to tend to a sick relative and would be away from work for six weeks if that was acceptable. Medora said it was, but did not believe the story, suspecting an explanation nearer the truth.

The truth. It was something that only Peggy and Upshaw actually knew. But John Marsh had once again been placed in the middle. From Peggy's defiled bed on Peachtree Street, Upshaw had gone directly to Marsh, confessed that he had attacked Peggy, claiming that she had provoked him, and then, after asking for a loan (which Marsh gave him), said he would agree to an uncontested divorce and would not return to Atlanta if Peggy did not press charges. He expected Marsh to act as an intermediary, and, indeed, that is the role Marsh assumed.

In view of the scandal a court case would create, Peggy, Stephens, and Mr. Mitchell thought that Red's proposal was the best solution. But then he left town before signing a paper agreeing to a divorce. The Mitchells were furious, but nothing could be done. Emotionally and physically battered and bruised from Upshaw's attack, her eyes blackened and her face swollen, Peggy at first refused to see anyone at all, but John Marsh insisted on visiting her even though, during the first week, he had to do so in a darkened hospital room. The evidence of Upshaw's brutality so shocked Marsh that he bought Peggy a small pistol, which she kept beneath her pillow as protection in case Upshaw should break his promise not to return.

Peggy and John now shared what she thought was an ugly, horrible secret. Knowledge of it drew them closer together and Peggy felt confident that John Marsh would not reveal what he knew. By the time she left the hospital, Peggy felt more beholden to him than she had to anyone else in her life, and John had never felt as needed or as appreciated by a woman. He showed his gratitude by keeping Peggy's secret, and she showed hers by tacitly agreeing to be his girl.

Mrs. John R. Marsh
1925–1936

Chapter Nine

*B*Y SPRING of 1924, Peggy was the leading feature writer on the *Journal*. Not only was she a respected newspaper woman, she had become a well-known local personality, a star reporter, and her name and face were familiar to all who read the Sunday *Journal*.

The *Journal* had a host of fine writers on the staff during the time of Peggy Mitchell's tenure. In addition to Erskine Caldwell there was Grantland Rice, Laurence Stallings (whose play *What Price Glory?* would soon appear on Broadway), Ward Morehouse, Ward Greene, Morris Markey, Roark Bradford, W. B. Seabrook, and William Howland. Peggy had quickly taken her place among them. Robert Ruark, a future best-selling author who was also on the *Journal* with her, said, "She walked straight into her stories without a lot of hemming and hawing."

One story that took her from the feature department downstairs to the newsroom was her interview with Harry Thaw, the Pittsburgh millionaire who had won front-page notoriety with his legal fights to escape the gallows and, later, the insane asylum, for the murder of famous architect Stanford White, the lover of Thaw's wife, Evelyn Nesbit.

His hair, still a thick shock which he brushes straight back in a long pompadour, is neither white, [nor] salt-and-pepper, nor iron-gray, but an odd slate color, the even gray of a Maltese cat.

His quick, noiseless movements are catlike, too, as if the years of confinement had bred in him a nervousness, an abruptness, bordering almost on suspicion.

Written in the same descriptive style as her features, Peggy's news stories did not really qualify as hard news, but were judged to be of more timely interest than those pieces that ran in the magazine.

Peggy made it her business to keep up with current fashion, and she wrote knowledgeably about "Society's darlings and their smart bobs." She was the *Journal* authority on the changing styles in slang, as well. In one of many articles on the subject, we learn that, along with "romping hieroglyphics and playful pharaohs" printed on the vivid dress fabrics of spring, 1923, Tutankhamen had invaded current slang. "King Tut" referred to "a well-meaning man who is continually putting his foot into it." A "mummy" was "a person without personality," but when "favorite mummy" was applied to a girl, it signified "the highest approval." And Peggy tossed in her own invention: "sacred ibis!" to replace "hot dog!" in moments of excitement. No one, she insisted, had a "sweetie" anymore, they had a "sheik." Other vivid phrases included "dizzy frog" (a dumbbell), "Wouldn't that tweeze your eyebrows?" (shocking), "Wouldn't that make you tear a toenail?" (unbelievable), "young ineffectuals" (would-be intelligentsia), "slipper-flipper" (someone who scorned serious thinkers), and "the eel's heels" or "the oyster's adenoids" (which replaced "the cat's meow").

Peggy's skirts were shorter than most, her language bold, and — in spite of the treatment she had received at the hands of Red Upshaw and her deepening friendship with John — she was still a tease and a flirt. She liked to surround herself with young men and felt a good relationship could stand such competition. She bore many traits of the flaming flapper and was part and parcel of the Zelda Fitzgerald era, of the aftermath of Camp Gordon in Atlanta in 1917 and what troops do to any city, of the rebellion of Southern women against the mores and patterns and restrictions of the past. She frequently suggested stories that involved her interviewing college boys and, invariably, she would win a heart or two along the way. But, she claimed, these "little flirtations were not for John to take seriously."

Sometimes she posed for the illustrations that accompanied her articles. One story, "Should Husbands Spank Their Wives?" featured a photograph of Peggy draped across the knees of a young art editor, who posed with his hand raised over her backside.

Medora Perkerson said of Peggy's *Journal* articles that they "mirrored the flapper era, almost as John Held, Jr., and Katharine Brush and F. Scott Fitzgerald did in their cartoon and fictional media. [Peggy] recorded the changing skirt lengths . . . the earliest boyish bobs, the strange slang of the 'Flaming Youth' period as reflected in Atlanta." She wrote hastily, but with care, to meet her deadlines, and Medora considered her a "genius at character delineation" and admired her "gift for sharply differentiating one individual from another so that each article had its special identity." Peggy had a talent for sketching memorable characters in a few short strokes. Certainly her description of Harry Thaw — with his hair "the even gray of a Maltese cat" and his "quick, noiseless movements" — brings him instantly to life.

On June 17, 1924, Peggy's divorce was filed in the Superior Court at Fulton County. The deposition she had made following Upshaw's attack was placed in evidence. She asked for an annulment of her marriage to Upshaw and restoration of her maiden name, but she waived a settlement or any form of alimony.

Peggy's marriage to Red Upshaw had caused great division in the Mitchell household. Her father had never reconciled himself to the marriage and believed she had demeaned the name of Mitchell by entering into such a union. But the divorce, rather than helping to ease the situation, worsened it. Divorce was unknown in the Mitchell family and was against the Fitzgeralds' religion.

Neither her father nor Stephens was present as Branch Howard, a family friend who acted as her attorney, presented Peggy's deposition to the court and she swore to its validity.

The foreman of the jury agreed that sufficient proof had been submitted to authorize a total divorce, but not an annulment or restoration of her maiden name. The jury's verdict did not discourage her and, on October 16, she returned to court before a second jury and underwent the entire painful experience again. This time she won her petition. She was again Margaret Mitchell, better known, however, as Peggy Mitchell of the *Atlanta Journal*.

Peggy's closest friend at this time was Augusta Dearborn, who had now moved to Atlanta, but her relationship with Medora was more active simply because they were in daily contact. Peggy admired Medora's professionalism and the way she had succeeded on her own at a newspaper where her husband was her boss. Not only was Medora a good editor and reporter, she also wrote the successful "Marie Rose" advice column. As Marie Rose, Medora received three or four large wire baskets of mail a week — letters numbering into the hundreds. She could only reply to a few of them in the paper, but she read each one of the others, somehow managing, in spite of her enormous work load, to answer all but the obscene or incoherent letters. Paying the costly postage herself, Medora was a one-woman social welfare team, enlisting the aid of doctors, ministers, and educators and giving, as Peggy noted, "sympathetic but hard-headed and practical advice when needed." This dedication to her readers, to people for whom she felt some responsibility because her column had provoked their letters, had a great impact on Peggy. In later years, when she was confronted with thousands of fan letters, she insisted on answering them in the same fashion, paying her own postage.

In the fall of 1924, Peggy did a brief stint as entertainment editor, covering "Pictures and Players." During this period, her by-line appeared on "Movie Stars Who Call Atlanta Home" — Ben Lyon, Mabel Normand, and Colleen Moore, who, as Kathleen Morrison, had been a Jackson Street neighbor of the Mitchells until 1908, when her mother had taken her to Hollywood. Perhaps Peggy's most famous interview was the one with Rudolph Valentino, in which she reported:

When he turned to bow and grip my hand in a grasp that made my rings cut into my fingers I suffered a distinct shock. Dressed in a fuzzy tan golf suit with tan sox to match and well-worn brown brogues, he seemed shorter and stockier than when on the screen as the Sheik. He seemed older — just a bit tired. His face was swarthy, so brown that his white teeth flashed in startling contrast to his skin, his eyes tired, bored but courteous; his voice low husky, with a soft sibilant accent . . . that held me with its well-bred, almost monotonous intonation.

She ended the article by saying that she "registered a world-beating blush" when the Sheik, in his knickers, picked her up in his arms, as he had Agnes Ayers on the desert sands, and carried her over the threshold of the terrace of his hotel suite into the sitting room.

None of this was timeless prose and no one was more aware of this than Peggy. Writing for a newspaper is the most transient of literary endeavors; the printed pages of a reporter's work last less than a day, ending up as wrapping for a piece of fish, or as a lining for a refuse can. But Peggy had grown good at her craft and had found her own niche in it. Her old friend from debutante days, Helen Turman, had married Morris Markey, and he was leaving the *Journal* to join the staff of the *New Yorker*. But Peggy had no high-flown ambitions to go on to a more prestigious newspaper job or to become a staff member on one of the many fine national literary magazines. Her opinion of herself was not much higher than it had been at Smith, and the fact that John could always find so many errors in her grammar and spelling, coupled with her incomplete education, made her feel not only insecure, but something of a literary fraud.

In December, 1924, John Marsh suffered a severe attack of hiccoughs that lasted forty-two days. During the first few days, Peggy tried all the home cures she had heard about, but John's hiccoughs persisted. By the end of the first week, he was so weak and exhausted from the seizure that the doctor put him in the hospital. No cause was found; no remedy seemed to help. There was concern that his heart was being overtaxed. Peggy spent every moment she could at his bedside. In what spare time was left, she began a thorough investigation into the causes and cures of hiccoughs, which she turned into an article, "What Causes Hiccoughs?", for the Christmas issue of the Sunday magazine. She persuaded the doctors to try some of the unorthodox methods she had uncovered, like applying ether to the skin over the diaphragm, which had no effect. Morphine and sleeping drugs were administered, but John hiccoughed as he slept. Finally, when the medics threw up their hands in despair, Peggy applied psychology, doing what she could to distract him and militantly supervising the conversations of visitors and nurses to make sure no one spoke about anything distressing.

And, as she stood vigil by his bed and in the corridor outside his room, knowing how weak and near death he was, she realized the depth of her feelings for him. She was terrified that he might die and did not know how she would cope with such a loss. Her need for his council had grown steadily, as had her dependence upon his editing ability. Before his attack, they had been seeing each other daily and were on the telephone several times during the day as well. It dawned on her at this time that she might well be in love with John Marsh, though this was not like the romantic love she had felt for Clifford Henry nor the passionate love she had experienced with Red Upshaw. With John, there was a sense of familiarity, of comfort, of never having to deal with emotional responses that sent her reeling.

The weeks progressed and John's condition did not improve. Finally, his brother Henry came down from Wilmington to see what he could do. Peggy met him at the railroad station. Henry was an intelligent, solid man who greatly resembled John, and Peggy was much relieved by his arrival. At the time, John's was the only case of this kind on record in which a patient hiccoughed thirty-one days and didn't die.

"I wish he had not picked such an elusive disease that doctor[s] know nothing about it," Peggy wrote to Frances. "It would have been much easier to treat if he had gotten delirium tremens."

A few days later, John had grown so weak that he had to be kept in an oxygen tent. Frantic about this turn, Peggy went directly from work to the hospital and remained by his bedside with Henry until midnight, when she called a taxi and went home. Her father and brother had already gone to bed and she went directly to her room, where she curled up on the bed and cried herself to sleep. When she woke, it was the middle of the night, and all she could manage was to kick off her shoes, set the alarm clock, and crawl under the covers, "clothes, stockings, hairpins and all." She awoke the next morning to find the downstairs lights on, as they always were when she was out. "They probably thought I was just being modern and leading my own life like the girls in the magazines that father continues to read while he condemns them," she wrote to Frances that morning. "I'll have to do some tall explaining tonight."

On the forty-second day, when the hiccoughs finally showed signs of abating, John spoke to Peggy of his deep love for her. But then, when the doctors reported that not only had his heart been weakened by the lengthy seizure, but that they had, in the course of their extensive tests, discovered that he suffered from petit mal, a form of epilepsy, he insisted they wait to talk about anything as serious as getting married until he was fully recovered and had had further tests.

He was dangerously thin and unable to eat without pain. The doctors diagnosed an infected gallbladder and removed the organ.

John spent all of March and April recuperating at home, and during this time he took an even greater interest in Peggy's work, penciling in his corrections on her copy as he had done before, but now adding comments that had whiffs of his schoolteacher's background. "Good!" he wrote on the margin of a story she did on One-Eye Connelly, one of the world's most famous gate-crashers. "Inconsistent," he chastised on a paragraph of an interview in which there were three different colloquial spellings of one word.

By May, John's health had improved. He'd gained weight, his skin looked less pasty, and he was able to work full-time at the office. Still, he was quite nervous. The long siege of illness had been costly and he was heavily in debt to the hospital and doctors. Perhaps even more disconcerting was the confirmation that he had epilepsy, that it could have been the prime cause of his hiccoughs, and that he had to be prepared for the possibility of another seizure — either hiccoughs or an epileptic fit. He was taught what to do in case of an attack and he gave Peggy instructions for handling the situation if she should be with him at the time. He asked that they wait to set a date to be married. To Stephens and her father's suggestions that John might be right, Peggy replied, "John and I are going to live poor as hell and get out of this jam."

But Marsh did not want Peggy to work after they were married, despite her claims that not only did she not *mind* working, she preferred it. Using Frances as an intermediary, she pointed out that her paycheck would help out on the expenses and, besides, it was more fun to work than to keep house. Furthermore, her best friends worked and she thought a mug of coffee at the Roachery far more interesting than a bridge or Mahjongg tea. John was not easily convinced. A few months later, Peggy was to write her only published magazine piece, "Matrimonial Bonds," for the *Open Door,* a local publication. Using the fictional names Nancy and Bill, she recreated the series of arguments she and John had had over whether they should wait to be married until she could be a "married lady of leisure."

> Bill has a sneaking, old-fashioned suspicion under his modern double-breasted coat, that Nancy's having held a job before her marriage had somehow unfitted her for wifehood. . . . He doesn't take into consideration that Nancy is a wise young person and will make a wise young wife. The reason for this is that Nancy has been through it all — been through the long hours of office work when employers were grouchy and she was tired, been through the long strap hangings on smelly homebound cars. She's learned how much a dollar means. A dollar is not just a shining silver disk or a crackling bit of paper. It's so many hours' wait when you want to be out swimming, so many hours of making tired fingers fly. And she won't be quite so eager to say airily, "Charge it!" After she is married, she'll think three times about buying chiffon stockings by the dozen. For if she loves Bill she can't help thinking how much of his sweat went into those dollars.

Her arguments were persuasive and they set Independence Day, 1925, as the date of their wedding.

In May, Peggy covered a tea dance at the Biltmore and, according to Medora, "brightened the occasion considerably for dowagers at a nearby table." She had attached brass bells to her garters and, as the photographer who accompanied her whirled her past the dowagers' table, "there was a flash of garter and bells tinkled from under her short skirt." It was Peggy's last lark as a single woman.

On June 15, John Marsh and Peggy Mitchell applied for their marriage license. Peggy lied about her age, listing it as twenty-two (she was twenty-four), said she had been divorced on grounds of cruel treatment in October, 1924, and then did not sign the document. John, however, did.

This time, Peggy's family was enthusiastic about the match. It was decided that the announcement and the wedding itself would be handled as a first marriage, and no mention of the earlier one was made in the newspaper accounts of either the engagement or the ceremony. Grandmother Stephens put aside her religious reservations for a second time to help with the plans.

Peggy's Sunday feature stories for July 5 and 12 were written between fittings and wedding preparations. For the story on the latter date, "Atlanta Boys Don't Want Rich Wives," she asked some seniors from the University of Georgia what they looked for in a wife. One of them, Sam Tupper, who was to become a close friend of Peggy and John, put "a civilized mind" at the top of his list; then, in descending order of importance, disposition, love of home and children, social position, personal appearance, health, religion, wealth, artistic talents, independence of spirit.

Mr. Tupper's peers agreed almost unanimously with these qualifications. One college senior said, "A girl who is successful as a homemaker is more of a genius than one who paints a beautiful picture or writes a best-seller." Peggy withheld editorial comment, though she slyly concluded her article with a quote from another student who thought "the clinging-vine type of woman" was "detestable" and was in favor of a woman "who does not follow a career, who is dedicated to her home and family, and yet is not above the necessity for honest, respectable toil, if need arise."

To understand Peggy Mitchell's future attitudes toward herself, it is important to consider the climate in which she lived. Maybelle was no longer at her shoulder encouraging her to be a free-thinking, independent woman, and Peggy did not have the self-confidence to do more than flout convention. The bells on her garters, the gift of a purple nightie, the boyish clothes she had once worn were gestures of independence, but she was never able or inclined to follow them up. Since her drastic misjudgment of Red Upshaw's character and the humiliation this had caused, her father's, Stephens's, and now John's approval had become most important to her. She harbored innumerable insecurities and feelings of inadequacy. If Maybelle had lived, she would have been disappointed in her only daughter; of that, Peggy was sure. She had not carried out her early dream of being a woman of medicine; she had not even graduated from college. Society had snubbed her. She had betrayed her first romantic, ideal love with a marriage to a scoundrel, a drunk, a pervert who had abused her physically, and she was certain that if the story got out, it would expose her weakness in allowing flesh to rule mind. She was also aware that she had chosen to go to work as an *out* and not as a *means*. In light of her future behavior, it seems obvious that Peggy thought the young gentlemen she had interviewed at the University of Georgia about prospective wives were probably right. All the things she was not and could not be were highly valued, and the things she esteemed — artistic talent and independence of spirit — were at the bottom of the list.

From the moment she and John decided to marry, certain things were tacitly accepted by each of them. Because of John's illness and the fear that the epilepsy could be passed on, there would be no children, a decision that seemed to relieve rather than disturb Peggy. She would work only until John was out of debt and they were able to sustain themselves on his salary; and they would not live in the house on Peachtree Street.

A few months before the wedding, Marsh wrote a long letter to his old girlfriend, Kitty Mitchell, telling her about his plans and his love for Peggy and including a photograph of them together. As the weeks went by and Kitty did not reply, John became distressed and discussed his feelings frequently with Peggy, who, in turn, told Frances that she thought Kitty was being ungenerous and that she should be "sincerely glad in the happiness of her old flame."

Actually, Kitty Mitchell had not had the depth of feeling for John that he had had for her, and now she was married and had a family and responsibilities of her own. However, just a few weeks before the wedding, a reply did arrive, congratulating him on his "good fortune at finding such a pretty and obviously clever young woman." Peggy wasted no time in conveying to Frances how happy this made John. Kitty Mitchell, she explained, was a sort of beloved legend to him and, after all, men had so few really beautiful legends that it grieved her to see one ruined in any way "with a touch of reality and human nature creeping in."

Though he might have harbored romantic fantasies of Kitty, there was no question that John Marsh was very much in love with Peggy. On her part, she respected John's honor and felt grateful that, after her degrading marriage, he considered her worthy of his love. John had a spotless reputation, and his willingness to overlook Peggy's past seemed to diminish its significance. He stood with her against Red Upshaw and acted as a buffer between herself and her father and brother. Too, he needed her and openly admired her.

Though Peggy gloried in feeling desirable and playing the Southern coquette, sex itself had been a painful, distressing experience for her. Marsh had made no demands upon her, and his nature was such that she felt confident he would never take advantage of his position as her husband if she did not want him to. Nor did he appear to be jealous, allowing her to bask in the flattery of the young men in her circle and those she encountered through the newspaper without censure. He even encouraged her to keep her relationship with Clifford Henry's parents alive.

Peggy's love for John Marsh was to grow with the years but, at the time, the marriage was undoubtedly a compromise for her, though one she felt was right and would bring no regrets. John Marsh was a perfect Southern gentleman, and with him Peggy felt safe for the first time in her mature life.

They were married at five o'clock on Saturday, July 4, 1925, at the Unitarian-Universalist Church on West Peachtree Street. Peggy wore a sleeveless chiffon afternoon dress in shades of pansy purple over orchid satin — the same color scheme she had chosen for her first wedding. Narrow silver and orchid ribbons, and tiny green and pink silk flowers adorned the waistline of her dress. An orchid picture hat of hand-woven straw trimmed with a cluster of matching moire ribbons, and a corsage of orchids, lilies of the valley, and pink roses added a touch of glamour to the costume and, she told Medora, made her feel "very Bebe Daniels." Her feminine sandals were responsible for some of her good feeling about her appearance. She had been adamant about this purchase, refusing to wear her heavy orthopedic shoes as a bride.

Being married on Independence Day struck both Peggy and John as a fine omen. The wedding was smaller and not nearly as lavish as her previous one and, perhaps out of deference to Eugene Mitchell's financial state, the guests came back to the house for tea and cake. A high spirit prevailed, for the guest list included many of John and Peggy's co-workers and a large quantity of alcohol was secretly consumed. When the bridal couple started for the car that was to take them to the mountains of North Carolina, they were "kidnapped" by a group of guests and taken down to the Peachtree Yacht Club, where everyone toasted the bride and groom again — and again. Peggy was later to confide to two close friends that a buddy of John's, the burly writer Ward Greene, had accompanied them on their week-long honeymoon. Greene was a part of the wedding party and, as he had no doubt imbibed generously, he might well have driven off with the newlyweds; whether he remained with them on their honeymoon is not known.

John and Peggy agreed upon two luxuries in their first home together: the services of a part-time cook–housekeeper, Lula Tolbert, and no stinting on the heat in winter. Even their combined salaries just barely covered necessities as they struggled to repay John's medical bills. So as not to add to these, John went to the Veterans' Hospital for a free general examination a few weeks after the honeymoon. To his surprise, the doctors concluded that his series of bizarre illnesses were service-oriented and of psychosomatic origin. Though he had not been in the trenches himself, the shock of seeing so many mangled, dying men in his medical unit and of hearing the constant sound of explosives had resulted in a severe nervous condition, which had been recorded on his Army records at the time of his discharge. The doctors told him he was eligible for government compensation provided that he sign papers that would state for the record that he was receiving this monthly stipend because he suffered from a "service-oriented psychosomatic illness."

The compensation offered was not a fortune, but it would have considerably eased John's financial pressures. Still, it seemed a serious move to sign a document that inferred he had an emotional or mental disturbance. Stephens was consulted and he advised his new brother-in-law to struggle on without the Army compensation, because one day it "might be misunderstood and embarrass you." Peggy agreed, so John refused the pension. But lack of money did not seem to inhibit Peggy's newfound happiness. She was finally mistress of her own home and could do whatever she wanted — keep the temperature up to a hundred degrees if she so wished, entertain anyone she liked, and leave stacks of dishes overnight and her bed unmade until Lula arrived.

The Marshes quickly named their small apartment at 17 Crescent Avenue the "Dump." Throughout the bitterly cold winter of 1925 to 1926, the Dump was probably the warmest, liveliest small place in Atlanta. Peggy set to work painting it herself. Furnished in an off-beat style with family hand-me-downs, the apartment could have been set in the heart of Greenwich Village. It consisted of two cramped rooms, a galley kitchen, and a bath on the ground floor of a three-story red brick building. Large, brightly patterned and tasseled silk scarves covered the faded, lumpy couch and the scratched surfaces of tables and chests. Makeshift shelves were jammed with Peggy's prized historical volumes and her collection of contemporary poetry and fiction. Maybelle's ancient sewing machine was pushed into the narrow hallway and covered with an old bedspread, with Peggy's Remington typewriter stored beneath it, to be brought out to turn the crowded narrow entryway into an "office" when necessary.

The building that housed the Dump abutted a shoe-repair shop and was only a few steps away from the Tenth Street shopping section. The neighborhood was called "Tight Squeeze" and had a colorful history. Before the Civil War, when the suburbs of Atlanta were infested with criminals, it had been a hangout for robbers. The road at that time had been narrow and crooked, running along a steep ravine, and it became a common saying that it took "a mighty tight squeeze to get through with one's life." At the turn of the century, the road was straightened and the ravine, which in some places was thirty feet deep, was filled in. There was a story that a bank robber had once been killed on the exact spot where the Dump was located, and this rather lurid history amused Peggy.

Peggy was a superb raconteur and, unlike most Southern women, she enjoyed a "man's" joke, was not embarrassed by strong language, and could hold her corn liquor. John was her best audience, prodding her to tell stories he had already heard several times, leading her into her punchlines. The Dump quickly became a gathering place for the Marshes' newspaper friends, who came carrying their own bottles. They noted the unusual relationship between the Marshes, who seemed to them to be more like bosom buddies than a married couple. Tacked to the front door of the Dump were two cards, reading, "Miss Margaret Munnerlyn Mitchell" and "Mr. John R. Marsh." The cards were indicative of the tone of their relationship and, to Peggy's delight, pleased her friends and shocked her neighbors. Marriage and moving away from Peachtree Street had a temporarily liberating effect on Peggy and, in the first few months at the Dump, there was a kind of buoyant recklessness in her attitudes. Whereas later she was to guard her privacy with a waspish tenacity, as a newlywed she not only opened her home to friends, she made it the center of their social world.

Peggy no longer fretted about her exclusion from Atlanta society, for she had found her own social circle. Her friends were the many newspaper people and young writers in Atlanta, and in her constellation she was a star — a feature writer with a by-line. The fact that she was earning only thirty dollars a week did not diminish her shine; most of her friends earned less. Weekends usually found six or seven of them each night for dinner, everyone bringing contributions of food and booze. There weren't chairs or space for more.

Peggy did not talk about Red Upshaw and, during 1925 and 1926, she saw less of Augusta, Lethea, and Medora, who knew about so many of the painful episodes of her first marriage. According to Augusta, Peggy displayed a "maternal attitude" toward her at this time, telling her she was not quite "developed" and "needed taking care of," almost as though she was purposely trying to undermine Augusta's self-confidence. Augusta had gone to New York to follow a cherished dream of becoming an opera singer, and she had, in fact, been accepted in a small opera company and appeared publicly in a supporting role in *The Magic Flute*. But Peggy did not think she had made a wise choice, and Augusta's beau, Lee Edwards agreed. Peggy supported his decision to go to New York and bring Augusta back with him to Atlanta. The older, more settled Edwards, an executive with Georgia Railroad who was twenty-six years Augusta's senior, convinced the young woman that her future was with him and not on the lyric stage. They were married in the Little Church Around the Corner, a theatrical favorite, and then, after a European honeymoon, came home to Atlanta.

Peggy and Lee were soon fast friends, even to the point, at times, of excluding Augusta. Peggy would call and say to her, "Put Lee on, I have a story to tell him he'll enjoy." Or, she would stop by and go off in a corner with him to tell him a joke that she thought Augusta might not like, and the two of them would roar with laughter. Augusta never seemed to mind this, nor was she offended that she was no longer part of Peggy's innermost circle, for her own marriage, pregnancy, and her music commanded most of her time.

Laughter was probably what Peggy sought more than anything during the first year of her marriage. She loved jokes and tall stories and "camping" about. Augusta still recalls with amusement the way "Peggy would pretend she was pregnant [in imitation of Augusta] with a big shawl draped around her and a beach ball under it rolling up and down."

Peggy began writing Jazz Age short stories in her spare time. When she had three or four of them, she gathered up her courage and, with John's prodding, sent them off to *Smart Set* magazine because she had heard Medora speak so often of its editor, H. L. Mencken.

Chapter Ten

AUTUMN, 1925. It was the height of the Jazz Age, and Peggy captured something of its spirit in her story "Matrimonial Bonds," in which she described the Charleston being danced by girls whose "short skirts swayed to the rhythm above their chiffon stockings and dainty slippers, their curly bobbed heads thrown backwards in exuberance and all the zest and joyousness of frolicsome — not flaming — youth shining from their sparkling eyes."

Marriage had not removed Peggy from the roll call of flappers in Atlanta. She had confided to Frances that she was the only happily married member of the gang she trailed along with, the only one who was not afraid to let her husband know that he was "the only one." The "pleasant result" of this frankness, as Peggy saw it, was that she had "all the dates with [her] ex-flames" that she wanted, as well as a "house full of Tech boys to tea time without scenes later, passionate and recriminating, with the man I live with."

For Thanksgiving, since the Dump lacked space, Peggy decided to cook the family turkey with Bessie's help at her father's house and invite a host of relatives. Stephens was keeping company with Carrie Lou Reynolds, a young lady from Augusta, Georgia, whom Peggy privately referred to as "the marshmallow" because she was so round and powdery white. Grandmother Stephens was invited, along with Aunt Aline and members of both the Fitzgerald and Mitchell clans. It was to be both a reunion and a chance for Peggy to display her talents in her new role of homemaker. Then, four days before the holiday, Angus Perkerson called her into his office and asked her to do a two-part feature that would require "a helluva lot of research and damn little time."

The five Confederate generals to represent Georgia in the immortal granite of the Stone Mountain Memorial had been selected, and work was to begin in the spring. What Perkerson wanted was a three-thousand-word sketch of the lives and achievements, in both peace and war, of Generals John B. Gordon and Pierce M. Butler Young. It would appear that coming Sunday, to be followed the next Sunday by a segment about Generals Thomas R. R. Cobb, Henry Benning, and Ambrose Ransom Wright. Could she do it? *Of course,* she agreed.

The Thanksgiving invitations had already been issued, and Peggy turned in desperation to Bessie, who promised to see to it that the turkey got to the table. Without a second thought, Peggy was on her way down to Carnegie Library to cover the most important assignment of her reportorial career. The selection of the five generals had only been made that morning, so she would be in a race to beat the *Georgian* to the story — one she knew she could write better than anyone else. Perhaps even more pressing was her need to prove herself a reliable historian after the disappointment and rancor that had followed her story on women in Georgia's history.

She worked until the library closed on Wednesday night and then went home with an armful of reference books and stayed up most of the night reading. On Thanksgiving morning, she began to write her first draft, scooting over to the house on Peachtree Street just in time to help Bessie put the finishing touches to the table and the platters.

Perkerson had the final draft, with John's small bit of editing, by Saturday and told Medora it was one of the best pieces Peggy Mitchell had ever written. There was a smack of authority in the writing, a kind of reverence coupled with plain good story-telling. The article was published the next day and was enthusi-astically received, and, after discussing it with Medora, Perkerson called Peggy back into his office to tell her that he had decided to stretch out the series for three more weeks, which meant she could devote three thousand words each to the remaining three generals. Peggy returned to Carnegie Library with added zeal.

"When General Cobb Wrote the Georgia Code" appeared on December 6, and Peggy, quite eloquent herself, wrote of how Cobb swept the state out of the Union and into the Confederacy with his eloquence, and how he had died at Fredericksburg on the Sunken Road, where thousands of others lost their lives.

His brigade was stationed behind a stone wall in the old road, the target of six consecutive attacks by Federal troops. Far away across the battlefield stood Old Federal Hill, the girlhood home of General Cobb's mother. It was from this old house that she had married and it was in the yard and the estate that the Federal batteries were planted — the batteries that were raining on Sarah Robinson Cobb's son.

General Cobb had dismounted from his horse, in one of the intervals of fighting, and was walking down the road behind the wall, encouraging the men, giving orders for the removal of the wounded, checking up, with saddened heart, the number of dead in the Sunken Road, when a bullet struck him. It severed a femoral artery and the General lived only a little while, dying on the battlefield with the roar of the guns in his ears.

The readers' response to the article was so good that Perkerson let her extend the next piece, "General Wright — Georgia's Hero at Gettysburg," to 4,500 words, rare for the Sunday magazine. And the readers were stirred with good reason as they read of General Wright. . .

charging up the green slopes, slippery with blood, with his yelling men behind him. Sword in hand, he led the advance, amid a rain of bullets and swirl of cannon smoke that would have daunted a less fearless man than he. But fear seemed never to have entered his heart, for, calling to the color bearer to follow close, he waved his sword and cried to his men — "Come on! Follow me! Do you want to live forever?"

Sometimes he turned his back on the enemy to harangue his men, climbing the slope backwards, calling for the flag to follow after him as banner-bearer after banner-bearer fell and the standard was snatched by willing hands before it touched the earth.

They reached the top of the rise, sprang over the captured guns, cheering as the enemy retreated down the opposite side of the hill.

When she returned to Carnegie Library the next week to do her research for "General Benning, Hero of Burnside Bridge," she realized that she was filling her notebook with extraneous stories and bits of historical information that intrigued her but had no place in the piece — incidents at Gettysburg, comments of survivors. . . . And, as she wrote about General Benning, she found herself almost more caught up in the story of his wife,

> a tiny woman, frail and slight, but possessed of unusual endurance and a lion's heart. The battles she fought at home were those of nearly every Southern woman, but her burdens were heavier than most.
>
> Left in complete charge of a large plantation, this little woman, who was the mother of ten children, was as brave a soldier at home as ever her husband was on the Virginia battlefields. She saw to it that the crops were gathered, the children fed and clothed and the negroes cared for. . . . While her husband was away she buried her aged father whose end was hastened by the war, comforted her sorrowing mother, cared for her bereaved sister-in-law, the widow of her brother, and her brother's children and nursed sick and wounded Confederate soldiers. And hardest of all things in those trying days, she went three times to Virginia to bring home her own wounded.

The last article appeared on December 20. By Christmas, Peggy had come to two significant realizations. First, aware of just how much she had come to value her marriage to John Marsh, she took down the two calling cards on their door and replaced them with one, which read, "Mr. and Mrs. John Marsh." Second, she realized that the itch to write something more challenging than a newspaper article had overtaken her.

John gave her two books for Christmas, *Barren Ground* by Ellen Glasgow, and F. Scott Fitzgerald's *The Great Gatsby*. Glasgow was from Richmond, Virginia, a Southern woman like herself, and Peggy was much impressed by this author's ability to so accurately recreate the world of the middle- and upper-class South. Like Fitzgerald, Ellen Glasgow was a stylist, the kind of writer Peggy most admired and thought she could never be.

For a few weeks after reading these books, her confidence deserted her. *Smart Set* had rejected her short stories, and she was sure that John was wrong about her writing potential. Then an idea came to her for a novel dealing with the Jazz Age.

She named her heroine, the daughter of a Georgian judge, Pansy Hamilton. The young men and women in Pansy's circle all bore a strong resemblance to the group that belonged to the Yacht Club. The story began with a wild party where bootleg booze was being consumed; this was followed by a fast, chilling auto chase, at the end of which the young man, who was the wildest of the crowd, crashed. His girlfriend, Pansy, came to his rescue, stealing into a locked pharmacy for medical supplies so that the injured man wouldn't have to be taken to the hospital, where she was certain he would be arrested for drunken driving.

Peggy wrote thirty pages and then was unable to continue — the hero too closely resembled Red Upshaw. She decided to leave the Jazz Age in the hands of the brilliant F. Scott Fitzgerald.

Throughout the spring of 1926, Peggy's schedule was that of a busy working wife. Lula arrived to clean the apartment after Peggy had left for the office, so there was always a sheaf of notes and instructions pinned to a bulletin board in the kitchen. Lula was only there an hour or two a day, and Peggy did all the grocery shopping and prepared dinner. She drew evening work at least twice a week and her assignments had begun to bore her. "What It Costs to Rush a Girl" occupied the front page of the magazine on January 10; "Spirited Heroines and Knee-Length Skirts," on January 31. She spoke to Medora, who gave her a story, "Conjuring the Wood Out of Alcohol," for which she had to go into Darktown, Atlanta's black ghetto. There was a possibility of danger about this that excited her. In Darktown, she was to interview the "Conjur" doctors and their victims, some of whom were paying as much as fifty dollars for voodoo charms that would allow them to drink bootleg whiskey without fear of sudden blindness, potash poisoning, or insanity.

" 'Conjur' folks," Peggy wrote, were "extracting dimes and dollars from the more superstitious members of their race," and taking "advantage of the different waves of terror" which swept over Darktown. She went on to describe the fraud and its perpetrators in plain, strong language.

When John heard she had gone to Darktown unaccompanied, he was frantic. Eugene Mitchell's maid, Bessie, was also alarmed when she saw the article. For a white woman to walk alone through this dangerous black ghetto was not much better than flaunting herself, as far as Bessie was concerned. Since Peggy had come through the experience unscathed — though, admittedly, a bit frightened — John was more concerned about the possibility of one of the maligned "darkies" (a word she used in the article) seeking revenge. She had handed in the story against his wishes and for several days after it appeared, John insisted on meeting her at the office and escorting her home. From the time of this incident, John pressured her into resigning from her job to stay at home and be Mrs. John Marsh, housewife. She argued that they could not afford for her to do so yet, and then, weakening, agreed to a compromise — when he received a raise, she would quit.

Forces were working in John Marsh's favor. The previous year had seen the sudden demise of hundreds of small-town newspapers throughout the country as the new tabloids and their star reporters had won the upper hand. Many people were dismayed at the depths to which the public taste seemed to have fallen, even though they might avidly buy the national tabloids or read the syndicated stories of the men and women who wrote luridly about lust and crime. The public lapped up coverage of sensational trials, such as the suit for separation brought by "Peaches" Browning against her husband, Edward "Daddy" Browning, who had a penchant for very young girls. One critic gave voice to a common complaint when he wrote that the press was having "a carnival of commercial degradation" and would soon be "drenched in obscenity."

The *Journal* did not lower its standards more than it had to in order to survive, but it *was* using the stories of a great many syndicated writers, like Faith Baldwin and Peggy Joyce and revivalist Billy Sunday. Peggy's job was never in jeopardy, but her stories were not as prominently featured as they had been. Even her interview with Tiger Flowers, Atlanta's own new middle-weight champion of the world, was pushed back to page nine, supplanted by a syndicated interview with a confessed murderess.

The Tiger Flowers piece was one in which Peggy took great pride because she thought she had successfully captured the sound of black speech:

> My wife used to be of the choir befo' we took to travellin' around so much. Uster sing powerful lot myself, but looks like I got hit in the mouf so much it plumb ruined my voice.
>
> Verna Lee and me learned to do the Charleston and I got to be a fool about it. Soon the congregation say, "Tiger, how you reconcile this Charleston with bein' a steward of the Church?"
>
> "Ain't I got to keep my wind," I say. "Ain't Charlestonin' better for the wind than skippin' rope and a heap more sociable?"
>
> "And the congregation say, 'Tiger, that shore is the truf.'"

In April, John received a raise and Peggy gave the paper one month's notice. She drew her last paycheck as a staff employee on May 3, 1926. But her writing days for the *Journal* were not yet over; she agreed to free-lance a weekly column called "Elizabeth Bennet's Gossip." The name had been drawn from Jane Austen's *Pride and Prejudice* and the title was misleading for, instead of gossip, the reader found a column containing amusing or informative anecdotes from Atlanta's history or about various leading citizens, past and present. The column at least took her out of the house and down to Carnegie Library, where she spent hours each day in the basement, looking through bound copies of old newspapers so massive and heavy that she had to lie on her stomach on the cold floor to read them. She filled her notebook with stories and details that had no place in the pages of the *Atlanta Journal,* brought these bits of information home, and put them in the drawer of the old sewing-machine table that served as her desk.

"Elizabeth Bennet's Gossip" was more challenging to write than one might suspect. It was humorous and anecdotal, an attempt to make Atlanta's past relevant without being irreverent. But as the summer passed, Peggy found it not challenging enough. She again began to consider stories she might write, and she told a close friend that she had "several hundred novels on my mind and have had them there since childhood."

To both her friends and her family, Peggy appeared to be a strong, healthy, young woman. She was tight and lean, still boyish in build, and she had surprising strength in her hands and arms and could lift heavy objects with considerable ease. She regularly consumed large quantities of alcohol with no apparent effect, smoked heavily, and never gave her sex as an excuse to get out of doing a man's job.

Her friends conceded that she was, unfortunately, accident prone but, despite this, in her reporting days she bloomed with good health. Yet, from the time Peggy Mitchell retired from the *Journal* to become Mrs. John Marsh, she seemed to be perpetually recovering either from injury or illness. She did, indeed, suffer a series of painful mishaps, but as she stood guard over John's shaky physical condition, she became increasingly obsessed with her own, even hypochondriacal.

With Lula Tolbert to clean, Peggy's housekeeping chores at the Dump were minimal. Most of her friends worked and could not indulge in womanly afternoon entertainments like bridge and the current fad, Mah-jongg. As autumn came around, her restlessness grew. About the same time, John was conscious of a testiness in their relationship. He wrote several people close to him that he was pressuring Peggy to try her hand at a novel but that she was pretty "bull-headed." Years later, she was to claim that she "hated writing almost as much as Wagner and tap dancing" and only because John "drove" her had she sat down at her typewriter. This happened one day in the fall of 1926, when her restiveness had made her cross and John had accused her of "putting her mind out to pasture." After he left for the office, she pushed the old sewing-machine table with her typewriter on it to a spot under the two high windows in the living room and, wearing a newsman's green eyeshade, one of John's shirts, and a pair of baggy men's overalls, she set to work on a story she first conceived as a novel, " 'Ropa Carmagin," but which, three weeks and a little less than fifteen thousand words later, had become a novella.

The story was set in the 1880s in Clayton County, in an area near the old Fitzgerald plantation, and included some of the grim, derelict houses that Maybelle had pointed out to her long ago with the warning that this was what became of people without moral fiber. The heroine, Europa Carmagin, was from such a family; the Carmagins had not been able to regain their antebellum affluence. The garden on the plantation was weed-choked, the fences rotting, the fields worked out, and 'Ropa was in love with a handsome mulatto whose mother had been a former slave on the Carmagin plantation. Under such circumstances, a happy ending was impossible. In grand opera style, 'Ropa Carmagin's lover was killed and her neighbors forced her to leave her ancestral home.

When Peggy had completed the novella, she gave it to John to read and edit. She thought she had written a good story, rich in true detail and on a theme — miscegenation — that was important enough to lift the work from the category of "romance" to "literature." John found the period and the background, and even 'Ropa Carmagin, fascinating, but he did not consider the novella worthy of his wife's talents and he did not like the theme at all. Nor did he believe 'Ropa's male lover was a true portrait of a mulatto. He suggested that Peggy put the manuscript aside and think about it some more before he made any notes for her.

Peggy was devastated. She moped about the apartment all weekend. On Monday, after John had gone off to work, she got into the car and drove out toward Jonesboro and Lovejoy, perhaps to see if a visit to the locale of 'Ropa's heartbreak might give her greater insight into the characters of her story, or perhaps without any motive other than putting distance between herself and the forty-five or so manuscript pages that were stacked up beside her typewriter. It was raining and she was preoccupied. When she came unexpectedly to a stop sign, she braked sharply and the car skidded, left the road, and hit a tree. Moments later she stepped out of the vehicle, miraculously unscathed except for a fast-swelling turned ankle.

A week later, and after competent medical treatment, the ankle proved so painful that she could not walk. It was X-rayed again but no break could be seen. It was, however, the same leg that had been injured in her two youthful riding accidents. Muscles had been pulled, and arthritis was suspected, but neither would have resulted in the crippling pain she suffered. Her ankle was placed in a cast for three weeks without successful results. Peggy spent several more weeks in bed, in traction.

Bessie came over to help out and made sure that "Miss Peggy" was well taken care of. Still, the pain persisted and she was bedridden.

Peggy gave up "Elizabeth Bennet's Gossip" because, she claimed, she could not write a word unless it was on the typewriter. John was filled with tender regard and tried to do everything he could to keep her spirits up. She read omnivorously and when her eyes tired John read the latest stories to her from literary magazines such as the *American Mercury*.

When she could, Medora dropped over during her lunch break. Augusta came by, and Stephens and Eugene Mitchell were attentive. Peggy didn't choose to see anyone else but, undaunted, Grandmother Stephens, whose own health was beginning to fail, came regularly, complaining about the shabbiness of the apartment, hinting that had her granddaughter been a better Catholic she might be in better health. Peggy preferred reading most of the day to seeing visitors. With her illness, the beaus and old flames had suddenly disappeared. She was completely dependent upon John.

On his way home from work, John would stop by the library to select novels, histories, and poetry to fill his wife's lonely days. They were having serious financial problems, with Peggy's current medical bills now heaped upon John's old ones, and neither one of them was in good spirits. John's health was still far from robust, but Peggy's depression worried him and he decided some drastic therapy was in order. The day she graduated to crutches, early in 1927, John came home from work with a stack of copy paper and told her that there was hardly a book left in the library that she would enjoy. "It looks to me, Peggy," he said, "as though you'll have to write a book yourself if you're to have anything to read."

"My God," she later confessed to thinking, "now I've got to write a novel and what is it going to be about?"

The next morning, after John's departure, she pulled on her baggy overalls, plunked on her green eyeshade, piled some cushions for her leg beneath the spindly sewing table, stuffed " 'Ropa Carmagin" into a big manila envelope and pushed it aside, put the stack of blank yellow paper in its place, and sat down. She knew she had a story she wanted to tell, the one she and John had discussed so often about women like her grandmother and Mrs. Benning, the general's wife. She didn't have to bother about background, for it had been with her all her life. She did not yet have a plot nor did she know who all of her characters were to be, but, as she sat before her old Remington, the sun from the high windows splashing over the blank page in front of her, she was glad that John's words had stirred her into a final decision. Now she knew why she had collected all those bits of historical information.

She had no outline, but her authentic background gave her guidelines and structure. The story would commence with the war and end in Reconstruction, and it would be the story of Atlanta during that time as much as it would be the story of the characters she created. She did not come to the typewriter cold. She knew the story would involve four major characters, two men and two women, and that one of the men would be a romantic dreamer like Clifford Henry; and the other, a charming bounder like Red Upshaw, and that of the women, one would be the essence of noble Southern womanhood, like Mrs. Benning; and the other — well, she would be a combination of her grandmother and herself, with a strong dash of hussy tossed in. From the beginning, Peggy knew that she wanted this fiery woman to be in love with the good woman's husband, and she always thought of the good woman as her heroine, even though, as she worked on the book, the second woman began to dominate its pages.

She began at the end because that was how all her *Journal* stories had been written; from the final denouement came the real thrust of a story. It was a bit like writing a murder mystery. She loved crime stories and read them avidly, and she was sure that their authors did not just amble along hit-or-miss. They had to plan the murder and catch the murderer first, and then go back to the beginning of the story so that they could lead their readers to a logical yet surprising conclusion.

The memory of that day when Red had gone off to Asheville, presumably for good, had always haunted her, as had the fact that she had never truly come to know the man for whom she had claimed undying love, Clifford Henry. Caution, of course, had to be applied. Fiction had to be based on some personal experience or observation to be good, but she had to cover her tracks well. Her father's whipping in her childhood was still well remembered, as were his constant reminders when she was working for the *Journal* of how easy it would be for people to sue her for libel. But, as she sat before her typewriter that morning, the possibility that anything she might write would ever be published seemed exceedingly remote. Probably her story would not be good enough to be seen by anyone but John, and if it was, well, she would think about what to do in that event later. With this thought easing her mind, she typed out the words:

She had never understood either of the men she loved and so she lost them both.

Peggy did not know it then, but with those words she had inalterably changed the course of her life.

Chapter Eleven

*H*APPY THOUGH she was in her marriage to John, the specter of Red Upshaw had not been exorcised from Peggy's thoughts, and the memories of the two confrontations she had had with Red before the divorce — the first, when he'd said he was leaving her to go to Asheville; and the last, when he had assaulted her — remained to trouble her. She had confessed to John and Medora some feelings of responsibility where Red's abuse of her was concerned. It had been wrong to insist on remaining in her father's house, for one thing; and, for another, she should not have brought up Clifford Henry's name and her own romantic feelings for him on her honeymoon. That had incensed Red, and nothing had been the same between them afterwards. Red had been a brute, there was no denying that. She could never forgive him for what he had done and lived in terror that he might return. Yet, at the same time, she remembered his first departure more vividly than the second — how bruised and battered she had felt as he drove away, even though that time he had not laid a hand on her.

Indifference, that was the cruelest blow you could receive from a man you had loved; it was worse, even, than hate. Red Upshaw had not fought for her love and, after the beating, when she had armed herself against him, he had not even bothered to appear at the divorce hearing and had never contacted her to apologize for his brutal behavior.

It was the pain she had felt at Red Upshaw's indifference, his detachment in doing exactly what she had forced him to do — leave Atlanta — that she used for the basis of the first scene she wrote, but this was a stepping-off point only. She had not given Red the time or chance to display any strength of character, and she had suffered some guilt about this, even though she now thought he was beyond redemption. But her hero had to be redeemable. No matter what kind of scoundrel he was, or how cold or brutal he might be to the woman who was to be his wife, if he was a loving father, he would gain some sort of absolution. So, two of the main characters would be partners in a violent marriage held together by their love for the child of that union. This much of the story was set from the beginning.

The name Rhett Butler was decided upon with some ease; it is the merging of two rather common Southern surnames. But, the names Red Upshaw and Rhett Butler are also alliterative, the first name of each starting with the same letter, and both names have an equal number of syllables. There were several other similarities that linked the fictitious and real men. Both were "masterful," "scoundrelly," and of "low morals," and both had been expelled from service academies — Rhett, from West Point; Red, from Annapolis. Both had been profiteers, Rhett using the war for profit; Red, Prohibition. Both took their sexual pleasures where they found them; and both were Southerners, but not Atlantans. But it was the volatile spirits of the two men that were most synonymous — the inner violence, the strong passions, the brilliant minds always so self-serving, and the animal magnetism that even faint-hearted women found hard to resist.

Atlanta and Jonesboro were to be Peggy's locales. Her heroine's plantation would be more of a farm, like her mother's ancestral home, than the stereotypical plantation, and it would be called Fontenoy Hall. She was not entirely satisfied with this name, but it was of her own making and she wanted to be sure that no plantation in Clayton County could be identified. She had read many more books on the Civil War during her months of immobility, but she had always known that her story would not be told from the military point of view but from that of those Southern women who had refused to accept defeat, even when their men were gone and the war lost. Grandmother Stephens's tales of Atlanta under Hood, with the Yankees closing in; of the fire; and of the terrible days when she had traveled to Jonesboro after the Union soldiers had plundered it, and there had been nothing to eat but a few root vegetables — they all came back to her, as did Mrs. Bennings's trials in caring for her dying father and all the other women and children and helpless "darkies" left on her plantation while her husband was commanding his troops.

The first day, she wrote about two thousand words — the last scene of the novel — and when John came home she read them to him, then he read them himself, and they talked about the story and the characters. This time he was not only supportive, he was enthusiastic. He went over her typed pages making notes in the margins and correcting small errors in grammar and usage.

Peggy was up early the next morning, retyped these pages, incorporating John's corrections and her own, and then she simply jumped right into the book at an early stage in the story, before the war. She was not sure this would be her opening chapter but, curiously, it did not seem to matter. The history of the period was so clear in her mind that she could pick up the story wherever she wanted and know fairly well what was happening in both Jonesboro and Atlanta at that time. Within a week or so, a pattern for her writing had formed. She worked six to eight hours a day, sometimes more, putting aside certain scenes that needed more research and would therefore have to wait until her leg had healed enough to allow her to go back to the basement of Carnegie Library. Still, this did not stop the flow of the story, nor did the fact that she often wrote scenes with several alternate endings. Contrary to the legend that grew up later, Peggy did not write her book in a nonsequential fashion. After the last chapter was written, she tackled the rest of the story more or less in chronological order, and chapters that were set aside to be researched later had outlines and explanatory paragraphs.

She kept index-card files for each of her characters, no matter how minor, and in this she was more organized and neat than in her actual writing. Angus Perkerson's lessons in professionalism had not gone unheard, and when Peggy was at her desk she went at the novelist's task with the same craftmanship that she had displayed as a reporter.

Perhaps this was why she wore the green eyeshade and the men's pants when she was writing — to simulate newsroom conditions. Her approach was entirely businesslike, and the image later evoked, of a tiny, genteel, Southern housewife beneath a counterpane, whiling away her spare hours by writing a novel "for fun," is a myth. As she wrote, Peggy Mitchell was once again a "working woman," and she wrote with the same fervor as she had at the *Journal* and sought John's praise just as she had once dedicated herself to winning Angus Perkerson's approval.

As she wrote, Peggy seemed to be in the presence of, as she described it, "something strange, something headlong and desperate." The wide range of emotions and experiences that she had known or had had described to her during her childhood and youth, and which had been accumulating within her all her life, suddenly began to dislodge themselves from her mind. But her insomnia, as she recalled the words of the Civil War songs her mother used to sing to her, persisted, and she still had nightmares associated with other bloody, graphic wartime descriptions heard in her childhood.

Only a few weeks after she began, John wrote his mother that Peggy was writing a drama that would contain "all the great elemental experiences of life: birth, love, marriage, death, hunger, jealousy, hate, greed, joy and loneliness." Except for this brief mention of it to Frances and his mother, John did not discuss the book with anyone at this point at Peggy's request. When people came into the house, she would toss a big bath towel over her desk to conceal the manuscript. His belief in her drove her on. She had no deadline, but each night when John came home and asked, "What have you got to read me tonight?" she felt compelled to deliver.

Within a short time, there was a stack of manila envelopes on the table and floor, each marked with an identification of the contents, like: "Family History," "Barbecue at Twelve Oaks," and "The Bazaar." When a day arrived when she could not seem to go forward or backward in the story, she would take out the pages from one of these envelopes, incorporate John's notes, and then rewrite the pages for both of them to discuss again. For several months, she wrote in this disciplined, compulsive fashion, often reworking a scene four or five times. A day seldom passed when she was not absorbed in work on the novel.

Peggy would always deny that any of the characters in the book were based on real people, except in the case of the black girl, Prissy, whom she admitted was patterned on Cammie. But Ashley Wilkes — another combination of two old Southern names — was a highly romanticized portrait of Clifford Henry, who, though not Southern, had also gone off idealistically to war and who had been a poet and a dreamer and a gentleman. And the similarities between Gerald O'Hara's grief over his wife's death and Eugene Mitchell's breakdown when Maybelle died are too striking to be dismissed.

Though Peggy claimed that the character she named Pansy O'Hara was in no way autobiographical, she did have the same first name as the girl in Peggy's abandoned autobiographical Jazz Age novel and as the girl reporter in the short stories that *Smart Set* had rejected. No matter what denials Peggy made later Pansy O'Hara had much in common with her creator; the parallels are there. Both were mavericks, constantly flouting convention and society, and both suffered identity problems caused by strong, righteous, Catholic mothers. Both had to care for their fathers after their mothers' deaths. Both were flirts and teases, both preferred the game of sex to the act itself, and both of them had been raped by a husband. Both turned their backs on the Catholic church. Both were women who drank in a society that frowned on such "unladylike" behavior, and both had set society against them. Both had had romanticized, unfulfilled first loves, a violent marriage, and a marriage to a steady reliable husband. And both were stronger than all but one of the men they loved. This autobiographical undercurrent gives the narrative a drive that it might otherwise have lacked.

But Pansy O'Hara was based nearly as much on Annie Fitzgerald Stephens as she was on Margaret Munnerlyn Mitchell, and there were enough similarities between the two women so that Peggy was reluctant to expose the book to her grandmother's sharp eye.

Peggy's leg was healing, but slowly, and she was still more or less confined to the apartment. Grandmother Stephens made a point of visiting regularly but, though Peggy and her grandmother finally made up their differences, Peggy never told her about the contents of the manila envelopes, for she was not at all certain that the old woman would appreciate having the most vivid events of her life turned into the stuff of fiction.

The O'Hara family had much in common with the Fitzgeralds, and had settled in Clayton County at about the same time. And, like Pansy O'Hara, Annie Fitzgerald Stephens had remained in Atlanta until the fire, had nursed the injured soldiers who had fallen or been brought there, had taken her first-born infant back to Jonesboro alone just after the fire, and had remained there, fighting starvation and carpetbaggers, until the men returned from the war. Also, like Pansy, Annie was just a few years younger than the city of Atlanta, and she did indeed think of it as "of her own generation," and was as proud of the way it had outgrown its crudeness as she was of her own achievements.

As Peggy got deeper into her story, she became convinced that her book could never be submitted for publication even if she were to finish it. Not only was there the problem of Grandmother Stephens, there was, of course, Red Upshaw. The fear of having the characters and incidents in the novel ever associated with real life became almost an obsession with her, and was, in fact, one of her major reasons for refusing to discuss the story with anyone, other than to say that the book she was working on had to do with the Civil War and Atlanta.

As she saw it, then, she was writing only for her own amusement, which made her something of a dilettante. She had no real goal, no deadline, nor could she see any possibility of ever getting paid for her hard work. This situation seemed to suggest that what she was doing was not worthwhile, and the more absorbed she became in her work, the less confidence she had in herself. Despite her disciplined routine, she could no longer say she was a professional writer; she was a housewife with a hobby that had possessed her, and that made her a less competent housewife at that. Had it not been for John's own excitement over the book, the way he involved himself so enthusiastically in the project, she might have forced herself to discontinue the work, the way one might put a stop to a bad habit. But any talk of this, or of her throwing the manuscript away, incurred John's wrath — and he was seldom angry at her otherwise. The manuscript had become like a child of theirs, and it meant almost as much to John as it did to Peggy.

🦃

Rain deluged the city that spring and Peggy did not dare to venture out on crutches and risk a possible fall. Arthritis had settled in the ankle joint to further complicate and retard her recovery, and the doctors warned her that she might never again walk without the aid of crutches.

In early March, John was given an award at Georgia Power for writing the best advertising copy of the past year. He was proud of his work and of the fact that not only was he paying off his debts, he was taking care of Peggy as a husband should do. Though their financial worries were far from over, he wrote friends and members of his family that he was happier than he had ever thought he would be and, though he never went into specifics, his pride in the fact that Peggy was writing a novel was apparent.

It is to be remembered that John Marsh's earliest dream was to become a man of literature, and that he had realized at a youthful age that he did not have the talent to succeed as a writer of novels or of nonfiction. Even as a reporter he had failed, but he had slipped quite naturally into copy-editing. Part of the reason he succeeded as a copy editor and failed on the more creative level was because, by his own admission, he was "a master flaw-finder and picayune-emphasizer." Yet, he had always sought the company of writers and other creative people, and, as with Red Upshaw, people who had stronger and more charismatic personalities than he. For himself, he had no further ambition than to do the best job he could at Georgia Power and, perhaps one day, to become advertising or public-relations director, which would greatly increase his paycheck but would still never make him rich.

Just as he had lived vicariously through Peggy when she was a feature writer for the *Journal*, he now did so with her work on the novel. His mind was too compartmentalized to think with

Peggy's sweeping vision or in terms of her amazing, labyrinthine story detail. It is difficult to guess how much he might have been able to contribute to her work if he had been faced with a huge pile of those manila envelopes instead of with the ten or so pages that he read through most evenings. He was Peggy's only sounding board, that is true. But there is no strong evidence that he contributed greatly to the development of the story. A conservative man, somewhat puritanical, he may have influenced her final choices in some scenes. Mainly, though, he made sure her writing was clear, precise, and to the point, and he corrected errors in usage and spelling. It was certainly useful to Peggy, but it was no more than a good editor in a publishing house would consider his or her job. Peggy, of course, being unacquainted with the publishing process, did not know this. She thought herself dependent on John, and, as she was now also financially reliant upon him, her love for him grew out of two emotions — gratitude and need.

Not surprisingly, as her love grew, her confidence in herself and her work was further diminished. She was, she later claimed, "singularly a prey to a disease known in this family as 'the humbles.' Everybody's stuff looks better than mine and a depressing humility falls upon me whenever I read stuff that I wish I could have written."

In the spring of 1927, Peggy fell into a terrible state of dejection after reading James Boyd's *Marching On*, a novel about the Civil War. She put a cover over the typewriter and for three months, in her words, her "life was ruined." Nothing could get her to sit back down and continue to write. It was hopeless, she cried to John, completely hopeless. She did not write with the intellectual power of Boyd, nor did she understand the Confederate strategy or the Union aims as well as he did. She was writing a book about the great war without taking any of her characters into battle, and she was convinced that it was cowardly for her to avoid such scenes, that it only proved how inadequate she was for the job she was attempting.

John argued that Boyd's book and hers were not comparable. Hadn't she said over and over that she was writing about the women who remained at home? Why, then, should she include battle scenes which — even if brilliant — would be gratuitous to the action of the story and, in fact, would disrupt the tremendous narrative drive that seemed to be gaining momentum even when chapters were disconnected? Not convinced, she let her eyeshade gather dust on top of the shrouded typewriter.

Peggy's "case of the humbles" may have been prolonged by Red Upshaw's reappearance in Atlanta. Upshaw, she heard, had gone out to the University of Georgia and had visited some of his old professors. He had even suggested that he might want to return for his degree. Through mutual friends, she learned that he was living in Asheville, North Carolina, and that he claimed he was sales manager for Reliance Coal and Oil in that city. It was reported that he was better-looking than ever, drove an even flashier car, and had been seen at a party with one of Atlanta's prettiest young women, a debutante of the current season. He could not have been in town more than a few days, and he left without contacting either Peggy or John.

On May 3, 1927, Stephens married Caroline Louise Reynolds in a Catholic service that the *Journal* society reporter said was "marked by impressive solemnity and simple dignity." It was one of the few times that Peggy had been out in public since her leg injury. Because she was still on crutches, she was not a member of the wedding party. After a wedding trip to New York, Stephens and Carrie Lou, who came from a respectable old Southern family, were going to live on Peachtree Street with Mr. Mitchell, and Carrie Lou would be caring for him and the household as he had always expected his own daughter to do.

A few days after Stephens's marriage, John took seriously ill and had to spend three weeks in the hospital. The doctors were unable to diagnose his problem, but he had been experiencing a lack of energy and had suffered a loss of equilibrium. His weight had dropped suddenly, and for no apparent reason, from 163 to 145 pounds. They tested him for countless diseases, but neither did they find a cause nor did he improve, and for the first two weeks of his hospitalization he was not able to lift his head from the pillow without experiencing violent nausea.

John's illness forced Peggy to rally. The crutches did not stop her from spending all the time she could with him at the hospital. Neither one of them ever lost their sense of humor. She gave him *Dracula* to read and she wrote Frances that "the book took a holt" of him in so big a way that it frightened "the liver and the lights out of him." The nurses, she said, thought him delirious because he suggested they get garlands of garlic to keep vampires from him. John claimed the shock was beneficial, and he began to get better.

He was released from the hospital in June and was back at work within two weeks, but the doctors knew only a little more than they had before his hospitalization. The cause of his dizziness was never established, but it did not return, and Peggy's main objective was to "fatten him up." Once the crisis had passed, she put on one of John's shirts, got back into her baggy overalls, pulled on her eyeshade, uncovered the Remington and returned to work. For the time being, her writer's block caused by "the humbles" was over.

Chapter Twelve

A LITTLE BEFORE 8:00 A.M. on the morning of May 20, 1927, a young man named Charles A. Lindbergh stepped into the cockpit of the small plane that he hoped to fly nonstop from Roosevelt Field, just outside New York, to Paris. Way back in 1919, a New York businessman had put up a prize of $25,000 to go to the first aviator who achieved this feat. Lindbergh was called "Lucky Lindy" and the "Flying Fool," and, although he had not yet become a national idol, he was a public hero. He was an appealing, modest man, and there was something so startlingly daring in his attempt to make this perilous flight alone in his small craft, the *Spirit of St. Louis*, that he caught the imagination of the nation. For the first time in nearly a decade, Americans were united in a hope — that Lindbergh would succeed. Through newspapers and radio broadcasts, they followed the young man in the *Spirit of St. Louis* across the Atlantic, praying for his safe arrival in France. Peggy and her newspaper friends gathered at the Perkersons' and listened in suspenseful silence as the news of Lindbergh's progress was broadcast.

Peggy's friends were ecstatic when the news broke that Lindbergh had landed at Le Bourget Air Field and was being mobbed by crowds of French admirers, but she herself was not so sure that he had performed "the greatest feat of solitary man in the records of the human race," as newspaper sellers on the streets shouted in their "extras" a short time later. Nor did she agree that his feat was worthy of the thousands of telegrams being sent him, some, hundreds of feet long and signed individually with as many as 17,500 names. Others had crossed the Atlantic by air, though not alone, and stopping to refuel in Newfoundland. Lindbergh's accomplishment was that he went nonstop by himself. Peggy admired the man's feat, but viewed it as little more than a daring stunt flight. Why, then, this sudden idolization of Lindbergh?

Others were able to see what Peggy could not. "For years," historian Frederick Lewis Allen explained in his fine book, *Only Yesterday*, "the American people had been spiritually starved, they had seen their early ideals and illusions and hopes one by one worn away by the corrosive influence of events and ideas — by the disappointing aftermath of the war, by scientific doctrines and psychological theories which undermined their religion and ridiculed their sentimental notions, by the spectacle of graft in politics and crime on the city streets and finally by their recent newspaper diet of smut and murder. Romance, chivalry, and self-dedication had been debunked; the heroes of history had been shown to have feet of clay, and the saints of history had been revealed as people with queer complexes. . . . Something that people needed, if they were to live at peace with themselves and with the world, was missing from their lives. And all at once Lindbergh provided it. Romance, chivalry, self-dedication — here they were." And they were being dispensed by a humble, modest man who could have been any one of his millions of admirers, had they been "touched" with his inspiration.

Considering Peggy's tremendous insecurities, it could never have occurred to her, even in the far reaches of the nightmares she often suffered, that a decade later she would be responsible for fulfilling the same needs in the American public and would be the recipient of that public's frenzied adulation.

Peggy's friends knew she was writing a book, but they did not ask many questions, for when they did, Peggy would just laugh, "Oh, it's a new kind of therapy for my leg."

She might have been telling a half-truth — as the summer and winter of 1927 passed, her leg grew stronger and, though it was still causing her considerable discomfort, she was able to put away her crutches and go down to Carnegie Library for short periods each week to do some necessary research. The rest of her time was dedicated to the writing of the book, which, she realized, was surely too long even at this stage and desperately needed organization, selection, and cutting. But she did not want to stop the flow of her writing to have John help her do this, for she was terrified that if she tried to read the book from the beginning to the point she had now reached — the death of Pansy's father, Gerald O'Hara — she might feel compelled to scrap the entire project. As it was, she was not at all sure that she could ever complete it anyway. Here she was, writing a book in which a major part of the plot had to do with a violent marriage and, with nearly 300,000 words already written, the marriage of Pansy and Rhett had not yet taken place.

Then, in the summer of 1928, to add to her difficulties, Peggy was struck once again with "a case of the humbles."

One afternoon, a friend named Frank Daniel, who reviewed books for the Sunday magazine, came by to discuss with her his current assignment, Stephen Vincent Benét's epic poem, *John Brown's Body*. Peggy was at the typewriter when he arrived, and she quickly covered up her work. Daniel praised Benét's writing and then insisted on reading passages out loud to her.

"This is the last, this is the last," he began in his softly cadenced Southern voice. As he read on, Peggy was so moved by the eloquence and horror and superb craftsmanship displayed by Benét in his lengthy Civil War poem that she asked Daniel to stop reading, fearing the final result.

Daniel did not take her seriously and continued, "in spite of the fact," Peggy later recalled, "that I had flung myself on the sofa and stuck my fingers in my ears and screamed protests. I had to read it all then. The result was that I wondered how anybody could have the courage to write about the war after Mr. Benét had done it so beautifully."

The cover remained on the typewriter after this incident for another three-month period. John was furious at her lack of self-confidence, but none of his lectures helped to restore it to her. Then, in late November, a Fitzgerald cousin died and Peggy went to Fayetteville for the funeral. When she got home that evening, she took the cover from the Remington and began a chapter on Gerald O'Hara's funeral.

At this time, she also decided on a new name for the O'Hara family home, "Tara," a name derived from the Hill of Tara, which was the seat of the high kings of Ireland from ancient times until the sixth century. But she did not take the time now to go back and change all the references to the former name, Fontenoy Hall.

In December, Bessie left the house on Peachtree Street to work full-time for Peggy. It was an extravagance for the Marshes, but Lula Tolbert had quit and neither Peggy nor John was able to take over the household chores. Peggy was not fond of cooking and felt she simply could not manage the shopping. According to Bessie, although her love and dedication to "Miss Peggy" knew no bounds, her first weeks in the Marsh household were less than pleasant.

In a letter to Medora, written years later, Bessie recalled, "Lula B. Tolbert . . . told me the likes and dislikes of Mr. Marsh. From her description of Mr. Marsh my first weeks . . . with them was hard and frightful. I were so afraid of Mr. Marsh until my clothes would seem to slip like a tight window shade at his appearance. But when I learned that he was an ex-school teacher, that he was rigid, that it was Promptness, Cleanness and good foods that it took to bring out that smile on his face — all was well."

Through Bessie's eyes, one can get a clear picture of life at the Dump. Bessie worked from 8:00 A.M. until after dinner and had Thursday afternoons and, supposedly, most of Sunday off.

I remember once being misunderstood by one of my friend maids. I told her that I were off each Sunday after breakfast. But that the reason I could not go to Church every Sunday A.M. was that Mr. Marsh would sleep some Sundays until 12 o'clock. She asked if they Both slept late. I told her some times Miss Peggy would have her Sunday A.M. breakfast and would slip out to visit her Father, or take flowers to the cemetery [for Maybelle's grave] and return befor[e] Mr. Marsh awaked.

She said it looks like they would have breakfast together on Sunday A.M.

I said No they never have Breakfast together, that Mr. Marsh lets her rest through the week and she lets him rest on Sundays. That Sundays was Mr. Marsh's day of rest.

And I thought that this maid friend understood this as I told it. But out of this conversation came a rumor that . . . Mr. and Mrs. Marsh were not congenial, that they never eat together. But what I said was they did not eat breakfast together.

Besides Bessie, the Marshes also had Carrie, the Mitchell laundress, come in and collect the wash and bring it back cleaned and pressed every Monday. Bessie received fifteen dollars a week and car fare, and would have received half that amount had she "lived in," and Carrie's wage was three dollars a week plus car fare. As John's salary was about seventy-five dollars a week and they had to allot most of it for their medical bills, food, rent, and utilities, the Marshes were left with almost no money for themselves. Not since their marriage had Peggy been able to buy a new dress. Frances was now married and pregnant and, knowing the austerity of Peggy's situation, sent her a blue velvet dress from her own wardrobe.

Peggy wrote back that she had thought she would have no new dress for the Christmas parties and had planned to put a new collar on a blue georgette that had been part of her Upshaw trousseau, when the blue velvet dress arrived. "I adore that type of skirt," she told her sister-in-law. "The flair makes me look taller. I really did weep but with joy and can hardly wait to get to work taking the waistline up."

Although life was not easy for Peggy at this period, she remained in good spirits. Nights out on the town were not missed because friends were often in and out of the Dump, and Bessie was such a good manager that there was always enough food to serve. An invitation to eat some of Bessie's fried chicken and collard greens was much prized within the Marshes' circle, and Bessie would buy the poultry at a butcher shop in Darktown, where prices were much lower than in white markets, and carry it to work with her.

The Dump was so small that Bessie and her employer could not help but become close. While Peggy worked at her typewriter, Bessie remained in the tiny kitchen and, amazingly, never asked her what the book was about. But they did discuss their personal lives. Peggy was still having difficulties with her father, and Bessie, who had worked for "Mr. Eugene" for ten years, understood the causes better than anyone. Bessie was a lean, handsome woman, ten years older than Peggy. A wise, religious person, she brought Peggy closer to the church than any member of her family had succeeded in doing. Bessie also believed strongly in the sanctity of marriage and that a man must be catered to, and Peggy was influenced by her convictions.

In truth, John Marsh's pragmatic personality was not always easy to live with. It took special care and tolerance on Peggy's part. He was in his daily life as he was in his copy-editing, "picayune and flaw-finding." Already set in his ways, he did not enjoy surprises of any sort, and disliked unfamiliar food and uninvited company. Overnight guests were an anathema to him. Luckily, the Dump was so small that the possibility seldom presented itself.

Neither of them were good sleepers and it was not unusual for either John or Peggy to be up roaming about the apartment or raiding the icebox at night. This was one reason they gave for not accepting invitations to stay overnight in the homes of friends and family outside of Atlanta (although later Peggy was to accept such invitations on her own). Peggy suffered frequent nightmares and insomnia, and John's idea of heaven was sleeping until two P.M. and then having Bessie serve him breakfast in bed.

Peggy wrote prodigiously throughout the final months of 1928, and then stopped abruptly in the spring of 1929. The arthritis in her ankle had suddenly shot up to her wrists and she was not able to use the typewriter. At this time, she pulled out all the envelopes and read their contents, penciling in new corrections and adjusting inconsistencies. She changed Fontenoy Hall to Tara throughout, heavily marking out the name each time it appeared and writing "Tara" above it. She did this, too, on the envelope that held the section of Pansy coming home after the burning of Atlanta, so that it read: "The Road to Tara."

When she had been through the whole manuscript once, she decided to put it aside for a while. It now filled twenty envelopes and was about six hundred thousand words long. Scenes remained to be written, mainly those having to do with the war and certain campaigns. She had rewritten and edited and then re-edited the opening chapter many times, and all those pages were together in one envelope, making no sense whatsoever to read. The problem of how to kill off Frank Kennedy, Pansy's second husband, was not yet solved, and she had written two different endings for this chapter. In one, Frank, never strong, died from exposure during the stormy night of the Shantytown incident. In the other, he is downed by a bullet during a Ku Klux Klan raid. Both occur after Pansy inadvertently goes into Shantytown alone on a buckboard and is nearly raped — a scene certainly culled from Peggy's own visit to Darktown but dramatizing John and Bessie's worst fears. Both versions also have the same effect on the story — Pansy is responsible for Frank Kennedy's death. Although dissatisfied with the way she had handled Pansy's first two children (she kept rewriting those scenes in which they appeared), Peggy apparently considered Bonnie, Pansy's little girl by Rhett, well drawn, for the passages with Bonnie remained pretty much the same in each successive draft, as did the majority of the confrontations between Pansy and Rhett.

John was too busy at the office for them to go over the entire long manuscript together — that would take months. And Peggy was not well enough to do the remainder of the research required for some scenes, nor was she certain how to fill in some of the remaining gaps in her story. She had no idea what the book might be worth as literature. Some scenes — like Gerald O'Hara's distraction after his wife's death; Bonnie's fatal fall from the horse, reflecting her own similar but luckier accident; and Rhett's near violence toward Pansy before he forces himself on her, bringing back incidents between herself and Red — were hard for her to evaluate. Reality became confused with fiction.

There were other problems that concerned her. She had modeled the one "bad" woman, Belle Watling, on a famous madam in Lexington whom John had told her about, and, though aging, Belle Breazing was still alive. Pansy's protector, Archie, the ex-convict who had killed his wife, was based on a real man, as was her Jonesboro character, Tony Fontaine, who murders Tara's former overseer. And, of course, there were Red Upshaw and Grandmother Stephens to think about, too. It made no difference to Peggy that Thomas Wolfe, in his newly published and acclaimed *Look Homeward, Angel*, had so realistically portrayed the people and town of Asheville, North Carolina, that a stranger who had read the book might have been set down on the main street of Asheville, found his way to the Gant house without asking directions, and could have recognized many passersby. Peggy was terrified of any potential risk of being sued for libel.

It would have taken about a year to finish the book at this point, but reading it had depressed Peggy severely. The work to be done was tremendous, and if she completed it — then what? How could she submit it anywhere when she feared lawsuits and dreaded professional criticism? And when she compared her work to that of Glasgow and Fitzgerald and Benét — how could she dare to think of herself as a true writer? She had worked hard and long hours, but that was not enough to qualify her as a literary figure. And she was sure that the authors she admired had no need of someone like John at their elbow, helping them all the time. Someday, perhaps, she would go back to the book, but at the moment, the entire project seemed to her like little more than a waste of time.

Peggy and John discussed her decision to put her work aside and, once he saw that there was no way to convince her that she was wrong, he helped her find places to store the stacks of envelopes so that they would not be constantly in the way. No sooner had this been accomplished than Peggy's arthritis grew even worse. She started on a round of medical consultations and, in an effort to diminish the arthritic pain, she had several badly decayed teeth, and then her tonsils, removed. A nutritionist eliminated all sweets and starches from her diet. The pain persisted and, during the summer, she received shots of small amounts of typhoid vaccine and underwent daily massage and diathermy treatments. Suddenly, as the New Year of 1930 passed and spring approached, the arthritis disappeared.

Although she had been away from the book nearly a year, John never let her forget that it was unfinished, and he accused her of being ungrateful for her ability to write, a talent he said he would have "given the world to possess." Years later, when a reporter asked her if she thought she might be inspired to return to her writing, Peggy replied bitterly, "I never met that lady Inspiration yet and I don't expect I ever will."

Certainly Peggy was not inspired in 1930, and she did not work on the book at all that year. Her energies were taken up with helping Grandmother Stephens, who was failing, and her elderly aunts in Jonesboro, who were also old and feeble. Friends, too, took much of her time now that she was no longer an invalid herself. She became involved in all their problems and was always available in an emergency. Later she claimed she had seen one friend "through three psychiatrists and a couple of neurologists, a divorce, and a happy new marriage."

Peggy was avoiding going back to work on the book and both she and John knew it. The blame was placed on all those close associates who required her services in illness and trouble. She ignored John's hints that she could say no, and did not even seem nettled when a friend commented, "Isn't it a shame that somebody with a mind like Peggy's hasn't any ambition?"

It looked as though the novel that John had so encouraged her to write and that had created such a closeness between them might never be completed. Such a possibility did not seem to disturb Peggy at this time, but it was the source of great dissatisfaction to John Marsh.

Chapter Thirteen

PEGGY TOOK UP the game of bridge because she was at a loss as to what else to do with her afternoons and Mah-jongg depressed her. She also joined the Atlanta Women's Press Club and, between these two activities, managed to stave off her boredom.

Never much of a gameswoman, she had chosen bridge because so many intelligent young women in Atlanta played it, and there was always good conversation at these bridge parties. After a luncheon at someone's home, the guests would draw for bridge tables, and one autumn Saturday afternoon in 1930 Peggy found herself seated across the table from a vivacious young woman named Lois Dwight Cole, whom she had not met before. Lois Cole had recently moved to Georgia to run the Atlanta branch of the Macmillan publishing company's trade department, and she was living in a rooming house a short distance from the Marshes.

As the cards were dealt, Lois asked, "Do you follow any particular conventions, partner?"

Peggy replied solemnly, "Conventions? I don't know any. I just lead from fright. What do you lead from?"

"Necessity," Lois replied, and Peggy broke out in a wide grin.

Lois Cole later recalled, "On the first hand our opponents bid four spades. My partner held six; I had two and two aces, and we set them five; whereupon we rose, solemnly if improperly, and shook hands across the table.

"As there was more conversation than bridge, it was soon established that I was the Yankee who had come down to work for Macmillan (everyone knew but it was manners to ask) and that I had gone to Smith where [Peggy] had been for a year. During refreshments, she edged around to me and asked if I would come to supper the following Wednesday with her and her husband, John Marsh."

Lois accepted the invitation, was served Bessie's best fried chicken, collard greens, and biscuits, and listened with delight to Peggy's tales of Atlanta and comments on books and people. Peggy told her stories "with such fun and skill and with such verve," Lois later wrote, that she never minded that her hostess was the center of attention the entire evening.

In a short time, the women became friends, and when Lois Cole married an Atlanta newspaperman, Allan Taylor, later that year, the two couples became a close foursome. Taylor, as both a newspaperman and a Southerner, had a great deal in common with the Marshes. They spent many evenings together and invariably there would be discussions about the Civil War. A typical evening found the couples at supper in the small front room of the Dump, with Peggy and Allan deep in conversation about Atlanta's trials at the hands of the Northerners. One such night, Peggy asked what prison Allan's kinfolks had been in during the war. He told her, and then inquired what prison hers had been in.

"What was the death rate in the prison your kinfolks were in?" she asked.

He responded with an exact figure, and then wanted to know whether pneumonia or small pox accounted for most of the deaths in the jail where her relatives were imprisoned.

To the two Southerners, there was nothing at all unusual about this conversation, and they spoke of it all as though from firsthand experience.

Lois looked at them blankly. "What I cannot understand about Southerners," she said, "is their obsession with the Civil War. We've forgotten it. Why can't you?"

"I can't explain without talking all night or writing a very long book," Peggy retorted.

It was about this time that Lois learned from John that Peggy had written a book about the Battle of Atlanta and the city's rebirth during Reconstruction. Lois had spoken to Medora and to several of Peggy's co-workers at the *Journal* and had an editor's instinct that Peggy Marsh could well have written a book that might be publishable. She prodded Peggy to show her the manuscript, but Peggy would not be swayed, nor would she even discuss any part of the plot, except for its historical background and setting.

In September, 1930, John was made advertising manager of Georgia Power and, to celebrate, they puchased a year-old, green Chevrolet. This gave them some mobility on weekends but also gave Peggy more responsibility than ever, as friends and family who did not have cars now called upon her in every emergency, large or small. However, the car also gave John the opportunity to "put Peggy back to work." He organized Sunday outings to include drives to the various Civil War battle sites in and around Atlanta. On seeing them, Peggy would recall stories she had heard, often ones she had included in the book. One blistering hot Sunday in early September, 1931, John took Peggy for a drive to Dalton, and on September 20 he wrote his sister:

> It was especially interesting to us because it was the scene of big events in the Civil War and in Peggy's novel. Seeing the place in the heat of summer gave us a keen sympathy for the men who battled over the section and dragged cannon up the sides of those mountains in July and August. One of the most interesting sections of Peggy's book tells of the approach of the northern army down the railroad line to Atlanta and the first awakenings of fear that the Confederacy might eventually be defeated as the army fought and dropped back to Dalton, Resaca, Big Shanty and then Kenesaw Mountain.

The short day trip refreshed Peggy's memories of the grim tales once told to her by the old veterans about the Battle of Dalton and, since it was Labor Day weekend and John was free from work, they decided on an impulse to drive on to Chattanooga, where the Confederate withdrawal to Dalton had begun. John's letter to Frances was the closest either Peggy or he had come to discussing with anyone the contents of Peggy's book. The trip to Chattanooga did stir Peggy to return to the basement of the Carnegie Library and resume her research. The manila envelopes came out of their hiding places and were once again piled by the typewriter.

As close as she was to Lois Cole, and even though Lois held an executive position in a publishing company, Peggy would not reveal the contents of the book to her and refused point-blank to show her any part of the manuscript. True, it was in a more confused state now than ever, what with all the new historical material she was inserting, but Peggy's secrecy regarding her book went much deeper than that. She had a low estimation of her own worth as a writer, and Lois was a professional, dealing with some of the best writers of the time. Peggy's father, whose approval was so important to her, had told her that writing was "a good enough way for a woman to occupy her time," but had never been interested to the point of inquiring about the book. He had not thought much of her journalism and he now ventured that he did not "expect that she could be writing anything worth time to read." John tried desperately to raise her self-esteem, but whatever he did or said could not negate the fact in her mind that it was John who put order and emphasis into her work and that without his constant help, the book would be in even a greater shambles than it was.

Peggy always claimed that she wrote the book only to amuse John and herself. But, weighing the evidence, that seems unlikely. She had spent several years of her life writing with no clear goal in mind, but now the end was in sight, and the time had come for her to admit the truth to herself, if she had not already done so unconsciously — she desperately wanted her novel published, to prove to her father and to all other detractors that she had talent and ability after all. Otherwise, she would not have bothered so at this stage about the accuracy of every small detail. She now spent days and sometimes weeks trying to determine, for example, whether there had been rain or sunshine on the particular date of a scene in the book. She found out all she could about Vicksburg and the defeat at Gettysburg, the Battle of Chickamauga, the bleak days when the Yankees under Sherman were above Dalton at Rocky Face, and all the fighting around Atlanta from May, 1864, until the city fell that September. She knew that if her father ever did read the book, he would be especially critical of any inaccuracies.

Certainly her insistence on authentic background material for the novel allowed Peggy a forum for her "obsession" — the war and what it must have been like to have lived through it — but, as the pages multiplied and the envelopes continued to bulge, her obsession with the war itself began to ease. At least from the time she became friends with Lois Cole, Peggy was torn between the desire to be published and fears that her best efforts would be rejected, her characters in the novel would be linked with people in her life, her father would become more critical of her, and friends — who were mostly of a literary bent — would be made aware of her failure. And, although John did not discuss the contents of the book with anyone but Frances, and even in her case did so only superficially, he did make it known that Peggy was writing a novel that he considered great and that one day would make people aware of his wife's tremendous talents.

❧

John received a small raise in 1932 and, as their debts were almost all paid, the Marshes now felt able to afford a few comforts. They moved into a larger, five-room apartment, filling it with Victorian furniture from Grandmother Stephens.

The new apartment, at Two East Seventeenth Street, was on the third floor and had a lovely bay window in the living room. The second bedroom was turned into an office for John, who often brought home extra work at night, and Peggy once again set her sewing table up in the living room and did her typing there. Since John was the breadwinner, his work was considered by both of them to take top priority and to warrant the privacy of an office. The neighborhood was a considerable step up from Tight Squeeze, although, since it was right downtown, it was quite commercial. Next door was the Northwood Hotel, a residential hotel, and there were shops up and down the road. Peggy particularly liked the apartment because light streamed in even on overcast days. The fact that her bay window overlooked the street, with its traffic, streetcars, and a constant flow of people, did not seem to disturb her.

According to Peggy, the main theme of her book was *survival,* or what she called gumption, and the second theme was the security found in the land. But Peggy never had any desire to own a house and land herself, preferring to live right in the heart of Atlanta. She felt a part of the city and loved it with all its blemishes.

Not long after they had moved, Red Upshaw appeared with no warning at Marshes' door — at an hour of the morning when he could be fairly certain that John would have left for the office. It was Monday, October 24, 1932, a date that might not have been recorded were it not the same day that presidential candidate Franklin D. Roosevelt visited Atlanta. Medora Perkerson had invited Peggy to a reception in his honor. While she was dressing for this occasion, the doorbell rang and Bessie answered it. The sound of Bessie's agitated voice carried into the bedroom, and Peggy hurried to the living room just as Bessie was preparing to close the door in Upshaw's face. Red made the best of the moment and stepped past Bessie and into the room. The indignant black woman stood guard, refusing to leave "Miss Peggy" alone.

Reconstructing this incident later for Medora, Peggy intimated that she could never have stood the shock of Upshaw's sudden appearance if Bessie had not been close at hand. He was much thinner than when she had last seen him, but he was as brash and handsome as ever. He told her he had a new job with another coal company in North Carolina and was just passing through, but she did not believe him because in the next breath he asked for a loan. It took her about ten minutes to convince him to leave, and she never revealed whether she gave him any money. Medora said that he refused to leave town before he had sufficient money to do so, and Lethea Turman seems to have heard a similar story.

A short while later, someone told Peggy that Red had married a rich socialite from the North; and not long after that, a rumor reached her that he had taken this woman for a large sum of money and that she was divorcing him. Again, neither of these stories was ever confirmed. His appearance in Atlanta, however, shook Peggy up considerably and renewed her fear that if her book ever was published, Red might well see fit to pay her another visit. Peggy's feelings toward Red were always confused. She hated, feared, and felt threatened by him. At the same time, his brief appearance in her living room once again made her question her own complicity in the violent end of their marriage. She discussed her doubts with John and Medora, but neither of them could dispel her nagging sense of guilt.

Every summer, John represented Georgia Power at the annual Georgia Press Association meeting, a convention to which large public companies came to advertise their products to the media. In the Depression summer of 1933, Peggy's spirits were as low as the rest of the nation's. Hoping it would do her good to get out of the city and away from her stacks of envelopes for a couple of days, John took Peggy with him to the meeting, being held that summer in the small town of Louisville, Georgia, near Augusta.

"Tobacco Road district and Erskine Caldwell to the contrary," Peggy wrote Lois, who had recently moved back to New York to become associate editor in Macmillan's home office, "the most charming people in the state inhabit these regions." Peggy welcomed the opportunity to attend the gathering, and especially enjoyed playing hostess for her husband's company, for this meant late-night gatherings in their room, where booze was dispensed to their guests in Dixie cups. Newspaper people sat on beds and on the floor, drinking corn and discussing job printing and the future of literature, and exchanging gossip and off-color jokes. Peggy loved it, downing as much corn as the most hardened of newspapermen. She was, in fact, right in her element, and press men and women alike found her an especially "grand fellow" and one of the best storytellers.

But once back in Atlanta, Peggy's restlessness returned. John prodded her to get back to work on the novel, but she made no headway. And when, in 1934, Stark Young's *So Red the Rose*, about life on a Mississippi plantation during the Civil War, was published, he refused to let her read it, fearing that if she did she might give up on the book altogether.

On February 17, 1934, Grandmother Stephens died, leaving Peggy a small inheritance. That April, Peggy was at the wheel of their green Chevrolet, John beside her, when a drunken driver careened into them, sending their car off the road. John was unscathed, but Peggy's back and foot were injured. Her doctor prescribed an elasticized girdle brace that she would wear underneath her clothes for a year. Sitting at her typewriter was now too painful to contemplate, she claimed, so she threw the old bath sheet over the sewing table and gave herself up fully to chauffeuring and tending relatives and friends.

❦

The morning that Harold Strong Latham arrived in Atlanta, in April 1935, Peggy had just been told that she could stop wearing her brace in a week's time. It was Medora's opinion that, not only was Peggy accident prone, but she had turned into a hypochondriac since her marriage. Yet, although Peggy's various physical complaints gave her an uncontestable excuse for staying away from her typewriter, she loathed the itchy girdle she had to wear and detested even more the low-heeled orthopedic shoes her injuries had demanded. Having always played the flirt and belle, Peggy sorely missed the swains who had once kept her feeling young and desirable, and who had long since ceased to pay her court. She was thirty-five, childless, the glamour of her newspaper days a decade past, and, with her brace and heavy shoes, she thought she walked "like a crotchety old woman."

But the doctor's good news had put Peggy in high spirits, and as she chatted with Latham later that day, at the luncheon and during their afternoon drive to Stone Mountain, she was the animated and entertaining Peggy Mitchell of old.

The next evening, after Harold Latham had left Atlanta with Peggy's manuscript in his possession, she and John discussed her impetuous act. John, who had always hoped Peggy would someday submit her novel for publication, did not at all approve of the way she had finally gone about it. Quite apart from the slovenliness of its pages, the missing chapters and transitional material, the sketchiness of some chapters and the multiple versions of others, the manuscript had been handed over with no title and no author's credit. At least six months were needed to pull the book into shape, and to give a publisher such a manuscript was unprofessional.

John agreed that Peggy should telegraph Latham to send back the manuscript. Latham wrote back from New Orleans that he would like to have the opportunity to finish reading it first. Judging by the sections he had read, he said, the book had great potential.

Peggy wrote him a curious letter the next day, spending an entire page touting an author named Emanuel Snellgrove, who was the city editor at the *Macon News and Telegraph* and a friend of a friend, before getting around to her own manuscript, in which, she told him, she was shocked he could find anything to commend. In a revealing admission she confessed, "I would not be at all surprised if my actions made you feel that there was something lacking in me that other authors real and fancied possessed — that passionate belief in the good quality of their work." So far, no one but Latham and John, who, she joked, "after all did promise for better or worse," had read the manuscript, and she was "more than a little frightened" that he was taking it to New York for a careful reading for many reasons.

Peggy then went on to warn Latham about the missing first chapter, and to explain that the second and third chapters were "not even satisfactory first drafts," and that a brief page and a half of explanatory material at the end of part one was missing, which shot "all of part one to hell and gone!"

Parts two and three, she admitted, stood up pretty well as an outline but lacked short explanatory sections. What most concerned her was a "terrible sag of interest and action" somewhere between parts three and four, as well as the confusion caused by the two versions of Frank Kennedy's death.

She then enumerated all the lapses in the manuscript in part four, concluding that there was a vast lack of political and social background in this section, which caused the story to be "appallingly thin" toward the end. Peggy was also fearful that she had presented a false picture of Southern men of the Reconstruction period by making it appear that only the ladies were valiant during those difficult times — an error she intended to rectify.

Finally, she apologized for having inserted three or four versions of the same chapters into the envelopes. They had been put there, she explained, for her husband's "convenience in comparing and throwing away."

She was certain, then, that the manuscript would give Macmillan a "dreadfully difficult time," and added, "If after you have read more you find that you can get some continuity out of the story then take it on to New York with my approval and thanks. But if on further reading you find it too scrambled to be intelligible, send it back to me and I will remove the extra versions and where chapters are missing put in a brief summary of what is contained in those missing chapters."

These words cannot be misinterpreted. Contrary to all the statements she made later — saying she had given the manuscript to Latham on impulse and had not only asked him to return it but had insisted that he *not* take it to New York — Latham brought the manuscript to Macmillan with Peggy's approval. It may well have been that her expectations for it were not high, but she could have requested that the manuscript be returned at this point — and she did not do that. Before Peggy had time to mail her letter agreeing to let Latham take the novel to New York, a second enthusiastic letter arrived from him, and she added a postscript to hers to tell him that his "encouraging words" had had a "more healthy affect on my back than all the braces, electric treatments and operations the doctors advise."

With Latham on his way to New York, the incredible journey of the untitled, unsigned manuscript that was to make publishing history had begun.

Chapter Fourteen

THE MARSHES told no one that Peggy's novel was with a New York publisher; neither of them expected it to be accepted. For now, Peggy had little choice but to put the book out of her mind. She had given Latham her only complete copy. There were stacks of rewritten and rejected pages that Bessie had stored away, but reconstructing any section of them would have been a difficult task. There was, however, no chance for her to enjoy her leisure, for just two weeks after Latham's departure, her father had a gallstone operation and Peggy spent her days nursing him at the hospital and then at Peachtree Street, as Carrie Lou now had two small boys to care for.

Then, in May, Peggy suffered her second car accident in just over a year's time. She was alone, "as tired," she said, "as a hound at the end of a hunt," and her leg was giving her some discomfort. The late-afternoon sun turned the hood of the car into a dazzle of reflections and she was having to squint to see. Suddenly, as she described it, a car came "hurtling out of a side street" and into her limited line of vision. She swerved sharply to avoid a collision, her car jumped the curb and then came to an abrupt stop, throwing her against the steering wheel. Except for the impact of the sudden stop, which aggravated the old spine and leg injuries, she was unharmed.

Peggy resisted wearing the brace again, but agreed to daily

diathermy treatment. Then, one evening at home, just two weeks after the accident, a guest — carried away in the enthusiasm of conversation — waved a bottle of whiskey in the air as he was getting set to pour himself a drink. The bottle slipped from his grasp. Peggy, who was at least a foot shorter than the man, stood facing him as he spoke, and the bottle landed on her head, knocking her unconscious. She was rushed to the hospital, but the doctors diagnosed only a slight concussion and she returned home to rest and recuperate.

Six weeks later, she was well enough to attend the annual meeting of the Georgia Press Association, held again in Louisville. It was the Fourth of July and the Marshes celebrated their tenth anniversary on the trip.

They returned home with Peggy feeling well for the first time in a year and with a new surge of energy that made her want to work. It had been three months since Latham had written that he was taking the manuscript on to New York. On July 9, she wrote to ask him to return it, explaining that she was one of those "clumsy or unlucky people who are always being run into by drunken autoists, sat on by horses, struck playfully with bottles by guests," or ill with influenza, battling arthritis, or in demand by friends at the births of their babies — the last being "far worse than the catastrophes listed above." At the moment, she was able and very anxious to work. "However," she wrote, "I realize that it is only a matter of time before I have an arm in a sling or my skull fractured again. With m[e], writing is sandwiched between broken bones and xrays and as I am all in one piece at present it looks like flying in the face of providence not to take advantage. So could I have my manuscript back please?"

Peggy went on to tell Latham that she would still look for Georgia authors for him. In May she had written him about a historian by the name of Marmaduke Floyd, who was writing a book, but Latham had not asked her to follow this up, and she wondered if he wanted her to continue to scout for Macmillan.

On the same day, Peggy also wrote to Lois that she wanted her manuscript back. Neither one of these letters gives the impression that Peggy was recalling the book because she had changed her mind about possible publication, but that she was afraid she might be spoiling her chances by allowing it to be judged in its disorganized state. She need not have worried, for a few days later she received this reply from Latham:

> Please hold off your request. I am very enthusiastic about the possibilities your book presents. I believe if it is finished properly it will have every chance of a very considerable success and for me you have created in Pansy a character who is vital and unforgettable. A number of your scenes have firmly fastened in my mind. As you have gathered I have taken a very keen interest in your book and I hope you will not insist on its return before our advisers are through with it.

Latham questioned the name "Pansy," which he thought had an "unpleasant connotation," and informed Peggy that the manuscript had been given to a Professor C. W. Everett at Columbia University to read and make suggestions about how the novel could best be revised and completed.

During the short time between Peggy's letter of the ninth, requesting the return of the manuscript, and the arrival of Latham's letter on the seventeenth of July, Bessie took seriously ill with meningitis and, in the first days of the disease, was on the critical list. Bessie was in the colored ward of Atlanta's one charity hospital. It was not that she could not pay for a hospital bed, nor that the Marshes were not willing to pay for one for her, but that Atlanta had no paying hospital facilities for blacks, which literally meant there was no place for them to receive top medical care. Peggy spent much of her time trying to see to it that Bessie was being well treated, but as soon as Bessie had shown good signs toward recovery, Peggy wrote Latham that she should be free to work in a week or so.

Macmillan already had the wheels in motion, however, and, on July 21, she received telegrams from both Lois Cole and Harold Latham in the same delivery. Lois wired: "MACMILLAN TERRIBLE [SIC] EXCITED YOUR BOOK I AM MOST EXCITED OF ALL STOP ALWAYS KNEW YOU HAD WORLD BEATER EVEN IF NO ONE COULD SEE IT STOP COMPANY PLANNING GREAT THINGS FOR THE BOOK HOW SOON CAN YOU FINISH IT STOP ALLAN [Taylor] AND JIM [James Putnam, a Macmillan executive whom Peggy had met once in Atlanta through Lois] JOIN THEIR LOVE AND CONGRATULATIONS TO MINE."

Latham's message confirmed the news: "MY ENTHUSIASM

YOUR NOVEL SHARED BY OUR ADVISERS WE WOULD LIKE MAKE IMMEDIATE CONTRACT FOR ITS PUBLICATION $500 ADVANCE ½ ON SIGNING BALANCE ON DELIVERY MANUSCRIPT ACCOUNT 10% ROYALTY FIRST 10,000 THEN 15% STOP MY RENEWED CONGRATULATIONS AND ASSURANCE WE UNDERTAKE PUBLICATION WITH TREMENDOUS ENTHUSIASM AND LARGE HOPES STOP DO WIRE YOUR APPROVAL COLLECT THAT I MAY SEND CONTRACT IMMEDIATELY."

Receipt of these messages put Peggy into a state which, she wrote Latham, "necessitated a Luminal tablet, a cold towel on the forehead and a nice, quiet nap" — but not before she rang John at the office and told him the news. Her worst fears and highest hopes had become reality.

It is apparent that if Peggy had been reluctant to publish the book, this was the opportunity to put off making a final decision. But when John came home that evening, she sent off two telegrams — one to Lois, the other to Latham — stating that her acceptance of Macmillan's proposal to publish her book was contingent only on the receipt of the contract. Then she sat down and wrote Latham a letter, asking if she would be required by the contract to deliver the finished manuscript by a certain, certified date, a condition she feared because she was "especially subject to acts of God" and never knew from one day to the next whether she would have "a broken neck or the bubonic plague, afflictions which interfere with the job of writing." She hurried to assure him that she did not anticipate any catastrophes and had actually gone as long as six months without anything happening to her. "But," she wrote, "I feel, in all honesty that I should tell you the possibility."

She asked to see Professor Everett's suggestions, "and the fuller the better," and then, pleading ignorance of the publishing business, she wondered whether Macmillan would let such suggestions pass into the hands of authors before the signing of a contract, expressing her concern that Professor Everett might suggest changes that she would be unwilling to make.

She did not give Latham an unqualified acceptance. "Coming of a legal family," she explained, "I do not like to accept any contract no matter how nice without seeing it, so please send it to me and I will give you an answer just as soon as I can look it over."

Peggy concluded her letter with a statement which, true or not, she was to make over and over again in the years to come: "I never expected to get an offer for the book because it was written just to please my husband and myself and to keep me occupied during the months I was lame."

Latham instantly sent Peggy C. W. Everett's enthusiastic report. Everett had managed to condense her 600,000-word story into five typewritten pages, and he ended his synopsis with the following critique:

This book is really magnificent. Its human qualities would make it good against any background, and when they are shown on the stage of the Civil War and reconstruction the effect is breathtaking. Furthermore, it has a high degree of literary finish. Take for instance, in the evacuation of Atlanta, the ridiculous appearance made by the aristocratic Mrs. Elsing in the morning as she drives furiously out of town with her carriage bulging with flour and beans and bacon. Then see Pansy leaving that night — with a worn-out horse and broken down wagon, and those literally beyond price so that only a strong man like Rhett could have secured them. And at Tara Pansy faces starvation. Yet there is no reference made by the author to the previous scene; it simply marks an increase in the tempo. It is perhaps in this control of tempo that the book is most impressive. When the writer wants things to seem slow, timeless, eternal, that is the way they move. But her prestissimo is prestissimo and her fortissimo is FFF. For like King Lear, Pansy learns "There is no worst as long as we can say 'this is the worst.' "

By all means take the book. It can't possibly turn out badly. With a clean copy made of what we have, a dozen lines could bridge the existing gaps. . . . There really are surprisingly few loose ends, and the number of times one's emotions are stirred one way or another is surprising. I am sure that it is not only a good book, but a best seller. It's much better than Stark Young [author of the recently published Civil War book So Red the Rose] and the literary device of using an unsympathetic character to arouse sympathetic emotions seems to me admirable.

The end is slightly disappointing, as there may be a bit too much finality about Rhett's refusing to go on. . . . Take the book at once. Tell the author not to do anything to it but bridge the gaps and strengthen the last page.

Peggy responded to Latham by special delivery two days later, on July 27, that she had not expected "so swell a report" and that it was only by "bearing up sturdily" that she kept from going to bed again with "Luminal and ice packs." Professor Everett did have some reservations about the author's use of certain words and phrases and, to Everett's suggestion that "the author should keep out her own feelings in one or two places where she talked about the negroes," Peggy agreed that he was absolutely right, and said she had tried to keep out venom, bias, and bitterness as much as possible. All "V, b and b in the book" were to come not from the author, she explained, but "through the eyes and heads and tongues of the characters, as reactions from what they saw and heard and felt." Everett had called her on her references to "Mammy's ape face" and "black paws," descriptions she was willing to change, although, she said, she had "meant no disrespect to Mammy for I have heard so many negroes refer to their hands as 'black paws' and when an old and wrinkled negro woman is sad there is nothing else in the world she looks like except a large ape. But I had not realized how differently this sounded in type."

She agreed with Everett at this time that there might be a bit too much finality in Rhett's departure, but added, "I think she gets him in the end." This seems to be the only time she ever made such a statement in a letter or interview. She conceded that it "might not hurt to hint as much a little more strongly," adding, "My own intention when I wrote it was to leave the end open to the reader. (Yes, I know that's not a satisfactory way to do!)" She had not read that section of the manuscript for two years and did not even have a copy. Her "vague memory" was that she had done no more than synopsize that chapter and she suggested to Latham that perhaps a rewrite would bring it closer to the more definite ending that Everett wanted.

At this time, she stated that she preferred the version where Frank Kennedy died of illness to the Ku Klux Klan one, exciting though that was, because "the Ku Klux Klan material has been worked pretty hard by others." She had written the Ku Klux Klan version when, in rereading that part of the book, she had felt that there was a "very definite sag of interest over a range of 6 chapters." The inclusion of the Klan was an attempt to strengthen that section without "a lot of melodramatic incident." She asked Latham to let her complete the book without the Ku Klux Klan version and if he did not like it and Macmillan's advisors did not like it then she would gladly go back to the first version. And, she went on, "The same applies to remarks written about the ending. If you don't like the way it looks when you get the final copy, tell me and I'll change it. I'll change it any way you want, except to make it a happy ending."

No one at Macmillan liked the name Pansy for the central character. In the North, the word was used to refer to effeminate men. But Southerners, Peggy explained to Latham, referred "to Pansies as Fairies or by another less euphemistic but far more descriptive term." She agreed, however, that if the name was offensive in the North, then she would have to try "to think of another name equally inappropriate."

As most of the chapters had not been numbered, Latham and Professor Everett had had some difficulty with the chronology of the story, and two characters — Pansy's first daughter, Ella; and Archie — appeared suddenly and without any introduction. To Peggy's embarrassment, she realized that the chapters in which these characters made their first entrances had not been given to Latham. With Bessie, who kept track of Peggy's papers, out ill, the search she made for them was not successful, although she did find the incomplete early drafts, and sent these on with the note: "The best way I can place these is to say that they come after the chapter on Gerald's death."

She had not said a word about receiving the contract, and Macmillan was considerably disturbed by this fact. Actually, the document had not yet arrived in Atlanta when Peggy wrote to Latham on July 27. Someone in the legal department had forgotten to send it by special delivery. On July 30, Latham wrote her:

My dear Mrs. Marsh,
   Your letter of July 27th has just reached me. I judge when you wrote it you had not received the contract as you made no mention of it. I hope by this time you have had it and found it satisfactory. If it isn't and you want it changed in any part, let me know wherein and I will see what can be done about it. I shan't be entirely happy until the contract is an accepted fact you see.

I am glad you liked the report. . . . I think your suggestion to withhold criticism on the Pansy–Rhett outcome until the book is in final form is just the thing to do. In fact, I think that is what we want to do with everything. We have large faith in this book — very large faith, indeed. We want it to be the best possible book it can be. We shall spare no effort ourselves to bring that about and once we publish it we shall spare no effort to make it the success which we are confident it should be. So don't think we'll hesitate to work with you to the limit. We are out to do just that sort of thing. . . . I wish I could make you understand just how I feel about this book. I think I am as happy over it as though I had written it myself.

     Sincerely yours,
     H. S. Latham

From the start, Latham felt certain that Peggy Mitchell Marsh had written a book that could give *Lamb in His Bosom* a run for its popularity. Mrs. Marsh had told a riveting story, managing to sustain suspense throughout over two thousand manuscript pages, and this despite the fact that the final resolutions of some chapters were still in question; the last chapter and the death of Frank Kennedy, especially. The motivations of the characters, however, were never in doubt. For, whether — as in the case of Frank Kennedy — death was to come by violence or illness, Pansy's responsibility for her husband's premature death remained. And either way, Frank's death reactivated the Pansy–Rhett relationship. And, by the end, Rhett had taken as much as a real man could from a castrating wife — he *had* to leave in the last chapter.

Later, F. Scott Fitzgerald was to observe that the book had "none of the elements that make literature — especially no new examination into human emotions." Latham felt much the same way. A fine and experienced editor, he did not think he had discovered a literary masterpiece. But he did believe the book was irresistible. Peggy Marsh possessed a natural narrative genius that gave an honesty and validity to her writing. And, more important, she was simply the best storyteller he had ever encountered in his job. She had managed to juggle hundreds of characters and incidents, never allowing the action to flag, and she had told a love story that sustained its passion to the very last page.

It was amazing to him that, despite the extraordinary length of the book, even the most minor characters were easily identifiable, as well as absolutely indispensable to the plot.

It was true that the main characters were not remarkably original. Pansy seemed to owe a lot to Thackeray's Becky Sharp; and Rhett Butler, to St. Elmo. But there was an immediacy to Mrs. Marsh's development of them, as if this was a first-hand account, not a story being retold, but one happening for the first time on the pages she had written. And not only was the book a page-turner, it was about the South and dealt fully with both the war and Reconstruction, something no other Southern novel had done. In 1935, it had a relevancy that was unique. The United States had not only survived a recent war, but it had also come through the worst of the Depression, in which people's lives had again been upended, and only those hardy souls like Rhett and Pansy had managed to turn the situation around to their own advantage.

Latham knew one thing; he was not going to let this book slip through his fingers. He was willing and ready to do everything he could to please this incredible Mrs. Marsh who, he was beginning to realize, was more naive than demanding.

Peggy received her contract in the mail on the first of August and, after going over it with John and her father, she composed a letter to Latham in which she questioned several of its terms.

For one thing, she wished to have the book identified more clearly, as her father, "a lawyer of the old school who can pursue a technicality to the bottom of the haystack," had warned her that failure to identify the property could render the entire contract invalid. To avoid this, she suggested that Macmillan replace "A Novel" with "A Novel of the South (*exact title to be determined*)."

She asked for approval of the jacket design, to ensure that nothing unsouthern should appear "to arouse mirth and indignation." And, in regard to the clause that stated, "Movie and dramatic rights shall remain author's prior to publication," she inquired, "How about *after* publication?" pointing out that they had worded serial rights in the same way. About the line, "Shall be apportioned as mutually arranged," she wondered what would happen if she and the publisher did not mutually agree. "Couldn't we arrange and agree now?" she asked, and then she considered another possibility: "What if Macmillan goes bankrupt?"

Latham showed her letter to Lois Cole. A chilly undercurrent now became manifest in the relationship between the two women. Lois always had the feeling that she was responsible for the discovery of Peggy's book, and she displayed great pride in this. Yet, a certain jealous competitiveness developed on her side of the friendship after Macmillan asked to publish the novel. Lois had written a nonfiction book herself, but she admired novelists and their books more than anything. On August 5, she wrote a rather snide letter to her old friend:

My dear Child,

May I take the liberty of pointing out that you are not dealing with a 5th rate . . . publisher? If your contract had come from Greenberg . . . your suspicions — in fact all suspicions — might have been easily understood. However, the contract came from us and it was the regular printed form which some 12,000 Macmillan authors have signed without a qualm! In fact, I signed one myself. The additional clauses are worded in the same way that thousands of similar clauses and similar contracts have been worded. If Macmillan goes bankrupt no one would be in any state to worry about what becomes of any novel. Gibraltar is no more firmly founded and we will go only with the last stage of the revolution.

　　　　Love,
　　　　Lois

Peggy received this the next day and was horrified that she might have acted in an unprofessional and unappreciative manner, perhaps even angering Macmillan to the point where they would decide against publication. Without further legal consultation or the advice of someone who knew and understood publishing contracts, she signed the Macmillan contract, asking only for small adjustments in the wording and accepting the size of the advance without comment, and without any realization that Macmillan might be anxious enough to buy her book to make the terms more attractive to her. On August 6, 1935, she sent the contracts off with a letter assuring Latham that she never suspected him or Macmillan "of bad faith and double dealing" and begging them to put such an idea out of their minds. She explained that she had only thought that a contract ought to be binding and valid on her as well as on them, and that was why she had written about the "three swell loopholes through which I could have crawled out should I have lost my mind and taken a notion." However, she had no idea of wanting to "crawl out," nor did she "suspect Macmillan in any way."

Peggy's only other request was that the contract be kept a "deep, dark secret." She told Lois that no one except John and her father — not even Stephens — knew about the contract at this time, and Eugene Mitchell had been told only because he would have "skinned" her if he had ever discovered she had signed a contract without his checking it over first.

Latham sent her back a confirming telegram as soon as he received the contract and her letter and, on the ninth of August, he wrote to contradict any unfavorable impression that Lois Cole might have made, assuring Peggy that he understood her questioning completely and would have done the same thing himself in her position. He also asked her for permission to tell Medora about the contract so he could write and thank her for bringing them together.

The next day, Peggy's manuscript came back to her by prepaid express. The receipt she signed for it said, "Manuscript of The Old South 27 sections." Bessie, recuperated now from her bout with meningitis, helped her unwrap the familiar scruffy envelopes that had started on a journey north four months before, and stack them on the sewing table. On the tenth of August, Peggy received a signed copy of her contract and a check for $250. And on August 15, Latham wrote her:

After I asked to have your manuscript returned to you I found I still had in my possession the novelette 'Ropa Carmagin which you gave me at the same time. I am returning this to you under separate cover. I have read this with a great deal of interest and very genuine admiration. It seems to me a splendid piece of work, expertly done. Its length is, of course, against it commercially speaking and of course it is too short for book form. I suggest that you hold it until after your novel is published. You may very easily be able to sell it to one of the better magazines after the appearance of your book. It confirms my very high opinion of you as a writer — if that needed confirmation — and shows you can handle more than one type of material and character. The novel is the big thing just now so don't worry about this or any other short material you have. There will be plenty of time for that afterwards.

Latham was right — the novel *was* the big thing now.

Chapter Fifteen

*F*OR THE FIRST TIME in nearly four months, Peggy was at work on her book. The yellow pages were now even more dog-eared than when Latham had stuffed them into his "please-don't-rain" suitcase. She looked at her work with a different attitude. Professionals had found it good enough to publish. Lavish praise had been given it by men and women whom she could respect. Professor Everett's accolades still rang in her ears. She set back to work with new enthusiasm.

One Saturday morning in early September, John came to her with several pages that she had just rewritten and shook them violently in the hot, still air. "In the name of God, what are these?" he shouted, and then read, according to Peggy, "a double handful of dangling participial clauses and dubious subjunctives."

With all the dignity she could muster, Peggy replied, "Tempo," the word that Professor Everett had used in referring to her marvelous sense of timing. After that, whenever she turned a couple of especially lousy pages over to John, he would say, "Some more of your goddamned Tempo, eh?"

The word became a family joke, and even Bessie, when she made her one and only failure of a lemon pie, commented gloomily, "I guess somethin' done gone wrong with my tempo!"

At the beginning of September, Peggy wrote Harold Latham that she was hard at work and that, for the first time in her life, writing was comparatively easy. According to John, she said, there was nothing like signing a contract, having a conscience about delivering the goods and burning your bridges behind you, to put a writer to work.

With John's help, she was trying to catch grammatical errors and loose ends, to eliminate repetitions, and to condense. She had gone over one-third of the book and at this time — provided, she warned, she did not come down with her "annual September 15th case of Dengue Fever" — she thought she would be finished in six weeks, especially since John was to get his vacation at the end of September and had promised to take his two weeks off to help her.

The problem of who was to be Peggy's editor on the book had still not been settled. Peggy had always shied away from the topic whenever it was mentioned. Lois had seemed the natural choice, as Latham was an acquisitions editor and did not work on manuscripts as a general rule. But Peggy avoided all overtures from Lois. This was not because she lacked confidence in her friend's ability, but because of her own insecurity; she feared that Lois would find her to be a literary fraud because of her "deficiencies" in grammar and spelling.

Latham offered her the use of a good editor, whom he would fly down to Atlanta to help her for a few weeks if she so desired. He even intimated that he would break precedent and come himself if that would make her feel more comfortable. Peggy, however, did not want outside help at this stage, before she and John had been over the entire manuscript themselves. She was convinced that without John's sharp editorial eye and tough criticism both Macmillan and Professor Everett would have rejected the book. Peggy looked up to John as the intellectual in their household. He had graduated from college, had taught English, and his vocabulary was far more extensive than hers, as was his knowledge of grammar and punctuation.

John Marsh's contribution at this point cannot be overestimated. He functioned as Peggy's editor and he was a good one, sensitive to just how much more rewriting Peggy had in her. By his own admission he was overly fastidious and, as he had been a copy editor and his handwriting was more legible than hers, he wrote many of the corrections on the final manuscript for her. The deeper they submerged themselves into the work, the more dependent she became upon him. He was not only acting as her editor, but as a teacher and coach.

By October, Peggy's self-assurance of a month before had begun to desert her. Bridging chapters and cutting others that had been duplicated was a more difficult task than she had anticipated. She had woven her story so tightly that when she cut or inserted anything, the whole picture seemed to fall to pieces like a giant jigsaw puzzle, and getting it back together again was the very devil. When she did, all the cracks seemed to show. It did not help that her father had finally read the material — somewhat reluctantly at that — and had praised its historical accuracy, for he had added that he could not understand why a company would want to invest money in it. She then gave it to Stephens, who would venture nothing more than, "It's competent." Her old doubts returned. Completing the book was now a challenge, but she had no great hopes for its success.

Paradoxically, Peggy could seldom refuse a challenge while, at the same time, she was terrified of change. Medora has said that all "the zip and bustle" that had characterized Peggy's early life, that had led her to "dare marriage with a wild man like Red Upshaw," and that had made her the newspaper woman she was, "somehow got buried with marriage to John Marsh." It is true that Peggy had managed to keep her sharp sense of humor, had remained stimulating company, and was still able to tell a story with verve and originality. But in her day-to-day life, she did rely on John enormously for encouragement and support. Medora suggests that John, out of fear of losing Peggy, had done all he could to make her feel beholden to him for saving her from social disgrace after the Upshaw debacle, as well as making her emotionally dependent upon him to such a degree that she could no longer function on her own. In Medora's opinion, John was "a villain" in Peggy's life and, about this time, she had a disagreement with him that was never really resolved. Sensitive to this, and yet not willing to give up her friendship with Medora, Peggy began to see her away from the house without John present, although the cause for this arrangement was tactfully ignored.

Medora was distressed by what she saw as the loss of Peggy's free spirit. But Peggy's youthful bohemianism and apparent emancipation had been a deception. She had not felt free enough to leave her father's house when she married Upshaw, and it had been John who had pushed her into becoming a newspaper reporter. True, she had taken to it immediately, but he had never let her try to make a go of it on her own, nor had Peggy resisted his involvement in her work. Medora knew that John had always functioned as Peggy's copy editor, but even she had no idea how paralyzed her friend felt without his assistance. The book had developed in the same way — John had pressed her into writing it and then had been there to help her along every page of the way. Later, Frank Daniel, who had worked with Peggy on the *Journal*, was to call the Marshes the "mama and papa" of the book, and that observation had much validity.

Medora, one of the few people who knew that Peggy's novel was to be published, was ecstatic about the news because she hoped it would bring her friend around once again to being the "bright button and talented independent girl" who had worked with her on the *Journal*, and that it might finally put "Peggy's energies to something beside family and illness." Medora was highly critical of John for having insisted that Peggy leave the *Journal*, and she later revealed that, after Peggy's leg had healed, her job had been offered to her again, and that Peggy had turned down the offer because of John's wishes. As Medora saw it, John was little more than a weight Peggy had to pull, which kept her off the main course.

Peggy was of the opinion that in no other section of the country were so many amateur writers working on books as in the South. A natural kinship developed among them and they looked upon those of their number who eventually achieved publication as literary gurus whose time and experience should be easily available. Peggy knew this from her days as a star reporter and she feared it with mounting anxiety, weaving a web of secrecy about herself and her activities to forestall the inevitable requests for her time and advice. She did not have to

A future Southern belle poses with friend, 1904. Even at the age of three or four, Margaret Mitchell liked stories about the history of Atlanta best.

(University of Georgia Archives)

The Fitzgerald plantation, where Margaret spent childhood summers, was destined for immortality as the inspiration for Tara. The house is shown here in disrepair, prior to its renovation in the 1960s.

(Jonesboro Historical Association)

Above left: Maybelle Stephens Mitchell, the fiery suffragette, with her children, Margaret and Stephens, 1904.
(*University of Georgia Archives*)

Above right: Eugene Muse Mitchell, the father whose passion was Georgia's history, 1908.   (Atlanta Constitution)

The Mitchell house on Peachtree Street constituted a move up in the world, but this imposing mansion was no place for an eleven-year-old tomboy who still delighted in wearing pants and throwing mudballs.

(*Atlanta Historical Society*)

Washington Seminary graduating class of 1918. Peggy Mitchell—as she now began to call herself—is center front. English teacher Eva Paisley (*fourth from right, top row*) encouraged her writing talent, and Peggy wrote her first novel while in her class. (*Private collection*)

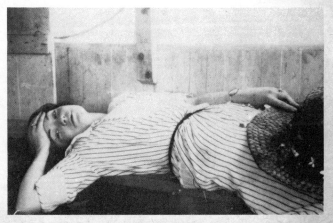

At Smith College Peggy was teased about her Southern accent, short stature, and naiveté, but the girls were impressed by her smoking skill and her daily letters from a serviceman overseas. (*University of Georgia Archives*)

Atlanta debutante, 1921. *(Atlanta Historical Society, Augusta Dearborn Edwards Archives)*

The *Atlanta Journal* reported: " 'The Apache Dance' by Miss Margaret Mitchell, one of the prettiest of the debutantes, and A. S. Weil, a student at Georgia Tech, was one of the striking features of the brilliant 'Mi-Carême' Ball given at the Georgian Terrace recently by members of the Debutantes' Club for the benefit of the home for incurables."

(Atlanta Journal)

Roommates Red Upshaw and John Marsh competed for
Peggy's affections. She chose Upshaw (*center*), and married him on September 2, 1922, but Stephens (*far right*)
told her she was marrying the wrong man. John Marsh
(*second from left*) was a gallant loser and even helped Red
select his wedding clothes.   (*Atlanta Historical Society,
Augusta Dearborn Edwards Archives*)

Within three months Peggy and Red were separated, and
she had landed a job at the *Atlanta Journal*.

Left: Star reporter chatting with Rudolph Valentino.
                                            (Atlanta Journal)

Right: Persistent suitor John Marsh.

                                        (*Frances Marsh Zane*)

Peggy posed at her Remington for a prepublication Macmillan publicity shot, 1936. *(Macmillan Archives)*

"Nothing could make me read it again," Eugene Mitchell commented. But he agreed to a publicity photo with his famous daughter and her best-selling novel.

(Macmillan Archives)

The crowds that gathered in front of Loew's Grand Theatre on the day of the film premiere, December 15, 1939, stood for hours in hopes of getting a glimpse of *Gone With the Wind*'s stars or the celebrated author.

(Atlanta Constitution)

He said she was "charming" and she said he was "grand," but, after social amenities had been exchanged, Clark Gable and Margaret Mitchell had little to say to each other.

(Atlanta Constitution)

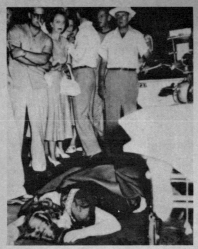

"I'm going to die in a car crash. I feel very certain of this," Peggy had written to Edwin Granberry. At the scene of the accident no one realized that the woman who had been struck down was Margaret Mitchell. (Atlanta Journal)

Margaret Mitchell, the legend.   (*Frances Marsh Zane*)

be a big success for manuscripts by local fledgling writers to choke her mailbox. People she had met once, or perhaps not at all, would appear at her door. There might even be local reporters looking for a story, and that was the last thing that she wanted, for she did not wish to have to fend off questions about Red Upshaw or to deal with snoopers of any kind. How she and John lived was their own business, as were her writing habits and any plans she might have for another book. She had been happy to scout for Macmillan for a fee, but the idea of reading other people's unsolicited manuscripts was so hateful to her that she wrote Lois that she and John had decided to ask for fifty dollars from anyone who asked.

As each day passed, another problem would erupt. Peggy's first estimates of the time it would take to edit now seemed to have been badly miscalculated and she had no idea how she was going to get the work done on schedule; nor did it seem possible to tell Macmillan she needed more time when they had set things in motion based on her original plans.

In all areas of her book except those dealing with actual military strategy — where she had relied entirely on her memories of stories told to her — Peggy's research had been meticulous. Before the book was sold, she said, "I saw no reason why I should plague my brain by studying 'military matters' which I cannot comprehend." Now, besides reading the accounts by the Civil War generals, she dug up all the notes she had gotten from eyewitnesses interviewed in her reporting days. And then, after clipping and studying every article ever written by Atlanta's most revered historians, Wilbur Kurtz and his wife, Annie, she turned to them for further help. She had met the Kurtzes only once, on an Historical Society excursion when the three of them had joined in a prank to try to deceive Stephens into believing that a factory-produced Indian carving was genuine Cherokee — and nearly succeeded.

Only two and a half chapters of the book dealt with military matters, but, she said, she wanted to have them "airtight, so that no gray-bearded vet could rise up to shake his cane at me and say, 'But I know better. I fit in that fight.' " She sent the chapters to Kurtz for his expert advice, along with a lengthy apology saying she knew she was imposing and that she had hated having manuscripts sent to her with similar requests when she was on the *Journal*, but that he was the only living authority she knew on the subject.

Kurtz obliged — a gesture Peggy never forgot — and, after reading the excerpts she had sent him, he wrote back that she had made only two errors. One was small — she had placed the Battle of New Hope Church five miles too close to the railroad; and one was rather vital — she had had the final fortifications of Atlanta completed six weeks too soon.

The pressure she felt to finish was too much for Peggy and, before John's vacation ended, she developed boils, not only over her body, but on her scalp, and the doctor had had to cut away small patches of hair the size of pennies and quarters from around them to prevent the infection from spreading. It didn't help, and the left side of her face became swollen just when Lois wrote requesting a new photograph for the publicity department. She replied to Lois that it was the worst possible time for a picture to be taken, for her scalp looked as though she had "just been rescued from the Indians, and not a minute too soon either." But she promised to try to get a good shot the next day, which she knew would mean hours at the beauty shop, and more hours for the "poor photographer trying to avoid the bald spots, Jimmy Durante nose and M[arlene] Dietrich cheek hollows."

Enclosed with the letter was John's finished copy for the "blurb" about the book and author that was to appear on the flaps of the book jacket, and a note saying that when it was edited she did not want the reference to Melanie to be eliminated, for, she wrote, "of all the characters she's the heroine of the book though I'm afraid I'm the only one who knows it."

The book was now being called "Another Day," which was Professor Everett's suggestion, but no one was particularly pleased with that title, nor had Peggy come up with a suitable alternative to the name "Pansy." When John returned to work early in October, Peggy grew frantic. She had extended her first delivery date from six to ten weeks, which meant the book should be in Macmillan's hands by the fifteenth of November, 1935. All of the publishing company's production staff had adjusted their schedules for that date. But Peggy knew she could not possibly have the manuscript ready for them. For one thing, the first chapter, which had defeated her throughout the writing of the book, was still presenting a tremendous problem for her. She knew she wanted to begin with the war looming close, the news of Ashley's betrothal, the preparations for the barbecue, and the introduction of Pansy, the Tarleton twins (more important in her first drafts than in the final), Gerald O'Hara, and the Wilkes family. But she just did not seem able to come up with the right tone in which to set the scene for what was to follow, and she tried it from every possible angle. Even John offered numerous suggestions, which she tried but which fared no better on paper than did her own ideas.

Finally, in desperation, on October 30, she turned to Latham and wrote him that it was "amateurish, clumsy, and worst of all self-conscious."

She had tried too often and too long on this chapter, and had developed some sort of mental block about it, and she explained to him that she did not exaggerate when she said she had written at least forty first chapters in the past two years, and that whenever she had nothing to do and nothing to read, she had written another first chapter and each one looked worse than the last.

She asked Latham to reread the chapter and tell her "what on earth is wrong with these first pages?" As soon as he received this letter from Peggy, he wrote an interoffice memo to Lois Cole: "Really I don't know what she is excited about. It is true probably that the first two pages of the manuscript are a little bit slow but from the middle of page three on the interest is held very intensely." And in his prompt reply to Peggy he wrote:

I at once dropped everything to read it and I am delighted to tell you how admirable I think it is. I think you want to forget this chapter now. It is absolutely all right. From the middle of page 3 to the end it holds interest without any question. The first two or three pages are necessary to set the stage and introduce the characters. I think you have accomplished a great deal on those two pages and I see nothing self-conscious or amateurish about them. They are, it seems to me, good writing and essential, I think to pick up intense interest as soon as you do and I am sure that begins on page 3 and is quite an accomplishment.

Reading this chapter now stirs in me the emotions which your entire book arouse, admiration for your style of writing, for the excellence of your characters and the very human note which predominates in it. I am especially grateful that we are to have the privilege of publishing this novel. I know we are going to do well with it.

He asked her to go on with the balance of the book and not give another thought to the first chapter. In the end, though, these first two pages were not to be the opening of the book, and Peggy was just as torn and confused about what to do about them after she had written Latham as she had been before. Two other important questions were settled at this time, however.

For about a month the book had been called "Tomorrow is Another Day," the previous title of "Another Day" having been decided against. But then, Peggy's old friend Sam Tupper, who was now doing book reviews for the *Journal*, learned that a book by that title had recently been published; at just about the same time, Lois wrote to confirm the fact. For a while Peggy considered "Tomorrow and Tomorrow," "There's Always Tomorrow," "Tomorrow Will Be Fair," and "Tomorrow Morning," all titles that she sent on to Lois as suggestions. But at the end of October, she wrote Latham that she was inclined to *Gone With the Wind* because, taken completely away from its context, it had movement and it could refer either to times that were gone "like the snows of yesteryear, or to the things that passed with the winds of war, or to a person who went with the wind rather than standing against it."

Latham liked *Gone With the Wind*, and he also thought the name she now suggested for Pansy had promise — "Scarlett." Both of these matters he promised to take up immediately with his editorial board.

But even as late as November 4, the title of the book remained in question and the central character was still named Pansy. Lois was resisting the name Scarlett because, she said, "somebody said it sounds like a *Good Housekeeping* story." Peggy had found the name in the text of her manuscript. The Scarletts, who were ancestors of the O'Haras, "had fought with the Irish Volunteers for a free Ireland and had been hanged for their pains."

At one point, Peggy even suggested her own name, as well as the name Nancy. Both were dismissed because there was certain to be a Peggy or a Nancy O'Hara. Not until after Thanksgiving was Scarlett O'Hara formally christened. This meant going through every page and catching each reference to her. The title was finally agreed upon at the same time. It had come from Ernest Dowson's poem "Cynara," and was the first line of the third stanza — "I have forgotten much, Cynara! gone with the wind." Peggy had come upon it while searching desperately through the Bible and all her volumes of poetry for a title. Ironically, she had used the phrase herself to describe Scarlett's feelings after the burning of Atlanta, when she was fighting her way home on the road to Tara: "Was Tara still standing? Or was Tara also gone with the wind which had swept through Georgia?"

Peggy had not anticipated the amount of work to be done, and pressure mounted as the end of the year approached. Macmillan offered, and she now accepted, the secretarial services of a young woman, Margaret Baugh, who worked in the Atlanta office. John managed a month's leave of absence from Georgia Power, and his secretary, Rhoda Williams, took on the formidable task of typing the final draft of the manuscript, which by this time was nearly illegible.

Had Peggy not been of a nervous nature, the task she had in putting her manuscript into publishable shape might still have been overwhelming. Basically, the entire book was written by this time, except for short historical links or the bridges where she had cut passages and left her narrative in an uneven state. But, as she had written many of the chapters in several versions, decisions had to be made about which version to retain and, once that had been decided, the manuscript had to be well vetted to make sure nothing that related only to an excised section remained. She also had to flesh out the last chapter. It was, however, the opening of the book that continued to bedevil her. It was not until a few days before her final relinquishment of the manuscript to Macmillan that she wrote the two pages that were to remain as the opening of the book. The problem was that the first chapter focused almost entirely on the Tarleton twins and by the time she had reached this stage in the writing, they had become minor characters. She needed to introduce Scarlett in the first two pages in such a powerful way that she dominated the scene between the Tarleton twins without being in it for the entire chapter.

The entire editorial process had become a horror to Peggy. Each day she awoke at what she called "can't see," not sure she could make it through the day again to "can't see." John worked on the grammar and punctuation until late at night. Bessie was functioning as cook-housekeeper-personal maid, trying to keep track of all the pages and sections of the book, making sure "Miss Peggy" ate to keep up her strength, and attempting to keep order in a household in constant turmoil. Preparing the book for publication might have been easier if Peggy had allowed Macmillan to send down a professional editor to work with her, or if she had asked for publication to be scheduled for fall of 1936 instead of in the spring, to give her a full six months more to do the required work. Latham even suggested this in one letter to her, but at the outset she seemed convinced that she could and would do all the editing in time for the Macmillan spring list.

She blamed the delay on the mental block she had on the first chapter, but it seems more likely that the mental block was due to her sudden realization of what she had committed herself to, and a fear that she might not be able to see it through if John was not home every day to assist her. He did, in the end, take more time off to help her in January, when a bargain was pretty well struck between them. No matter how many books she might eventually write — although even at this early stage she vowed she would never write another one — she was first and foremost, Mrs. John Marsh, and, as he was the man in the house, his career was to take top priority. This later was to become an impossibility as the book's success began to take over their lives. But Peggy tried to maintain the illusion throughout her life, even at a high cost to John's health, for she insisted he not give up his career and, at the same time, she depended upon him for "almost everything" in her own career. From this point forward, John Marsh was always to hold two jobs as long as he was well enough to work. During the day, he was advertising director of Georgia Power. At night, he handled all foreign matters for his wife, as well as much of her business correspondence, seldom quitting before 2:00 A.M. He appears to have preferred it that way, and Peggy never did anything to persuade him it might be too much.

The job of editing the book was so exhausting to Peggy that, at the beginning of January, 1936, she spent two weeks in bed, turning over most of the final work to John, under her supervision. Rhoda Williams came by before and after work to pick up and deliver the typed pages she was doing for them in the evenings, and Margaret Baugh did what she could during the day. Three-fourths of the manuscript was mailed to Macmillan on January 19, and John, in an eleven-page letter to Lois two days later, reported that "Peggy collapsed as soon as it was sent off." Word had come to the Marshes that Lois was expecting Peggy to come to New York for the publication of the book, and John had immediately become protective of his wife's health and privacy. A pattern was forming — one that had contradicting ramifications. On one hand, John would guard Peggy against any and all demands upon her, and then, on the other, he would initiate or encourage a public-relations scheme that would pull her right into a pressured, time-consuming situation, the likes of which he claimed he was trying to avoid at all costs.

John Marsh did have a protective personality and Peggy had always felt she could lean on him. Augusta Dearborn Edwards states that she had felt this protectiveness of John's for many years, and that he had been equally protective of Red Upshaw during the two years of their friendship. Even so, the odd letter that he wrote to Lois Cole on Peggy's behalf seems unnecessarily hostile; indeed, he implied that Macmillan was to blame for Peggy's health problems:

It may be that she will *never* come to New York and if she comes at all it will be because on the day she gets on the train she feels able to come and wants to come. The reasons are partly financial but chiefly physical. After two automobile accidents in less than a year, she is in no shape to undertake anything that puts a strain on her . . . and a trip to New York for the first time in many years would be a major strain. The reason why she has been in bed the past two weeks is the fact that getting the book delivered to you involved the most prolonged strain she has had to undergo in many years. She hasn't recovered from the injury to her back which she received in the [first] automobile accident and those injuries included injury to the nerves running from the spine at the point where she got the twist. Sitting up for hours at a time, day, after day, over a period of weeks, typing, editing the manuscript, handling heavy reference books, etc. was about the worst possible thing she could have done. She stuck it out until the job was finished, except for checking the typewriter copy, correcting errors, etc., which was work I could do under her supervision and then her ailments got her down and the doctor ordered her to bed.

The doctor thinks she may yet have to have an operation, one which she might have had a couple of months ago except for the book and her whole concern is to get herself rested up and postpone the operation at least until after the proofs are ready and the job is finished. It won't help her resting a bit if she thinks Macmillan is making plans based on her coming to New York when she may not be able to come. . . .

He promised Lois that the remaining chapters could be finished in a week, which would leave merely a final polishing to be done. With some surprise, he commented that he did not know that publishing houses had copy editors, but that Peggy did not want anyone to do more than change her commas (she thought now she had used too many in the first half of the book), and no one was to alter the dialect under any circumstance because a house Negro talked differently than a field hand. Peggy, he explained, had tried to make the Negroes talk like Negroes without at the same time putting every single word into dialect and thereby making it difficult to read. The dialect was thus a careful compromise between what he called "true nigger talk" and what could be, from a practical standpoint, translated into type. "Please don't change this," he wrote Lois.

Lois, understandably taken aback by this letter, replied: "I assure you my remarks were prompted by Southern hospitality I learned from my Atlanta friends. I took it for granted that the author of a first and successful novel would wish to have some of the fun connected with the success. . . . Had we known Peggy was endangering her health so seriously and drastically by working on the book we would not have asked to have it finished for Spring publication. It could have been put off for a year. . . . But once publication was set — a deadline was inevitable."

That deadline was now extended, and the May 5 publication date was set forward to June 30. But now Lois faced an even greater problem — Latham had gone to Europe for two months, leaving her in charge of the project during his absence, and when she received the manuscript from the Marshes, she was taken aback. She had known, of course, that Peggy had written a long book, but as there had been so many duplicate chapters in the first packets Macmillan had been given, no one had been able to project the final page count.

Now, with the arrival of the last package, on February 8, Lois Cole's fears were confirmed. The book was over four hundred thousand words long. Though she had expected a long manuscript, when she finally received it Lois was shocked by its size. She now wrote Peggy that, because of its length, the book would have to sell for three dollars and not two-fifty as Macmillan had originally planned. Even at that, she claimed, the company could not hope for a penny in profit unless ten thousand copies were sold. She therefore asked Peggy to agree to accept a reduced royalty schedule of a straight 10 percent on *all* copies, the alternative being to cut the book drastically.

There were runaway best-sellers like *Tobacco Road* and *Anthony Adverse* and *Lamb in His Bosom* that sold into the hundreds of thousands of copies, and Macmillan could hope for that kind of success with *Gone With the Wind,* but the odds were against any book selling such numbers at the high price of three dollars during those spartan days of the Depression. Realistically, at this stage, Macmillan set a goal of 27,500 copies and planned a first printing of 10,000 to be followed, if warranted, by a printing of 7,500, then 5,000, and 5,000 again. The Macmillan people remained positive in their feelings about the book's potential, but were not ready to assume it would become a big best-seller. They were at this time waiting for a sign — a Book-of-the-Month Club selection, film interest, something of that sort — and that would not come until the book was in galley proof. In the meantime, they were faced with a much higher manufacturing cost than they had anticipated.

Upon receipt of Lois's letter about the lower royalty, John again took to the typewriter and wrote her a single-spaced, ten-page reply.

Discounting the duplicate chapters, the manuscript was shorter than before, not longer, he protested. It wasn't Peggy's fault that Macmillan had not realized the length of the book, he added, for she had always thought no one would print it at that length unless they did it in two volumes, and she had been in a state of "constant mystification" ever since Macmillan had bought it, because of their insistence that she should do nothing to it but bring it together and deliver it back to them intact. She expected to be told in the beginning that it had to be cut and when nothing was said about it, she had surreptitiously cut to improve the story herself, so the manuscript was now fifty to seventy-five pages shorter than before. According to John, they had now deleted a thirty-page chapter in which Rhett lends Hetty Tarleton some money to buy her mother some horses; a long chapter that went into detail about what happened after Sherman went into Atlanta, because it slowed the action at a time when all interest was focused on what was happening at Tara; a seven- to eight-page section in part five where Mammy finally leaves Scarlett and goes back to Tara, which was condensed to three paragraphs; and several pages describing the education of a young lady in the old South. Peggy also condensed a section in which Miss Pittypat talked at length about how the carpetbagger gentleman got her property away from her, and two long sections on what happened to minor various characters after the war. And the original Reconstruction material, John explained, was concentrated into two rather long chapters, which Peggy had written before she had done all her research, when she had still been under the impression that Reconstruction arrived with a bang right after the war ended. Her further investigation had shown that conditions were relatively pleasant in 1866 in comparison to the worse horrors that developed over a period of years. This had made it necessary for her to split up the background material and string it out through the chapters dealing with the years from 1866 to 1872.

This last gave the book a slightly different look, John felt, and perhaps because of it it did *seem* longer, but, on balance, the book was shorter now. He closed saying, "From the length of this and my previous letter you may get the impression that I wrote Peggy's long novel which I didn't. I wish I could write as well as she does. Personally I am much more enthusiastic about the book in spite of its length than she is."

His protestations notwithstanding, Marsh enclosed a letter of agreement signed by Peggy, stating she would accept the lower royalty arrangement. If Latham had been in New York, there is a good chance this arrangement would never have been requested, for a royalty graduating to 15 percent was standard, and Latham, for one, had had a good idea of the book's length since the beginning, and had even warned his production staff in an early memo that the book would be "about as long as *Anthony Adverse* and there's no use trying to trim it down much because it doesn't seem to have any chapters or characters that aren't absolutely germane to the story."

The fact that Peggy Mitchell had a book that would soon be published by Macmillan had become public knowledge following a statement given to the press by George Brett, president of the company, during a short trip he had made to Atlanta in January.

As soon as the Atlanta newspapers printed the news that Macmillan was publishing a book by an Atlanta author, Mrs. John Marsh, the telephone began to ring off the hook at the Marshes' apartment. Macmillan had asked them to adhere to a "shush-shush" policy on news about the book so that the first major statements would come from the publishing company. But in a place like Atlanta, and with a couple whose best and oldest friends were all members of the newspaper world, that was nearly impossible. Yolande Gwin, at the *Atlanta Constitution*, was the first one to get a story from Peggy. John described the interview in a letter to Lois: "It wasn't much. It got the headline but as publicity it was grade x. More social than literary. Yolande referred to her [Peggy] as 'this clever young writer,' but Yolande liked it and she'll say something good later on."

About this time, the manuscript was put into the capable

hands of Miss Susan S. Prink, a copy editor at Macmillan. Just when Peggy thought the bulk of her work was done, a package arrived with the first thirty-five galleys of proof, each page liberally marked with Miss Prink's queries and punctuation. Peggy was later to say to Latham that "Miss Prink and I went through the war together," and, indeed, it seems they did, as Miss Prink not only questioned every one of Peggy's unorthodox dashes, but asked the weary author to check, once again, all historic dates and give her sources.

After a flurry of furious letters from Peggy to Miss Prink, which were answered with cool implacability, compromises were reached. Most of the dashes were removed from the book and the Negro dialect in some passages was spelled more phonetically for easier reading. But for a while there was a stand-off on the matter of Scarlett's stream-of-consciousness dialogue that ran through the entire book. Miss Prink felt this should be in quotes; Peggy did not. Scarlett's thoughts presented the book's point of view and, as such, were more telling than much of the action. Peggy explained, not too pleasantly, that they propelled the story forward and she did not want any gratuitous punctuation to distract the reader. Four letters passed between them on this point. Miss Prink proved stronger than Peggy and, in the end, when Scarlett says to herself, "I'll think of it all tomorrow, at Tara," she does so in quotes.

It was only fourteen weeks before publication when it suddenly came to someone's attention that, since the manuscript had been submitted without a title page, it was still missing the author's credit. There was a Mary Mitchell who was publishing a book that spring and Lois asked if Peggy would *mind* being credited as "Margaret Marsh," to avoid confusion.

Peggy sent back a title page that read:

Gone with the Wind

by

Margaret Mitchell

And she asked that the book be dedicated:

To J. R. M.

The manuscript contained another set of initials, too. At the end of chapter thirteen, Belle Watling gives Melanie some gold coins wrapped in a man's handkerchief. Scarlett knows that the handkerchief belongs to Rhett Butler because the monogram on it, RKB, matches the monogram on a handkerchief Rhett had given her to wrap some flowers in the previous day. It is never revealed in the text what the K in Rhett Butler's monogram stands for. However, RKB were all initials that belonged to Red Berrien Kinnard Upshaw.

Chapter Sixteen

IN FEBRUARY, 1936, when Macmillan announced its spring–summer list, *Gone With the Wind* was given prominent placement. Inquiries from Hollywood were immediately forthcoming and galleys were sent to several of the story editors of leading film companies. Samuel Goldwyn wrote a personal letter to Harold Latham asking for the *Mary* Mitchell galleys of the new book, *Gone With the Wind*, but decided against the book two days after receiving them. The Hollywood story editors, most of whom were women, tried desperately to get their bosses — all of whom were men — to buy the rights, but any fervent enthusiasm for the book as a viable film property seemed to stop at the movie moguls' desks.

Louis B. Mayer was reported to be somewhat interested, but Irving Thalberg, MGM's reigning creative genius, was quoted as telling him, "Forget it, Louie. No Civil War picture ever made a nickle."

Thalberg was right. Stark Young's *So Red the Rose* had failed at the box office, as had MGM's own *Operator* 13. Exhibitors had been complaining that costume pictures were not bringing in audiences and box office receipts proved this to be the case. Therefore, Macmillan's first efforts to sell the book to the movies, through E. E. Hall in their own subsidiary-rights department, met with no success. Hall called a meeting with George Brett, Harold Latham, and Lois Cole, and suggested they turn the property over to an agent who could work full-time selling the book. Hall, after all, had the whole Macmillan list to deal with, and not only for movie rights, but all subsidiary sales, and, as *Gone With the Wind* would be a costume film, expensive, and hard to cast, it needed a hard sell. Lois proposed Annie Laurie Williams, an agent with a company that had often done business for Macmillan in the past and who had sold John Steinbeck's *The Grapes of Wrath* to Twentieth Century-Fox for a tall sum.

Peggy resisted the idea of an agent from the very beginning, but wrote Lois on March 14, 1936, that if taking Miss Williams as her agent would make things easier for Lois, she would agree and would not hold Lois responsible if Annie Laurie Williams didn't sell the book. Peggy had never thought a film company would buy her novel, for she did not see how it could possibly be cut to film length. With the failure of Macmillan's subsidiary-rights department to interest Hollywood's producers, the possibility of Miss Williams doing so seemed unlikely to her. As she understood it, Miss Williams was being employed by Macmillan, and was therefore technically not her agent, so all fees for her services would be paid by the publishing company.

Handed the ball by Macmillan, Annie Laurie Williams ran with it. Short and stocky, a twang of Texas in her cigarette voice, Miss Williams rammed her way into the opposing team's territory with alarming quickness and then did some clever end running. Within a few weeks, Hollywood began to react. Darryl Zanuck at Twentieth put in an offer of $35,000. Doris Leroy Warner, representing her father, Jack Warner, topped Zanuck's bid with a $40,000 offer, hoping the purchase of the book with the great role of Scarlett O'Hara would appease their female star, Bette Davis, who was threatening to walk out on suspension.

Annie Laurie Williams now trotted out her trick play. She refused these offers and insisted that she would not take less than $65,000. All this was duly reported to Peggy, who resented terribly the fact that someone had turned down such a fortune without consulting her. Had she known of it earlier, Peggy might well have insisted on accepting Warner's $40,000 offer. It was too late for that now, but she began a barrage of letters to Lois stating in no uncertain terms that she did not want Annie Laurie Williams to represent her any longer. Apart from the fact that Miss Williams was building a momentum that might be costly or even disastrous to interrupt, Lois Cole found it difficult to understand her friend's reactions. The book's success was Lois Dwight Cole's goal, and she found it downright perverse of Peggy to jeopardize a film sale that could help catapult *Gone With the Wind* to the top of the best-seller list. So she kept on pressing Peggy to endorse Annie Laurie Williams as her recognized agent, while doing nothing to change Miss Williams's status.

Peggy received a letter from her old Smith friend Ginny Morris, now a free-lance magazine writer, congratulating her and also inquiring about the rumor that she had turned down $40,000 for film rights. Peggy replied, "It seems a very widespread rumor, but there is no truth in it. Now, I ask you, can you imagine poor folks like me turning down $40 — much less $40,000?"

From the booksellers' large first orders in March, it began to look as if *Gone With the Wind* would be more than moderately successful. But what Lois and Macmillan were still waiting for was some outside spark that would help it make the best-seller lists. Then, on April 15, George Brett received a letter from the editor in chief of the Book-of-the-Month Club, informing him that *Gone With the Wind* had been chosen as a main selection, to be sent out to subscribers in either July, August, or September at their option. The Book-of-the-Month Club planned to take fifty thousand copies of the book to start, and agreed to pay $10,000 for exclusive book-club rights.

John was away on a trip to Savannah for Georgia Power when Lois called to tell Peggy this news. George Brett sent a confirming letter setting out the terms of Macmillan's agreement with the Book-of-the-Month Club. For several days, Peggy kept the news to herself. Long-distance telephone calls were considered a great extravagance in the Mitchell–Marsh family, and so she was reluctant to call John to share the news with him. Finally, she took Brett's letter over to show her father, who, she told Lois, was not only her father, but her severest critic. According to Peggy, Eugene Mitchell said frankly that "nothing in the world would induce him to read the book again and that nothing in the world except the fact that [Peggy] was his child induced him to read it originally." It seemed to him "very strange that a sensible organization should pick this book," an idea with which, at least in her letter to Lois, Peggy heartily concurred.

When John returned home several days later, Peggy was in despair. She thought the book would fail miserably as a Book-of-the-Month Club choice and embarrass everyone involved. John told her blandly that she was "a fool."

As soon as Medora was informed of the Book-of-the-Month Club news, the *Sunday Journal* ran a story on it. Lois was furious because she thought Macmillan should have been the first to break the story, and she crowed a bit about the three-page advertisement for the book that Macmillan had placed in *Publishers Weekly*. Peggy was pleased with the advertisement (*The characters are people with whom Miss Mitchell has lived, the atmosphere is the same she has breathed since birth*), but she thought the picture of her that had been used made her face look "long and pointed instead of square" and gave her "a loathsome ratlike Levantine look," and she wrote to Lois, "I have become hardened to looking like a cat but never a rat." Actually, the picture was a flattering one — her eyes look large and alive, and her smile is wistful and charming.

The "ratlike" photograph was to appear in the Book-of-the-Month Club bulletin and Peggy asked Lois to withdraw it and replace it with a new one she sent. She also requested that the bulletin, in describing Bessie, substitute the words "colored maid" for "colored lady" for the benefit of Southern readers.

In April, *Publishers Weekly* gave the novel its first advance review. "*Gone With the Wind* is very possibly the greatest American novel," it concluded, after lavishly praising its character development, story, and historical authenticity. The *New York World Telegram* said in its book column, "The forthcoming Civil War novel, *Gone With the Wind*, will undoubtedly be leading the best-seller lists as soon as it appears."

Peggy was already a star Macmillan author, but she refused to think about the success that might be ahead. Lois warned her to prepare herself, and asked her to please, *please* reconsider

Annie Laurie Williams as her authorized film representative because now, with the Book-of-the-Month Club deal, they had the leverage to demand a high sum for the rights. But Peggy had taken an intense dislike to Miss Williams and to the idea of anyone except the lawyers at Macmillan handling any subsidiary-rights offers she might receive. "I *know* you, I don't know any other agents," she wrote Latham. To Lois she wrote that she had not realized she would have to give Annie Laurie Williams 10 percent of a film sale.

From the start, everyone in the Mitchell and Marsh households regarded *Gone With the Wind* as a one-shot fluke, which meant that whatever sums Peggy received from it had to be handled well, and the three men in her family intended to watch her investment closely. It didn't occur to them that Annie Laurie Williams was in a position, and had the expertise, to negotiate a far more lucrative deal for Peggy than Macmillan's lawyers could have done.

In addition, and despite the fact that Annie Laurie Williams was a Texan and so considered herself a "sister Southerner," Peggy thought the agent's tactics pushy, and it did not help matters that Annie Laurie Williams innocently chose the evening of April 24 to call Peggy in the hope of ameliorating their relationship. It was a Friday evening, and the Marshes were to attend the opera. Because of some weakness she was experiencing with her eyes, Peggy had planned to spend most of the day in bed. But there had been one demand upon her after another. Before breakfast, a woman who had read an advance galley of *Gone With the Wind* and reviewed it for a small Georgia paper appeared at Peggy's door wanting to meet the author. Flattered by the woman's praise, Peggy had let her talk most of the morning — until a call came from a friend whose mother had broken her hip and whose child could not be left alone. Peggy agreed to take the injured woman to the hospital for X rays, and so she had not had any lunch either.

The afternoon had proven equally as difficult, for Bessie had reached her at the hospital with the news that a poor and ailing old-lady friend of Peggy's was being evicted from her house. Attending to this situation took up the rest of the day and Peggy had arrived home with only twenty minutes to eat and dress and get to the opera when Annie Laurie Williams called. Peggy told her she had been ill and could not talk at that time, rather than explaining that she was late for the opera. Miss Williams continued her conversation, saying she was sorry to hear that but she had understood that Peggy had wanted her to proceed as her agent in the matter of the movies and she thought they should discuss how Peggy's best interests could be represented. At this point, as Peggy told Lois, she "blew up" and told Miss Williams that she had given her no such authority. The indefatigable Miss Williams ignored this, and insisted that she would come down to Atlanta to talk the matter over. Peggy told her she had no intention of deciding anything now because "when sick people make decisions they are always wrong." Moreover, she declared, if Miss Williams had read the book, she would know it was not good movie material. Annie Laurie Williams *had* read the book and disagreed, but the call had only worsened the impasse between the two women.

In truth, Annie Laurie Williams's only mistake was inadvertently calling Peggy at an inconvenient moment. But, strange as it may seem, Peggy never forgave Miss Williams for this call. In letters to Lois, Harold Latham, and George Brett she complained that Miss Williams was the cause of her going to the opera hungry, and she described in detail how she had been forced to miss meals throughout the day. Even in much later letters she referred to Annie Laurie Williams as "the lady who's bent on starving me to death."

Harold Latham arrived in Atlanta that Wednesday to discuss the problem with Peggy. She and John were not just resisting Miss Williams, but the whole idea of anyone other than Macmillan working in their behalf. They trusted Macmillan, and they did not know what to expect from a stranger, nor did they see why they should have to hire an agent when Macmillan would have to be present at any negotiations anyway. Latham carefully explained to them that no matter how fine the relationship between Peggy and his company, Macmillan would be looking out for its own interests first, and so should she. But neither of the Marshes could be convinced of this.

Even more distressing to the Marshes was the fact that Peggy was suffering from severe eye strain caused by the months of checking data for the book and proofreading the galleys. She claimed she never counted them, but that her references ran into the thousands. She left nothing to chance or criticism — what time of day the news came of Hood's defeat at Jonesboro, the weather conditions at the time, the hour the retreat began and the hour the last outpost withdrew, the exact positions of the munitions trains, the exact time they were fired. Then, of course, there were hundreds of details, such as when hoop skirts went out and bustles came in, the price cotton sold for in Liverpool in 1863 ($1.91 a pound), the way pistols worked, "and, well, hundreds of other unimportant but important things."

Peggy did tend to exaggerate. It is doubtful that she had to "look through nearly a *million* old Bibles, old letters and more geneological records" before she found the name "Scarlett" — which had actually been in the text all along as a surname. But, once she knew the book was going to be published, she did reexamine old tax books, muster rolls, land lotteries, hospital records, and old directories and war land grants from Savannah, Atlanta, and Clayton County; she even went through historian Franklin Garrett's voluminous list of tombstone names in Atlanta and its environs, to make double sure that none of the names she had given to characters in the book had once belonged to a real person. One such name was found. Cathleen Calvert's husband, who was originally named Wilson, thus became Hilton, a name chosen when the book was in galleys.

Bed rest had been prescribed for Peggy on the day of the opera because of her eyes. But whatever the ailment, it is extremely difficult to judge just how ill she really was. She did suffer a great many injuries due to accidents. She had chronic trouble with her leg and back, a condition that was apparently more painful when she sat at her typewriter than when she tended family and friends, chauffeuring them around the city, handling their most difficult emergencies, doing battle with hospital staffs and civil employees. Her eyes *had* been strained in the last eight months of work on the book and were to bother her throughout the coming year, but she had no disease of the eye. The fact was, her ill health and the ill health of any member of her family had become a convenient excuse to use at any time and at the slightest provocation. Her state of health was discussed in almost every letter she wrote, no matter how slight her relationship with the recipient. Excuses for tardiness — in replying to a friend or fan, returning an article she had bought, paying a bill — were invariably pinned on her ill health. Those who knew her only through her letters believed that they were dealing with a frail, brave, sick woman. It was due to this impression, which she herself furthered, that rumors of her dire physical condition circulated so often after her book was published.

Anyone who knew Peggy thought of her as a vibrant, vital woman. But from the time *Gone With the Wind* was published, she propagated a very specific public image, utilizing every opportunity to call attention to her physical condition. In the first publicity release she gave Macmillan she wrote, "I am very small. I don't *feel* small. Like most small people I feel myself as big as anyone else and twice as strong. But I am only 4' 11" tall. By working hard all the time and drinking lots of milk I manage to keep my weight at one hundred pounds."

She also managed, in the space of less than five hundred words, to explain why she had written about the Civil War ("I was reared on it"), and to deny ever having read *Vanity Fair*, to which her book had already been compared, until "a year and a half ago after my auto accident," adding, "I was on crutches for about three years." She said that she read voraciously and rapidly and had hoped to study medicine, "but while I was at Smith College my mother died and I had to come home to keep house." Except that she claimed she was fifteen and a half years old when she left Smith, the above statements were probably true. But they underscored her way of relating time and experiences to the "disasters" in her life. References to accidents and crutches and long years of convalescence just before the book's publication created an aura of sadness about her. Further talk of darkened rooms and bandages and orders not to try to read even a telephone number was certain to create rumors of serious illness and advancing blindness — and so it did. Then, upon hearing or reading these rumors, Peggy would become unaccountably incensed — even though they brought with them warm responses of sympathy and protectiveness.

Latham returned to Atlanta in May, bringing Peggy the first bound copies of *Gone With the Wind*. He asked her to look for any further typographical errors before the first large printing, a task she could barely face. She wrote Lois that she "nearly threw up at the sight of it," adding that one should not feel that way about one's first and only child, but that seeing the book reminded her "of the nightmare of getting it ready."

These advance copies were being sent out to reviewers and to the film studios, even those who had already received galleys. Annie Laurie Williams was making her grandstand play, and one of Latham's motives for coming to Atlanta was to try one last time to convince Peggy that she must endorse Miss Williams, as it would give her greater authority in her negotiations. Peggy and John refused to do this and Latham returned to New York disheartened but certain that Macmillan must carry on as they were with "Bonnie" Annie Laurie, who, Peggy complained to Lois, would probably be the cause of "me laying me down and deeing before we get to the end of the row."

When Latham got back to New York, he put through a request for a five-thousand-dollar advance on royalties to be sent immediately to Mrs. Marsh. It would be months before, under the contract, she would have received any of her earnings and, as the book's orders were now well over twenty thousand and there was the Book-of-the-Month Club money to come as well, Macmillan agreed. Until this point, Peggy had received only her full advance, five hundred dollars.

Yolande Gwin at the *Atlanta Constitution* had been sent one of the advance copies of the novel, as had other book people in Atlanta. Suddenly, it seemed, everyone Peggy had ever known in Atlanta wanted to throw her a party, and she accepted them all, but when Latham renewed Lois's invitation for her to come to New York for publication, Peggy refused because, she said, "I'd hate to land in New York looking like a hag and with my eyes hanging out so far you could wipe them off with a broomstick."

Since she would not come to New York, Macmillan's Atlanta office tried to get her to do as much publicity on that end as possible, and, with Margaret Baugh's prodding, she finally accepted an invitation to speak at an Atlanta Library Club supper before an audience of about fifty people. She had spoken a few weeks earlier at the Macon Writers' Club Breakfast, but, despite an audience of two hundred and fifty people, that had been "like talking with friends." This was different and, as she told Latham, she spent "anguished days" going through her bibliography planning to tell the "library ladies just how dull the job of writing was." Then, on the day of the dinner, Alma Hill Jamison, head of the reference department of the Carnegie Library, introduced her as "an author whose book has been variously compared to *Vanity Fair, War and Peace,* and *Gentlemen Prefer Blondes.*" This upset her so badly, she wrote Latham on June 1, 1936, that she drew a blank and forgot even the titles of the reference books she had had in mind and when she "came to," she realized she was telling "indelicate stories." And, after a glance at Miss Jessie Hopkins, the head librarian at Carnegie Library, she thought she was perfectly safe from having to address librarians in the future.

However, she did turn right around and speak at a banquet given in her honor at the Georgia Press Association's annual meeting, held that year in Milledgeville from June 10 to 12, and at which she was treated as a celebrity instead of as John Marsh's wife, as in years past.

Though the book was still in the hands of only a select few (fifteen hundred advance copies had been shipped at this time), Peggy was already a celebrity, at least in her hometown and to her friends in the Press Club. News of Hollywood interest in the novel and of the Book-of-the-Month Club edition had appeared in film columns and the local papers. Reviewers had read the book, and in some cases had published early reviews, all of which were laudatory and dealt with *Gone With the Wind* as a literary event.

No one was more overwhelmed by her emerging eminence than Peggy herself, and her shock and disbelief did not decrease with the affirmation each new review brought. From the beginning, she made a point of replying to each review. To Joseph Henry Jackson, whose advance critique appeared in the *San Francisco Chronicle*, she wrote:

> I suppose you could call my reactions "pleasure and happiness"
> even if I did have to go to bed with a cold pack on my head and

an aspirin after I read your words. God knows I'm not like my characters, given to vapors and swooning and "states," but I was certainly in a state. I have always been able to bear up nobly under bad news but your good news floored me. I suppose it was because it was so unexpected.

She then went on for several pages telling him about her childhood, and ended by thanking him for his remarks about her style, which he had called "simple and utterly sincere."

I haven't any literary style and I know it but have never been able to do anything about it. I am very conscious of my lack in this particular and I was expecting more brickbats about it than any other thing. I wish I could tell you how very happy you have made me! Just saying thank you seems too inadequate!

When she replied to Harry Stillwell Edwards's glowing review in the *Atlanta Journal* on June 14, she fell back to being the Southern belle of old:

My dear Mr. Edwards:
    Only a very small remnant of decorum prevents me from addressing you as "my *very* dear Mr. Edwards," or "you utterly darling person," or "you kind, kind man." But I will try to remember my raising and merely address you as —
    My dear Mr. Edwards:
    May I thank you first for the happiness you brought to my father? You see, he was especially anxious that Southerners and Georgians should like my book and especially afraid that they wouldn't, although the book is as true as documentation and years of research could make it. He didn't like the notion of my offending the people of my state, nor did I. And when he read your perfectly marvelous review his mind was set at ease. "If Mr. Edwards likes it — etc."

Of those prepublication months, John Marsh was later to write:

April, May and June of 1936 saw, first a stirring of suspicion, then a rapidly growing certainty, that something remarkable was about to happen in the book world. A tremor of excitement rippled up, here and there, in far distant parts of the country. It was one of those phenomena that modern communication methods cannot explain. "One-person-tells-another," the original communications method and still the best, flashed the news along in a manner almost magical. From mouth to mouth, the word spread, and spread still further that a book was coming that you must not miss. Bookstores doubled and redoubled their orders.

Though Peggy was thrilled by the flattering reviews, she found them hard to believe. She waited anxiously for the complete Southern verdict on the book, and even when the good opinion of her "home folks" was forthcoming, she was fearful that the next voice that spoke up would be a dissenting one, for, as Medora was to say later, "Wasn't her heroine a baggage, with nothing to recommend her but courage? And wasn't her hero a scoundrel, who profiteered at the expense of the Confederacy? And didn't her book contain the shameful truth that there were some deserters from the Confederate Army?"

The Marsh household ticked with excitement, but neither John nor Peggy had any real idea of what was to come. Lois and Latham felt certain that *Gone With the Wind* was going to be a publishing phenomenon and tried again to prepare Peggy. But she still thought it was all a bubble that would burst as soon as the book appeared in the bookstores.

On May 25, the question of a film agent was finally settled. Peggy signed a contract with Macmillan giving *them* the right to sell the book to the movies. She wrote to Latham that she felt "very relieved about having it in your hands instead of any agent." If someone was "mad enough to buy the book for films," Macmillan promised to try to get her final say on the scenario, because she did not want "tough-mouthed Harlem accents in southern negroes' mouths." And she asked, "By the way, is your new agency department going to handle dramatic rights too?"

In the one questionable action in the Macmillan staff's otherwise long and loyal relationship with Peggy Mitchell, not only had they led her to believe that E. E. Hall would now be handling the rights, but they secretly signed an agreement of their own with Annie Laurie Williams assigning their rights of representation of the book to her. George Brett sent memos to Miss Williams, Latham, and Lois Cole, warning them, "Mrs. Marsh is to know nothing of this." Macmillan was to split the commission (their agreed upon 10 percent) for their role as film agent fifty-fifty with Miss Williams. This meant that she received only 5 percent for her services. And Peggy, whether she sanctioned it or not, still had "Bonnie Annie" representing her.

🍃

Bette Davis claims she was about to leave for England in defiance of her studio, Warner Brothers, when Jack Warner called her into his office and told her he was about to buy a book with a marvelous part in it for her.

"What is it?" Davis asked.

"A new novel. It's called *Gone With the Wind*."

"I'll bet it's a pip," the lady says she replied, and walked out of Warner's office to take the first available boat to England. *Gone With the Wind* sounded exactly like the kind of melodrama she was willing to take a suspension and loss of salary to avoid.

But, curiously, on May 28, Harold Latham received the following telegram:

DEAR MR LATHAM HAVE HAD OPPORTUNITY READ BOOK GONE WITH THE WIND BY MARGARET MITCHELL AND AM TERRIBLY EAGER TO PLAY THE ROLE OF SCARLET[T] STOP KNOW THAT I COULD DO GREATER THINGS WITH THIS ROLE THAN MY PART IN DANGEROUS WHICH WON ACADEMY AWARD LAST YEAR STOP UNDERSTAND WARNER BROTHERS NEGOTIATING FOR MOTION PICTURE RIGHTS IN GONE WITH THE WIND AND MY PERSONAL DESIRE TO PLAY IN IT IS SO GREAT THAT I AM SENDING YOU THIS WIRE ON A PURELY PERSONAL AND SELFISH BASIS TO URGE THAT YOU DO NOT SELL IT TO ANY OTHER COMPANY AS THIS WOULD MEAN I WOULD LOSE THE PART WHICH WOULD BREAK MY HEART.
    BETTE DAVIS

Miss Davis swears she did not send this telegram. That raises the possibility that Warner Brothers sent it, risking an allegation of fraud to get the rights to *Gone With the Wind* for the $40,000 they had offered and hoping that Miss Davis's name would soften Macmillan's heart. Perhaps Miss Davis's agent sent the telegram without her knowledge. But whoever was the true author of the telegram, its context suggested that Hollywood had changed its tune. Forty thousand dollars had been the price paid for *Anthony Adverse*, the highest price to that date for the film rights to a first novel. Annie Laurie Williams was determined to get more. Negotiations were going forward with David Selznick, but Lois wrote Peggy that a deal was "far from in the bag."

Annie Laurie Williams had also sent the novel to Katharine Brown, head of the New York office of Selznick-International Pictures, at about the same time that it was being read at Warner. The book instantly excited Miss Brown, and she sent Selznick, who was on the West Coast, the memo: "I beg, urge, coax, and plead with you to read this at once. I know that after you read the book you will drop everything and buy it." Selznick, to her disapppointment, cabled back a week later: "MOST SORRY TO HAVE TO SAY NO IN THE FACE OF YOUR ENTHUSIASM." A few days later, after his wife, Irene, had read the book, he revised his opinion, but he still did not think the book was worth a purchase price of over $40,000. His decision now was to wait until publication and see how well the book did.

News of the book's potential spread throughout the publishing world. European countries were already clamoring for foreign rights. ("Translate dialect," Peggy wrote Lois, "God forbid!") And Macmillan's English office, headed by Harold Macmillan, was competing with W. A. R. Collins for the British rights. At home, orders for the book were exceeding even Latham's wildest predictions.

Peggy was kept in daily touch with the rush of events, but things were happening too fast and seemed unreal to her. She still harbored deep insecurities about the book and wrote Lois, "I shouldn't even think about such good things. Something terrible is bound to happen." But John suspected a measure of what was to come, and engaged Stephens and Mr. Mitchell on a professional basis, with an established fee for their services, so that Peggy would be protected in any further dealings regarding subsidiary rights. Characteristically, the Marshes did not want to bring in outsiders, but the choice of a law firm in Atlanta that knew absolutely nothing about films or publishing and that had never had to deal with the kind of powerhouse legal staffs that large companies employed, was naive. Mitchell and Mitchell had remained patent and real-estate lawyers throughout the years. Stephens Mitchell did have some knowledge of copyright laws and certainly Eugene Mitchell had always been a watchdog of copyright infringement but, because the firm placed such emphasis on copyright matters, it was shortsighted in other matters of negotiation.

The winds of fame were blowing toward Atlanta. Peggy was getting calls from book-page people all over the country, one of whom referred to her as "the latest literary Goliath." The book buyer at Atlanta's Davison's department store told her they had ordered several hundred copies of her book and asked if she would come and autograph them on publication day, now firmly set for June 30. She agreed. Lois reported that the first edition (incorrectly dated May, 1936) of ten thousand copies had all been shipped and Macmillan was now considering a major printing of twenty thousand more, since large orders had just come in from Macy's and other department stores. Macy's was also planning a book luncheon on publication day, but Peggy said she could not attend.

Macmillan knew by now that they had a best-seller, and George Brett, acting in good faith, wrote to Peggy three weeks before publication to tell her that they were going to reinstate the terms of her original contract, at least to the extent that she would receive 10 percent on the first twenty-five thousand copies and 15 percent thereafter. She answered him with surprise: "I wasn't expecting it, and had forgotten all about the original royalty arrangement . . . such good news coming like it does is doubly good and exciting like Christmas coming twice a year."

Foreign rights were being handled by Macmillan at this time and the company received 10 percent of all the sales they made, while their foreign representatives received an additional 10 percent. But in the case of the English rights, they were dealing directly with a branch of their own company, and so *Gone With the Wind* was sold to Harold Macmillan for only two hundred pounds plus the usual royalties — a lower price than Collins had offered Latham when he had been in Great Britain in February. This created quite a stir between the two English publishing companies, but Harold Macmillan held fast to his "rights."

In the last week before publication, response to the book had reached a fever pitch. Besides the glowing early reviews, expressions of praise came in from literary celebrities Ellen Glasgow, DuBose Heyward, Mary Ellen Chase, Storm Jameson, Julia Peterkin, Constance Lindsay Skinner, and Kathleen Norris. "The best to come out of that generation," "one of the greatest man-woman stories ever written," and "unsurpassed in American writing," were some of these comments.

Due to all this public acclaim, bookstores were sold out of their shipments before *Gone With the Wind* was officially on sale. There were now nearly 100,000 copies of the book in print. Never before had there been a first novel that had sold like this before publication. In letter after letter, Lois Cole and Latham and Brett warned Peggy to prepare herself for the onslaught of fame. Peggy never took their advice seriously, refusing to believe that their predictions would ever come to pass. As always, she had a "bad sign" to look to — yes, the early reviews had been stunning, but, she wondered, why had not one New York paper published a review yet? Miss Greeve, in the publicity department of Macmillan, explained to Peggy that New York was the heart of the publishing industry and that, because of it, the reviewers were bound to Macmillan's original request to wait until publication day before printing their reviews.

On publication day, two reviews did appear in the New York papers. Edwin Granberry in the *New York Sun*, a morning paper, was bold in his praise of the novel and also predicted its impact on American literature in an unprecedented 1,200-word review:

> We are ready to stand or fall by the assertion that this novel has the strongest claim of any novel on the American scene to be bracketed with the work of the great from abroad — Tolstoi, Hardy, Dickens and the modern Undset. We have had more beautiful prose from American writers; and we have had those who excel in this or that branch of the novelist's art. But we can think of no single American novelist who has combined as has Miss Mitchell all the talents that go into the making of the great panoramic novel such as the English and Russians and the Scandinavians have known how to produce.

The *New York Post*'s Herschel Brickell referred to the book as a "striking piece of fiction, which is much too sound and too important not to pass into the permanent body of American literature," and he said it came "closer to telling the whole story of the most dramatic episode in our history, the War Between the States and the dark and bloody days that followed the breaking up of a culture, than anything that has ever been written or printed. . . . It is far and away the best novel that has ever been written about the Civil War and the days that followed."

Peggy did not read these two reviews on publication day. She went to Davison's early that Tuesday morning, and found herself in the center of mayhem. Even with the several hundred books Davison's had ordered, the demand was greater than the supply. Customers were tearing books out of each others' hands. A zealous fan ripped a button from Peggy's silk jacket for a memento. Another surprised her by snipping off a lock of her hair. Peggy remained remarkably good-natured through it all. "Southerners, especially Atlantans," she said to Medora, who accompanied her, "consider their folks' success belongs to everyone." She left the department store with Medora and Norman Berg, who worked in Macmillan's Atlanta office, and went over to station WSB, where Medora interviewed her on a live radio show. Although Peggy claimed they were both in "a lather of apprehension" since they had no idea what to do or say, the interview went better than either of them had expected, for Medora led Peggy right into the heart of what she could talk about most colorfully and easily — her youth and the stories she had been told so often about the days of the Civil War and Reconstruction.

Peggy arrived home just as John was returning from work, to find Bessie in a state of near hysteria. The telephone had been ringing almost nonstop. Telegrams and special deliveries arrived in a deluge, and people kept buzzing the doorbell and thrusting books at Bessie to have them signed by the author.

Peggy Mitchell had become an overnight celebrity.

Margaret Mitchell, Author

Chapter Seventeen

*P*EGGY MITCHELL had never had a desire for fame and now it had been thrust upon her with staggering rapidity. Bessie recorded that within twenty-four hours of publication, the telephone rang every three minutes until midnight and about once an hour after that; the doorbell chimed at five-minute intervals throughout the day; a telegram arrived every seven minutes; and a line of at least ten people kept a round-the-clock vigil at the front and back doors of the apartment house, waiting for the author of *Gone With the Wind* to appear and sign their books. Within a few days of the novel's publication, the postman was delivering Peggy's mail in large satchels. She could not go out on the street wihout being instantly recognized and set upon, and once, when she was in a dressing room at Rich's department store trying on a dress, five women flung back the curtain, to reveal her only half dressed. "She's small breasted like a boy!" exclaimed one as Peggy grabbed something to cover up her nakedness and demanded that they leave her cubicle at once.

The book, of which she would have been pleased to sell five thousand copies, had sales of 178,000 by the end of three weeks, that number accelerating so steadily every day that Macmillan was soon convinced that close to a million copies would be sold by the end of the year.

Margaret Mitchell had become a folk heroine. Despite her

publisher's warnings, what made the change in her life so difficult for her to grasp was the complete unexpectedness of it. A woman of a conservative and thrifty nature, she had thought it highly unlikely that great masses of people would purchase her novel at the unprecedentedly high price of three dollars when, in such lean times, that amount would buy more than a day's food for a family of four. Neither Macmillan's predictions nor the various signs and portents — the Book-of-the-Month Club sale, the large early printings, the first reviews — had mitigated Peggy's pessimism. For the first few days, she was certain the public acclaim would rapidly subside. When it did not, she began to suffer extreme anxiety.

Reporters plagued her for interviews. Readers by the hundreds called to ask if Scarlett and Rhett ever got together again. Others telegraphed their congratulations or questions. The most trying fans were those who appeared on the front steps of her apartment building to ask advice on personal matters, beg for loans, or leave manuscripts that they wanted her to read. The mail was flooded with requests for her to appear in public, give lectures, and endorse organizations, products, and other books. By the end of the first week, she had been sent more than three hundred copies of *Gone With the Wind* to be autographed. Most fans expected her to return the signed copies at her own expense.

It had all come too fast. Peggy Mitchell simply had not had the time to prepare herself for being a literary celebrity even had she wanted that role. "Fame," Rilke had said, "is the sum of misunderstanding that gathers around a new name." Peggy did not know how to deal with the image that fame was creating around her. She felt brutally victimized, as though her precious uniqueness as an individual was being torn from her, and she was determined to hold on to it at all costs.

The truth was that she had begun her novel without any grand plan. Although she had entertained hopes that it might someday be published, at no time in the writing had she ever considered that her book was other than an unusually authentic historical novel. Over and over she had repeated how otherwise "rotten" it was. She never thought of it in terms of its possible relevancy to the 1930s nor as a book that could catch the fancy of the nation. Part of her unpreparedness for the book's success was due to her lack of self-confidence, but there were other factors.

There had been no outside editor. John had functioned in that capacity and he had been no more farsighted than she. Nor was his intellectual and sociological perspective any more sophisticated. Their personal correspondence after the publication of *Gone With the Wind* shows their tremendous dismay at the sociological importance placed upon the book by the reviewers. Peggy herself had no intent other than to tell a good story and to describe a difficult period in her city's history with impeccable accuracy. It is doubtful that either Peggy or John was aware of the novel's timeliness, and Macmillan's vice-president, James Putnam, was later to say that they published the book with the "sole and innocent intention of making a few honest dollars." Perhaps *Gone With the Wind* succeeded on such a grand scale for *exactly* these reasons. It had been written sincerely and spontaneously, and it never smacked of clever artifice, jingoism, or social dogma.

In many ways, the devastating effects of the Depression were comparable to those of the Civil War — a fact that made *Gone With the Wind* seem uncannily contemporary. Scarlett O'Hara's refusal to be blown away by the winds of change, her impressive strength, her vow that "As God is my witness . . . I'm going to live through this, and when it's over, I'm never going to be hungry again," strongly appealed to readers who had struggled to keep life and home together during the long Depression. Many of the letters that Peggy Mitchell received from fans said, in essence, that if Scarlett could survive the awesome struggle she had had to endure, so could they. But there was still another, perhaps even more basic, reason for the hysterical fervor the book generated.

Never had America's self-image been so low. The United States had never been a leader in music, ballet, art, or literature, although, for many years, it had been in the forefront in business and industry. But the dollar had been devaluated, at home and abroad, as one large company after the other had gone into bankruptcy. Roosevelt's New Deal seemed to be floundering, and the public did not know whom or what to believe. Politics had divided the nation almost as critically as the Civil War had once done, and all the average man could concern himself with was personal survival.

And so, in the summer of 1936, the nation hungered for some sign of the reemergence of its former glory, and the people wanted it to come not out of a military victory this time, but out of individual achievement. Peggy could not have guessed it, no matter how prescient she might have been, but the publication of her book marked a real upturn in America — not only in publishing, but in the American people's pride in their own accomplishment.

Gone With the Wind was instantly seized upon as a harbinger of what might one day be called a national literature. It celebrated the American past in a way that the novels of Willa Cather, William Faulkner, and Thomas Wolfe had not. Unlike the Realist novels of Theodore Dreiser and his followers a quarter of a century before, it dealt with American history on a grand scale rather than dissecting regional American mores. And, though the story took place totally in the South, and specifically in Atlanta and its environs, it was still more national than regional because it dealt with the greatest and most devastating schism the country had ever had to endure, and it did so in a unique fashion — not through men and war and politics and power, but through the women and the hardships they had had to overcome in order to mend the South's wounds and bring hope, pride, and prosperity back to their men and their homes. And then there was the ending — Peggy had not passed final judgment on Scarlett. It was anyone's guess as to whether she did or did not get Rhett back, which meant that readers could decide this for themselves according to their own sense of justice and romantic fantasy.

Except for Charles Lindbergh's overnight celebrity, there had never been an instance of immediate national adulation that was even comparable to that which Peggy Mitchell experienced. It was not only that the book's sales were so staggering — for there had been other best-sellers — but that the public treated *Gone With the Wind* as more than just a novel. Its characters almost instantly became folk heroes along with their creator. The book's fame spread swiftly to Europe. Frank

Daniel, Peggy's friend from the *Atlanta Journal*, wrote her in a memo after a friend of his had just returned from Europe that the

> decks of the Queen Mary were littered with copies of Gone With the Wind, by all odds the most popular book abroad, one in nearly every deck chair. . . . The demand for the book in London and Paris book-stores is something momentous and . . . advance orders for the English edition (to appear October 1, isn't it?) are record making. . . . Henry Fonda was on the Breman coming back [from Europe], and he got so excited about the book he radioed Selznick for an immediate interview to discuss his playing Rhett . . . an odd notion, perhaps, but it just goes to show that if Macmillan continues to buy large ads in the Atlanta Journal (which, after all, covers Dixie Like the Dew), your little novel stands a fine chance of becoming known.

When the *Queen Mary* docked in Southampton on its first Atlantic crossing that summer, Scarlett and Rhett were names as familiar to passengers as King Edward VIII and Wallis Simpson. It did not take long before dinner parties in London buzzed with discussion about America's new best-seller, perhaps a welcome relief from all the speculation about the king and his mistress.

Peggy often said in those early days of the book's phenomenal success that she felt besieged, and so she was. All of her press statements mentioned that her married name was Marsh, and John Marsh's telephone number and address were in the Atlanta telephone directory. The apartment house had no doorman or security system, and when John was at work Bessie and Peggy were left alone to man the telephone and the door. Telephone callers were often shocked to find they had reached Margaret Mitchell directly, and uninvited visitors were taken aback when the door was opened to their urgent rings by a small woman who *had* to be Margaret Mitchell.

There were also daily news items about the motion-picture rights. Whether the rights had actually been sold to the movies or not did not seem to concern the public, whose national pastime now was casting the movie version of *Gone With the Wind*. On July 3, Peggy complained to Lois that people were driving her crazy asking for handouts because she "wouldn't miss the money out of her millions." Friends, she said, plagued her as to "why in Hell" she "persisted in driving a 1929 model car and wearing four-year-old cotton dresses and fifty-cent stockings." She claimed someone had even called her "an old Hetty Green" to her face. The day before, she admitted to Lois, she had had "the tired shakes so bad" that she had gone to bed in midafternoon in tears. When John came home that evening, he insisted she had to get away from Atlanta for a few days even if he could not go with her. Her plan was to leave on the next Monday, she told Lois, and "just get in the car and ride." She intended to go to the mountains, where she thought she would be less likely to run into people who might recognize her, but she assured Lois that if Macmillan needed her they could wire John, for she would be telephoning him each night.

On Monday morning, July 7, a short time after John had left for the office, Red Upshaw telephoned Peggy. Later, she described their conversation to Medora:

"After reading your book I figure you still love me," Upshaw said.

"Why would you think that?" she asked.

"Because Rhett Butler is obviously modeled after me," he replied.

She denied it and asked him what he wanted. He promised to tell her someday in person and then hung up.

Peggy was in a terrible panic as she dressed for the interview she was to have in the apartment that morning with three representatives from the Associated Press. Hearing Red Upshaw's voice had been a shock, but it was the smirky way he had accused her of basing Rhett on him that had alerted her to possible danger.

He could, she suspected, sue her for libel. She had made Rhett Butler a scalawag, had left those incriminating RKB initials on his handkerchief, and had had him expelled from West Point, all of which might give a judge pause. Butler's profiteering days had something in common with Upshaw's adventures in bootlegging, as well. She was probably right in thinking that a lawsuit with Red Upshaw would be a scandal, for it could have meant that the court deposition she had made following his assault upon her would be exposed.

Peggy did not have much time to decide what she should do before Bessie ushered the Associated Press reporters into her modest living room. Afterwards, she wrote that they had subjected her to "a brisk workout that lasted three hours." She fended questions about her past, present, and future with much evasiveness, using her Southern-belle wiles to such good advantage that "the boys from the AP" did not even realize that they weren't getting straight answers to their questions about the years between her mother's death and her marriage to John Marsh.

As soon as they left, Peggy had Bessie pack a small bag and, with an air of melodrama to her exit from Atlanta that rivaled Scarlett's, she got into her car and headed for the mountains. Dramatic, detailed letters describing her escape from "the hell" of fame were written and sent to at least eight well-known writers and newspaper people. In each, she told a vivid, pathetic story that made her trip to the mountains appear to be an act of sudden and total desperation — although she had had five days, since her letter to Lois, to plan it. That evening, from Gainesville, Georgia, the first stop in her "escape," she wrote to several people about the three-hour press conference that, she claimed, had left her in such a state that she had telephoned John and told him she had to get away and that, if she could get through the lines at the front door, she would drive to the country just to spend the night someplace where she would not be recognized.

In a five-page letter written that night to Herschel Brickell, whom she had never met, she said that her intention when she left that morning had been to "hide out in the mountains where there are no telephones and no newspapers and no one reads anything but the Bible — and to stay there til my money ran out. Or til my local fame ran out. And from my experiences as a reporter, I recall that local literary celebrities usually last three weeks."

She had left the house, she wrote in another letter, with a bundle of reviews, her address book, four mysteries, five dollars, and her typewriter, but she claimed she had not taken her toothbrush or even a change of underwear.

The fifty-five-mile trip to Gainesville took her about two

hours for, since her last accident, she had gotten into the habit of driving less than twenty-five miles an hour. She checked into a modest motel off the main street of Gainesville, a small town nestled into the foothills of the northeast Georgia mountains. She signed the register "Mrs. J. Marsh, Atlanta" and paid three dollars in advance for the room. Although no mention was made of it in her many "runaway" letters, she also had her checkbook and there was a branch of her bank in the town.

Peggy wasted no time in setting up her typewriter and opening and reading the latest reviews, which had arrived in the mail from Macmillan just before she had left home. After calling John, she wrote the letter to Herschel Brickell, who, John had told her, had called to say he was coming South shortly and would like to meet her.

> As you may observe from the postmark, I'm not at home in Atlanta. I'm on the run. I'm sure Scarlett O'Hara never struggled harder to get out of Atlanta or suffered more during her siege of Atlanta than I have suffered during the siege that has been on since publication day. If I had known being an author was like this I'd have thought several times before I let Harold Latham go off with my dog-eared manuscript. I've lost ten pounds in a week, leap when phones ring and scurry like a rabbit at the sight of a familiar face on the street. . . . Utter strangers collar me in public and ask the most remarkable questions and photographers pop out of the drains.

She told him, however, that she would "come home with the greatest pleasure" if he decided to come to Atlanta. "It will be marvelous if I could meet you," she wrote, "because I have long been an admirer of yours." Peggy also commented at length on Brickell's review:

> Thank you for going on record that while my story "bordered on the melodramatic" at times, the times of which I wrote *were* melodramatic. Well, they were but it takes a person with a Southern background to appreciate just how melodramatic they really were. I had to tone down so much, that I had taken from actual incidents, just to make them sound barely credible. And thanks for your defense of Captain Butler and his credibility. I never thought, when I wrote him, that there'd be so much argument about whether he was true to life or not. His type was such an

ordinary one in those days that I picked him because he was typical of his times. Even his looks. I went through hundreds of old ambro-types and daguerreotypes looking at faces and that type of face leaped out at you. Just as surely as the faces of the pale, sad looking boys with a lock of hair hanging on their foreheads were always referred to with a sigh as "dear cousin Willy. He was killed at Shiloh." (I've often wondered why the boys who looked like that were *always* killed at Shiloh.)

In the matter of Captain Butler I am caught between crossfires. Down here, folks find him so true to life that I may yet have a lawsuit on my hands despite my protests that I didn't model him after any human being I'd ever heard of.

"Good Heavens I am running on," she wrote halfway down the fifth page, adding, a few lines later:

Well, perhaps you contributed to a practical nervous collapse and are really the cause of me being on the run! I just can't take it. Come to see me. I'll give you a party if you want a party or I'll feed you at home and sit and listen to you talk. My cook's a good old fashioned kind, strong on turnip greens and real fried Schicken and rolls that melt in your mouth. Personally, I'd rather listen to you talk — and thank you — than give a party.

The morning after she arrived in Gainesville, Peggy wrote Edwin Granberry, who had reviewed the book glowingly for the *New York Evening Sun,* an extraordinary eight-page letter that was even more revealing than the one to Brickell:

My dear Mr. Granberry:
I am Margaret Mitchell of Atlanta, author of "Gone with the Wind." Your review of my book was the first review I read, and it made me so happy that I tried to write you immediately. I have been trying to write you for over a week, but you can see just how far my good intentions have gotten me!
As soon as I read what you said, I had what I thought was a perfectly marvelous letter to write you, a letter which would tell you just exactly how much I appreciated your kindness. But that letter has gone, disappearing somewhere along the road of this last nightmare week and I find myself tonight here in a hotel in Gainesville, incoherent from exhaustion and from gratitude to you. So forgive this letter its inadequacies.
I didn't know that being an author was like this, or I don't think

I'd have been an author. I've led so quiet a life for so many years, quiet by choice because I'm not a social animal, quiet because I wanted to work and quiet because I'm not the strongest person in the world and need plenty of rest. And all my quiet world has blown up recently. The phone has rung every three minutes, the door bell rings and perfect strangers bounce in asking the most extraordinary and personal questions, photographers arrive with the morning coffee. Reporters arrive too, but I don't mind them for I used to report myself and I can't help realizing what a tough go-round they're having with me. For I'm perfectly normal, not eccentric, had no romantic experiences with the writing of my book. So they can't find anything hot to write about me! And then teas and parties, the first I've been to in years, have about ruined me. Yesterday it got too much and I climbed in the car and set out with no baggage to speak of: a typewriter, four murder novels, and five dollars. When I reached here I was too tired to go on. So I'm staying here till tomorrow and then I'm going back into the mountains where there aren't any telephones and no one will recognize me from my pictures and ask me if it's hard to write a book.

I did not mean to fling all my troubles upon you, a stranger, who has been so kind to me. But I'm trying to explain my seeming discourtesy in not writing to you sooner; explain, too, why this letter is such a hash.

I don't believe I can make plain to you how much your review meant to me unless I tell you something about the background of the writing of my book. I wrote it so long ago. It must have been nearly ten years ago, and I'd finished most of it by 1929. That is, I'd about stopped writing on it both because pressure of illness among friends and family never seemed to let up, and because the thing didn't seem worth finishing. I know it sounds silly for me to write that I thought the book too lousy to bother with retyping and trying to sell, but I didn't think it humanly possible that any one would buy it. It seems silly to write that when I see by this evening's paper that the fifth printing sold out the day after the publication date, but I know good writing and mine didn't seem good. So I never tried to sell it.

After Mr. Latham came along and pried it out of me last year and got me to sign the contract, I was utterly miserable. I thought I'd been an awful fool to let a job like that go out where people could see how bad it was, where people could remark on its badness at the top of their lungs and in the public prints. My only comfort was that there wasn't much criticism they could give me that I hadn't already given myself. Criticism wouldn't hurt me (and it hasn't!) but it would upset my family, especially my father. So you can see what my frame of mind was when I got an advance clipping of your review. . . .

Thank you for your kind words about Scarlett, for saying that she still keeps your sympathy and explaining why. It never occurred to me while writing her that such a storm of hard words would descend upon the poor creature's head. She just seemed to me to be a normal person thrown into abnormal circumstances and doing the best she could, doing what seemed to her the practical thing. The normal human being in a jam thinks, primarily, of saving his own hide, and she valued her hide in a thoroughly normal way. . . .

You have been so kind, have made me so happy and my family so happy. (My reserved and unenthusiastic father simply purred when he read your review — and why not?) I wish there was some way I could tell you how much I appreciated everything you said. I wish I could see you because I talk better than I write and perhaps I could make you understand what your review meant to me. And I hope I do see you sometime.

Granberry had won the O. Henry Award for the best short story of 1932 and had published a few books of moderate critical success. A professor of English at Rollins College in Winter Park, Florida, he was not the *Sun*'s regular reviewer. It is doubtful that Peggy knew much about Granberry's background, and she did not claim to have read his books. But the fact that he had reviewed her book for a major newspaper had impressed her.

She wrote numerous other letters that day — to George Brett at Macmillan; to Gilbert Govan, who had reviewed her for the *Chattanooga Times* on July 5; to Hunt Clement, who had been lavish in his praise of her in the *Atlanta Journal* on the seventh; Julia Collier Harris who had devoted a long column to her and the book a few days before; and to a number of others. In fact, she typed out something over seven thousand words — or about the equivalent of an average chapter of *Gone With the Wind*.

The next day, she left her motel room long enough to go to the bank so that she would have enough money to continue her escape from the public. On her return to her hideaway, she wrote Stephen Vincent Benét this "preface" to a seven-page letter replying to his review of the book in the *Saturday Review*:

> I am not in the best condition to write you the kind of letter I'd like to write you, the kind of letter that would adequately tell you how much I appreciated your review, how happy it made me. I have just made my escape from Atlanta after losing ten pounds since my publication day, after having photographers with the morning coffee, and strangers collaring me at the bank and ladies' societies at me on the phone all day wanting me to make a "little talk." . . . And now, some fifty miles up the road toward the mountains, I find myself even tireder and more flabbergasted than ever. For I never dreamed the book which I didn't think worth retyping and trying to sell would ever sell, or having sold, would ever get a kind word from a reviewer. But I want to write you now and thank you for when I do get up to the mountains I know I'll go to bed and not get up for a week.
>
> I must admit that when I heard that you were to review me my heart sank. I suppose that needs some explanation. . . . Your "John Brown's Body" is my favorite poem, my favorite book. I know more of it by heart than I do any other poetry. It means more to me, is realer than anything I've ever read by any poet, bar none, and I've read an awful lot of poetry. . . .

The tone, the length, and naiveté, and the desperation in Peggy's letters to reviewers she had not met combined to ensnare the recipients into correspondence with her. The recipients of such letters could not help but be flattered, first by her compliments and second by her humility. Here was a lady who had just won praise from almost every respected reviewer across the nation and whose first book was being hailed as a masterpiece, and she was bowing to their own "greatness." The sense of flattery was followed by sympathy and pity for a woman so ravaged by an adulatory public that she had had to run away and hide out all alone in a small-town motel among traveling salesmen and their temporary companions. It was impossible to turn away from such helplessness without some pang of guilt. After receiving their letters, Brickell and Granberry were eager to help this innocent Southern lady whose life had suddenly been uprooted by unsought fame. Benét, to Peggy's delight, replied in a sympathetic manner and suggested that they meet whenever she was in New York.

Reading the great body of letters that Peggy Mitchell dashed off during her three-night sojourn in Gainesville, one is stunned by the overwhelming pleas for sympathy they contain. She seemed to be struggling with her own ambivalent emotions. On one hand, she was terrified of the changes fame would bring to her life and her marriage; on the other, fame was making a fantasy come true. Her name was being linked with those of the great writers whom she had admired all her life. Now she actually had good cause to write to literary celebrities and expect that they might reply. Peggy wrote Donald Adams of the *New York Times* on July 9, "For all I know of literary etiquette an author should keep haughtily silent." (She doesn't, of course, her letter to Adams being of even greater length than those to Benét, Granberry, and Brickell.) The fact that she replied to almost every good review, major or not, can be attributed to Southern politeness to a degree, but Peggy had not been much of a letter writer before the publication of *Gone With the Wind*. For a number of years, John had handled the bulk of their correspondence to his family and their mutual friends. Therefore, to write such long, personally revealing letters to people whom she had never met seems a curious thing for her to have done. But Peggy was in deep emotional water, and the letters were as much calls for help as they were expressions of thanks.

She had written a book that had dramatically altered the pattern of her life, and she did not know how to cope with the changes. She began to hate the existence of the book while, at the same time, enjoying the personal glory it brought her. The letter to Donald Adams, perhaps the most pitiable of the "runaway" letters, is filled with a list of trials she had survived that nearly equaled Job's. Toward the end, she vowed that she would never write another book:

> I wouldn't go through this again for anything. When I look back on these last years of struggling to find time to write between deaths in the family, illness in the family and among friends which lasted months and even years, childbirths (not my own!),

223

divorces and neuroses among friends, my own ill health and four fine auto accidents which did everything from fracturing my skull to splintering my vertebrae — it all seems a nightmare. I wouldn't tackle it again for anything.

Peggy Mitchell's heroine, Scarlett, was almost completely fearless when it came to plunging into tomorrow, but her creator feared any whisper of change. And, unlike her second heroine, Melanie Wilkes, Peggy did not accept her trials with quiet courage. People would be expecting things of her now that she was a famous author — speeches, comments, appearances, another book — and she knew she could not handle any of those pressures. She had known her greatest security as Mrs. John Marsh, and she did not think she or her marriage could withstand a fame that kept her constantly before the public. Nor did she ever want to write another book. If she was not to be looked at askance by those literary men and women who mattered so to her, then she had to have their sympathy and understanding.

From Gainesville, she wrote George Brett at Macmillan:

Life has been so much like a nightmare recently that it was all I could do to stay on my feet. . . . I finally ran away from town yesterday. A brisk three hour work out with three Associated Press boys and a couple of photographers finally finished me and I left town with practically no clothes and no money. I do think it's awful when you've sent me a check for five thousand dollars that I haven't had time to buy me a new dress, or have my car overhauled! I didn't know an author's life was like this.

I've started for the back of beyond in the mountains and stopped here because I was going to sleep at the wheel and I was afraid I'd kill myself in a ditch. When I reach a place where there aren't any telephones and no newspapers for my picture to be in, I'll stop and write you a letter to tell you just how much I appreciate the check and all you and Macmillan have done for me. Good Heavens! With all those ads and the grand publicity the newspapers have given me, Macmillan could have sold Karl Marx up here in these hills!

However, Peggy did not continue any farther into the hills, for that evening, July 9, when she called John he read her a telegram she had just received: "WE HAVE A WONDERFUL HIDEAWAY

PLACE COME AND HIDE OUT HERE. YOU ARE MOST WELCOME NO NEWSPAPERS ONLY OTHER WRITERS EDWIN AND MABEL GRANBERRY, BLOWING ROCK, NORTH CAROLINA."

Blowing Rock was the summer campus of the English Department of Rollins College. Edwin Granberry and his wife, Mabel, were so moved by the "pathetic note" in Peggy's letter to him that they had decided to offer her refuge, although they did not think she would accept. They were, of course, total strangers, but Blowing Rock was a writers' colony and, coincidentally, Herschel Brickell was also due to arrive to give a series of lectures.

Early the next morning, Peggy called John to tell him that she was coming right home and that he should make arrangements with the Granberrys for her to arrive at Blowing Rock on July 13, with the provision that her visit be kept secret. It seems perverse of her to have run off to stay with strangers in a writers' colony where the other writers were not to be informed of her presence, but she was driven by desperation. It was true that the number of telephone calls and cables and gushing strangers had not diminished in her absence. However, she could have gone to New York and stayed with Lois (who begged her to do so); Augusta's sister had offered her shelter at Saint Simons Island; and there was Frances in Wilmington, ready to do anything she could to help her harassed sister-in-law. The public would not have invaded her privacy in any of those places. But it was not just the public Peggy feared. In her letter to Herschel Brickell, she had revealed the source of her greatest worry. "*In the matter of Captain Butler,*" she had written him, "*I may yet have a lawsuit on my hands despite my protests that I didn't model him after any human being I've ever heard of.*"

There was always the danger of a physical attack in a confrontation with Upshaw, as well, and this possibility terrified her. Blowing Rock seemed to be a perfect hideaway — it would give her the opportunity to meet two writers who had praised her book; and, while Red Upshaw was clever enough to get through Macmillan's lines, knew Augusta's sister's house at Saint Simons very well, and could easily have tracked down Frances, he would never suspect her of going, without John, to a place where *everyone* was a stranger to her.

Chapter Eighteen

THE MARSHES had celebrated their eleventh anniversary on July 4, 1936, but, in the brouhaha caused by the book's publication, they had not exchanged presents. Medora had sent Peggy's favorite flower, roses, and their arrival had reassured her that a shred of normalcy still existed in her life. She had tried not to let her sudden fame affect her, but it had been impossible to disregard it; it was there and she was conscious of the fact that now, when people saw her name or photograph in the newspapers, they conjured up a strange image of a Margaret Mitchell whom she did not know.

There was nothing in Peggy's appearance that would have led one to suspect that they were in the presence of a celebrity. Because of her diminutive size she was forced to buy her clothes in the teen sections of department stores, and her outfits had a curious naiveté to them that often jarred with her choice of flirtatious hats, her rather large pocketbooks, and the heavy orthopedic shoes she wore. Shopping for clothes had long been an unpleasant and unsatisfying experience for her, and dressing for any special occasion was generally traumatic, the choice of what she was to wear often throwing her into panic and ending with her simply grabbing for anything easy to put on, regardless of how appropriate it was for the occasion. She seemed to like to play up the little-girl quality in her appearance, and always dressed as a small child for costume parties. (She attended one of these affairs as Baby Snooks.)

The marking of more than a decade of marriage to John prompted Peggy to reassess their relationship. For the first time, she discussed her marriage in her personal letters. To Lois Cole, she joked that she and John might have grown like Darby and Joan, so mutually dependent were they upon each other. To a family member, she confided that her marriage was sound because she and John could reveal to each other what they could tell no one else. They both did, indeed, thrive on the secrets they shared about each other's lives. With Peggy, it was Upshaw; with John, his epilepsy.

John's condition had been fairly dormant for a number of years but, during the final year of work on the book, he had had a number of seizures. Most were not severe and none had required hospitalization. However, Peggy was certain the recurrence of the attacks had been caused by the strain of editing the book, and she suffered a sense of guilt on this score.

Until the wild reception of *Gone With the Wind*, neither of the Marshes had imagined that the book would change their lives much or that it would be a threat to their diligently guarded privacy. When the three AP reporters had set upon her the morning she had run away to Gainesville, Peggy realized that not only could her life with Red Upshaw suddenly be revealed, but that her place in the limelight could also cause John's illness to be exposed. She was, as Edwin Granberry had perceived, deeply troubled. The invitation to Blowing Rock, North Carolina, therefore, seemed like a godsend; there, she would have time to think things out, and no one except John would know where she was.

Not only was Peggy running away from Upshaw, her fans, and the press, but from the need to make an important decision. As far back as June 14, David O. Selznick had made an offer of $50,000 to Annie Laurie Williams for the film rights to *Gone With the Wind*. Macmillan had passed it on to Peggy, who had telegraphed her acceptance, pending approval of the contract, on July 8 from Gainesville. But no sooner had she done this than she began to have doubts about whether she was doing the right thing. News of her acceptance had not been released to the press. The contract had been dispatched with great haste and had arrived in Atlanta just a few hours before her planned departure for Blowing Rock on the thirteenth. Peggy refused to look at it, leaving it to John to read and explain to her, but she wanted him to be certain Macmillan knew they must not yet issue any statements about its existence.

Be that as it may, the press had been casting *Gone With the Wind* for two weeks, with Clark Gable and Janet Gaynor the favorite choices for Rhett and Scarlett. "Not Janet Gaynor! Spare me this last ignominy!" Peggy wrote Lois Cole. It is in this same letter, written the day she left for Blowing Rock, that Peggy — for the first and what seems to be the only time — "cast" the major roles in her book. "Miriam Hopkins has been my choice for Scarlett from the beginning, but I knew what I had to say wouldn't matter so said nothing." Hopkins, she thought, had the voice, the appearance, the personality, and the sharp look. Elizabeth Allan, who had played David Copperfield's mother in the recent movie, was her favorite for Melanie. And she wrote, "I wish Charles Boyer didn't have a French accent for he's my choice for Rhett. Next to him, Jack Holt [a Western star] is the only person I can think of."

From the contents of this letter, it does appear that Peggy saw her book as a film, fully intended to sign the contract, and already believed that by doing so she was losing her control.

On Monday morning, July 13, with perhaps even less attention given to her dress than ever, Peggy started off on a railway journey that involved two train connections and ended in the small town of Hickory, North Carolina, forty miles from her destination. John had made the arrangements with Edwin Granberry, who was to be waiting for her at the depot with his wife and brother-in-law to drive on to Blowing Rock. There, she was to stay in a boardinghouse across the street from the Granberrys and their three small sons. As promised, Granberry had told no one but his wife's brother, who was visiting them, and Herschel Brickell that Margaret Mitchell was arriving in Blowing Rock.

There were numerous people on the platform when Peggy stepped off the train, and she immediately feared someone might have told the press of her arrival. She had traveled in a rear car, which meant she was a short distance from the station house. Certain that the Granberrys would be waiting inside for her, she left her baggage on the platform and darted around the side of the country depot to the front door and went inside. The Granberrys were not there and, believing she had out-witted the press, she sat down to wait until they either arrived or came back inside to find her. There were, however, no re-porters. When the train had emptied, with no sign of Margaret Mitchell, Granberry decided she had changed her mind and was not coming to Blowing Rock, and that somehow the tele-gram telling them of this had not reached them before they had left to pick her up. The July sun was hot and the three of them stood in the shade of the station house as they discussed what they should do. Out of the corner of his eye, Granberry saw what he was later to describe as "a small, plain, wren of a woman, dressed in a housewife's cotton" (she had worn a printed calico smock that looked like a housedress) come out of the building, peer around, speak to a man near the tracks, and then walk toward the one taxicab waiting nearby. It never oc-curred to the Granberrys that *this* was Margaret Mitchell. They had a published photograph of her in which she looked quite striking but, of course, it did not show her small stature. They had just agreed to call John Marsh in Atlanta when Granberry felt someone touch his arm and he looked down at, as he said later, "this little elf."

"Can you be Edwin Granberry?" she asked.

They insisted Peggy sit in the front seat with Edwin, who was driving. As the car twisted and turned up the steep narrow road to the crest of the Blue Ridge Mountains and to Blowing Rock, her conversation, which was highly spirited at first, be-came sparse. About halfway, she fell silent for about ten min-utes and then said in a small, terrified voice, "Would you please stop the car. I'm afraid I'm going to throw up." He did — and she did — and the rest of the journey was anything but jolly. Once in Blowing Rock, however, she wrote John that she knew she had done the right thing in coming. Not only were the Granberrys delightful people, but the town, which was four thousand feet above sea level and was situated directly on the Park-to-Park Scenic Highway through the Shenandoah and

Great Smoky Mountain National Parks, commanded a spectacular view and was both cool and charming.

During the greater part of the ten days Peggy spent at Blowing Rock, she remained aloof from both lecturers and students, spending most of her time with the Granberrys and Herschel Brickell. Brickell had telephoned her the day before she had set out for Blowing Rock, and she later wrote him that she knew he was going to be nice from the sound of his voice. A lantern-jawed Mississippian with the manners of a Southern gentleman, he appealed to Peggy immediately. He had come without his wife, Norma, who had remained at their home in Ridgefield, Connecticut, and he and Peggy often joined the Granberrys for meals at their house or at the little hotel on the main street of the village.

Granberry, a slight, dark man with a trim mustache and a rushed way of speaking, and Brickell, with his soft drawl, were both good speakers, and Peggy enjoyed attending their lectures. For the most part, however, she remained in her room when she was not with the Granberrys or Brickell. It was no use trying to keep her identity secret among the school's faculty and students, for the news that she was on campus had quickly circulated. But there seemed to be no reporters in town, and people accepted her presence among them in an interested but respectful manner. At the Granberrys', Peggy felt impelled to talk about herself, though always with great humor and vivacity. Discussion centered on the book, the reviews, and the new pressures in her life caused by the suddenness of her fame; but, because the book was such a success story and the author such an enigma, people liked listening to her and were fascinated to learn what they could about *Gone With the Wind* and its author.

The only intrusion on Peggy's Blowing Rock respite was a series of rather disconcerting letters from John about the Selznick film contract. In the first of these letters, written on Wednesday, July 15, he explained that the contract was about ten pages long and was filled with highly technical language. John seemed to feel it was acceptable, except for one point — it was an outright sale and did not give Peggy any right to approve the scenario nor to have any say-so about what Selznick did with the book once she had accepted her check. John told her not to worry about it, however, as he had spoken to Lois, and he and her father would go over the contract and try to get it all settled by the time she returned home.

But then, in his second letter, on July 16, he went on about the problem at great length, although repeating once again that she should not worry about it and that "Mitchell, Mitchell, and Marsh" would handle it for her.

> My idea is that there is no need for you to come back to Atlanta while the "lawyer" stuff is being wrangled over — hence the course of action which I outlined above and submitted for your approval. But if it doesn't meet with your approval, if you rather I would *not* deal directly with Macmillan without consulting you in advance on each point, just let me know. If the latter course is your preference, you had better wire me or phone me as soon as you get this letter. A wire, "Please submit everything to me before taking up with Macmillan" will be all that is necessary.
>
> My affectionate and husbandly advice is that you enjoy your vacation and let us bother about these preliminary legal technicalities. You understand, of course, that you will have the final say-so on the whole matter. Nothing that we do will be final until you put your name on the contract, and if you don't like what we have done, you can change it all when you get back to Atlanta.

He suggested that she might want to discuss the issue with Granberry and Brickell, who perhaps could advise her from their own experience or from that of their author friends. Peggy did discuss the contract with Granberry and Brickell, who both told her they did not think she would be able to get approval of the film script. Granberry felt she should not sell at this time, that she could achieve better terms at a later date.

John's first letter had been extremely affectionate, but, as the letters went back and forth from Atlanta to Blowing Rock, "Sweetheart" became "Darling," and then just "Dear Peggy." For, after John's letter of the sixteenth, she had telegraphed him to make no decisions without her.

Just before she had left for Blowing Rock, Peggy had had an interview with Faith Baldwin. The two women had hit if off extremely well — so well, in fact, that John wrote Peggy on July 17 that she should write to Faith Baldwin for another "expert opinion" on their current problem. Then he added, "It occurred to me that we might insert a clause on this page of the contract stating that the movies would *not* have an option on your next book unless they did right by you on this one. Of course, the joke is that you don't intend to write any more books, but the fact that Selznick is sufficiently interested in you to *want* an option on your future production might prove to be a lever through which you could retain some control over what is done in making a movie out of this book."

He signed the letter cooly, "John" — no "Love," "All my love," or "Best love," as in previous letters. The following day, he wrote her that Macmillan was waiting for her to sign the contract and was concerned that she might have changed her mind. However, Peggy did not cut short her vacation. She left Blowing Rock on the twenty-second, arriving home that evening. The next morning she received a telegram from James Putnam of Macmillan: "IS THERE ANY DIFFICULTIES [sic] REGARDING MOVIE CONTRACT HAVE BEEN EXPECTING SIGNED COPIES DAILY."

Everyone, including Selznick, had said no to the high price Annie Laurie Williams had first asked for the book. Selznick had been the only one to come back with a counter offer, and Putnam was nervous about Peggy's delay in returning the signed contract, fearing that the deal would fall through. Peggy wrote Latham on her arrival home that she had not been able to oblige Macmillan as she was in "a lather of rage about the contract, and ready to throw it in the movie company's face," and that she thought it was a contract that no rational person could sign regardless of the amount of money involved, for her father had found that it held her liable "for so many things, such as damage suits." It was, in her opinion, not only worded "idiotically," but it was "the stupidest contract" she had ever seen. Latham was considerably upset by this letter and memos flew fast and thick in Macmillan's offices as the various executives sought a solution. In the end, they decided to wait until they heard from Peggy the specific points in contention.

Life was no calmer after Peggy's return from Blowing Rock — she was living in a "goldfish bowl"; the telephone jangled constantly; fan mail was still arriving in bags every day; crowds followed her on the street and the interest of the press had not slackened. She wrote Lois Cole on July 25, "The pressures are worse than before Blowing Rock and I've hardly had a word with John except about contracts."

The Selznick contract had created new and greater pressures in their lives. On July 27, Peggy and John and Stephens had a five-hour conference about the various clauses they considered unacceptable. Immediately afterwards, John wrote Lois an eleven-page, single-spaced letter setting forth their reservations, and sent it off special delivery. No sooner was this done than the two men decided Peggy and Stephens must go up to New York the next day to settle the matter in person, and they got on the telephone and told Brett and Putnam at Macmillan that she would not sign anything if they told *anyone* she was in New York.

Peggy complained to Lois that she had "no clothes, no hats, not even a change of underwear or an extra pair of stockings," but that it seemed she was coming to New York just the same. This letter to Lois was written at 1:00 A.M. on the night Stephens and John had made plans for her to go to New York. She dared not use her typewriter because John was asleep, and, in a scrawling hand, she told Lois about an interview, supposedly on modern fiction, that she had had that day. The reporter had asked her what kind of uplift brassiere she wore, and when she said falteringly that she didn't wear one at all, he was "terribly shocked."

Herschel Brickell had returned to his home in Ridgefield, Connecticut — about an hour's train journey from New York City — and, the next day, Peggy telegraphed him and his wife, Norma. Her plan was to spend the first night in New York at a hotel with Stephens and then to go the next evening, when negotiations should be concluded, to the Brickells' for a few days.

Peggy and Stephens arrived in New York early on the morning of July 29 and, after checking into the Grosvenor Hotel, near the Macmillan offices on lower Fifth Avenue, they attended their first meeting. Among those present were two lawyers for the Macmillan Company, two Selznick lawyers, Kay Brown, and Annie Laurie Williams. Harold Latham was on a holiday at his home in Tannersville, New York, and Lois had not been included. This was the first meeting between Peggy and Annie Laurie, and Peggy was cool as they sat facing each other at the table. The meeting went on for several hours, with Peggy initiating most of the discussion. The issue of an indemnification clause that left Peggy open to a libel suit if someone claimed a character in the film was based on a living person and the matter of copyright were settled in Peggy's favor at the first meeting. That left the controversy over final script approval. Peggy had no desire to be involved with the making of the film itself, but she did want the contract to spell out more clearly what the final product would be. She particularly wanted to protect its historical authenticity, as well as the dialects of the characters. Selznick's people were not willing to include a clause to this effect and, therefore, at the end of the day they hit an impasse.

That night, Stephens and Peggy had dinner with Lois Cole and her husband, Allan Taylor. Lois and Allan, who were more knowledgeable about such matters, pointed out that Selznick had given her radio, television, and dramatic rights, and that the purchase price of $50,000 was to be paid immediately upon signature. They impressed upon her that no one would pay more than Selznick, that if she pressed too hard, she could lose the deal altogether, and that David O. Selznick was a man of good taste who had successfully brought novels like *David Copperfield*, *Anna Karenina*, and *A Tale of Two Cities* to the screen. It seemed unlikely that he would not employ experts to assure the authenticity of the background and of the speech. This sounded sensible to Peggy and she went into the meeting on the second day ready to cooperate.

Of that meeting, Peggy wrote Latham on her return to Atlanta, "The Selznick lawyers were mighty nice. So were the pretty young ladies in the Selznick office. They smoothed me down. They made concessions and I made concessions and the contract was rearranged so that it was possible for me to sign it."

The Selznick company, on their part, had feared that Peggy Mitchell would hold out for better financial terms. Stephens did not raise the issues of either escalating clauses or box-office percentages, and never questioned the fifty-thousand-dollar purchase price. The amount was the highest price ever paid to that date for a first novel and had Peggy not insisted that this figure be kept secret, it would have seemed, at that time, impressive. Later, during the wartime boom, books sold to the movies for as much as two hundred thousand dollars. But when Peggy sold the rights to *Gone With the Wind,* no one could have predicted that a war would finally end the financial struggles the nation had so long endured.

In addition to the rights for live dramatization, television, and radio, Peggy had rights of approval if a sequel was ever to be made, and a 50 percent share in a shortened version of the book, with photographs from the film. In the area of indemnification, the revised contract was certainly much more protective of the author than the original. But commercial tie-ins — an issue that would cause future problems between Selznick and Peggy — belonged to Selznick International, including the use and license of the title and character names in advertisements or in connection with manufactured items. John wrote Granberry, "Peggy has gone to N.Y. to take Selznick's skull and has done it."

As soon as the contract had been signed, Stephens left for Atlanta and Herschel Brickell picked Peggy up in New York and took her to Ridgefield. By the time they arrived, she was in a state, having suffered a sudden and frightening "stroke of blindness" en route that had lasted nearly ten minutes. Brickell put her on the train to Atlanta on August 2 "in a bad way" after his eye doctor had diagnosed a relapse of the eye strain she had suffered as a result of the final eight months of editing the book.

As Peggy's train pulled into Atlanta's Terminal Station, John was boarding another one for Wilmington to see his mother, and they hardly had time to exchange more than a few words. Her eye problems did not deter John from continuing his trip and he remained in Wilmington for a week.

Peggy's Atlanta doctor concurred with Brickell's, and she was confined to a dark room for ten days and then had to remain in bed for another eleven days of complete rest. Although she had adamantly refused to have a radio before, asserting that the invention was an invasion of one's privacy, she now allowed

Bessie to hook one up next to her bed. Incoming mail was read to her and she managed to dictate a few letters to Margaret Baugh, who had taken a leave of absence from Macmillan's Atlanta office to help Peggy during what John called "the six weeks that rocked the Marsh world." From Atlanta, Peggy wrote Lois that she must remain for long hours in "a dark room with a black bandage over my eyes," but that she was still glad not to have gone blind. She did not see how the vicissitudes of fame could last much longer, and if they did, she said, her disposition would not.

Peggy was hearing from people with whom she had lost touch years before, but there was no further communication from Red Upshaw. Ginny Morris wrote again from New York. Divorced and the mother of a small girl, she was employed by United Artists Film Corporation in the publicity department during the day, and worked as a free-lance screen magazine writer after hours. "Is this the same girl who used to borrow my toothbrush and who left her stockings in a heap in the middle of the room?" she joked.

A lighthearted correspondence began between the two old friends, with Ginny sending Peggy articles about her from the trade papers not covered by Peggy's various clipping services — and usually adding irreverent comments. In the margin of a publicity release that stated Peggy was born in 1906, Ginny quipped, "What a precocious smallfry of twelve you were when you tumbled out of your Henshaw Avenue bed to celebrate the Armistice!"

Margaret Baugh opened and sorted the mail so that Peggy did not have to read the crank letters and pleas for money. She was given all other correspondence and chose to reply personally to a large percentage of it. She never liked dictating and, once her eyes were better, she managed to answer about a hundred letters a week, always making carbon copies. Replies to fans' brief hand-written notes were often single-spaced, three-page, typed letters that revealed far more about herself and the book than the correspondent had asked to know. And, although Stephens was her lawyer, she answered numerous legal letters.

To stay on top of this avalanche of mail was impossible, and just attempting to do so involved a shocking amount of work.

In the month of September alone, Peggy wrote Macmillan executives sixteen rather complicated letters pertaining to foreign rights, publicity, monies, autographing books, and a clipping service, as well as advice to someone who suffered from arthritis. The shortest of these is two pages long and several others range from seven to nine pages, always single-spaced. John continued the correspondence with his family, but Peggy wrote the Granberrys and the Brickells. She was also still signing books sent to her in the mail. In the same month, Peggy received well over a thousand fan letters and two hundred books. As an apology for her tardiness in replying, she nearly always fell back on her numerous health problems. Literally hundreds of strangers who had written to her were told that she had been confined to a dark room with black bandages over her eyes and that it was still difficult for her to spend more than a few hours writing letters. It was during this time that Louella Parsons reported in her syndicated Hollywood column that Peggy was going blind. "I am not going blind and never intend to go blind," Peggy replied indignantly.

Now that she was a public figure, Peggy's personal affairs were grist for the gossip mills. In early September, another rumor flew. John Marsh, it was reported in a Hollywood column, had suffered shell shock in the war and had a nervous disorder. No one knew the genesis of this report, but Peggy and John suspected someone who had seen or heard about one of his small seizures. In a fury, Peggy wrote Edwin Granberry that she could stand anything anyone wrote about her, but she could not stand lies about John or any member of her family. "It isn't their fault that I wrote a best-seller," she said. "They were just innocent bystanders. Let them say anything they want about me. Anybody who is fool enough to publish a book deserves anything that lands on them. But not their kin."

In this, her second letter to Edwin Granberry since "the old eyes blew their fuses," she discussed a trip that she and John were planning to Winter Park, Florida, where Granberry taught at Rollins College. John's idea of heaven — rising late and having breakfast in bed — and their "habit of eating at odd hours and singing in the bathtub" were given as reasons why they would prefer not to stay with the Granberrys.

The first weeks in September were happy ones — or, at least,

237

they were less unhappy than any time since the publication of the book. Peggy's eyes were healing, and the visit in Winter Park was brief but relaxing. Eugene Mitchell, who had not been well, had improved. And, to handle things while they were away, Margaret Baugh was given the assistance of two additional typists.

Peggy had convinced herself that the worst might be about over. She wrote the Granberrys on her return home that she felt sure book sales would taper off in short order, along with the tumult the publication had caused. But *Gone With the Wind* was not only number one on the *New York Times* best-seller list, it had been reported as the best-selling novel in every one of seventy leading bookshops from coast to coast. On September 25, Peggy received a check from Macmillan for $45,000, her share of the money from the sale of *Gone With the Wind* to Selznick.

This was when Peggy learned for the first time that Miss Williams had been acting as her representative at the conference table and that the Macmillan lawyers and executives had appeared at the conference not on her behalf, but solely to protect the interests of the Macmillan Company itself. That same day, she wrote Harold Latham that she considered this a reprehensible action on the part of Macmillan, who knew her strong feelings about Annie Laurie Williams. She ended, characteristically, by saying what a low blow it was to have this disloyalty taking place at a time when her eyes were in such a weakened condition that she had been ordered to bed with bandages over them and could neither read nor write.

Lois, in rebuttal to this letter, parried with a thrust of her own, "But my dear child, Stephens, as your lawyer, was *also there!*" — a point Latham himself had made upon handing the letter over to Lois.

Another problem arose when, after receiving a Scarlett O'Hara doll from a reader who had made it herself, Peggy forwarded it on to Ginny Morris as a gift for her little girl. An alarming letter arrived from Ginny — didn't Peggy know the vast sums of money that film people like Walt Disney had made on commercial tie-ins, dolls and watches and "God-knows-what else"? Didn't Peggy have these rights? There followed a list of various profits that could be made from such tie-ins. Ginny's letter opened up another area that had not been explored — the right to use the title and names of the characters for exploitation that did *not* tie up directly with the movie. Peggy passed the letter on to Stephens who, in turn, wrote Latham a long legalistic letter upbraiding Macmillan for their deception both in this and the matter of Annie Laurie Williams. Peggy now wanted the tie-ins to be designated as *her* right, but Selznick felt she had sold him those rights — which, though perhaps inadvertently, she had — and Macmillan felt caught in the middle.

In his reply to Peggy on this matter on October 6, Latham pointed out that everyone at Macmillan had been enthusiastic about her book and had done the best possible job promoting it. "Now there is an impasse because of the film contract," he wrote. "I don't know whether this situation could have been avoided had I been there. From what Mr. Putnam tells me, I judge that it could not for apparently although we were your agent in effecting the sale of the motion picture rights you were represented in the negotiation of the sale by your own attorney who approved the contract that you signed."

They were right, of course. Stephens had been at the conference table, but — not being familiar with publishing and film terminology and, perhaps, being somewhat overwhelmed by his seat at such a table — he had not disputed the clause. Peggy's loyalty to Stephens never waned due to this, and she fought valiantly on his behalf in the next confrontation they were to have with "the film people."

Chapter Nineteen

THE FIRST of the false rumors that Peggy had written *Gone With the Wind* in collaboration with John appeared in the *Washington Post* on September 29, 1936. Under Secretary of the Interior Harry Slattery had taken great offense to what he called the "slanderous use of his family name" in the book because the character Emmy Slattery had been referred to as "white trash." "Under Secretary Slattery threatened to sue," the *Post* declared in an article in which Slattery was interviewed, "but an exchange of letters and conversation with the young Atlanta author [have] convinced him that no malice was intended." Peggy had never heard of Mr. Slattery, and she was appalled at the ridiculous untruth of his statement, as well as of the *Post*'s further claim that, "The world might know her as Margaret Mitchell but she is first and foremost the wife of John Marsh. She still cooks breakfast in her little flat in Atlanta and he keeps working at his job, in spite of the fact that they suddenly came into a fortune. Atlantans have tried to fete and exploit them — they wrote the book in collaboration over a period of seven years — but they keep their heads and decline all invitations."

Four or five days later, Peggy wrote Slattery, pleading with him to ask the *Washington Post* to print a retraction of the statement that her husband had collaborated with her in the writing of *Gone With the Wind*. "I am so upset about this error I have been unable to do anything but cry ever since I read the clipping," she wrote. "I have given so many years of my life to the writing of this book, injured my eyes, endangered my health and this is my payment — that I didn't write it! And I did write it, every word of it. My husband had nothing whatever to do with it. In the first place he is not a Georgian (he was born in Kentucky) and no one but a Georgian with generations of Georgian ancestors could have written it. In the second place, he has a very responsible position and works very hard and he seldom gets time to play golf much less to write books.

"In fact," she stated, "he never even read the whole of my manuscript until after the Macmillan Company had bought it." She explained that it was not that she did not want him to read it, but that the book had not been written in chronological order and he could not have been expected to follow the story. "Not all the financial rewards I may receive can make up to me for this," she wrote in conclusion. "Moreover, it puts me in such a dreadful light before the world — that I had concealed my husband's work on this book. And he actually had no part in it except helping me with the proof reading when my eyes gave out and my deadline was upon me. . . . Of course, the story has already gone out into the world, to rise up and plague me all my life but a retraction would help some. You see, it is my whole professional reputation which is at stake — my reputation which has been ruined through no fault of my own."

Why Peggy wrote to Under Secretary Slattery to approach the *Washington Post* rather than doing so herself or through Stephens, her legal counsel, remains a mystery. An apology but not a full retraction was printed in the *Post*, and Peggy never was able to squelch the rumors that John had collaborated on the writing of *Gone With the Wind*. But neither had she been completely fair to John in her letter to Slattery. John had not read the manuscript through from beginning to end before she gave it to Harold Latham, but then, neither had she. It had been written in sections over nearly a decade, but her habit was to read John the sections as she completed them, discuss the work with him, and allow him to make notes and corrections on her manuscript. Early letters of hers to Latham reveal that John had suggested several chapter openings. It is doubtful that he contributed any historical background or helped her with research, but his encouragement and support had been given freely throughout. Before its publication, Peggy had confided to Lois that John had driven her to write the book in the first place and had then prodded her on at every juncture. She had told Latham quite frankly that the book had benefitted from John's "tough criticism along the way," but her attitude about any public knowledge of John's contribution to the development of the novel once *Gone With the Wind* had been published contains more than a touch of paranoia.

The *Washington Post*'s article had been untrue, possibly even libelous. However, it is not too difficult to trace its roots. John had many newspaper friends in Washington from the days of his job with the Associated Press. The secrecy that surrounded John's editorial help on the book, combined with the knowledge many of his Atlanta and Washington press colleagues had of his involvement in it, caused them to suspect his contribution had been more than it was. And Peggy's silence fed these suspicions. The book had contained no acknowledgements of assistance; there was only the dedication to J.R.M. To those people who liked to speculate, it could have seemed that Peggy had something to hide.

The question of her sole authorship did irreparable damage to Peggy's confidence. Some people thought she did not have the capabilities to have written the book on her own, and she herself confessed to Lois that she could not have done it without John.

Gone With the Wind's tremendous success presented its author with responsibilities that she could not shoulder. Her life had been upended as Maybelle had predicted it might be one day, and she was not prepared for it. She could not help but entertain the thought that her mother had been right — education would have helped her to overcome at least a portion of her problems. She did not feel adequately educated for the role of a literary personality.

In *Gone With the Wind* Peggy had dealt with what she knew best, and her span of knowledge was limited to that subject — Atlanta during and directly after the Civil War. She had thought the publication of the book would renew her stature in

Atlanta, that friends would stop saying she was wasting her life, and that the literary crowd would regard her with a small measure of respect. But she had not suspected that her life would be so disrupted. Not until the Book-of-the-Month Club chose *Gone With the Wind* as their July selection had she thought she would make more than a thousand dollars from its sale. At the time, the Marshes' finances were such that the amount would have been the difference between debt and solvency. Now, suddenly, she had become a business.

In September, a royalty check had arrived from Macmillan for $43,500 and, in October, another came, for $99,700 — a veritable fortune in the heart of the Depression. In addition to these earnings were the original $500 advance, the $5,000 paid on behalf of the Book-of-the-Month Club, Latham's authorized $5,000 advance on royalties, and the $45,000 from the film sale. Peggy was a rich woman and growing richer with each passing day. The large amounts she was earning seemed unreal to her. She was certain it could not continue and yet she was implacable in her decision that she would not write another book. This meant that royalties from *Gone With the Wind* had to last the Marshes a lifetime.

Court orders were much on Peggy's mind as Stephens conferred daily with her on all the manufacturers of clothes and cosmetics and toys who were infringing on her copyright by using her name, the title of the book, and the names of its characters in advertising their products. Organizations — professional and amateur, and including church groups — were quoting the book without permission. Stephens's best talents were now put into action. He became the guardian of her copyright and, although it is doubtful that many transgressors slipped past him, the Marshes were kept in a state of constant litigation. All legal and business entanglements were reported each day to Peggy. And not only were people swooping down, as she said, "like buzzards to a carcass" to infringe on her copyright, but impostors were appearing in California, Mexico, and New York who claimed to be Margaret Mitchell, gave statements to the press and, in one case, tried to use her name to establish financial credit.

No day seemed to pass without a flurry of agitated calls from

Stephens. Whatever little free time the Marshes had was taken up with conversations dealing with the subjects of Stephens's calls. Peggy was short-tempered and sharp-tongued, and not easy to live with. It now appeared to her that the world was filled with "thieves and chiselers" and that they were all feeding on her good fortune. This cynical attitude manifested itself in her dealings with Macmillan.

Peggy now felt she had not "taken the Selznick skull" at all, but that Macmillan had failed to alert her to how much money could be made by the commercial tie-ins should Selznick decide to lease rights for Scarlett O'Hara dolls or Rhett Butler wristwatches. Some angry letters went from Peggy, John, and Stephens to George Brett and Lois Cole. Convinced by Stephens and John that Macmillan had been remiss in protecting her best interests, Peggy insisted something be done to amend the contract. George Brett wrote that her lawyer should, perhaps, come up to New York to discuss the matter and that Macmillan would "pay the costs." The Marshes and Stephens naively assumed that this meant Stephens's legal fees, as well as his travel and hotel expenses, and Stephens wrote Brett a curt letter setting this forth. Appalled by the tone and content of this communication, Brett withdrew his offer.

At this point, relations between Peggy and Macmillan became severely strained. Lois was especially upset over the situation and Allan Taylor, her husband, stepped in to smooth Peggy's ruffled feelings. He wrote her a long, placating letter on Lois's and Macmillan's behalf, but Peggy's strong family loyalty had been put to the test. She defended Stephens's position to the wall. Perhaps to ease the situation, Macmillan gave Peggy back all foreign rights except the English. But the Selznick conflict was not settled until a later date.

Despite the Marshes' feeling that they had been ill-served in these last two disagreements, it is only fair to say that Macmillan had always bent over backward to do the right thing for Peggy. Even their decision to employ Annie Laurie Williams was an effort on their part to have Peggy competently represented. No matter what its merits, they *had* accepted a manuscript in shocking condition, altered original contracts to her advantage on two occasions, given her monies before her royalty payment was due, and produced, published, and distributed her book with great care and attention. Along the way, Peggy had repeatedly written to Latham and Lois, "I never knew publishers could be so nice." But once the success of her book was guaranteed and the film sale completed, Peggy seemed to feel that Macmillan's niceness was a way of taking advantage of her former naiveté.

On October 9, she wrote Herschel Brickell that Stephens would arrive in New York the following Tuesday for conferences with George Brett and the Macmillan lawyers, and that she would now pay his expenses.

> This present business and legal tangle in which we are now involved has about exhausted us all. It has ruined what ever disposition I had, taken all John's time after his working hours and most of Steve's after-office time too. I think if it can just be settled perhaps I will begin to get well. . . . I hope Steve can settle it all by a trip North. Of course, I should go with him as there will be papers to be signed but I would as soon stick my head in a lion's mouth as leave this house. You haven't any idea how *peculiarly* people can act around a new celebrity. Really, we've been living behind a barricade for weeks. . . . I wasn't cut out to be a celebrity.

Then, for the first time, she expressed her puzzlement at the mass appeal of *Gone With the Wind*.

> Herschel, sometimes, when I have a minute I ponder soberly upon this book. And I cannot make head or tails of the whole matter. . . . I can not figure what makes the thing sell so enormously. . . . Here in Atlanta, the fifth and sixth grade students are reading it — obstetrical details and all. . . . The old people, God bless them. . . . The bench and bar like it, judges. . . . The medical profession — most of my letters and phone calls from men are from doctors. Psychiatrists especially like it. File clerks, elevator operators, sales girls in department stores, telephone operators, stenographers, garage mechanics, clerks in Helpsy-Selfy stores, school teachers — oh, Heavens, I could go on and on! — like it. What is more puzzling, they buy copies. The U.D.C.s [United Daughters of the Confederacy] have endorsed it, the Sons of Confederate Veterans crashed through with a grand endorsement too. Debutantes and dowagers read it. Catholic nuns like it.

Now how to explain all of this. . . . Despite its length and many details it is basically just a simple yarn of fairly simple people. There's no fine writing, there are no grandiose thoughts, there are no hidden meanings, no symbolism, nothing sensational — nothing, nothing at all that have made other best sellers best sellers. Then how to explain its appeal from the five year old to the ninety five year old? I can't figure it out.

In retrospect, of course, the mass appeal of *Gone With the Wind* is not too difficult to analyze. It contains something for everyone.

A lurking sensuality pervades the book from the moment Rhett Butler appears on page ninety-nine, representing the ultimate in masculine appeal. But the author teases the reader by having Scarlett always ready to give herself to the paler Ashley Wilkes, while Rhett's powerful presence is constantly felt. Not until twenty-five pages from the end, and after 1,015 pages of Scarlett's pursuit of the chaste Mr. Wilkes, does she discover what the reader has known all along — that Rhett is the man she loves and passionately needs. For Scarlett to lose Rhett at this point is a stroke of story-telling genius. What romantic could resist such a tantalizing story? And no wonder readers of the book clamored for a sequel and deluged the author with letters begging her to reveal whether Rhett and Scarlett ever reunited.

For the children, there was a story of adventure and war told from a point of view — the women and children left at home — that could have been theirs had they lived in those times. Old people were dealt with in the story with great reverence and, in 1936, there were still many old folks who recalled with great nostalgia childhoods spent in wartime both in the North and in the South, and the hard times that followed. The book contained enough medical data to interest doctors, and there was history told first-hand for all the history buffs. The South and Southerners were meticulously drawn for die-hard Confederates. Scarlett's independent spirit was attractive to modern women, Eleanor Roosevelt among them. Melanie's exemplary goodness was often spoken of from the pulpit (permission granted by Stephens). Scarlett's rejections of Rhett's sexual advances after they were married were understood by many a dissatisfied wife, and Rhett's final departure was cheered by their husbands.

Theories explaining the cause of the book's success were always being discussed in the press. The most often repeated conjecture was first proposed in a book by Dr. Henry Link in 1938, and was condensed in the *Reader's Digest* the following year. Dr. Link attributed the book's popularity to the fact that Scarlett, though in many ways not an admirable person, was a woman who remained the master of her world rather than its victim, and who exemplified personal triumph over social upheaval. Scarlett, he claimed, experienced "more tragedies than most people ever dream," but she "rushed to meet disaster and emerged with courage unimpaired." The book's million-plus readers, he asserted, were "victims of a machine concept of social security, a people still faintly protesting the loss of personal responsibility and power." Peggy pondered this possibility for four years and then wrote to Dr. Link in 1941 that she still wasn't sure his theory was correct.

Whatever the reason, one year after publication, *Gone With the Wind* remained the top-selling book in America and it did not look as though sales would wane in the near future. That is not to say that the book did not have its detractors. "Left Wingers," as Peggy called the liberals, derided the novel for its condescending portrait of blacks, the glorification of plantation life, and its lack of a political and social point of view. However, the literary reporter for the Communist paper the *Daily Worker* had to quit his job after giving the book a favorable review. English reviewers endorsed the book heartily, although some of them said the entire novel was an anachronism, as it took a 1920s or 1930s heroine and placed her in the 1800s. And Franklin D. Roosevelt commented that "no book need be that long."

Peggy had made certain that her contract with Selznick guaranteed that she would have nothing to do with casting or publicity, nor would she act as a technical advisor or as a script consultant, although the latter were usual requests by a film company when buying rights to a historical novel in which the author had demonstrated special expertise. Selznick had offered $25,000 to come to Hollywood, but Peggy's fear of Southern censure should the film be unfaithful to the book despite her efforts, overrode her usually acquisitive nature. She simply did not want to be held responsible for the film company's mistakes, which she was certain were inevitable. Since the Selznick company had refused to grant her final script approval, Peggy wanted to make sure that "Hollywood's historical inaccuracies" could in no way be attributed to her. But as soon as *Gone With the Wind* had been sold to the movies, it was impossible for her to remain completely detached. "Life has been awful!" she wrote Kay Brown. "I am deluged with letters demanding that I do not put Clark Gable in as Rhett. Strangers telephone me or grab me on the street, insisting that Katharine Hepburn will never do. It does me no good to point out sarcastically that it is Mr. Selznick and not I who is producing this picture."

Selznick took Peggy at her word that she did not want to be involved in the casting of *Gone With the Wind*, yet the end of the year found her writing to Kay Brown to ask for information, pleased that a search in the South might be initiated to find an unknown to play Scarlett O'Hara, and pleased also that George Cukor was being signed to direct the film and Sidney Howard to write the screenplay. Both of them were planning to come to Atlanta to begin the talent search. Inconsistency now crept into Peggy's relationship with the Selznick company. On November 18, 1936, she wrote Kay Brown:

> I think the whole idea of scouting through the South is a swell one for if you don't find anyone who will do it, it will still be worth a million dollars in publicity. . . . Count on me for any help you need.
>
> I don't think you know anything of my back ground so I must explain . . . I worked here on the Atlanta Journal. . . . My husband has worked on the Journal and the Georgian. . . . Most of my friends are on these papers and they have been kinder than anyone can imagine to me since the book came out. I have found myself . . . the best little bit of copy in town . . . [and] they all look to me for news breaks on everything connected with my business or the book or movie. . . .
>
> So I'd like, if possible, to give them a break on your trip south.

. . . The very idea that a movie company thinks enough of a story to send a talent scout and a director and an adaptor down here will go over big. And moreover, it makes people who've always refused to go to any movie about the south think very kindly of Mr. Selznick and makes them feel that he honest to God wants to do a real southern picture with real southern color. Oh, yes, it will be a big story. I know your outfit isn't averse to publicity and publicity will be a great help to you in your search for new faces. . . .

So — could you wire me when you are coming, where you are staying, whether you are willing for me to break the story of your trip immediately and if Atlanta is your first stop on the way South? . . . I hope you'll let me give you a brawl of sorts — probably a cocktail party to meet the press.

This letter was understandably interpreted by Miss Brown to mean Peggy would cooperate with them on this trip and that she was endorsing it. Russell Birdwell, Selznick's publicity manager, when informed of this, instantly wired Peggy a story his office was planning to release that stated she was hosting a cocktail party for the Selznick group. Peggy was now fearful that she would be dragged into the group's activity and be blamed for any chaos their arrival might cause in Atlanta. The word "cocktail" also alarmed the Mitchells, who did not want Peggy involved in a public affair where liquor was being consumed because that might open the way to attacks on her character. This was Stephens and the Marshes' first overt act in creating the image of Margaret Mitchell that would persist for years — that of a teetotaling Southern lady of genteel breeding and nineteenth-century manners.

Within hours of her telegram from Birdwell, Peggy wired him back:

WHEN MISS BROWN AND OTHERS COME TO ATLANTA I WILL FEED THEM FRIED CHICKEN, SHOW THEM STONE MOUNTAIN AND INTRODUCE THEM TO ANYBODY THEY WANT TO MEET BUT ALL PARTS OF FILM JOB ARE ON THEIR HANDS AND NOT ON MINE STOP AM RELEASING STORY TO ATLANTA AFTERNOON PAPERS TODAY AFTER DELETING REFERENCES TO ME. . . . PLEASE MAKE THE SAME CORRECTIONS IN ANY RELEASES YOU GIVE OUT STOP ON THIS AND ANY FUTURE STORIES I WANT NO REFERENCES MADE TO ME EXCEPT AS AUTHOR OF THE BOOK.

Birdwell issued the release pretty much as he had written it, altering it only to the effect that the party was to be a "tea," but retaining the original implication that it was in honor of the Selznick people. Peggy's temper flared. "If your story goes out making it appear that I am giving the tea for the Selznick representatives, I will have to recall my invitations and hold no tea. I am giving this party for my friends in the press who have been so kind to me and for my book. And it's *their* party and in *their* honor. I thought it would be very nice if Mr. Cukor and Mr. Howard and Miss Brown were here to attend it so that they could meet people who might be of assistance to them. But my invitation to them to attend the tea is purely a *social* courtesy."

This last was a final blow to Sidney Howard's ego. He had been working on the screenplay for nearly three months and had written Peggy that he might have to ask her help in the writing of additional dialogue for the "colored folks."

Peggy hastened to write him that she had "no intentions of doing anything about additional dialogue or even looking at the script. . . . Not for worlds or for money would I put myself in the position where if there was something [Southerners] didn't like in the picture they could say 'Well, you worked on the script. Why did you let this, that and the other get by?' I would never live it down and I could never explain that I really had nothing to do with the script. It won't matter to them if there is something in the movie they don't like that you may be responsible for. You didn't write the book and you do not live here in Atlanta and if they do not like something then you will be excused."

In effect, Peggy was saying she *expected* Howard's screenplay to contain inaccuracies. There is a large degree of petulance in her attitude toward the script of *Gone With the Wind*. She was certain that without her final approval it could not be accurate, and she was still a bit miffed that Selznick had not given in to her on this point. Her retaliation was an adamant refusal to have anything at all to do with the script.

Neither Cukor nor Howard made the trip to Atlanta at this time, but on December 2, Kay Brown and two other Selznick employees arrived in town. Madness ensued. There had been a notice in the paper that auditions for the four major roles only

— Scarlett, Rhett, Melanie, and Ashley — would be held in the ballroom of the Biltmore hotel, although it was added that candidates for Aunt Pittypat or the Tarleton twins would be welcomed. Hundreds of aspirants for all the roles turned up. Many of them had traveled by any means available to get there and were not Southern at all. There were to be numerous fictional plays, films, books, and magazine stories about the search for Scarlett O'Hara, which was to last for nearly two years. The real search was no less peopled by promoters, con men, and pimps, and many a young woman's hopes were smashed and her life ruined in her attempt at the role.

Almost as much avidity was displayed in the crush for the smaller roles. It was as though there was a mass clairvoyance that foretold success to anyone cast in the film. Even before the talent search was initiated, Peggy had felt under attack. Once it began, it became as bad, she said, "as being in the path of Sherman's cavalry and waving a Confederate flag." She could not walk down a street or go shopping or eat in a restaurant, for hopefuls pounced upon her the moment she appeared in public. One day, a mother with her small girl done up as a prospective Bonnie, in tight curls and wearing a riding habit, appeared at Peggy's hairdresser's and pulled the dryer from Peggy's head so that the child's recitation of a Confederate poem could be heard. Another time, a woman with a young boy suddenly rose up from the back seat of the car as John was driving Peggy to the dentist. The woman demanded that Peggy audition the youth for the role of Wade Hampton, Scarlett's son, on the spot. It turned out that the woman was not the boy's mother, but an "enterprising" talent agent.

Even Eleanor Roosevelt, as her husband waited to be inaugurated for his second term, caught the *Gone With the Wind* casting bug. In August, 1936, Mrs. Roosevelt had written in her syndicated column, "My Day," "I can assure you that you will find Scarlett O'Hara an interesting character." In December, Mrs. Roosevelt wrote Selznick requesting that her maid, Lizzy McDuffy, be tested for the role of Mammy. Miss McDuffy did make a test but was not cast in the film. On her way back from Hollywood to Washington, she stopped in Atlanta and visited with Peggy for an hour or so.

It was toward the end of 1936, when she was feeling particularly beleaguered, that Peggy let it be known that she would no longer sign autographs or books. The result was that people went to the most remarkable lengths to get her autograph. As she explained to Lois:

John turns them down by scores every day, poor Father's life has been made a misery by the people who sit in his office and take up his time telling him that he should force me, by parental authority, to sign their book. Steve and Carrie Lou and all of my relatives lead hunted lives because perfect strangers descend upon them, leaving copies with them and instructions that they *make* me sign them. When I make a business appointment with someone they usually turn up staggering under a dozen copies which their friends have wished upon them — and oh, my God the pressure that's brought to bear by charitable organizations wanting an autographed copy for raffling purposes!

At a tea given for the library, the only large social affair that she had attended in months, other than the tea she herself had given for the press, her sash was torn off, her veil "yanked" from her hat, punch and refreshments "knocked" from her hands, and she was poked at with sharp fingernails by "ladies from Iowa, Oklahoma, and Seattle."

The incessant ringing of the telephone did not stop, but Peggy avoided most callers. She wrote to Granberry, "Bessie answers gently in that cooing voice of hers, 'No Mam, I can't tell you whether or not Miss Scarlett got the Cap'n back or not. No Mam, Miss Peggy she don't know either. Yes, Mam, I've heard her say a hundred times she didn't have no idea than the next 'bout what happened to Miss Scarlett after she went home to Tara!' "

For the length of one unusually frenetic day, the Marshes discussed the possibility of Peggy going to Europe for a few months and inviting Augusta to go along with her. But she did not want to leave John for that long a time. As a compromise, John agreed to take a three-week vacation with her to return to Winter Park and visit the Granberrys over Christmas and New Year's. They departed on December 17, 1936, with Peggy at the wheel of the car. The Granberrys had been warned not to tell anyone they were coming.

Peggy was exhausted but, as they headed onto the highway, she felt somehow free for the first time in over a year. They were alone. There was no telephone, no doorbell. They were using the alias "Munnerlyn" and were stopping along the way at places where they felt they would not be recognized. John looked thin and worn and Peggy noticed a slight tremor in his hands. The year had been difficult for him, too. And now he had the foreign rights to deal with along with all her other problems and his own work. Seldom did he turn off the light in his small office room until 2:00 A.M.

It would not have been possible for either of them to have anticipated the events of the past year or to have prepared for them. There had been good things, of course. Now they would never have to worry about being in debt again. Two days earlier Peggy had received the one-millionth copy of the book. The praise upon the publication of the novel in England in October had been as overwhelming as on its American debut. Danish reviews had just come in establishing its critical success in that country. *Gone With the Wind* looked as if it would bring her international, as well as national, acclaim. And on Thanksgiving, she had received word that the novel had been nominated for a Pulitzer Prize.

Margaret Mitchell should have been the happiest woman in America. Why, then, wasn't she? Drastic changes had taken place in Peggy's life and she was incapable of accepting them; nor was it possible to return to her former obscurity. She had not gone "high hat" and it was doubtful that she ever would, but an intractable hostility had replaced her former good nature. She was rich and famous; she could have realized almost any dream — a trip around the world, a palatial home, jewels, expensive cars — but she wanted none of them. What she wished for was a return to the way things had been and that wish could never be granted. So, she became defensive and decided that it was Margaret Mitchell against the world. Ironically, her background and training had prepared her for adversity, but not for fame and wealth, and she became almost obsessive about retaining her privacy and a semblance of ordinary life.

While the Selznick film negotiations were going on, Peggy

had received a letter from Ginny telling her she had been approached through Annie Laurie Williams — certainly not a name to warm Peggy's heart — to do a "Mitchell story" for *Photoplay*. Ginny had seized on the idea, for she badly needed the money to take her daughter, who suffered from respiratory problems, to a milder climate. Explaining her reasons for considering the offer, Ginny assured Peggy the article would be entirely innocuous and would deal with their college days at Smith in a casual manner, which she did not think Peggy would mind.

The two women had seen each other two months earlier, when Ginny had stopped in Atlanta for a couple of days on her way back from a trip to Florida. Peggy had played "guide" (later, Ginny was to describe the Mitchell house on Peachtree Street as "Tara on streetcar tracks") and had invited her old friend for dinner, and Ginny felt their friendship had been reestablished.

To her surprise, Ginny received a furious reply in which Peggy claimed that such an article would stir up the movie-mad public and make her life hell again. Peggy stressed the fact that many Atlantans *could* have written "I-knew-her-when" stories and had not, and she said she would not comply with Ginny's request for an interview (which, in fact, Ginny had not requested), offering instead, to loan Ginny the eight hundred dollars she would have been paid for the story. Ginny indignantly rejected this "embarrassing compromise," and wrote:

The only thing about the whole business that disturbs me is the distraught undertones of your letter. It's indeed a shame, Peggy, that you can't enjoy the terrific success of your book. Such a windfall is probably what everybody in the world dreams about. Wouldn't it be feasible to just get on a boat and go places where people didn't know you for a little while at least?

The night I got your letter I went to hear Thomas Mann give his only lecture in English. He talked about Goethe (the subject of his next novel) and I got a great kick out of it when he went quite thoroughly into the heavy and annoying fame that went with Goethe's first terrific popularity. . . . people used to get so excited at seeing him walk thru the streets that they'd faint at his feet . . . so, kid, as long as you haven't yet started to step over prone bodies, you've something to be thankful for!

Incidentally, I think a little of my sympathy still clings to the dopes who like to know something about The Personality Behind The Book — as I discovered I wasn't nearly as interested in what Mann was saying about Goethe as I was in the fact that Mann's collar was too big for him and that he had that indescribable moth-ball aura about him that was characteristic of the professor who used to teach me French when I was a kid.

If you don't mind a word or two of wisdom, the tabloid mob which is getting all steamed up about Rhett and Scarlett in the movies is for all the world like a big harmless mutt of a dog who never thinks of snarling at you until you look scared and run away. So sometimes the simplest way out is to "give" a little to the fans. I've always been convinced that Lindbergh would lead a much more peaceful life if he mingled a little and got it over with.

Ginny had been dealing with the foibles of fame in her capacity as a publicity woman for United Artists for nearly fifteen years, and she felt herself qualified to explain to Peggy that life did not have to be as Peggy had made it for herself, that she had to understand "the dime-store minds" that had plagued her and realize that a great percentage of the fans who followed movie stars and films formed part of her own reading audience, and that if she tried to understand them, she would not feel so angry at them nor so in need of fortification. "Why don't you change over to an unlisted number?" Ginny sensibly suggested.

And if you can't get away on a boat trip because of John's job, how about moving off the bus route? You've told me your present apartment is too small anyway. Mary Pickford's correspondence is appalling. And the amazing part of it is that it has been for over 25 years without a let-up. She has the most marvelous [staff] and all this correspondence is handled with grace and tact without making Miss Pickford a martyr. Couldn't you find some capable people to do a job like this for you? . . .

You could also hire a service that handles such things and have Macmillan send your incoming letters directly to them — or an agent. Why don't you have an agent? They would be able to place a protective wall around you. All publicity calls would then go to them and only the people you wanted to have contact you referred. Can't your father's office handle all your legal matters without you having to be so *rattled* by them?

Peggy did not take well to this "chemical analysis" of her fame, but within a month the small dispute between the two women seemed to have been forgotten and when Stephens had to go up to New York, Peggy asked Ginny to please see him privately if she could, to help advise him on the ways of films and film people before he had to go into a meeting with the Selznick representatives. Ginny obliged and Stephens came back extolling her help and intelligence.

The truth was, Peggy Mitchell simply did not know how to rise to the occasion of her fame, and she feared it might somehow destroy her marriage. But John Marsh enjoyed his position as the husband of America's best-selling novelist. He was proud of Peggy's accomplishment and her fame, which reflected upon him. Later, when the momentum was finally to slow down, he was even responsible for fanning the flame. It was Peggy who thought it important that he keep his job at Georgia Power and that they live on his salary, remain in an apartment *he* could afford, not take on the responsibility of live-in help (which would require a larger home), and that they live exactly as they had before the publication of *Gone With the Wind*. Less than six months from the time of the book's appearance, it was obvious this would be impossible.

She had been right; the world looks at new celebrities in a peculiar way. No one in Atlanta would ever treat her in the same manner as they had treated Peggy Mitchell Marsh. The fame that had been thrust upon her was sudden, demanding, unwanted, cruel sometimes, always a burden, but there it was — her load, and there was no magical way in which it would simply disappear.

Since her marriage to John Marsh and her retirement from the *Journal*, Peggy had placed great emphasis on what Atlantans thought of her. Maybelle's daughter, for all her sassy tongue and feisty nature and her former delight in shocking people, believed deep down that her role in life should be subordinate to her husband's, and that the world she respected would not respect her if she was married to a man whose career was not as important as hers. One would have thought that her fame would have established her self-confidence. Instead, it threatened to rob her of the one thing she thought really mattered — the security she felt in her marriage to John Marsh.

Chapter Twenty

JOHN "MUNNERLYN" and his short, unfashionably dressed wife checked into Winter Park's one small but pleasant hotel a few days before Christmas, 1936. The sun was shining so brightly that Peggy felt dazed when she stepped into the semidarkness of the modest lobby. The first thing she saw when she was able to focus her eyes was a Christmas tree decorated with artificial snow. For some reason, this sent her into a burst of giggles, and she and John were in high spirits as they unpacked. A short time later they arrived at Mabel and Edwin Granberry's bungalow. For the next three days, they spent their time picking oranges, reading to the Granberrys' youngest son, Edwin Jr., and talking about *Gone With the Wind* and a novel that Edwin Granberry was proposing to write.

Peggy was relaxed and happy for the first time in many months. She felt comfortable with the Granberrys, who treated her with a mixture of admiration and protectiveness. Conversation was lively. Granberry, like Lee Edwards, Augusta's husband, shared her love for a good story and laughed easily at her humor. Mabel was a good cook and hostess and never showed any resentment at being "on duty" most of the time during the Marshes' visit.

It was during this trip that Granberry approached Peggy about the possibility of his doing an article about her for *Collier's*. Since Ginny's aborted request, there had been stories in several national magazines and, just before leaving Atlanta, she had given Faith Baldwin an interview for the March issue of *Pictorial Review*. But the Baldwin interview had not contained much more than the items generally known. Granberry was suggesting something more in-depth and promised that, if she agreed, the Marshes would have a part in the writing of it as well as final approval. In Ginny's case, Peggy had been fearful that facts would have been reported that she did not want known — her true age, her poor grades at Smith, Clifford Henry and his death, and who knew what else — for Ginny had been her closest confidante at Smith. But Granberry could only write what Peggy revealed to him. It seemed a perfect opportunity for the Marshes to get certain things into print that would refute all the false rumors and that would present Peggy to her reading public as she wanted to be perceived. They agreed to the plan after extracting a vow from Granberry that *no one*, not even *Collier's*, would ever be told they had had any hand whatsoever in the piece except to approve it. Granberry enthusiastically concurred. For a year he had been submitting pieces to Kenneth Littauer at *Collier's* and they had all been turned down. Littauer had intimated that if Granberry could get Margaret Mitchell to agree to an article by him, he would gladly publish it. Littauer could well have had an ulterior motive, for he badly wanted Peggy to write a short story for *Collier's* and he knew that the Marshes and the Granberrys had become good friends.

The Marshes discussed the material Granberry's article should include and John promised that as soon as the first draft was ready, he and Peggy would make their revisions and suggestions. Peggy was feeling so well when they parted that night that she agreed to a small, impromptu party the next evening, Christmas Eve, with some Rollins faculty members as long as it was "very hush-hush." She also took Edwin aside and explained to him that John might suffer a small seizure (he had had one en route to Florida), and that if Edwin saw her lean over John, pressing a spoon between his lips, he was to try to distract the rest of the guests. To Granberry's relief, the party went smoothly and both of the Marshes enjoyed themselves.

The next morning, an item appeared in the local paper revealing that the author of *Gone With the Wind* was visiting their town over the holidays as a guest of Professor and Mrs. Edwin Granberry. Alarmed that newspapermen from all over would deluge them shortly, Peggy packed their bags while John telephoned Granberry to announce their departure. Because it was Christmas Day, Peggy was confident that they had a day's jump on the press. Edwin, terribly upset, came over to the hotel to say good-bye and to make sure the Marshes did not hold him responsible. (Peggy wrote Herschel Brickell, "With the best intentions in the world, Edwin let the cat out of the bag and we had to pack up early Christmas morning and get out of town, one jump ahead of the newspapers and dinner invitations!") They spent the rest of their vacation in small hotels in small towns and had, she said, "a wonderful time."

As soon as they returned home, John was operated on for hemorrhoids, a condition that embarrassed John and Peggy, for, in mentioning the operation to Brickell, Granberry, and even Lois Cole, Peggy did not explain what was wrong, a fact that led to some fear and speculation that his condition might be more serious than it was.

The seven days that John was in the hospital proved to be a test for Peggy, but, though she spent much of her time with him, their whereabouts and his hospitalization were successfully kept from the press, and even from friends. No visitors ever came. The nurse who was drawn in as a confederate to maintain the secrecy later described Peggy as "not outgoing, but positive in her viewpoint . . . almost mannish in appearance — short hair, thick coke-bottle glasses, blue eyes, and her shoes — (I remember them well) heavy, low-heeled orthopedics." It was the first time that Peggy had worn glasses in public, although she had gotten them when her eye problems began. As the lenses were a strong prescription, it must have been difficult for her to see well without them.

The nurse, Mrs. Gaydos, recalls that also in the hospital at this time, "there was a retired nun who was quite old. She was a cousin [of Peggy's] — second or third — named Sister Melanie. Mrs. Marsh would stop in to see her. She told me that was where the name 'Melanie' came from."

Granberry sent the first draft of his article to the Marshes while John was recuperating. Not able to sit at the typewriter yet, John responded in longhand with a twenty-six page critique, carefully noting the page and line of each of his corrections and inserts. Peggy added only one page of her own comments. The combined document is most revealing.

Peggy corrected Granberry only in the telling of a certain experience she had had. In one of her "escapes" from her fans during the first weeks of her fame, she had driven out to Jonesboro and had stopped at five different gas stations, asking each attendant if he knew where Tara was. All of the men had given her directions, which, of course, could not be true because there was no Tara. When she told the last man who she was, he did not believe her. Struggling to find some proof, she had finally taken a Confederate map out of her glove compartment, which had convinced him that she was the author of *Gone With the Wind*. Peggy had Granberry cut all descriptions of the filling-station attendants that made them appear gruff, money-hungry, or stupid, and asked him to say at the end of the story that Tara was entirely fictional and that no such house existed.

John, on the other hand, insisted on excising the word "sober" because "the word is too easily associated with drinking." John also wanted to include direct denials of all the most recent rumors — that Peggy was blind, that she had left her husband and her two children, that John had written her book — and he wanted the denials to appear at both the beginning of the piece and again in the text, so that the readers would remember the denial and not just the rumor. Peggy should not be described as "unknown to the public" before the publication of *Gone With the Wind* — that should read "unknown outside of the state of Georgia." She was not a "*very* young woman," he wrote. "She would like to have the word 'very' eliminated." And he asked Granberry to please not "involve *me* in any scheme [during the writing of *Gone With the Wind*] to throw the manuscript away. I would have given her a good cow-hiding. (Please don't mention that in your article.)"

But the important thing is that John not only corrected grammar, caught errors, demanded deletions, and replaced Granberry's observations of the Marshes with his own, but that, with a simple "here goes with a suggestion for a substitute paragraph," he ended up writing long sections that appear to have been published verbatim from his penciled notes. One of his inserts is a 1,200-word preachment on the tortures Peggy had endured since the publication of her book. Yet, in the context of this narrative, he illogically reveals, "There is no secret about Miss Mitchell's address. Her telephone is listed. It is but part of her determination to continue to live her life as she has always lived it."

Numerous other passages in the article were initiated by John, all of them stressing Peggy's need for privacy and rest. Why, then, did he allow a magazine with one of the largest circulations in the country to print the information about how she could be easily reached, and, further, that she gave no more autographs but was personally answering and signing replies to all the letters she received? And to reveal the intimate confessions contained in some of those fan letters, as he did do, could only work to encourage more confessional letters from Peggy's reading audience and increase the load of her correspondence.

Of these letters, Marsh says the majority were

of a kind that could not be answered with stereotyped politeness.
. . . Many of them, written under the fervency of emotion
aroused by the novel, have the note of the confessional about
them. Miss Mitchell might perhaps ignore them . . . but having
unwittingly been the cause of the desperate tone of some of
them, she feels an obligation she cannot evade.
Wives write that the tragedy of Rhett and Scarlett has opened
their eyes to similar tragedies under their own roofs and has
moved them to correct estrangements from their husbands before it is too late. Husbands write that Rhett's separation from
Scarlett after he had loved her so many years had kept them
awake at night, fearful that they might also lose beloved wives.

The categories of unhappy, possibly disturbed, readers who found salvation in the pages of *Gone With the Wind* goes on to include "men broken by depression," "idealists who could not survive change," and "proud wives whose men have been thrown out of work." As soon as the article appeared, Peggy was deluged with more calls and letters than she had conceived possible. Whatever John had been attempting to accomplish through the *Collier's* article, it had boomeranged. Kenneth Littauer was later to say that he had assumed that, since Marsh was an advertising and public-relations man, the article had been intended by the Marshes for publicity purposes.

When Littauer received Granberry's piece, he was not happy. He had hoped for a more personal story, one that would reveal some of Margaret Mitchell's public and private opinions and that would give an inside picture of her life before, during, and after the writing of *Gone With the Wind*. But, if the piece was to appear in the March issue as planned, in order to compete with Faith Baldwin's *Pictorial Review* interview, due to hit the stands during the same month, there would be no time for a rewrite. The magazine was already half set in galleys, and Granberry had warned him that the Marshes (whom Littauer had heard were extremely tough with magazine and news writers) would never allow any alterations or changes. It was obvious to the *Collier's* editor that it was either the article as it was or no article at all; anyway, as he observed to Granberry, "the subject matter was self-promoting and would get itself read no matter what we did short of printing it in Chinese." Littauer agreed to print the story as it stood, hoping that in return Peggy Mitchell might oblige him one day with that short piece of fiction in demand by every other magazine.

John had not exaggerated about the emotional letters that Peggy received every day, and he was telling the truth when he said she answered them all. Although the reason she replied personally to such an enormous number of letters might have been, as he said, her sense of responsibility for the book having stirred its readers' emotions, it is more likely that there were other motivations — some of which she may not have understood herself. The letters — which were much like those Medora had received as Marie Rose, the magazine's "Advice-to-the-Lovelorn" editor — may well have stirred Peggy's old desire to be a psychiatrist. Perhaps they also brought her a gratifying feeling of power, and the act of writing them belonged to her as nothing else did anymore. Most important though, the letters kept her from writing anything else. She wrote them in much the same way that she had once written her book. Thoughts poured out of her and onto the page — long, detailed, and sometimes quite intimate. Often she shared her own problems with her correspondents. Although she said she hated making carbon copies, she always typed these letters in duplicate. To see the files containing these copies is an eye-opening experience and visual proof of why Peggy didn't have time to write another book, at least during this phase of her life. During the first four years following the publication of *Gone With the Wind*, the author wrote nearly twenty thousand letters with Margaret Baugh's help, all quite lengthy — an average output of about a hundred letters a week.

In February, to the Marshes' distress, it was rumored that they were getting a divorce. "If this is *true*," she responded, "I can't imagine who the gentleman in the pajamas is. He sleeps in my bed and calls himself John Marsh, but I am beginning to wonder!"

Every time a rumor came back to Peggy — she had a wooden leg, she had taken a room at the Piedmont Hotel and had been drunk for weeks, she was to play Melanie — she agonized over it. The Marshes' lives were further complicated by a spate of lawsuits. Susan Lawrence Davis, author of *An Authentic History of the Ku Klux Klan, 1865–1877*, charged in a 6.5-billion-dollar suit that *Gone With the Wind* plagiarized her work. Despite Miss Davis's 261-page brief, in which she accused Peggy of using the same "historical facts" that she had, her case was not only insubstantial, but ludicrous. Nonetheless, the action had to be answered. (It was later dismissed.) Peggy wrote Lois:

> To tell the truth, I was relieved when the letter announcing her claim arrived. I had been waiting for months for the first racketeer to open fire. It had been a marvel to us all that some chiselers hadn't opened up on me sooner. We didn't know what form it would take, extortion, attempted blackmail, suits of every kind. . . . We were glad that the opening gun was a pop gun. It might have been one of those bad affairs where some one alleges that you've run over them and permanently injured them on a day when you weren't even in your car.

The next suit was initiated by Peggy. Theatrical entrepreneur Billy Rose had included a satire of *Gone With the Wind* in his spectacular Aquacade, and Peggy sued him for violating her copyright. The case had not yet been settled when a pirated Dutch edition of *Gone With the Wind* appeared in the Netherlands. Stephens appealed to Macmillan's New York law firm for assistance on this case, and a suit was initiated to establish Peggy's right of copyright all over the world. This last legal action was to strain the Marshes' relations with Macmillan even further and was to remain unsettled for a number of years.

Authorized translations were now either underway or had already been published in sixteen foreign countries besides Canada and England: Chile, Denmark, Finland, France, Germany, Holland, Hungary, Japan, Latvia, Norway, Poland, Sweden, Romania, Italy, Brazil, and Czechoslovakia. In Germany and Japan, sales had reached nearly two hundred thousand copies. The correspondence that foreign rights entailed kept the Marshes' hands full, and a secretary was hired to work evenings from six to ten. While John dealt with foreign rights, Peggy wrote as many letters as her eyes and the hour allowed.

With unusual vehemence, Peggy refused a request from Lois that she allow Macmillan to publish one printing with her rubber-stamped facsimile autograph. "I feel pretty violently about autographs and always have," she wrote. "When a stranger asks me for an autograph I feel just like he (or she) had asked me for a pair of my step-ins. . . . If I could buy back every autographed [copy] and destroy it, I would."

Not long before this, Peggy had learned that people had been selling her autographed books at a profit, and this had incensed her. In many cases, signing the books had been a chore, and she had paid for the postage out of her own pocket. The retail price of the book was three dollars; autographed editions were selling for twenty dollars the spring of 1937. Including the books whose endpapers she had signed for Macmillan, there were about thirty-five hundred copies inscribed "Margaret Mitchell." She seldom wrote more than her name unless she knew the owner of the book.

Despite the continuing pressures and problems, Peggy had regained some of the weight she had lost, and John wrote to Frances, "She looks prettier and is much pleasanter to live with. The battle still rages, but she is learning some of the ways and means for combating it." Peggy was now allowing herself a nap in the afternoon, and she had acquired a new, secret office.

Upon their return from Florida in January, the Marshes had rented a room for $32.50 a month in the Northwood Hotel, next door, for Peggy to use as an office. Margaret Baugh was hired on a permanent basis and the lease was made out in her name. Elaborate precautions were taken to maintain the privacy of the office, and the owners and occupants of the residential Northwood Hotel were sworn to secrecy. Peggy would slip out of her apartment after Bessie had reconnoitered and had sounded the "all clear," then the two women would bolt to her retreat. A couch was installed there, but not a telephone. If an important call came in, Bessie would make her way back and forth through the subterranean bowels of one building to the other, often having to interrupt Peggy's badly needed afternoon nap.

Peggy still relished a good earthy anecdote and had a fund of "indelicate" jokes that she delighted in telling whenever she got a chance to visit with Lee Edwards or other old friends. She was proud of her collections of pornographic French postcards and literature with bawdy passages, and liked to share these with friends she knew well. But she could no longer attend those parties she called "brawls," and she missed the chances they gave her to be herself — to use her peppery tongue and indulge her taste for "corn likker." She liked to drink, particularly with good friends, and she liked "drunken brawls" — meaning such gatherings as the Georgia Press Association bashes, where quite a bit of alcohol was consumed. Peggy had always felt that she had "a good head for likker," but now she was inhibited about attending affairs where it was served. Out-of-state reporters (she always trusted the Georgia press) were bound to get wind of her harmless good times and the next thing she would find was that she was being written about as an alcoholic. In fact, it seems probable that Peggy did have a drinking problem, though she refused to admit it and never seemed to allow it to control her life.

Peggy was inordinately fond of slapstick movies, and they became her one uncomplicated means of entertainment. There was a movie theatre within walking distance of the apartment, and she and John were friendly with the manager, who was always protective of Peggy when she called to say she was coming. She saw three or four films a week and loved "those movies where people get hit with pies and fish get put down your neck." She was crazy about the Marx Brothers, never missed a Buster Keaton film, and, as Medora recalled, at a Three Stooges comedy "you could always locate Peggy by her big haw-haw."

Although Peggy had insisted she have no hand in the casting of *Gone With the Wind*, she made a point of seeing the latest movie of any likely candidate for the roles of Scarlett and Rhett. To Kay Brown she confessed, "I've even refused as much as five hundred dollars to name the cast I'd like because I thought it might embarrass y'all." She kept out of the movie production, but she did suggest to Lois that "the Selznick folk" take her friend Susan Myrick, a reporter on the *Macon Telegraph*, "out to the coast in some capacity while the picture is being made . . . to pass on the authenticity and rightness of this and that, the accents of the white actors, the dialect of the colored ones, the minor matters of dress and deportment, the small touches of local color, etc." Susan Myrick was hired and worked for Selznick throughout the making of *Gone With the Wind*.

George Cukor; his assistant, John Darrow; and the set designer, Hobart Erwin arrived in Atlanta the first week in April. Peggy threatened to throw herself "on the mercies of the Atlanta newspapers and ask them to run appeals to the public not to devil me but to devil Mr. Cukor." In the end, she enjoyed the "Selznickers' " visit more than she had anticipated. She wrote to Herschel Brickell that she had driven Mr. Cukor and his technical staff over all the red-rutted roads of Clayton County. The dogwood was just coming out and "the flowering crabs blooming like mad." Cukor wanted to see old houses that had been built prior to the Civil War and Peggy obliged, but she was sure the film people were disappointed not to see the white-columned mansions that seemed to be Hollywood's notion of the South. She begged them to "please leave Tara ugly, sprawling, and columnless." There were, of course, quite a few white-columned houses in Georgia, but Clayton County and Jonesboro had only a few, and Peggy had always thought of Tara as a working farm like the Fitzgerald place.

This second trip to Atlanta by the Selznick people, who had held auditions in Charleston en route, was even more frenetic than the first. Peggy remained sequestered in her secret office much of the time, leaving Bessie and John to deal with the scores of hopefuls who turned up at the Marshes' door. But Cukor was, indeed, "bedeviled" from the time he arrived until he boarded a train bound for New Orleans five days later. One Scarlett hopeful — a Dixie belle whom Peggy always referred to as "Honey Chile" — did not receive an audition with Cukor and was so furious that she bought a ticket for New Orleans, planning to corner Cukor on the train and make him listen to her read for the part. Unwisely, the girl telephoned Yolande Gwin at the *Atlanta Constitution* and announced her plan, whereupon Yolande took it upon herself to warn Cukor. A chase to rival any in a Keystone Kops comedy followed. Yolande got a note to Cukor, who posted his assistant, Darrow, at the door of his railway car. When the determined "Honey Chile" appeared, Darrow jumped down and grabbed the girl by the arm, pulling her away from the train, and promising her he would listen to her read.

"I don't want to see you. I have already seen you," Honey Chile shouted when she saw Darrow. "My God, *anybody* can see you! I must see Mr. Cukor!"

"He's already gone to New Orleans by motor," she was told.

But Honey Chile would not be discouraged, and when it looked as if she might storm the train, Darrow drew her toward the front of it, several cars up from Cukor, hoping his boss would have time to hide before she spotted him. Then, as the train began to move, Darrow made a running leap to board it — but only after it had picked up enough speed so that he was certain Honey Chile, in her high heels and slim skirt, could not follow. The indefatigable Honey Chile turned up later at the New York offices of the Selznick company and also at Peggy's Aunt Edyth's in Greenwich. She was never to have an audition with Cukor, but Peggy had been right — the search for Scarlett O'Hara was a front-page story across the nation, and it remained news until the film was finally cast.

Harold Latham arrived in Atlanta on the third of May, 1937, for a three-day visit, once again scouting manuscripts. There had been a driving rainstorm the night before and now a warm sun was drying the streets. Latham was extremely happy to be back in the city where he had first discovered Peggy Mitchell and her astounding book. Now, slightly less than a year after its publication, it remained the best-selling book in America, where, at Macmillan's most recent accounting, 1,370,000 copies had been sold. Latham suspected its critical and popular acclaim might be crowned by the winning of the Pulitzer Prize, to be awarded the next day. This possibility had influenced the timing of his arrival in Atlanta, but he had not told Peggy because, in all her letters, she had refused to believe that her book stood a chance for such an honor.

Latham planned to dine early at his hotel, then make a call at the Mitchell home to meet the ailing Eugene Mitchell, and then go to hear the Marshes' cook, Bessie, sing with her church choir. Latham was a devotee of Negro spirituals and was highly excited about being invited to attend a late-evening choir practice at Bessie's church. About eight-thirty that evening, Lamar Ball, the city editor of the *Atlanta Constitution*, and a staff photographer appeared at the Mitchell house on Peachtree Street. Ball announced that he had trailed Peggy "all over town for a statement."

"On what?" she asked.

"Why, Peggy, don't you know? The Associated Press has already put it on their wire service. You've been awarded the Pulitzer Prize."

Of course, there had been much speculation about her chances of winning. Brickell and Granberry had assured her that it would happen, and Kenneth Littauer had dryly commented, "Even a Pulitzer committee couldn't miss that one!" But now that it had occurred, Peggy kept thinking there was a mistake. In all the excitement, she had said yes when Ball asked if his photographer could take a picture, even though she had been refusing all such requests since the previous September. Peggy later said she didn't know what had impressed her more — winning the award or having the city editor leave his desk at the rush hour on her account. After the photographer had taken his shot, she realized that they were already late for the singing, but, she wrote Brickell afterwards, she "didn't dare intimate where [they] were going because old blood hound [Ball] would have accompanied us with great pleasure, shot forty pictures of us and the colored choir and written a hell of a story about where Miss Mitchell went to celebrate winning the Pulitzer Award."

The Marshes, Stephens, Carrie Lou, and Latham finally made their escape, but Peggy was uneasy all during the singing for fear that Ball was lurking somewhere in the back of the church. Bessie presided and the guests all rose from their bench seats and expressed their pleasure at being there. The congregation was pleased to have them, but, according to Peggy, they "didn't slop over. They just took it for granted that naturally Bessie's Madam and Bessie's Madam's publisher wanted to hear them sing and oh, how they sang! One old sister got to shouting and I thought Harold Latham would have a spasm he enjoyed it so much."

The fact that she had won the Pulitzer Prize did not seem real to Peggy even when she arrived home at 1:00 A.M. and found a telegram from the committee chairman, Frank D. Fackenthal at Columbia University, telling her the public announcement would be made the following morning, a Tuesday. Although forewarned, she was not prepared for the clamor at her door at 8:00 A.M. when Bessie arrived for work. Flashlights from cameras blazed their way into the living room and, Peggy said later, reporters were "slithering out of cracks in the floor." Peggy had always claimed that public speaking was not her strong point, but she drummed up her courage that day and, supported by John, Medora and Latham, went on the radio to express her gratitude for the award. She had had little opportunity to prepare an adequate statement and she said afterwards that she must have sounded "awfully dull" and swore it would be her last radio appearance.

By noon, Latham had managed to put together a party in her honor for that night. All day the telephone "rang off the wall." There were telegrams and flowers from all over the country, and the house was filled with family and friends. She went to the party — where "barrels of champagne" were served — decked out in big, gorgeous orchids, and feeling, she said, like a "Kentucky Derby winner." She arrived carrying a small footstool, which she explained to the guests, she needed to keep her legs from dangling when she was sitting down.

Peggy wrote to George Brett that even at the party she still could not convince herself that she had actually won the award, but that she kept glancing down to look at the corsage, which he had sent to her, and telling herself that she certainly would not be wearing this massive orchid display if she had not won something. But it was not until May 8, when she received the check that went with the award, that she confessed to Brickell, "The $1,000 was sure proof that I had won."

Chapter Twenty-one

Gone With the Wind went off the best-seller list for the first time in twenty-one months on April 8, 1938. Over two million copies had been sold in the United States, and a million copies abroad. Yet, Peggy did not consider herself a professional, but a lucky amateur. Letters still consumed a monumental part of her days but, except for those times when the Selznick publicity department issued a release about new casting developments, she was getting something of a respite.

She now allowed herself the luxury of redecorating the apartment, and hired a painting contractor to strip off all the old wallpaper and paint the rooms in cheerful shades of apple green and Georgia peach. The old couch was re-covered to match, and Peggy's one household purchase — a sumptuous Aubusson carpet in muted greens — pleased her.

John, however, continued to handle both his daytime job at Georgia Power and the late-night work on Peggy's foreign publications, and the strain was sapping his strength. By the following autumn, his weight had dropped to a low 132 pounds, he had little energy, and his breathing was often labored.

Certain that a holiday would revitalize him, Peggy arranged for them to spend Christmas with the Granberrys in Winter Park. After the holiday, they drove through the small towns of Florida and Georgia to Blowing Rock, for a visit with novelist Clifford Dowdey and his wife, Helen, whom Peggy had recently met through the Granberrys. From there, they traveled to Wilmington to see John's mother, and then down to Washington, D.C., where they tried to convince the State Department to help them in fighting the Dutch piracy case.

Along the way, the Marshes stayed in small hotels, and Peggy used the time away from home to catch up on some of the popular fiction she had not had time to read since the publication of her own book: John O'Hara's *Appointment in Samarra* and *Butterfield 8*, James M. Cain's *The Postman Always Rings Twice* and *Serenade*, Elmer Rice's *Imperial City*, and others. "Reading them so close together," Peggy wrote to Brickell, "the impact was strong. What depressed and bothered me was the tiredness of everyone concerned. These characters did not leap gaily in and out of strange beds as did the characters of the jazz age, nor did they commit murder, forgery et cetera with passion, enthusiasm or regret. They did all these things — for what reason I cannot say. Certainly, they got no pleasure from any of their sins, nor did they have any sense of remorse."

An urgent desire to write "a story about a girl who went wrong and certainly did regret it" overcame her, and she told Brickell, "I think it would be colossal and sensational. I could not find in any of the books I read the perfectly normal feminine reaction of fear of consequences, of loss of reputation, of social disapproval or of the good old-fashioned Puritan institution, conscience. I suppose my desire to write such a book puts me definitely in the Victorian era. But then 'Gone With the Wind' was probably as Victorian a novel as was ever written."

This urge to apply "her rear to a chair" before her typewriter was short-lived. With *Gone With the Wind* off the best-seller list, the Marshes' life had quieted down a bit — the telephone did not ring as often, the tourists were more discreet in their interest, and the mail dropped off to a level that, with the help of Margaret Baugh and her staff, was manageable. Unless the film caused a resurgence of interest in Peggy, it looked as though the Marshes could look forward to a normal life again — except for the lawsuits that Stephens was handling, the tax problems, the business correspondence that no one but Peggy or John could deal with (or rather, that they preferred not to delegate to others), and the fact that, in their present financial circumstances and with their new position in the community, they no longer knew what *normal* meant. *Gone With the Wind* might no longer be a best-seller, but the book remained a demanding business. A second book that might add to all these pressures was too much for Peggy to consider, and she quickly abandoned any ideas of attempting a novel about a woman with a moral dilemma.

Though she wouldn't have admitted it, Peggy's interest in the progress of the movie was as avid as that of her fans. She wrote Kay Brown frequently for the latest news and was pleased to have a personal letter from David O. Selznick (they had not yet met) telling her that the movie would positively go into production before September. She went to see the Warner Brothers film *Jezebel*, starring Bette Davis and, despite all the publicity it was receiving on this count, saw no similarities between it and *Gone With the Wind*, except for period costumes and some dialogue about the approach of the war. For once, she found no need for legal action, as she did not feel she had "a copyright on hoop skirts or hot-blooded Southerners."

"He ought to be a landslide," Peggy commented to the press when it was announced on June 23 that it appeared Clark Gable and Norma Shearer would be cast as Rhett and Scarlett. Never keen on Shearer in the role, Peggy hedged her opinion by saying obliquely, "She's a good actress." A new onslaught of press interest in Peggy began with this publicity release and, fearful that all the old hoopla was to start up again, she telephoned Herschel Brickell to ask if she might come to Connecticut for a brief escape. He cordially invited her to Ridgefield, and she remained in Connecticut a week, not traveling into New York to see Kay Brown or Lois Cole, who was pregnant. Only after she returned home did the Brickells tell her the shocking news that they were divorcing.

On August 1, Peggy was relieved to read that Norma Shearer was not going to play Scarlett O'Hara after all. Miss Shearer said she was convinced that the majority of fans "who think I should not play this kind of character on the screen are right."

A few days later, Gable was officially signed by Selznick to play Rhett Butler. Filming was now set to begin on February 1, 1939. Georgia historian Wilbur Kurtz, recommended by Peggy along with Sue Myrick, had been in Hollywood for nearly a year as the film's official historian, and Sue had arrived a short time later to help the performers with their dialects and accents. Through her two close friends, Peggy was kept up to date with what was happening at the Selznick studio. She had thought that Sidney Howard's screenplay was finished and in final form, for as far back as February of 1938 Wilbur Kurtz had written her that Howard had ended his stint. In his own diary entry for February 2, 1938, Kurtz had written:

> Well, over the [drawing] boards Sidney Howard walked in. He said this was his last day. His manner of being preoccupied never deserts him. But on his way out, he wheeled, threw back his large shoulders and with incisive speech somewhat on the sardonic side, orated, "Yes, I'm through. It's not a movie script. It's a transcription from the book. But what else can I do? I just used Miss Mitchell's words and scenes." All with an air of talking down his trying efforts and the results he got. No one seemed to agree with him. "See you later." And he was gone.

Howard was, in fact, to be called back to rewrite a number of scenes and finally, as late as October 12, not satisfied that he had a shooting script, Selznick turned to Peggy for help. An invitation was extended through Kay Brown for Peggy to join her, Selznick, and his wife, Irene on a boat trip to either Sweden or Bermuda so that she could go over the script with him in the most relaxed atmosphere. Peggy flatly refused. A counter suggestion was made — Selznick would meet her near Charleston or any place she designated. Again Peggy refused, using her social engagements and her father's ill health as excuses. Selznick now had Kay Brown explain that he was planning to cut scenes from Howard's script and needed "bridgeovers," or transitions, and if she would only consider assisting in this one thing, he would be happy to keep her involvement a private matter. He also offered her a large sum for her time.

Fearful that any contribution of her own would not remain secret for long, Peggy replied with an adamant no. At this point Selznick, accepting the fact that Margaret Mitchell meant what she said, employed a series of well-known authors to work on the script. Oliver H. P. Garrett was the first, and Kurtz reported, "The revision seems to be along the lines of condensation. . . . The Tarleton twins turn up *missing* and only a few glimpses of Belle Watling are vouchsafed."

F. Scott Fitzgerald, to Peggy's great pride, was engaged next. A few weeks later, he was off the assignment and wrote his editor at Scribners, Maxwell Perkins, "I was absolutely forbidden to use any words except those of Margaret Mitchell, that is when new phrases had to be invented one had to thumb through [*Gone With the Wind*] and check phrases of hers that would cover the situation."

Selznick then proceeded to work on the screenplay himself. Letters and telegrams went to and from Kurtz, Myrick, Brown, and Peggy, making their way back and forth across the country like frenzied hen tracks. Sketches of costumes and even of Mammy's head rag arrived for Peggy to approve. She answered some of Selznick's questions — Rhett would not drive publicly with Belle in a carriage, it was "ungentlemanly"; Rhett would not be rude to Belle; Belle must not be familiar with the coachman; Scarlett would converse freely with the coachman, but Belle could not because Belle was "not nice"; a coachman would show disdain for Belle but not impertinence; poor whites hated Negroes and Negroes did not like or respect them; Rhett could never alight from Belle's carriage in front of Aunt Pittypat's house as it would show disrespect for Melanie and Scarlett, and no one would be able to receive him after such a social blunder. Peggy made one creative suggestion (not used): if a scene between Rhett and Belle outside of Belle's infamous house was necessary, then Belle could be seen following Rhett from her front door to his horse. Despite these spurts of cooperation, Peggy still would not comment on the script or okay any sketches.

Script queries were not the only disruption in Peggy's life during the fall of 1938. Her father's illness now demanded a great deal of her attention. Too, she was hounded by a constant flow of reporters hoping for a news break on the casting of Scarlett O'Hara. It did no good to repeat over and over that she knew no more than they did; the press refused to believe this. Through Sue Myrick, who was coaching all possible Scarletts in their accents, Peggy knew who was the latest actress being tested, but no more, and she seems to have lost interest in her own speculations. During these last frantic weeks before the start of principal photography, the race had narrowed to three contenders, all well-known Hollywood ladies — Paulette Goddard, Jean Arthur, and Joan Bennett.

What Peggy did not know about were the financial problems besetting Selznick at this time. In the three years since he and his backer, John Hay Whitney, had bought the property for films, he had spent a fortune of the investor's money and Whitney had finally lost his patience. Either Selznick must set a definite starting date and stick to it, or he would withdraw his support. Selznick, always a big gambler, took a daring chance. On a clear, crisp December evening shortly before Christmas, he ordered the burning of Atlanta to begin on the back lot of his studio. The scene was to be shot with doubles so it did not matter that he had not cast the female lead.

A large robust man, well over six feet tall, Selznick stood on a high, railed platform and gave the order to his crew to turn on the gas jets that would start the fire. As seven technicolor cameras began to roll, flames leaped up to devour the false fronts that had been created to simulate the Atlanta of the American Civil War period. Doubles for Scarlett and Rhett jumped on a buckboard and raced alongside the fire. Sweat poured down Selznick's face and he had to remove his glasses to wipe them clean. An assistant swore his boss had actually shed tears as the shooting of *Gone With the Wind* finally began with an incomplete script and no Scarlett O'Hara.

Selznick stood for a moment, squinting, as the flames consumed what remained of the set. The back lot was a maze of men and fire equipment. Suddenly, as he replaced his glasses, he caught sight of a woman, dressed starkly in a black dress and a wide-brimmed black hat, coming up the steps of the platform. Beside her was Selznick's brother Myron, an actors' agent. A wind had risen, fanning the flames and making it hard to stand too close to the railing. The woman turned her head to the side and held onto her hat as she approached him, and he could not see her face.

"Here, genius," his brother said. "Meet your Scarlett O'Hara."

Selznick stared with stunned disbelief as the woman turned

to face him, tilting her head back and removing the halo hat so that her dark chestnut hair blew wildly behind her. Here, indeed, was his Scarlett O'Hara — English film star, Vivien Leigh.

Selznick did not even recall that he had been sent a print of one of Vivien's films, *Fire Over England*, in February of 1937, by Kay Brown, who had been caught by Vivien's ability to project charm and femininity and, at the same time, a duality of personality that she knew her boss had been looking for. At this time, Selznick had telegraphed Miss Brown: "I HAVE NO ENTHUSIASM FOR VIVIEN LEIGH, BUT AS YET HAVE NEVER EVEN SEEN PHOTOGRAPH OF HER. WILL BE SEEING 'FIRE OVER ENGLAND' SHORTLY, AT WHICH TIME WILL OF COURSE SEE LEIGH." But Selznick had never run the film because he had been so certain in his mind that an English woman would be wrong.

A rough test was shot of Vivien. There was an indescribable wildness about her, and when Selznick saw the rushes he was deliriously happy. One hurdle remained to be jumped — whether she could master a Southern accent. Sue Myrick was put to work, and three days later Vivien shot another test. There was no doubt in anyone's minds when this test was run — Scarlett O'Hara had finally been cast.

Photographs of Vivien were sent to Peggy, and she was offered a copy of the English actress's film test. She decided not to view it, fearing that if something should happen and the decision should somehow be reversed, she would be involved. Anyway, she trusted Sue Myrick, and Sue felt Vivien Leigh would be a marvelous Scarlett O'Hara. Peggy did not reply to the question that Selznick put to her — was Vivien Leigh Scarlett O'Hara as she had imagined her? But she did write Lois how shocked she had been when she saw the photograph that had been sent to her — for Miss Leigh bore a remarkable resemblance to Margaret Mitchell in her early twenties.

Once production of *Gone With the Wind* began, on January 26, Peggy avidly followed the progress of the film and was disconsolate to learn, less than three weeks later, that the cameras had stopped rolling because George Cukor had been fired. Peggy read about it in Louella Parsons's column before hearing from

Sue Myrick and Kurtz, and she immediately dispatched a telegram to Sue, who replied two days later:

> It is really and actually true; George finally told me all about it.
> . . . We sat down and he talked — not for publication he said, but
> because he liked me, felt responsible for getting me into a mess
> and wanted me to know the truth. . . . He said he is an honest
> craftsman and he cannot do a job unless he knows it is a good job
> and he feels the present job is not right. For days, he told me, he
> has looked at the rushes and felt he was failing. He knew he was a
> good director and knew the actors were good ones, yet the thing
> did not click as it should.
>
> Gradually he became more and more convinced that the script
> was the trouble. . . . David, himself, thinks HE is writing the script
> and he tells Bobby Keon [the script assistant] and Stinko [Oliver]
> Garrett what to write. And they do the best they can with it, in
> their limited way. . . . And George has continuously taken script
> from day to day, compared the Garrett–Selznick version with the
> Howard, groaned and tried to change some parts back to the
> Howard script. But he seldom could do much with the scene. . . .
>
> So George just told David he would not work any longer if the
> script was not better and he wanted the Howard script back.
> David told George he was [a] director — not an author and he
> (David) was the producer and the judge of what is a good script
> (or words to that effect) and George said he was a director and a
> damn good one and he would not let his name go out over a lousy
> picture and if they didn't go back to the Howard script (he was
> willing to have them cut it down shorter) he, George, was
> through.
>
> And, bull-headed David said "OK, get out!"

The next Peggy heard was that Gable had been asked to
choose Cukor's replacement from a list of three directors.
Gable took Victor Fleming, who had directed him the year
before in *Test Pilot*. Selznick had given Gable his choice of directors because he had been sulking under Cukor, who, he complained, had given more directorial assistance to the women in
the cast than to him. Fleming's first comment to Selznick after
reading the screenplay was, "David, your fucking script is no
fucking good." Selznick now had no alternative but to call in
another writer or see if he could get Howard back.

Sue Myrick and Kurtz were so embroiled in the machinations

of each daily crisis that neither of them had written Peggy of this latest development. Finally, on March 11, Peggy wrote Kurtz asking if they had a script yet, for she had read in a theatrical paper that the last people who had been hired to do the script had refused to do a day-to-day job and had said they had to be at least ten days ahead. This had sounded to her as if the script were not completed yet. She had also heard that Robert Benchley was one of the writers being considered, which, she claimed, had moved her to conjecture that "Groucho Marx, William Faulkner, and Erskine Caldwell would probably be on the script before this business is over."

None of these men were employed by Selznick, who had already hired writer and director Ben Hecht. Hecht worked day and night for two weeks, at the end of which he collapsed from exhaustion and was hospitalized. Hecht's main contribution was to resurrect an idea of Sidney Howard's that had been discarded, that of connecting the chief sequences of the film with a series of titles.

On March 12, Sue Myrick informed Peggy that John Van Druten, the playwright, and John Balderston, who had written *The Prisoner of Zenda* for Selznick, were now working on the screenplay. "We have 60 pages marked 'completed script,'" she wrote, "but every few days we get some pink pages marked 'substitute script' and we tear out some yellow pages and set in the pink ones. We expect blue or orange pages any day now."

Fleming then turned to Sue Myrick and asked her to write some additional dialogue, telling her, "God knows they'd had fifteen writers," and that she might as well try her hand at it as it "probably couldn't be any worse than the others!"

Filming had resumed on March 3, seventeen days after Cukor had walked off the lot, and Fleming had been shooting scenes without any idea of what was to come or whether the sequence he was directing might be cut when more pages were delivered to him.

"SIDNEY HOWARD IS BACK ON THE SCRIPT!" Sue Myrick wrote triumphantly on April 9. "I haven't the faintest idea how many folks that makes in all who have done script . . . all I know is that Howard is somewhere around the sixteenth, though he may be the twentieth."

Peggy replied, "I would not be surprised to learn that the script of the other sixteen had been junked and Mr. Howard's original script put into production."

Howard reworked the screenplay in five weeks and, when he went to say good-bye to Miss Myrick again, he said that he had no doubt that Selznick would rewrite it and then call him back again to rewrite it once more. Sue also told Peggy that the current scenario was now fifty pages longer than the original Howard draft, and that the film's running time would be at least four hours. Louis B. Mayer's comment on hearing the projected length of the film was supposedly, "They'd stone Christ if he came back and spoke for four hours."

Selznick did retain most of Howard's final script, and both Kurtz and Sue wrote Peggy ecstatic letters. Sue informed her, "The street scenes are so fine I think the thing is a *Birth of a Nation*. And the new script we have for the scene with Scarlett and Dr. Meade in the hospital (Howard's replacing Garrett's) for the wounded men is thrilling as can be."

During the time of the filming of *Gone With the Wind*, it was almost impossible to pick up a magazine that did not have an unauthorized story or rumor about Peggy, one of the cast members, or Selznick. In view of this avalanche of publicity, Ginny Morris now thought the time appropriate for the article she had discussed with *Photoplay* two years earlier. This time, she did not ask Peggy's permission, but wrote, on March 13, 1939, and told her she had sold the article to the film magazine and that it was not an "intimate portrait" by any means, and that since, following their last exchange of letters, Peggy had done interviews with Faith Baldwin and Edwin Granberry, she did not think that Peggy's former position was valid.

Peggy's reply was to insist Ginny stop the publication of the story because, she said, "I would like to keep my childhood and my girlhood and the rest of my life to myself." She offered to pay Ginny whatever *Photoplay* had paid her and warned that "its [the article's] publication will mean the end of any friendship between you and me."

When Ginny received this "ghoulish document," as she was later to call Peggy's "shocking attempt to buy off the freedom of the press," she filed it away without heeding its threat. The friendship was over as far as she was concerned, and she published the piece. Although the article was, as she said, "innocuous enough," it did record the fact that Peggy went to Smith in 1918, that she had been married twice (a fact not widely known then), that she *had* read the "gigantic filmscript," and that she greatly admired George Cukor, "who had come to Atlanta to consult her." Ginny also stated that Peggy was a millionaire but that "the government has taken half her revenue in taxes," and she attributed the success of *Gone With the Wind* to the fact that Peggy "ignored the mothball approach to the past and put 1929–1936 souls into 1865 people."

Peggy was furious about the article and wrote *Photoplay* asking them to retract certain statements made by Ginny, all of which were essentially true, except perhaps for the claim that Peggy had read the filmscript of *Gone With the Wind*. The magazine printed her letter without a retraction in a later issue, but neither the article nor the letter brought in an untoward amount of reader response.

Officially, filming was completed on *Gone With the Wind* on June 27, 1939, but retakes, montages, bridgeovers, and technical effects were still to come. A brief scene was inserted as late as November 11, just after the film had been exhibited at a sneak preview at the Warner Theatre in Santa Barbara. Preview cards indicated an overwhelming success, carrying comments such as, "the screen's greatest achievement of all time," and "the greatest picture since *Birth of a Nation*." Nevertheless, it seemed to be the general opinion that the film was uncomfortably long. Selznick decided to divide the picture into two sections and have an intermission, a possibility that he had considered earlier. This meant there had to be a new piece of film shot with which to open the second half.

Selznick's special effects department sorted through all their existing footage and put together a montage with an ominous, warlike effect — soldiers on the march, caissons churning up the red dust of Georgia's dirt roads, then the superimposed title, "Sherman." With this bridge, the filming of *Gone With the Wind* was complete, although the score, by Max Steiner, was still not recorded. It seemed to be rushing things, but Selznick announced he would premiere the film in Atlanta on December 15, 1939. Peggy's life was once again under attack.

Chapter Twenty-two

*A*FTER THREE AND A HALF years' experience with the sudden tides of public interest, Peggy knew in October, when the date of the premiere was announced, that a tidal wave was certain to follow. She spoke on the telephone to virtually no one outside her family and rarely left the apartment except to see her father. Still, as Peggy wrote Lois, the waves came in "steadily, harder, and higher," adding, "we're so inundated and battered that we can barely keep our ears above the water line."

A false front of tall, white columns was already being erected on the facade of Atlanta's Loew's Grand Theatre to make it look like the Tara conceived for the film — which, of course, bore no resemblance to the O'Hara plantation in Peggy's book. Georgia's Governor Eurith D. Rivers had proclaimed December 15 a statewide holiday, and Atlanta's Mayor William B. Hartsfield had extended the one-day holiday into a three-day festival and had urged Atlanta's female population to don hoop skirts and pantalets, and its male citizenry to wear tight britches and beaver hats, and to sprout goatees, sideburns, and whiskers. The celebration was to include a parade with a brass band stationed at every corner for a mile in the center of metropolitan Atlanta. For the entire state of Georgia, having the premiere of *Gone With the Wind* on home ground was like winning the Battle of Atlanta seventy-five years late.

Peggy kept Lois Cole apprised of what madness took place in

the pre-premiere weeks. All of the stars of the film — except for the blacks — would be in Atlanta for the festivities, along with David O. Selznick and his wife, Irene; Clark Gable's wife, film star Carole Lombard; Vivien Leigh's future husband, Laurence Olivier; and Claudette Colbert, who was there because Selznick had heard that she was Margaret Mitchell's favorite movie star. All the visiting celebrities, governors from five former Confederate states, and anyone who was anyone in Atlanta were invited to a huge costume ball to be held the night before the premiere. Peggy was expected to be the guest of honor but, to everyone's shock, she declined the invitation, claiming her father was ill and that she could not be away from him two consecutive nights. In truth, refusing to attend the ball was Peggy's way of squaring an old grudge, despite the fact that it meant depriving herself of a great personal tribute. The costume ball was sponsored by the Junior League — the same women who had once barred her entrance into Atlanta society.

Only a privileged 2,031 persons, the sum total of all the seats in the Grand Theatre, were to attend the premiere, and from the moment of the announcement it seemed to Peggy that "the whole of Atlanta — and apparently the South" and, in fact, "everybody in Christendom" was on her neck in a grim and desperate struggle to obtain tickets. She and John had been given only the four tickets that they had requested, for themselves and Stephens and Carrie Lou. The folks at Macmillan wrote her that they were concerned about not having enough tickets for the executives who hoped to come to Atlanta, but Peggy was unable to help. In the end, Selznick gave Macmillan enough tickets for Latham, George Brett and his wife, and the Taylors. There was one extra ticket (presumably because they thought Latham was married), and it proved to be a problem, as all the other executives at Macmillan fought to claim it. Sue Myrick and Wilbur Kurtz and his wife, all now officially "home from the war" were, of course, attending. Peggy had the three of them to dinner, which was not an altogether happy occasion, for they all mourned the tragic death, only a few months before, of Sidney Howard.

Peggy had been suffering from abdominal adhesions for six months and the doctors now planned to operate in January.

Eugene Mitchell's condition had steadily worsened and Peggy was in daily attendance. The movie premiere in her hometown should have been a glorious moment, but now, as always, she cast her startling blue eyes on the dark side, and the closer December 15 came, the less certain she was that she would have the stamina or the time to be at her own premiere. The Selznick people were up in arms when they heard about this, and finally she promised that she would attend.

Selznick had taken the same extravagant care in staging the premiere as he had in filming *Gone With the Wind*. Howard Dietz, the film's public relations man, received a telegram from Selznick before the premiere that read, in part: "I WANT YOU TO BE VERY CAREFUL OF THE PAPER YOU SELECT FOR THE PROGRAM STOP SOMETIMES THEIR CRACKLING MAKES IT DIFFICULT TO HEAR THE DIALOGUE STOP PROMISE YOU WILL ATTEND TO THIS STOP."

Selznick also sent down an advance photographer weeks before to photograph still backgrounds against which portraits of the stars could be taken. Therefore, many of the pictures of the stars that appeared in press releases were "process shots." By taking the foreground and background separately, stars could be photographed anywhere, indoors, or out, without the distraction of the crowds who always followed them in public.

Everyone connected with the film company was besieged with requests for tickets. Dietz tells the story of the elderly lady who followed him wherever he went, repeating, "You don't understand. I am president of the local chapter of the D.A.R."

At the end of his patience, Dietz replied, "But you don't understand, madam. This picture is about another war."

Crowds larger than the combined armies that fought the Battle of Atlanta lined up for seven miles to watch the procession of limousines from the airport to the Georgian Terrace Hotel, where most of the visiting celebrities were staying. There were said to be three hundred thousand people waiting at the airport to greet the stellar performers. A forty-piece band blasted out "Dixie" as Vivien Leigh alighted, and to Dietz's horror, she naively exclaimed, "Oh, they're playing the song from the picture!" "Dixie" was, in fact, played almost nonstop, and both the American and the Confederate flags were flown. Confetti littered the path from the airport to the hotel and the

Rebel yell echoed through the streets as star-watchers whistled, cheered, and goggled.

On Wednesday evening, December 13, Peggy had the Selznicks, Vivien Leigh and Laurence Olivier, Olivia de Havilland, Sue Myrick, and Annie and Wilbur Kurtz to the apartment for drinks. She was tremendously impressed with Miss Leigh, whom she found to be extremely knowledgeable in Southern history. Gable and Carole Lombard were not due to arrive until Thursday morning, when the crowds came out again to welcome them.

At the Atlanta Municipal Auditorium the following night, nearly six thousand celebrants, dressed in Civil War-period gowns and uniforms, danced to Kay Kyser's music at the Junior League ball. All of the film's stars were present. Gable danced with Mayor Hartfield's daughter and sent one debutante into a faint when she was introduced to him. But the author of *Gone With the Wind* held to her vow and was not present at this gala affair.

Peggy made her first public appearance the next day, Friday, at a luncheon in honor of the Macmillan executives. To her delight, Julia Peterkin and Marjorie Kinnan Rawlings, both Pulitzer Prize-winning authors, also attended. John was to join Peggy later that day at a cocktail party in the Marshes' honor given by the Altanta Women's Press Club at the Piedmont Driving Club. Invitations had been limited to a few official guests, Press Club members, and local reporters and photographers. The ladies of the press had gone to great lengths to keep the time and place of the party out of the newspapers. Unfortunately, they guarded this information so well that there was a mix-up about the hour. Peggy had thought the party was to begin at 6:00 P.M. and so had not yet arrived when, at 5:30, police sirens announced the approach of the Selznick contingent. Only the officers of the Press Club were there to greet the celebrities and there was much scurrying about as the waiters rushed to provide them with mint juleps.

Gable and Selznick exchanged nervous glances. Where was Margaret Mitchell? Would she fail to show up again? To everyone's relief, the Marshes finally arrived at 6:10 and, after greeting everyone, Peggy talked with Clark Gable for the first time. Gable was struck by her diminutive size and sat down with her in a fairly quiet corner so that she would not have to look up at him and strain her neck. Peggy, a coquettish velvet hat in the shape of a large bow precariously secured to the back of her head, was flushed and a bit insecure as flashbulbs exploded close by. Her glance caught Gable's. He smiled down at her and then, on impulse, jumped up and spirited her into one of the smaller adjoining rooms, for a private chat about herself and the book. Gable, towering over Peggy, was in full command as he shut the door to curious eyes. Later he said she was "charming" and she said he was "grand." But, in fact, they remained behind those closed doors for less than five minutes, so it would appear that once social amenities had been exchanged and they were alone, Margaret Mitchell and Rhett Butler had little to say to each other.

A throng estimated at a hundred thousand people or more packed the brilliantly klieg-lighted block of Peachtree Street that held Loew's Grand Theatre as the privileged ticket holders began to arrive. The audience members were well aware that they were participating in a national event, that they were about to see enacted a story that it had taken Margaret Mitchell seven years to write. They were also aware that it had taken two years to find an actress to play Scarlett O'Hara, that the film was the third most costly picture Hollywood had ever produced, and that it ran three and three-quarters hours, making it one of the longest pictures ever filmed. "Above all," *Time* was to say in its story on the premiere, "most of them knew by heart the love story of Rhett Butler and Scarlett O'Hara, and they were there to protest if it had undergone a single serious film change."

Nowhere in the voluminous correspondence that survived the later destruction of her personal papers did Peggy record what she felt as she and John sat on the plush rear seat of the limousine Selznick had supplied, on their way for the first time to see her book and characters brought to life. But she did comment on the luxuriousness of the vehicle, the first of its kind she had ever ridden in. And Bessie, who helped her into the bouffant, pale pink tulle gown she had chosen for the opening, said, "Miss Peggy wished she had been able to see the picture by her own self 'til the very last minute."

The theatre was only a five-minute ride from the Marshes'

apartment, and Dietz had staged Peggy's arrival to come last. The crowds had been standing all day in hopes of getting a glimpse of members of the famous assemblage as they arrived, and by this time they were in a near frenzy. There was a crisp breeze and the evening was a cool forty-two degrees, but people had their coats off and were waving their hats along with Confederate flags. The moment they had been waiting for had arrived. Their own Peggy Mitchell was on her way to the theatre where Atlanta's history would be recreated, and, in a few moments, she would emerge from the sleek black car that was flanked front and rear by caterwauling police cars. When she did, careful her gown did not reveal her low-heeled, heavy shoes, she flinched in the extraordinary glare. The square before the theatre had been brilliantly flood-lighted, powerful beacons criss-crossed in the sky, and searchlights threw arcs of dazzling light up and down Peachtree Street.

Mayor Hartsfield stepped forward, took Peggy's hand and led her onto a platform in front of the theatre where a microphone had been set up. She glanced back over her shoulder to watch John get out of the car and then turned again and waved to the crowds, who could not possibly have heard Julian Boehm's introduction above the shouting and whistling. Howard Dietz was at Peggy's shoulder, between her and John, and helped her down from the platform and across the short red-carpeted area to the entrance of the theatre. As Margaret Mitchell disappeared through the columned doorway of "Tara," a great and thunderous cheer arose from the crowds.

Four aged veterans (the youngest was ninety-three) who had fought in the battle of Atlanta — each proudly dressed in Confederate gray — had been seated on the aisle. As she came down it on the arm of Howard Dietz, Peggy paused, leaned over, and shook hands with each of them. Then she continued down to her own seat.

Only a few minutes after Peggy's arrival, the houselights dimmed. Later she was to say that she was somewhat aghast when Ben Hecht's first title moved across the screen: *There was a land of cavaliers and cotton fields called the Old South . . .*

"Cavalier" was not a word she liked associated with the South. But Vivien Leigh had not pouted on the screen for more than five minutes before Peggy, along with the rest of the audience, was convinced no better choice for Scarlett O'Hara could have been made. She did not speak letter-perfect middle-high Georgian, but no one watching her really cared. "She is *my* Scarlett," Peggy told Medora during the intermission.

Throughout the entire film, the audience clapped, cheered, whistled, and wept in turn. There were cheers when Scarlett shot the Yankee deserter, loud sobbing at the scene of mass desolation as the grieving folk of Atlanta read the casualty lists after Gettysburg, and cheers again as the Confederate band dispelled the mood of tragedy with a rousing chorus of "Dixie."

Peggy's "haw-haw" could be heard during moments when Prissy (Butterfly McQueen) was on screen, and when Mammy (Hattie McDaniel), whom *Time* dubbed "the sly, leather-lunged devoted Emily Post of the O'Hara's," lifted her skirts to show Rhett Butler her red petticoat. Peggy told Medora, who reported it in her *Journal* coverage the next day, that she felt desolate that Hattie McDaniel was "the only big star of the picture who isn't here — and a *real* star, too. The scene in which Mammy walked up the stairs with Melanie after Bonnie's death was one of the finest I ever saw."

When the lights came up at the end of the film, there was hardly a dry eye in the house and, when Peggy was escorted down the aisle by Mayor Hartsfield and onto the stage to stand with David O. Selznick and all of the actors and actresses who had come to Atlanta, she unashamedly dabbed at her eyes with a lace handkerchief. The entire audience was on its feet, yelling "Bravo!" and applauding at the same time. Mayor Hartsfield stepped in and guided Peggy to the microphone. There was silence for a brief moment as the master of ceremonies announced, "Ladies and gentlemen, Miss Margaret Mitchell of Atlanta."

He lowered the microphone to her height, but it was fully three minutes before the wild, enthusiastic cheering was finally silenced. She stood there looking incredibly childlike, her cheeks flushed, eyes red-rimmed, a coy pink bow holding back her hair on one side. "It was an experience," she finally said in a trembling voice. The audience laughed nervously. "And I'm so glad you liked my Scarlett." She finished by thanking Mr. Selz-

nick and all the film people for "doing such a fine job of bringing my book to life."

Whatever adverse literary criticism had been laid upon the
book — that perhaps its love story was too "women's magazine"; its history, sectional; its length, pretentious; its writing,
lacking in style — the film avoided. In the three years since its
publication, *Gone With the Wind* had been recognized as the
incarnation of not one, but two American legends — one, a
vivid, moving account of the war between the states, told from
the viewpoint of the South; and two, the heroic and tragic love
story of two people who were strong and brutal enough to have
survived the first. The advantage of filming two great legends
in one picture was that Selznick had two great pictures in one
— "a surefire Rebel-rouser for the South, a surefire love story
for the rest of the country," *Time* said.

Peggy never doubted the film's success as she had once
doubted the success of the book. And as she was escorted out of
the theatre, having to stop every inch of the way to accept
tearful congratulations, she whispered to Medora, "Oh, I do
hope the madness isn't going to start up all over again!"

After a series of "premieres" in Los Angeles, New York, and
Chicago, *Gone With the Wind* was booked into theatres all over
the country on a reserved-seat basis. Ticket prices began at
twice the normal movie-house admission. Yet, despite the high
tariff and the necessity of purchasing seats far in advance, box
office receipts were extraordinary. Scalpers bought and resold
tickets at such exorbitant prices that in New York live theatre
was frequently a less expensive form of entertainment. Even
people who, because they were not readers, had been unaware
of either Margaret Mitchell or *Gone With the Wind* before the
film's release, now could not help but be thoroughly aware of
both. Say what she would about Annie Laurie Williams, Peggy
had been assured her name would appear above the title as a
result of Miss Williams's perseverance. And now the words
"David O. Selznick Presents Margaret Mitchell's *Gone With the
Wind*" seemed to appear on towering billboard posters *every-*

where; they dominated the highways that led into major cities and were plastered on the sides of buildings and the backs of buses. Her name and the title of the book even flashed on and off in garish neon high over New York's Times Square. And the first week in January, "Margaret Mitchell's *Gone With the Wind*" occupied the covers of eleven major national magazines. The mail once again had to be delivered in satchels and the telephone rang off the wall.

Peggy and John went to Tucson, Arizona, to visit Helen and Clifford Dowdey for Christmas. One of the enhancements was that Herschel Brickell was also there. "We did have a good Christmas, didn't we?" she wrote him upon her return. As Brickell was deeply depressed over his divorce problems at the time, and the Dowdeys were struggling through financial reverses, the question seems especially poignant. She had helped to cheer everyone up with stories about the premiere. Her friends had not yet seen the film and she expounded on its merits and demerits, "discussing every angle of the thing." The Marshes had both been back to see the film a second time and, in retrospect, as John wrote the Dowdeys, they thought that "the novel was followed much too closely"; Leigh was "unqualifiedly marvelous — she *was* Scarlett"; Gable seemed "only adequate"; de Havilland, "good"; and Howard, as Ashley Wilkes, "wretched beyond compare." Peggy was delighted with Mammy, but now felt moments of her performance were "a little on the Show Boat side." Miss Pittypat was poor, and except for the "excellent" Carroll Nye, who played Frank Kennedy, all of the supporting performers were "adequate." Twelve Oaks was "too lavish" a set; and Tara, "not nearly plain enough;" and the house Rhett Butler built for Scarlett "could have been in Omaha so little does it resemble any dwelling in the Atlanta of the Reconstruction period." But on second viewing, both of them had agreed that the feeling of the old South was stronger than they had originally thought, and Thomas Mitchell's performance as Gerald O'Hara, much more moving.

Neither of the Marshes had been well when they had left for Arizona. Peggy had her abdominal operation to face on her return (now scheduled for January 13) and was in a moderate amount of pain, and John just seemed exhausted. Home again in Atlanta, they were plunged back into the madness the film had stirred up, and they also mourned the demise of the newspaper the *Georgian*, which had employed many of their good friends. Wistfully, Peggy commented to Brickell, "It seems like a pleasant but improbable dream that we all managed to get together in a far place. I'll always think the first batch of eggnog we made was the best I ever drank, and I wish I had the energy to make some right now. But I have decided that the best flavor eggnog can have is when it is made by the combined efforts of a very few people and these people are good friends."

In personal terms, the year 1939 had been the most rewarding since the publication of *Gone With the Wind*. In early June, Peggy had traveled to Smith College to receive an honorary Master of Arts degree. For three years her friends had been aware that she hoped Smith might so honor her one day. To Edwin Granberry, in refusing a similar honor from his school, Rollins, she had ruefully mentioned that she was as illustrious a Smith alumna as Anne Morrow Lindbergh, and that, although she must say no to Rollins, she would accept an honorary degree from Smith if asked. Ginny was not at the commencement exercises, but Red Baxter and some of the other girls from Ten Hen were there. Lois, also a Smith alumna, met Peggy on campus and they drove back to New York together through the rich green countryside of Massachusetts and the rolling verdant hills of Connecticut. Peggy felt good about herself. Twenty years after her departure from Smith, Margaret Mitchell had achieved the recognition of her classmates and her school as one of the "top."

The premiere and the adulation she had received during that week in December had been the apogee of her sudden and meteoric rise to fame. It was not just her fans, but *all* of Atlanta who had paid her homage. It seemed doubtful that anything further could occur in her life that would equal the sense of accomplishment she had felt as she stepped out of the Selznick limousine before the Loew's Grand Theatre, unless it had been the moment when she had stood alone, front and center of the Grand's stage, waiting for the ovation that was being given her to subside. At that moment, she later confessed to Medora, she felt assured that Atlanta was proud of the film and proud of her, and that she never again need worry about losing the esteem of her hometown folk.

To an old friend living in California, she wrote, "The crowds on the streets were larger than those which greeted Lindbergh and President Roosevelt. . . . I was so proud of the town I nearly burst."

John's comment to the Dowdeys was, "Whatever else might be said about the picture it certainly made a splash."

Chapter Twenty-three

I N JANUARY, 1940, Peggy went into the hospital for the abdominal surgery that she had been putting off until after the premiere. She spent three weeks recuperating in the hospital and expected it to be at least a year before she felt fully recovered. However, when she arrived home it appeared that John's condition was even more precarious than her own. He had been running high fevers and feeling listless. The doctors suspected undulant fever and put him in the hospital, but none of the tests were positive. He came home in a few days, but for six weeks he was extremely weak, with no one seeming to know what was the matter. As the Georgia summer pressed in upon him, John wrote to his mother:

> Have I written you that we did acquire the bookkeeper I told you we were thinking about? . . . And from the first evening when he started to work, I have had a great feeling of relief. Keeping books on Margaret Mitchell, Author, isn't an especially onerous job in and of itself, but *trying* to keep them on top of doing all the other work that's had to be done around this house the past three years is the most onerous thing imaginable. I have been the bookkeeper — after a fashion — and one of my most nagging bothers has been the ever-present thought that I was from two to ten months behind on entering up expense items, etc. . . . Now that burden is off my shoulders from now on, and I feel like kicking myself for not having turned the job over to somebody else long

ago, for the cost of it is surprisingly small. The man can handle the work on one or two evenings a month, and as we pay him by the hour the expense won't be great. But what a relief it is to know that that's one job Peggy and I can be free of in the future!

Of course, I find myself rolling on the floor, metaphorically, screaming with laughter at the thought of the firm of Mitchell and Marsh having a bookkeeper. It's one of the droll incongruities of this strange situation that will always seem strange to me. But I can put up with an incongruity or two if they help me to get loose from working day and night, seven days a week. The idea of even *one* more summer of continuous sweaty night work is something I dread and I don't aim to do it if there's any way to avoid it.

It was now diagnosed that John did have undulant fever, and he took a leave of absence from Georgia Power that lasted for several months. "Trips are a pipedream," Peggy wrote the Granberrys, "but I keep dreaming." However, that summer, although John was not well, the Marshes had their first real respite from the rigors of fame. The bookkeeper handled their accounts; Margaret Baugh took care of the other office matters; and Bessie oversaw the rest of the household. Although Mr. Mitchell was ill, Carrie Lou helped Peggy keep an eye on him. And her fan mail had taken a sharp decline. All of which should have given Peggy time finally to do some of the things she claimed she had been deprived of doing for several years.

But, she wrote Granberry, now she could not go out on the street because people stopped her and asked about the rumors of a sequel to *Gone With the Wind* called, she joked, *Back With the Breeze*, and which she humorously described as a highly moral tract in which everyone, including Belle Watling, underwent a change of heart and character and reeked with sanctimonious dullness. Because she had been in the hospital and then back and forth to see John while he was there, rumors had circulated that she had an incurable blood disease and she told Granberry she was "forced" to write innumerable letters disputing this. She also wrote several of her friends to tell them not to believe the rumor that Selznick had given her a fifty-thousand-dollar bonus. "Not true!" she insisted.

Financial security still worried Peggy, despite the fact that the book remained a fast-moving title in bookstores across the country and, even with the troubles that had beset Europe, foreign royalties were sizable. As well, there were the royalties from the Selznick film book that Macmillan had published and the revenues from the commercial tie-ins, which Selznick had finally agreed to share. John had invested their money well and they lived on a modest scale. Peggy's one extravagance, a fur coat, had been stolen from the apartment during their last trip to Winter Park, and she had not replaced it. The Marshes still drove their nine-year-old Chevy. In September, 1939, they had moved to a new apartment, at the Della Manta at 1268 Piedmont Avenue, a few streets from their old one. The block was more residential, however, and the building faced the Piedmont Driving Club with its lovely gardens. The apartment had an extra room and rented for $105 a month, a sum still afford-able on John's salary, especially since they now gave up the office at the Northwood and used the additional room on Piedmont Avenue as an office for Margaret Baugh during the day and for the accountant on the evenings he was there. But piracy cases in several countries continued to plague Peggy, and with John's ill health and her own propensity for "disaster," she claimed she could not help but be concerned. After all, no one knew better than she that when she said she would never write another book, she truly meant it.

Peggy would always be a celebrity, but the attention paid her had tapered off somewhat as the excitement over the film and its stars also began to flag. In June, the film was withdrawn from road-show houses, the plan being for it to remain inac-cessible until Christmas, when it would be rereleased at popular prices for the first time. *Gone With the Wind* had won nine Academy Awards in February — including Best Film, Best Actress (Vivien Leigh), Best Supporting Actor (Thomas Mitch-ell), and Best Supporting Actress (Hattie McDaniel) — and taking it out of the movie theatres for six months and before the average film-goer had a chance to see it was expected to result in a tremendous publicity boost.

On the morning of October 25, 1940, the Marshes took off in a brand new Mercury to see their friends the Dowdeys in Rich-mond, Virginia. Before they left, Peggy had made arrangements to meet Richmond residents James Branch Cabell and his wife, as well as Rebecca Yancey Williams, author of *The Vanishing Virginian*. Literary stars still very much intrigued her, and since the publication of *Gone With the Wind* she had made a concerted effort to meet those writers who had been her favorites. Quite contradictorily, she did not consider that her own desire for privacy might well be shared by other literary luminaries. She had tried to start correspondences with such writers as Stark Young, Stephen Vincent Benét, Hervey Allen, Julia Peterkin, and others, but her gestures had not been picked up as they had by Brickell, Granberry, and the Dowdeys.

At the back of her mind as she set off for Richmond was the hope that she might be able to meet Ellen Glasgow, who was now elderly and ill. Cabell was Glasgow's nephew and a friend of Herschel Brickell. A meeting between the author of *Gone With the Wind* and the distinguished Virginia writer whom she had always idolized was finally arranged, but not without difficulty. Glasgow was so frail that Peggy went to visit her without John.

This meeting, which took place in Glasgow's bedroom, was considered by Peggy to be one of the few great things that came to her because of the book (the rest, John explained to Frances, were the friends she had made through its publication). Ill as she was, Ellen Glasgow was working on a book, *In This Our Life*, and Peggy was in awe of the woman's dignity that, as she wrote later, "has no stuffiness and . . . graciousness that has no condescension." Peggy gave her homely advice about "taking things easy," and commented on how well the prolific and revered writer had carried success and public acclaim, "not just a brief grassfire flare of notoriety but solid success that grew from year to year, which was based on true worth of character and back-breaking work."

After winning the Pulitzer Prize the next year and receiving a congratulatory telegram from Peggy, Miss Glasgow wrote to her, "I have a charming recollection of your flitting in and spending an hour by my bedside."

By the time she got back from this trip, preparations were underway for a "second premiere" of *Gone With the Wind*, to be held December 15, one year to the day after the first one. Although Peggy was not directly involved in the plans, she fretted over each new development and complained to Helen Dowdey about the "furore" the film people were creating in her life. The term "second premiere" was a ridiculous contradiction in terms, but Selznick had thought it would add a note of glamour to the film's switch from a reserved-seat, raised-price policy to a regular run. Selznick oversaw the publicity campaign himself and high on the list of directives he sent to his underlings was the instruction, "DON'T write publicity stories about Margaret Mitchell." Still, when news of the premiere came to the Marshes, Selznick was surprised at the support they gave the plans. In the month of October, only 1,600 domestic copies of the original three-dollar book had sold, and the film book had been temporarily withdrawn during the six-month film hiatus. John Marsh wrote the Dowdeys that the second premiere probably would not put the book back on the best-seller list, but that it certainly would not "hurt sales" either.

Proceeds from the second premiere were to go to British War Relief. Therefore, it seemed fitting that Vivien Leigh be the honored *Gone With the Wind* star. But Selznick, conscious of the publicity *two* Academy Award winners would produce if they were on stage together, announced that Hattie McDaniel would come to Atlanta, too, and that she and Miss Leigh would re-create the famous corset-lacing scene live, on stage. Furious that Selznick would impinge on her stage rights, Peggy raged to Lois, "Of course I could have sued the hell out of them and I would have done it except for the unfortunate and innocent ladies of the Atlanta British Relief."

Her concern was unnecessary because Hattie McDaniel, claiming she was otherwise committed, declined to visit segregated Atlanta. Miss McDaniel, the first black actress to win an Academy Award, had been born in Wichita, Kansas, and raised in Denver, Colorado, and, though Sue Myrick had coached her meticulously on the dialect and ways of a Georgia black woman, she had no desire to go to Atlanta, where she would have to stay in a substandard room in the city's black ghetto.

This time, there was none of the "whoop-to-do" that had prevailed at the first premiere. There were crowds, but none to equal the first. Vivien Leigh came, but her heart was not in it — her country was at war, her home in London had just been destroyed by the Germans and, in ten days, she and Olivier were to board a boat to return to England so that Olivier could serve his country. Storms brewed the day of the "premiere" and the wind and rain were so strong that Miss Leigh's plane was late and Peggy had to be the official hostess to the press. The attending crowds walked through the Grand's portals — Tara's facade having been dismantled — with a different attitude than the one they had had at the original opening night. In fact, all through the week before the event (referred to as "the second coming" by some of the Marshes' more irreverent friends), Peggy had noticed a diminishing of excitement.

The tidal wave she had expected had not come this time and, rather than feeling relieved, she felt let down. At this time, as Peggy began to fade from the limelight, the contradictions in the Marshes' attitude toward her fame became more apparent. She wrote almost plaintively to Herschel Brickell, "I think the war, of course, had something to do with the cessation of public interest in me, and the election naturally diverted attention."

This statement seems to imply that Peggy had begun to believe that the furor over *Gone With the Wind* would go on forever, and that she was even a bit resentful that the election in November, 1940, of President Franklin D. Roosevelt to an unprecedented third term and the threat of the United States being drawn into the war in Europe had intervened to make that no longer possible. If that was the case, and her letter to Herschel Brickell leaves little doubt of this, then it would seem that the false conceit of fame had claimed Peggy Mitchell its victim.

Chapter Twenty-four

*L*IKE SCARLETT O'HARA, Peggy Mitchell was never able to endure a conversation of which she was not the subject. From early in 1936 to the spring of 1940, either she or the book or the film or the "chiselers" who were all out to rob her had been the center of conversation and correspondence. This was no longer the case, but she was reluctant to place that part of her life behind her. In July, 1941, George Brett wrote and asked her if she would be one of twenty-five authors to write a few words for the National Endowment for the Arts redefining "The American Way." She asked Brett several pages of questions as to who might be behind this organization and who the other writers were — for she didn't want to find herself "waking up in bed with fifth columnists and pinkos," but in the end, she confessed that since his letter came she had not been able to think of a single idea to put down on paper for him. "My rustiness amazes even me," she admitted, "but then for four years I have neither written nor thought about writing. Everything has conspired to crowd ideas out of my mind." No, was her final answer. She felt she was rusting away, but, even if she did not want to write again, handling the business affairs of "Margaret Mitchell, Author" did not have to be her only alternative.

She could have ventured into something that would have used her talents — fund raising (which, indeed, she was later to do), historical preservation, newspaper work. She could have concentrated on just being Mrs. John Marsh, as she had always insisted was her aim. But with several dozen editions of *Gone With the Wind* displayed in a newly purchased bookcase, and twenty oversized scrapbooks stuffed with clippings gathered from all over the world by three clipping services as constant reminders, it does not seem she was ready to retire Margaret Mitchell to the role of housewife. The truth was that Peggy now had a new image of herself, an image perceived as much through the eyes of others as through her own. The fortifications she had constructed to stave off change had been dismantled from the inside.

❧

Peggy had always disliked Roosevelt's "New Deal" policies, not because she thought the New Deal was doing too much for the blacks, which was the opinion of many Southern politicians, but because, as she wrote a young man who feared he might be called to fight, "ever since the New Deal came into being the young ones have been told that they are God's chosen creatures, that the world not only owes them a living but a good living and an awfully good time." Forgotten, obviously, were her own salad days with the Peachtree Yacht Club. Though she did not support the New Deal, Peggy applauded the president's indications that he planned to help the Allies; but, at this point, the war in Europe held little interest for her. She had no husband or sons or brothers to lose, and Stephens's sons were too young to go to war. And what had she chosen for herself but a warm chimney corner and a sense of security?

In fact, Peggy marched through 1941 battling in the service of her own interests — her rights on *Gone With the Wind*. The Netherlands was occupied; the fate of the Dutch agent and the publisher, unknown, but Peggy persisted in her fight to overturn a first court decision in their favor — that her copyright did not cover the publication of *Gone With the Wind* in the Netherlands. This suit turned out years later to be a landmark copyright case and did, in the end, help to win protection abroad for American writers. But at this time her fight was not a popular cause, and even Latham and Macmillan thought she should desist. Nor did she allow the war in Europe to cut her off from publishers of her foreign editions in countries not directly under Nazi occupation. John kept ledgers on all of them and Peggy was proud to say in the late forties that almost all had paid the revenues owed her. She seldom turned down requests for loans from close friends or associates, but she kept businesslike records of them and photostats of all checks that had been exchanged.

The rest of Peggy's time was spent nursing her father, rolling bandages, and answering every letter that came to her. All of her out-of-town friends were involved in their own personal problems. The Dowdeys were still in financial straits, and the Granberrys, whose son, Edwin, Jr., had been nearly blinded in a freak accident, were struggling through hard times.

Herschel Brickell had reunited with his wife and, as the Marshes had sided with him during the period of the incompleted divorce proceedings, their relations with Norma were strained. Jealousy on Norma Brickell's part could have added to this problem. Her husband had been known to wander from time to time and was presently involved with another woman — a situation much discussed in the letters that passed between Peggy and the Dowdeys. It is doubtful that Peggy ever had an affair with Brickell, but she was, as close observers have said, "taken with him," and her letters to him are more revealing than to anyone else. Seldom did she discuss Norma or direct more than cursory regards to her in their early correspondence. After the Brickells' reconciliation, Peggy wrote a chatty letter to the two of them, but she later confided to the Dowdeys that she "never heard from Herschel anymore."

In Atlanta, the Marshes had a dwindling social life. Peggy was called upon for autograph parties for local writers and teas at the Atlanta Historical Society, but when it came to friends as close as the Dowdeys, the Marshes had few in Atlanta. There were Stephens and Carrie Lou, but the two women had never had much in common. Medora and John still bore their old grudges toward one another, and Augusta was eternally involved in playing hostess to visiting opera companies and attending concerts that Peggy found boring. Frank Daniel came by occasionally, but he had published an article about Peggy in the *Journal* that she had not liked and their friendship had cooled. The Marshes had so thoroughly convinced people that they must leave Peggy alone so that she could have some peace and privacy that most old friends were afraid that by inviting John and Peggy for dinner they would appear to be "celebrity showers-off" and would be committing a transgression of their friendship.

Peggy was known by almost everyone in Atlanta, and old friends felt honored that they had once been a part of her circle. Many had a favorite Margaret Mitchell story that they relished and told and retold. Those fortunate enough to have a signed book displayed it prominently in their living rooms or libraries, but few of them still felt that they could telephone Peggy just to chat or ask to visit with her on the spur of the moment. Peggy was seen in public now — she gave a party for Medora when her mystery book, *Who Killed Aunt Maggie?*, was made into a film and previewed in Atlanta, and she attended, for the first time in several years, a Georgia Press Association meeting with John. She was coming out of her shell, but no one's attitude toward her was the same. The wasp waist was gone; the bright blue eyes, heavy-lidded; and years of indulging her taste for "corn likker" had made her face puffy. A small, select coterie of young men — admirers of *Gone With the Wind* who were somewhat awed at being acknowledged by its famous author — came often for tea or drinks, and to them Peggy was her "charming, funny self." In essence, she was being treated like an aging film star whose glories were behind her but who had become "a legend in her own time." There was always talk around her of "the *Gone With the Wind* years"; it was as though she had created an era — and had then outlived it.

A new cruiser, the U.S.S. *Atlanta*, was to be launched on August 9, 1941, at the Navy shipyards at Kearny, New Jersey, and Lieutenant Commander E. John Long, U.S.N., invited Peggy to come North to christen the ship. She swiftly accepted and, in an eight-page letter, asked the Lieutenant Commander all kinds of questions, with what she should wear topping the list. If a bouquet was to be presented to her, she requested that it not be large, explaining, "I am small, not quite five feet tall. On several dreadful occasions in the past I have found myself presented with arm bouquets made of flowers with stems a yard long." She wondered if it would be "violating one of the Navy's sacred traditions" if she had no flowers at all, or if she could lay them down someplace when it came time for the launching for, because of her smallness, she preferred to have both arms free so she "could take a good two-handed swing with the bottle."

She also inquired of Lieutenant Commander Long whether it was customary for a sponsor to present a gift to the ship she christens. And if so, would "some after-dinner coffee cups which our Atlanta Historical Society had made by Wedgwood in England" be suitable? Each cup featured a small scene from old Atlanta, but they were small and delicate, and she realized that probably "Navy officers like cups which hold a quart. Please tell me," she went on, "if you think the gift of the after-dinner cups would be inappropriate to such a highly masculine set of people as Naval officers."

Frankly, the Lieutenant Commander did not think the demitasse set appropriate, but he simply replied that although her gesture was greatly appreciated, her presence at the launching would be gift enough to the U.S. Navy. He also provided her with the specifics she had requested and sent along a photograph of Eleanor Roosevelt swinging a large bottle against the side of a ship, in the hope that this would give Peggy some idea of what ladies usually wear to a christening. This did not satisfy her, however, and she wondered whether different attire would be required for a morning launching than for an afternoon one. Then, too, Mrs. Roosevelt's heavy coat led her to believe that *that* launching was in the fall or winter, and August was dreadfully hot in places like New York and New Jersey.

Next to the honorary degree from Smith College, the invitation to christen the U.S.S. *Atlanta* was one of the most meaningful honors in Peggy's life, and she was determined to do the correct thing by it. Shipyard strikes delayed the occasion and finally September 6, a Saturday, was set. She arrived on the Thursday before and, with a great deal of secrecy, reminiscent of her days at the Northwood, sneaked out of the Waldorf Astoria where she was staying, to see the Dowdeys in their new apartment on East Eighty-second Street. She had agreed with Macmillan that on the next morning, September 5, she would hold a large press interview in her suite. A table was set up along one wall, where she and the Macmillan publicity director were seated; extra chairs had been brought in to accommodate hosts of newspapermen and press photographers. Pinned to Peggy's pale blue dress was a large white orchid sent to her by Mr. George Brett who, she remarked, "most probably doesn't know I'm not the orchid type."

Laughter.

Reporter: "Miss Mitchell have you ever christened a battleship before?"

MM: "Battleships are named after states, cruisers after cities. But no, I never have christened either one and I'm sure the newsreel will probably show me swinging one minute and dripping the next. Everyone in Atlanta has been thinking of everything that could possibly happen. I will hit it so hard I will knock a hole in it [the ship] and they will arrest me for sabotage. I am an old baseball player. I swing from my right. I was pitcher until I was fourteen but I was never good at hitting a ball so perhaps if I bunt it I won't have to worry."

Laughter again.

Reporter: "We were given photographs of you in a Red Cross uniform. Are you active in the Atlanta chapter?"

MM: "Oh yes. I'm the smallest in the class and the one always being demonstrated on. Classes are held in one of our very swanky clubs in the ballroom and the colored attendants were outraged at seeing me used for the fireman's drag!"

With that, she stood up and to her audience's delight, walked around the table, fell to the floor and demonstrated, while members of the press stood up on their chairs to get a good view.

MM: "You enter a burning building, tie the hands like this [crossed] lay them on their back, then on all fours crawl and drag them between your legs. To tie the hands you take any piece or strip of clothing from your outfit. [And then, she popped up to her feet and made her way back to the table.] The air is better on the floor than higher up."

Applause.

Reporter: "What was it like just after *Gone With the Wind* was published?"

MM: "The phone rang every three minutes for twenty-four hours and the doorbell every five minutes."

Reporter: "And now?"

MM: "Well, there is still a lot of business connected with the book. It is published in nineteen foreign countries including Canada and England and that means working under nineteen different copyright laws, nineteen different financial setups, nineteen different sets of unwritten customs. It all takes a great deal of time."

Reporter: "Do you have an agent?"

MM: "A foreign agent, but I have no American agent. My husband is my business manager. My father and my brother are lawyers."

Reporter: "Why did you file a second suit against the Dutch for copyright infringement?"

MM: "So that American books would be safe anywhere."

Reporter: "How many copies of *Gone With the Wind* have been sold to date in the United States?"

Grinell: "2,868,000 copies."

Reporter: "Do you hope to get back into writing?"

MM: "All I need is paper and opportunity."

Reporter: "Someone said writing was an application of seats, pants, and chair."

MM: [laughing] "It means just that and . . . well, I would rather do anything else than write and I never ran across that lady, inspiration."

Reporter: "What were your most vivid memories of the prefilm days?"

MM: "Girls who had run away from their homes to try out for Scarlett O'Hara came to my door. 'No, sugar, I can't help you get into pictures,' I'd tell them. Then they'd beg for me to ask their schools not to expell them and their mothers not to tell anybody [that they had tried for Scarlett O'Hara]. It all took a lot of time. Then, there were people posing as me. One even tried to collect my royalties."

Reporter: "The premiere in Atlanta in December, 1939, must have been exciting for you."

MM: "Yes, it was, but there was a lot of unpleasantness because of the tickets. I only had two, and those only five hours before the show was to begin. About 300,000 people wanted to go and there were only 2,000 tickets. Some Atlanta women could say they had been to the unveiling of the Jefferson Davis Monument in 1884, but their daughters — if they had been 'privileged' — can now say, 'Mama was there when Jefferson Davis came, but I was at the premiere [of *Gone With the Wind*]."

Reporter: "If you write another book would it be of the South?"

MM: "Sugar, I don't know anything else."

The reporters left the press conference in high spirits, won over by Peggy's own good humor. Afterwards, a luncheon for Peggy and fourteen members of the Macmillan staff was held in a small private room at the Waldorf. Mint juleps were served first and then Peggy was seated, at her request, with her copy editor, Miss Prink, on one side and George Brett on the other.

At 10:20 the next morning, in a navy outfit trimmed in crisp white, and a hat that looked as if it just might take sail, Peggy stood on the dock surrounded by Naval officers and photographers. The sun blinded her vision and she swung and missed three times before the bottle hit the side of the ship. "In baseball I would have been out," she told Admiral Bowen, who was beside her, as a cheer rose from the rest of the spectators.

Talk of war was in the air morning, noon, and night. Unlike her Scarlett, Peggy was not bored by it nor did she necessarily think it was "men's business, not ladies." Christening the *Atlanta* had kindled in her a new sense of patriotism, and she threw herself into the task of rolling bandages and putting together "care" packages to send overseas. She protested loudly that she could not see how the United States could stay out of the war or how they were to stand with any degree of pride if they did. She was never to become a Roosevelt supporter, but she felt — much like her own character Stuart Tarleton — that the country would "have to fight or stand branded as cowards before the whole world." She said it came as no surprise to her when the Japanese attacked Pearl Harbor on December 7, because she had never trusted those "varmints worth a damn." Just before Christmas, Peggy went back to the Brooklyn Navy Yard to attend the commissioning ceremony of the *Atlanta* and then had luncheon aboard the ship, where all the men from Georgia lined up to meet her. The day after Christmas she wrote the U.S.S. *Atlanta*'s captain and asked if she could contribute something to the ship's seamen's fund, but the cruiser had begun its wartime service and was already heading out for enemy waters.

The following November, Peggy received the sad news that the U.S.S. *Atlanta* had been sunk off Guadalcanal and all the men on board were missing in action. It was not an easy thing for her to accept, for she felt a great sense of personal loss. But more than that, the sinking of the U.S.S. *Atlanta* brought back her old nightmares and, with them, a terrible foreboding about her own violent death.

Chapter Twenty-five

THE WAR gave Peggy's life a direction it had not had since the final manuscript of *Gone With the Wind* had been turned over to Macmillan. She did everything she could to aid in the war effort — the new Mercury sedan the Marshes had bought before Pearl Harbor remained garaged to conserve fuel; she continued to roll bandages; both she and John became street wardens; and they coped with the shortages of sugar and butter and meat. Still, they felt fortunate when they thought of the British.

Peggy read all the books about the war that she could lay her hands on, and all the war coverage in the local newspapers. Each month she purchased a sizable war bond, and she worked relentlessly on a bond-selling campaign to raise $35 million to buy another cruiser to replace the U.S.S. *Atlanta*. One windy, freezing day she stood outside selling bonds for five hours.

"We had all the Atlanta Marines with us," she wrote to a young Atlanta marine who had become a correspondent, "and they fired off a cannon every time anybody bought a thousand dollar bond. We were deafened and frozen but we had a wonderful time and raised $500,000."

It is doubtful that any other woman in America could have raised the $65 million that Margaret Mitchell brought in in a matter of six weeks. It was enough money to replace the U.S.S. *Atlanta* and to pay for two destroyers as well. All of her fears of public speaking seemed to have been dispelled. In fact, there were vestiges of Maybelle in Peggy's small person as she stood on boxes before microphones in factories and schools and city squares trying to shout her way into the hearts and pocketbooks of rich and poor.

The *Gone With the Wind* fan letters had all but stopped by this time, but Peggy's postage expenses were larger than ever, as she carried on heavy correspondences with dozens of servicemen who hailed from Atlanta or from other Southern towns. Some she had known before the war; most, she had not, but often they were related to family or friends of hers. To Leodel Coleman of Statesboro, Georgia, after telling him all about civilian "hardships, shortages and the likes," she explained, "I [want] you to know about the changes that are going on back here at home and the way civilians live. You and the other boys are so far away from us that if we do not tell you of the little things which make up the big changes in American wartime living, then you will never know about them."

She griped quite a bit in these letters but thought griping was a "normal and healthy sign . . . symptomatic of a free country where people can and do squawk and criticize the government. People of Germany can't do this."

The Marsh apartment on Piedmont Avenue had an open-door policy to servicemen, even those known only tangentially, and Peggy appeared to enjoy the informality of wartime life as she had never enjoyed the crush of fame. She behaved much in the way she had before *Gone With the Wind*, flirting harmlessly with the young men, who succumbed quickly to her warmth, good humor, and charm. Clifford Dowdey was amused by this when he and Helen came through Atlanta for a night, and he wrote Peggy later that she "must be having a return to her debutante days."

In late March, just after her strenuous war-bond campaign, Peggy had an operation at Johns Hopkins in Baltimore to remove the cartilage between the lower lumbar vertebra and the vertebra above it, for the cartilage was pressing on the nerves that ran down her legs and into her feet. The doctor promised an end to her chronic backaches and the freedom to wear shoes of her choice, and she was in high spirits following the surgery, convinced that she owed her recovery to the Southern roots of the neurosurgeon. She wrote the Dowdeys that one day when this doctor and a group of interns were standing around her bed, she was moved to tell them about her Grandpa Mitchell back during the Civil War, and about "the gallantry, courage and the plain stupidity that made him stick his head up above the corn to lay his rifle across a splitrail fence. A minié ball went through the back of his head, fracturing it in two places." At this point, she said, she put her best creative and reportorial efforts into the inspiring saga of her grandfather's hitchhike to a Richmond hospital and his further travels on a flatcar to Atlanta, still without any medical attention. Then, to impress upon them how tough her grandfather was, she told them of his two marriages after the war, his begetting of twelve children, and his amassing of "a whacking amount" of Atlanta real estate and cash. Finished, she fell back "limply" on her pillows, ready for praise about her grandfather's stamina.

The doctor considered her story in silence for a moment and then said, "How often did he have convulsions?"

"What do you mean, convulsions?" she asked. "Grandpa never had a convulsion in his life."

"No convulsions? But he must have had convulsions with a brain injury at such a place," the doctor countered.

"He never had any convulsions," Peggy insisted, but, trying to be helpful, went on to admit that he had had the worst disposition and the shortest temper "of any good-looking man between the Potomac and the Rio Grande." She thought she had impressed her surgeon, she wrote the Dowdeys, but he rose ponderously, summoning his entourage of white-coated interns.

"No convulsions," he said, shaking his head indignantly. "I never heard the like." And he took himself off, convinced, she was certain, that she was "several kinds of a liar."

Peggy came home from the hospital on April 19, 1943, and was able to sit up half the day strapped up in a brace, which, she confided to Helen Dowdey, "improves my figure below but does nothing for my above, as thirty pounds below the waist have been displaced to the north. John says with the addition of a few medals I'd be a dead ringer for General Goering."

To one of two brothers, former pressmen, who were both overseas during 1944, Peggy wrote that it was somehow difficult to think of them in uniform since, the last time she'd seen them both, at a Press Institute party, they had been in costume — dressed up like inhabitants of Dog Patch, with bare feet, torn clothes, a fishing pole, and a jug.

> I enjoyed that tacky party enormously and my greatest enjoyment came from something you have probably forgotten. Do you remember how I knocked on your door to see if you were ready and you two came roaring out looking like *Tabacco Road* or something William Faulkner wrote about and chased me, screaming, down the hotel corridor, making gestures at me with jug and fishing pole? My own costume as you recall of hoop skirts and plumed hat and large doll was a bit strange to see. And just then those Yankee tourists got off on the wrong floor and caught a glimpse of us and decided that everything they had ever read about the South was true. I've often thought those poor tourists went back and lectured before culture clubs on their experiences in the South.

It was so well known among servicemen abroad that Margaret Mitchell would reply to their letters that Bill Mauldin, the syndicated cartoonist, published a cartoon that showed one of his "feet-itchy," exhausted combat soldiers writing on a pad, "Dear, Dear Miss Mitchell" by the light from nearby artillery fire. Peggy wrote Mauldin that his cartoon had "raised her stock with youngsters to extravagant heights."

A temporary building was set up for a Red Cross canteen in Piedmont Park, a short distance from the Marsh apartment, and Peggy was often there to help servicemen by mending uniforms, sewing on new chevrons, reattaching buttons, and reknitting gloves. And, as she worked, there would always be a crowd of young soldiers around her chair, sitting on the floor or leaning against the wall, laughing and rallying with her, or listening quietly while she told a story.

She remained an extraordinary tale bender and she collected stories to tell her young uniformed admirers:

> A soldier was stationed near Boston and became infatuated with a young lady in that city. The government moved him to Missis-

sippi. Shortly after his arrival in Mississippi he received a letter from her stating that she was "elected" and knew that he wanted to do the right thing by her and please send her some money and she would come on down to Mississippi. He replied in about ten days, telling her that she had better stay where she was; that after careful inquiry in the community he believed a bastard would have more chance in Boston than a Yankee in Mississippi.

Peggy's network of servicemen correspondents brought news about the fate of *Gone With the Wind* in war-torn Europe, although she had no way to keep track of foreign sales. Many of the publishers she had been contracted to had been liquidated by invading armies. Still, *Gone With the Wind* was read. The Germans at first allowed its circulation in Occupied France, feeling the Yankee oppressors would serve German propaganda well in discrediting the United States as the "land of the free." When they realized that this plan had boomeranged, and that the French wholly empathized with the portrait of Southerners as a people who would not accept defeat, publication was halted in France and all copies that could be found were confiscated. Indomitably, *Gone With the Wind* then turned up on the black market at about sixty dollars a copy, a price that could have purchased the rare luxuries of a pound of butter and a dozen eggs in Holland, Norway, and Belgium. According to the reports of her correspondents, people had been shot for possession of a copy of the book.

A tide of gallantry rose in Peggy during the war years, and, at the same time, her middle-aged jowliness evolved into a stalwart maturity. When she spoke, she kindled the fire of pride and sacrifice and heroism in her audience. She wholeheartedly believed in the war, and sacrifice was to be borne proudly. When news came back to her that one of her "pen pals" had been killed in action and her letters to him found in his knapsack, she framed the letter. In February, 1944, she received an invitation to christen the new U.S.S. *Atlanta*. It afforded the Marshes an opportunity to travel up North to visit with John's family and to see the Dowdeys, who, they had just learned, were having marital problems. They arranged for Helen Dowdey to dine with them alone in their suite at the Waldorf Astoria on the night of February 8. Since they knew there had been another woman involved, they were not surprised to hear that Helen planned to go to Reno for a divorce. Peggy tried to convince her that this would be a legally unsound move, for if she ever was to remarry and to have children, that marriage might not be legal, nor would the children of that marriage have their rights of inheritance protected. But Helen would not be swayed.

As summer, 1944, approached it looked as though the war was near its end. Peggy's happiness over this was dimmed by Eugene Mitchell's severe kidney problems and rapidly deteriorating condition. She wrote Helen Dowdey that her father was "just as easy to handle as a wildcat in his prime." Eugene Mitchell had grown even more irascible with the years, and his illness now required that he be tended twenty-four hours a day. Good nursing help was hard to find and, to make matters worse, Mr. Mitchell harassed the orderlies Peggy was able to hire, was rude to the doctors, and refused to take so much as an aspirin unless Peggy administered it.

Eugene Mitchell died on June 17, 1944. Peggy was torn by her ambivalent feelings toward her father and his death. For six years his illness had been an excuse for her nonattendance and nonapplication to anything that she was opposed to doing. In 1941, she had written the Dowdeys that if it were not for her responsibility to her father, who used up all her energies, she would be writing again. To Douglas S. Freeman, Robert E. Lee's Pulitzer Prize-winning biographer, she wrote much the same thing in 1944. It was not true, of course. She had filled her life during those years with her wartime activities — the letters, the bond drives, the canteen appearances, Red Cross work, street-warden duty, and packing and sending gifts to soldiers: food, sweaters, chewing tobacco, snuff, and even, in one case, a country guitar.

Magazines still approached her frequently to write a story for them, and she always refused. Selznick had tried to reopen negotiations to buy the stage rights to *Gone With the Wind* for "an agreeable figure," but Stephens and John felt they would be worth more at a later date. And Macmillan often inquired through Lois and Latham about any new "literary activity."

The inconsistency of Peggy's attitude was that she was always trying to galvanize other writers into beginning new works, whereas she remained caught up in her *Gone With the Wind* fame. She even wrote Stark Young, begging him to begin a new book soon; and, after the publication of *A Tree Grows in Brooklyn*, she wrote to Betty Smith, whom she did not know, "I hope the world is not too much with you and that you will have time to write more books."

Evidently the world was too much with Margaret Mitchell, because even her father's death did not get her back to the typewriter, at least, not in any literary pursuit. The "business" of *Gone With the Wind* remained to take up the time and energy she was not giving to the war effort. To an under secretary at the State Department, in a letter dated October 14, 1944, she confided her fears that perhaps she might be considered to be "trading with the enemy" if she continued doing business with her French publisher, who was a suspected collaborationist. She asked: "Has a policy or procedure been established by the provisional French government or the Allied nations for the handling of the property and assets of collaborationists? If such assets have been taken over by some governmental agency, what is that agency and what would be my line of action in protecting my right? Would I be expected to deal directly with that agency in France or through some agency of the United States Government in this country?"

A few days later, she was battling with the editor of the *New York World Telegram* because they had published two stories that repeated the statement that *Gone With the Wind* had been sold to the movies in galley proof for fifty thousand dollars:

"Gone With the Wind" was not sold in galley proof and I have never made any statement as to the amount I received. . . . I have been correcting this misstatement ever since 1936. But here we go again!

I finished reading galley proofs on "Gone With the Wind" in March. It is highly doubtful that anyone read it in galley proof. If they did no offer was made to me at that time. . . . I sold the motion picture rights on July 30, 1936, as the date of my contract will show. As the pre-publication sale was something between 50,000 and 90,000 copies, I knew my book would be fairly successful. "Gone With the Wind" had sold several hundred thousand copies by the time I disposed of the motion picture rights.

I do get tired of seeing this error crop up about once a month, in spite of my denials. . . . If ever you . . . are writing on the subject of the sale of moving picture rights, I hope you omit mention of "Gone With the Wind" or else state that it was not sold in galley proof and that, far from being hornswaggled by Hollywood, the rights to "Gone With the Wind" brought the highest price ever paid for a first novel by an unknown author up to that time.

Working backwards in Peggy's letter to the *World Telegram*, it would seem she did not want anyone to think she had been fool enough to sell *Gone With the Wind* as cheaply as its original purchase price now appeared. But of course, it *had* been sold for $50,000 to Selznick and, furthermore, not only had Kay Brown received galley proofs from Annie Laurie Williams in April of 1936, but so had Doris Warner, Samuel Goldwyn, Louis B. Mayer, and Darryl Zanuck. Warner's first offers had been made in April and there *were* no books of *Gone With the Wind* until early May. And, in Macmillan's files there remains an order for twelve sets of galley proofs.

But the point is, why was Peggy still expending so much energy on the maintenance of her legend and that of her book? The answer is all too sad and clear. The critiques on the book were all in, the excitement long past, the film accepted as a classic. With no new book on the horizon, Margaret Mitchell was no longer news. Keeping the legend alive was the only way Peggy knew to sustain interest in herself and, during this period, she seems to have been involved in a small game in which she wrote to friends in the newspaper world and told them, for instance, about *Gone With the Wind* playing for five years to queues in wartime England, or about Hitler having a private showing of it in Berlin with his "four closest boyfriends." These nuggets would then appear in the press, much to Peggy's "consternation."

Margaret Baugh noted a change in her employer's appearance and attitude around Christmas, 1944. Peggy's sense of humor did not surface as often, she was careless of her grooming, and her letters to her fans lost all their variety and verve.

The two Margarets — who had now spent over nine years in each other's daily company, and under particularly close circumstances — were always on a slightly formal basis. Peggy was tremendously fond of Margaret Baugh and grateful for her help and her loyalty. But a line was drawn, and the employer-secretary relationship was meticulously maintained. Margaret Baugh kept a sheaf of notes about Peggy's moods and made certain close observations which indicate she might have been considering writing a book about Peggy at some future date.

Before Christmas, 1944, Margaret Baugh noted that Peggy was "generally cheerful." After that, she entered a "glum" period. The only time Margaret Baugh ever saw Peggy cry was in February of 1945, when a nylon stocking she was rinsing out in the kitchen sink somehow slid down the drain and was lost. For some reason known to Peggy alone, this stirred her emotions, and she stood leaning against the sink sobbing bitterly, unmindful of Margaret Baugh standing helplessly and with some embarrassment in the doorway.

The Germans signed an unconditional surrender in Rheims on May 7, 1945. America was still at war with Japan but, during the summer of 1945, many Atlanta boys returned home. Their return contributed to Peggy's bouts of depression. She explained to her few close friends that she could not help but think of all the Georgia boys who had been left dead on foreign soil. Images of death paraded through her night dreams. She was suffering insomnia again, and she wrote Edwin Granberry an odd request — not to destroy her letters no matter who should ask him to do so. She added, "I'm going to die in a car-crash. I feel very certain of this."

Chapter Twenty-six

WITH THE WAR OVER and her father dead, Peggy finally had
to face up to the fact that she would never return to her "writing desk." In January of 1945, Peggy had written George Brett
that procrastination was one of Scarlett O'Hara's basic weak-
nesses — she kept putting off until tomorrow coming to terms
with her own conscience — and that she guessed she was guilty
of the same vice. Someday she would try to understand why she
had not written anything but letters since *Gone With the Wind* —
but, for the present, that day would have to be tomorrow.

Nine years had passed since the publication of her book.
During that time, she had made notes for only one story idea,
which she had discussed with John and Margaret Baugh. It was
to be a fictionalized account of her own sudden fame — its
cause and effect. But Margaret Baugh later told friends that by
1945 Peggy had long since abandoned this idea and that she
had made no story notes for years. The creator of Scarlett
O'Hara had fallen into the trap that her heroine had avoided —
Margaret Mitchell was the victim, not the master, of her world.

With peace came a brand new surge of activity in the sales of
Gone With the Wind, both domestic and foreign. In October and
November of 1945, the book even reappeared at the bottoms
of the best-seller lists, and the rise in sales in Europe was
astronomical. The daily business of the foreign editions was
complex. The Marshes still had a bookkeeper two evenings a

month, and he recorded all monies coming in and going out. But John was in charge of the foreign rights. In 1941, the Marshes had dealt with a foreign agency for a short time, but the association had ended unpleasantly when Stephens accused the agents of not giving their best effort to the problems the book was having in the Netherlands. The fact was, the Mitchells did not trust strangers; and John now made himself responsible for such matters as finding out which foreign publishers had survived the ravages of war, and what laws now governed them. Letters had been sent to Peggy's "storm-battered" European publishers and they were "checking in." She reported to Lois, "Still no news from Poland, where I know my first set of publishers were Jewish. Nothing from Latvia, but the Russians have them. No news from Finland at all. They were a fine set of people, and I recall that when the Russians were almost at the gates of Helsinki and the old gentleman of the firm was running the business while his boys were at the front, they still came through and paid my royalties."

The "foreign stuff," as she called it, was keeping the Marshes busy. Peggy's network of servicemen overseas and her foreign admirers had reported to her the incredible sales of *Gone With the Wind* in occupied countries during the war, and she was determined that this information now be verified so that her foreign publishers could do the "honorable thing" by her and square their debts. She was aware that the book had been banned by the Nazis, and that, therefore, it had been sold on the black market and a true accounting could never be had. But John wrote letters whenever he could trace a publisher's address. In most cases, he received replies, and eventually — since the firms wanted to continue publishing the book — royalties.

Since June of 1945, John had had a fever that persisted without any sign of abating, and the doctors once again were baffled. One diagnosed the return of undulant fever but, as there was nothing he could prescribe for it, John continued both his work at Georgia Power and on the foreign affairs of *Gone With the Wind*. By December, Peggy was alarmed. "He is always so fatigued it frightens me," she wrote a friend, "but there is nothing much to do about it except 'supportive' treatment. Perhaps by spring this new drug, 'streptomycin' [sic] will be out of the experimental class and we can try it."

John wrote to Helen Dowdey that they never did seem to get caught up on the work that had to be done. Despite this, he and Peggy were going to go to Sea Island, a resort off the Georgia coast, for Christmas to get a few days' rest. Early on the morning of December 24, they arrived by train in Jesup, Georgia, where they then had to change for Brunswick and Sea Island by private transport. A station wagon was scheduled to meet them, but when they left the train — in a driving rainstorm and a hundred feet from the depot — there was no porter in sight and no station wagon. Peggy, a coat over her head for protection, ran for cover as she shouted to John to leave their suitcases and follow her. Ignoring her order, John juggled the bags uncomfortably and started toward the station house. Halfway there he was seized by a sharp pain up his arm and stood frozen for a few moments. Then, as the pain began to subside, he made his way shakily to Peggy's side. His face was drawn and tissue-paper white, but he assured her he was all right. A few minutes later, the station wagon arrived.

As soon as they reached the Cloister Hotel at Sea Island, John went to bed. An hour later, he suffered a severe heart attack. There was no doctor in the hotel, no doctor on the island. Peggy was frantic and she finally commandeered the hotel's station wagon and got John to nearby Brunswick, where there was a hospital. On Christmas Day, John Marsh nearly died, but then slowly, he began to revive. It was three weeks before he could be moved to Atlanta's Piedmont Hospital. Two months later, he was still there, and Peggy wrote Lois: "There is a faint hope that John will be home in a week by ambulance. How long he will stay upstairs [in their apartment] I do not know. . . . The whole truth of his recovery will not be apparent until he starts to take up normal or semi-normal life again."

That was not to be for a very long time and, in fact, John Marsh never did recover from this attack; from the time of his heart attack on Sea Island he lived what Peggy called a "semi-normal life." He was brought home from the hospital on a stretcher ten weeks after the attack, and for months he could do nothing but lie flat on his back. The doctor had wanted him to remain in the hospital, but Peggy did not think he was strong enough "to stand the hospital," where it took "forty minutes for the nurses to come," and where the orderlies stopped work at

8:00 P.M. "with the sanction of the hospital" and let "the patients wet the bed if they so desired." She was a martinet at trying to get things done for him in the hospital, but still complained that it was sometimes sixteen hours between supper and breakfast, and that the dirty plates and greasy tableware were more than she could bear.

Peggy hired a young black man who was studying to be an orderly to come home with John. For months, the house was turned into a hospital, with Peggy helping with the nursing and Bessie putting in extra hours for a "second shift." By July, 1946, John was able to be propped up in bed for twenty to thirty minutes. "It seems wonderful to him. It is wonderful to me, too," she wrote to Helen Dowdey. But the future was unknown. At present, she was grateful for the small progress he had made. But, she said, she did not want to think about "how long it will be before John can think of getting out of bed, nor how free or limited his activities will be when he does get up."

She confided to Lois in July that she did not think John would ever again be able to carry the double load of the job at the power company and her foreign affairs. "To be frank," she wrote, "at present I do not know if he will ever be able to carry *any* load at all." To her mind, his illness could not have happened at a worse time. There was a "four-cornered dog fight of a piracy suit" in Yugoslavia, another one in Belgium, her Spanish publisher was misappropriating funds (she subsequently regained them), there was a "mad rush" to get money out of France before the devaluation of the franc, there were three new contracts to sign, and on top of all this, there was still the unresolved piracy suit in the Netherlands.

She had won her case at the retrial, but the war had intervened and settlement had not been made. The payment was finally delivered in the summer of 1946, and Peggy felt elated by it for, in her opinion, the lawsuit and settlement was of international importance and touched directly or indirectly "the rights of every author in this country." She wrote to George Brett, "I don't know of any other author who has made such a fight to establish the legality of the copyright and I do not know of any publisher who has taken the trouble as you did to test it."

Without question, Peggy was a terrific fighter. Just give her a cause she believed in, and she stuck it out to the bitter end. When her battles were not in her own interest, they were usually on behalf of close friends or family. Bessie and the Marshes' laundress, Carrie, who had been with them for over twenty years, figured in that category. Carrie was dying of cancer the week that John came home from Piedmont Hospital. The Holbrooks were proud people who had never taken charity, and they appealed to "Miss Peggy" to try to find a noncharity hospital bed in which Carrie could die more comfortably than at home. Peggy tried every paying hospital in the Atlanta area, but none of them would take Carrie. Finally, Peggy threw herself upon the sisters of Our Lady of Perpetual Help, and begged them to violate their rule that patients should be friendless and without money. Carrie was taken in and a "donation" was arranged. Three days later, she died.

Peggy now took up the cause of Atlanta's "Negro problem" — mainly, the need for a paying hospital to afford better medical care for those blacks who could pay and did not want charity. As soon as John was able to move from his bed, Peggy began to raise funds to build a pay hospital for blacks. She helped to sell the plan to the trustees of the Fulton–DeKalb Hospital Authority and to the Fulton County Medical Society, and she gave them their first pledge, of one thousand dollars.

Before Christmas, 1946, with John not well and his future looking bleak, Peggy set out to try to buy a one-story house in their general neighborhood, so that John would not have to climb steps. She found a perfect house, but she felt the price was too high and she decided she would not make a move until the following spring, when, she predicted to Lois, prices were "bound to come down."

The Marshes' domestic situation had been difficult that summer. Bessie had been out ill, and her daughter, Deon, had come to cook and clean for them. Then Deon had left to have a mastectomy performed. The young orderly had quit too, and there had been nothing else for Peggy to do but to put John back in Piedmont Hospital until Bessie was able to come back to work in September. On John's return home, a sixteen-year-old orderly was hired and, from that time, John's progress was steady but unspectacular. By Christmas, he could sit up for several hours at a time, an improvement that gave Peggy an idea.

The Marshes had always loved movies, so Peggy now rented a sixteen-millimeter movie projector and sent the janitor to town every day to get them films to show. They especially liked the old films, and within a few months they had seen all the vintage Chaplins, as well as such movies as *The Last Mile, Scarface,* and *Hell's Angels.* To Helen Dowdey she wrote, "Machine guns rattle every night here and the tom-toms of 'South of Pago-Pago' awake the echoes."

Peggy hardly went anywhere except to the grocery store, and she seldom saw anyone other than Medora Perkerson and her old friend, Sam Tupper, who would sit and watch films with them. It was not a satisfying life for Peggy, but she was thankful John was alive and she wrote Helen Dowdey, "As God is my witness I have never had so much business, domestic and foreign, and as some [letters] include checks [that] I never expected to see . . . I know I should not kick." Still, tending John and handling all their domestic and foreign affairs left her no time for anything else. She was, she confessed, almost as confined to the house as her patient.

The revival of foreign interest in *Gone With the Wind* that had begun with the war's end continued as war-torn countries overseas went through their own reconstructions. And, with the book's reappearance on American best-seller lists, there was a small resurgence in 1946 of the "rubberneck" autoists, the bus tours, and the stacks of mail. Peggy now wrote to Edwin Granberry that she had made a revolutionary change in her life — she would no longer be hauled out to lunch to see "visiting firemen," she did not care if she ever spoke publicly again, she would not be an "unpaid Chamber of Commerce greeter," she would not be on public display "like Stone Mountain and the Cyclorama," and there would be no more lunches with "the President of the Daughters of I-Will-Arise of Opp, Alabama." Peggy Mitchell would once again be her own woman. Rather late in the game, she decided to remove her name from the Atlanta telephone directory and get an unlisted number.

This "revolutionary change" seems to have been more of a trade-off, however. With John incapacitated, Peggy was now the protector and the collector general for "Margaret Mitchell, Author," and she scrapped in her own behalf with amazing tenacity. All the "chiselers" were back, "anxious to turn a penny." She wrote to George Brett, "Even some of the hotels and boarding houses have glibly pointed out this or the other place as where Aunt Pittypat lived and I have *forced* them to desist." There was a professor at Western Reserve University in Cleveland who had tried to copyright a detailed map of the Atlanta of 1861, including possible locales of homes and incidents in *Gone With the Wind*. Peggy forced him to "desist," too, writing the professor that she had gone to a great deal of trouble and had spent much time mixing up the topography of Atlanta so that no house could be located, and that she had done this purposely to avoid embarrassing anyone and encumbering herself with legal battles. Did he realize, she inquired, that a perfectly respectable family had lived in the house he ascribed to Belle Watling?

Peggy handled the complicated business of foreign rights with equal competence. Her head for business had always been good, but she had resisted running her own affairs in the past because it had seemed "unfeminine." The war and John's illness had changed her thinking about that. Women had always been able to take over the running of things during wars, when men were out fighting, and they were seen as "stalwart," not unfeminine, at such times.

By September, the Marshes knew John would never go back to his job at the power company. They had been expecting this news, and it did not disturb them unduly. He was able to be helped across the street to the Piedmont Driving Club every afternoon, have a drink, and stay about forty minutes. In the evening, Peggy often sent over to the club for champagne cocktails and dinner to be brought over and served by one of the waiters in their living room. It was an "extravagance," she felt, but worth the expenditure, as it was one of the few pleasures they could enjoy together.

❦

It had been a little more than a decade since the madness over *Gone With the Wind* had begun. Peggy was now forty-six years old. Medora, who was older, looked younger and still put in her full day writing. Lois looked surprisingly youthful. But Peggy thought she herself had aged badly. She had gained thirty pounds since John's heart attack, her hair had begun to thin, and, too, there was the puffiness about her face and under her chin. But more distressing than her matronly exterior was the fact that she was beginning to *feel* old, and it nagged at her that she did not have many years ahead of her. Intimations of these feelings appeared in her letters to the Granberrys and the Dowdeys during this period. People in Atlanta stopped Stephens on the street and asked if everything was all right with Peggy because she looked so weary.

Her scale of living had certainly not altered much since pre-*Gone With the Wind* days. She lived only a few streets from where she had been raised and twice married. Over the years she had fought obstinately to hold on to the past, to anything and everything that made up her history, to those things and people who were part of her sphere. Matters to do with the book she treated the same way — possessively. But change had come nonetheless, as it has a habit of doing as one ages. A unique mixture of Southern belle, young tomboy, and crusty woman had always dominated Peggy's personality, and the first two had overshadowed the last to give her a distinct charm. But, at age forty-six, the young boy and the coquette were gone.

Chapter Twenty-seven

ANNE MORROW LINDBERGH once said that fame is a kind of death. That was certainly true in Peggy's case. From the summer of 1936, when *Gone With the Wind* had been published and fame had intruded upon the Marshes' world, all of her energies had been spent in either barricading herself against it or in coping with its entrapments. And so determined was she that fame would not change her way of life that she ceased growing emotionally and intellectually from the time of the publication of *Gone With the Wind* — and what is that but a kind of death?

Time that could have been spent writing, or at least in exploring new avenues of thought, had been given over to the stultifying task of maintaining a correspondence with thousands of strangers on two subjects only — *Gone With the Wind* and the minutiae of protecting her rights in it. That is not to say that if *Gone With the Wind* had not been such a grand success, Peggy would have written a second book, or anything more at all, for that matter. But she might have been a happy woman. Reading her personal letters to the Granberrys, the Dowdeys, Herschel Brickell, Lois Dwight Cole, and Ginny Morris, as well as John's letters to his sister, Frances, one is struck by the unhappiness that pervades their pages. Delight in *anything* is a rare occurrence, and when it does appear, it is of a curious nature — the wild goings on at a Georgia Press party, a "chiseler" stymied, a Southerner who approves of the book. There is a sense of Peggy's deep love for Georgia and for the city of her birth. But even that was not a living, current thing, but a passion that had been fixed some time long past, in her childhood — before Roosevelt and the New Deal, before *Gone With the Wind*, before her marriage to John, and before her marriage to Red Upshaw.

In fact, much as she loved her city's history, Peggy's feeling toward Atlanta ever since the Junior League matrons had turned their backs on her in 1921 had been one of defiance, an "I'll-show-you" attitude. And, when all of Atlanta, including the ladies of the Junior League, was at her feet, she chose to remain aloof but visible. There was a knob of retribution in her choice. Except for Medora, and later, Sam Tupper, both of whom she had known since her reporting days, her best friends had not been Atlantans. Of course, she was fond of Augusta and Lee Edwards, and she loved Stephens. But she did not often see them socially. Nor did she encourage her new friends to come to Atlanta; she preferred going to them. Loyal as she had been to her father, she almost always spent Christmas away from him.

A wistful note clings to John Marsh's letters. It was not he who felt so dedicated to their modest lifestyle in Atlanta nor, for that matter, to his job at Georgia Power. But he did think it would be bad for Peggy's image to have gone "high-hat," and he did believe that any change in their lifestyle would give that impression. Peggy's fame was a kind of death for John Marsh too. Not only did it take its physical claim on him, but it put an end to his ambitions and dreams as well. To leave his job for any reason but ill health, he feared, would have started tongues wagging. As far back as 1936, Marsh had felt he had gone as far as he could at Georgia Power. That same year, a major railroad had offered him a public-relations position with a chance for national prestige. But, by then, *Gone With the Wind* had been published, and he had put aside his own considerations.

By 1948, the *Gone With the Wind* fan letters had fallen back down to a trickle. Since the war, there had never been a time when the film was not being shown somewhere, and the book had never been out of print. But a curious thing had happened, perhaps because of the war's intervention. Both book and film had become legends in the matter of one generation and, due to this, new readers and viewers of *Gone With the Wind* assumed the author must be legendary as well and, if still alive, quite elderly. The best-seller lists were crowded with books about the Second World War and its survivors. The popularity of *Gone With the Wind* right after the war was attributed by many book people to have been due to its relevancy — war and its aftermath. But there were many new readers now who thought the book had been written by a woman in the nineteenth century. Sales rose each year and, with the appearance of an inexpensive edition as well, the book had more circulation than ever. But Peggy no longer had to worry about protecting her privacy from the invasion of the curious.

In the fall of 1948, however, she felt she did have cause to worry about Red Upshaw. After more than a decade of silence, news had reached them of his activities. The story was that he had spent the war years in the Merchant Marines and was now an incurable alcoholic and a bum, that he had been in several Southern cities, and that he had written mutual friends of the Marshes and asked them what Peggy was doing and why she had suddenly disappeared from the pages of the Atlanta telephone directory. The friends had written to the address he had given, telling him the Marshes were still in Atlanta, but their letter had come back marked "addressee unknown."

On a cold, windy Sunday in November of 1948, Peggy decided to make a new will to replace an earlier one made in 1936. A five-page document, the will is written in longhand in a simple, unlegalistic style, almost like a letter, with heirs referred to by their nicknames. According to Stephens, she had called him to come over a few days before this, and they had had a series of in-depth discussions about her finances as well as his own. She was surprised to learn, he said, that all her payments to him for legal services had gone into the family law firm in which their uncle was also a member, and that he had not accrued any personal wealth due to her. The money he did have had been earned from knowledgeable real-estate investments. He also said that at this time Peggy told him she wanted all her personal papers destroyed in the event of her death, as well as all her writings and manuscripts. She did not, however, mention this wish in her will.

Peggy's greatest concern was Bessie, and a house that she held the mortgage on and that Bessie was paying off. There was eight hundred dollars left on that mortgage, and Peggy wanted to make sure that Bessie got the house free and clear upon her death, and that the debt would then be cancelled. She said this twice in the will. Her bequests were not generous, except perhaps, in the case of Margaret Baugh, to whom she left a small annuity for life. Bessie, Bessie's daughter, Peggy's nephews and John's nieces and nephews, her godchildren, and Augusta Dearborn's son were all left token amounts of between one hundred and one thousand dollars, as were the Atlanta Historical Society and the Margaret Mitchell Library at Fayetteville. The rest of her estate was to be divided so that three-quarters went to John and one-quarter to Stephens. All rights to *Gone With the Wind*, all her personal papers, all the household furnishings, and her own personal possessions went to John. The names of three witnesses appear on the last page below her own, but as the will was drawn on a Sunday, it seems unlikely that it was witnessed that same day.

What is important about this will is, first, that Peggy said nothing in it about a wish to have her papers destroyed (a major issue later), and, second, that she left all rights to *Gone With the Wind* to John Marsh, a man even then at death's door, without specifying who should succeed him when he died. For a lawyer's daughter — as she was proud to boast she was — who had spent her entire adult life living the letter of the law, it is a confounding omission. As John had not made a will at that time, it meant that if the Marshes had died together, that "unscrupulous chiseler" Peggy was always fearing could well have stepped in and claimed to be Margaret Mitchell's child (perhaps from the first marriage), holding up the estate in a costly fight that would have created great problems for her legitimate next of kin — Stephens or her two nephews.

In January, 1949, Peggy received a newspaper clipping in the mail. Margaret Baugh had opened the envelope and debated whether she should show it to John first, but as he had not been well that day, she decided to give it to Peggy, warning her that it was about her first husband. Peggy's hand trembled as she held the clipping.

"Are you all right?" Margaret Baugh asked when Peggy put the clipping down.

Peggy did not reply. She sat there not moving for a moment or two. "Did you read it?" she asked Margaret Baugh.

"Yes," the secretary answered.

"What a terrible way to die," Peggy said quietly, and then she got up and went into her room and did not reappear for the remainder of the day.

Margaret Baugh wasn't sure what to do with the clipping, but she finally pasted it on a piece of paper and filed it in the four-drawer file of clippings that Peggy had collected over the last thirteen years, under *U* — for Berrien Kinnard Upshaw.

January 13, 1949 — Galveston, Texas

The possibility that Berrien Kinnard Upshaw, killed Wednesday in a drop from the fifth floor of a downtown hotel, was ill was voiced Wednesday night by a Salvation Army worker who had talked with him shortly before his death.

Mrs. Una M. Dean, corps sergeant major, said the 47-year-old seaman had passed out Tuesday at the Salvation Army home in a "kind of a fit" and when he recovered appeared in a dazed condition and claimed he couldn't remember his name.

Upshaw was discovered lying in the alley behind the hotel by Steve Connell, clerk of corporation court.

Justice of the Peace James L. McKenna returned an inquest verdict of death due to jumping from the fifth-story fire escape of a building, resulting in self-inflicted multiple traumatic injuries, suicidal.

According to the hotel clerk, Upshaw was sharing a fifth-floor room with three other men.

Upshaw's roommates said he arose a little after 6 A.M. Wednesday and went out of the room without saying anything to any of them. That was the last they saw of him.

Detectives William Whitburn and James Fox, who investigated the case, said they found a hall window leading to the fire escape open when they arrived at the scene.

Mrs. Dean said she didn't know how long the man had been in

Galveston. She said he called at the Salvation Army home Tuesday and asked for supper and a bed.

It was while he was waiting for supper that he had what she described as a "fit."

The body will be sent to Raleigh, N.C., Thursday under direction of Malloy & Son Funeral home."

Nowhere in the article in the *Galveston Daily News* had it said that Berrien Kinnard Upshaw had been married to Margaret Mitchell, author of the internationally famous *Gone With the Wind*.

❧

The Marshes' world now consisted of the few square blocks of the section in which they lived. Movies were still their best entertainment. As the spring of 1949 approached, John had made enough progress to be able to cross the street to the Piedmont Driving Club for dinner occasionally, or to go to a neighborhood film. On May 5, they went to see *Gone With the Wind*, and the next day Peggy wrote Harold E. George, the manager of the theatre, how pleased she was to see "the theatre packed and even the front rows in use." She noted that many in the audience were "repeaters" who knew beforehand what was going to happen and "started laughing or crying . . . before the cause for laughter or tears appeared on the screen."

In July, Peggy was made an honorary citizen of the town of Vimoutiers, France, in gratitude for some help she had given this old Normandy village in obtaining American aid after the war. She was pleased with this, but concerned about the ramifications and she wrote for advice from Dr. Wallace McClure in the State Department, who, over the years, had become something of a special advisor to her on various copyright matters. The honor made her more conscious than she had ever been of the problems now besetting foreign countries, and she confided to Dr. McClure:

I lie awake at night wondering about the publishers, agents, newspaper critics, and just plain letter-writing friends who have suddenly become silent and disappeared as Russia rolled over their countries — Bulgaria, Roumania, Hungary, Poland, Yugoslavia, and now Czechoslovakia. The Communists have attacked

"Gone With the Wind" in this country and every other country. . . . My Czech publisher has just had his publishing house "Nationalized." He is still alive and still at liberty but I do not know for how long.

At night I pack food and vitamins and clothing boxes, always wondering if they will ever reach the people to whom they are sent. Sometimes when I am out in crowds I find I do not have too much conversation about what is going on in Georgia because I have been wrestling with international financial regulations and wondering about people who cannot possibly escape from the encirclement of Russia.

Sometimes I discover I know things about some foreign countries which are not public property. I tell you this so that if ever my experience can be of help to you I hope you will call on me.

And, on July 28, in a letter refusing a request from Governor James M. Cox for an autographed copy of *Gone With the Wind* to place in a case in the *Atlanta Journal* building, she wrote that she was sending him a copy of the Yugoslavian translation of *Gone With the Wind* — for reasons that the governor never quite understood, although she explained:

In Yugoslavia, as in all Communist countries, the press denounced *Gone With the Wind* at the top of its lungs, stating, to my great pleasure and pride, that the book was a glorification of individual courage and individual enterprise (both qualities being highly obnoxious to Communists) and revealing in a hideous, bourgeois fashion the love of a person for their land and their home. The Communist critics observed virtuously that any school boy knew how vicious such ideas were because the STATE is everything, the individual nothing. To love one's home and fight for one's land is the act of a traitor.

The summer of 1949 was wickedly hot and, to escape the heat of their apartment, the Marshes often dined across the street on the porch of the Driving Club, overlooking the pool. On the night of August 11, their plans were to go there for dinner with Richard Harwell, a young friend and historian. But the day was an especially draining one for Peggy, and in the late afternoon she asked John to call Harwell and ask if they could postpone their engagement until another evening. Harwell, of course, agreed. Peggy had been unduly depressed all day and, after a light dinner, John talked her into going down to the Peachtree Arts Theatre to see the English film *Canterbury Tales*. If they were going to make the first show, Peggy had no time to change, and so she kept on the bright cotton peasant-style housedress she was wearing, which looked a bit as if it belonged on a Swiss schoolgirl. She helped John down the stairs and then they drove the few short blocks to the theatre. She was still in low spirits as she parked the car, at quarter past eight, on the west side of Peachtree Street. The Arts was across the street, at the corner of Thirteenth and Peachtree streets, the latter being a main thoroughfare and a dangerous crossing. There was no traffic signal or marked crosswalk and, for about a hundred yards both north and south, Peachtree Street curved sharply, blocking the view of anyone crossing to the theatre at the point the Marshes chose.

Why Peggy did not drive the car around to Thirteenth Street and park in a public lot, or even on the side street, is not clear. But there were only a few minutes until the film was to begin and she probably thought it best simply to pull into the first available space.

Peggy got out of the car first and went around to help John. He still walked with a lumbering step and had to be helped up and down curbs. Conscious of the dangerous spot she had chosen to cross the street, Peggy waited with John until Peachtree Street, according to John's police report, was free of traffic "from one curve to the other, except for two cars already abreast of the Thirteenth Street corner."

Her hand supportively under John's elbow, they started slowly across. They had just passed the center line and were heading for the opposite curb when Peggy saw a car to the right of them, speeding down the middle of Peachtree Street, and advancing fast enough so that she must have known instantly it would hit them unless they got out of its path. She screamed something unintelligible and, in that split second when a decision had to be made, panicked, withdrew her support from John's arm, pivoted sharply, and — leaving John standing immobile in what at that moment looked like the advancing car's path — started to run *back* toward the curb where her car was parked.

Terrified spectators on the street knew at that moment exactly what would happen, and there were screams from both sides of the road. The driver, suddenly aware of the danger and in a last-ditch effort to avoid an accident, swerved to the left on an impulse, never expecting either pedestrian would turn and go backward. He jammed on the brakes, but the car plunged forward in a sixty-foot skid, and Peggy fell under the wheels and was dragged another seven feet before the driver could bring the car to a tire-shrieking stop. Peggy was eleven feet from the sidewalk, unconscious, bleeding profusely, obviously critically injured.

Someone at the theatre called for an ambulance, and someone else helped John back across the street to Peggy's side. He dropped to the asphalt beside her and knelt there over her prostrate body refusing to let anyone touch her or try to move her until the ambulance came. No one knew at this time that the injured woman was Margaret Mitchell. The young man who had driven the car hung back, watched by two men, until a police car arrived. Twelve minutes from the time of the impact, the ambulance from Grady Hospital was on the scene. By coincidence, the intern on ambulance duty that evening was Dr. Edwin Lochridge, Lethea Turman Lochridge's son, a young man whom Peggy had known since he was a child. John rode in the ambulance with Peggy to Grady Hospital and, after X rays and emergency treatment, she was wheeled up to a private room on the third floor where the battle for her life began.

Peggy had a skull fracture that went from her brain to the top of her spine, a concussion, internal injuries, and a fractured pelvis.

The doctors debated whether to operate to relieve pressure on her brain, but they feared she would not survive surgery. On the third day, she seemed to rally a bit and mumbled incoherently. A nurse reported that she drank some orange juice and said, "It tastes bad." Someone else said she moaned that she hurt all over. Stephens and John hardly left her bedside and the rest of the Mitchell family was always close by, as were Augusta and Lee Edwards and Margaret Baugh.

From the moment it was known that Margaret Mitchell, author of the most celebrated of all American novels, was the victim of a car accident, the hospital was inundated with calls and invaded by people who wanted to see her. Medora mobilized all the friends she could think of to assist the telephone operators at the hospital at their overloaded switchboard. Thousands of people called throughout the five-day vigil that followed, including President Harry S Truman. Instantly, Peggy became a symbol for everyone who had suffered similar brutal and needless accidents. As she fought for her life, newspapers across the country published articles about the need for more traffic lights and tougher driving regulations in metropolitan areas. And the twenty-nine year old Atlanta taxi driver, Hugh D. Gravitt, who had been at the wheel of the car that had struck Peggy down, also became a symbol — of the deeper causes behind reckless driving. Gravitt had a long history of traffic violations as a cabby and had always gotten off easily. This time, however, he had been in his private car, and the victim was Atlanta's most famous citizen. He was held on counts of driving while intoxicated (he had had a beer four hours before the accident) and reckless driving, and was released on $5,450 bail, with homocide charges pending until it was seen whether Margaret Mitchell would survive.

On the morning of the fifth day, Peggy's condition seemed to have stabilized, but the doctors held little hope of her recovery, and both John and Stephens accepted the grim truth that Peggy's death was imminent. For four days they had kept a close vigil at the hospital; now there were practical matters that had to be dealt with.

For business and tax purposes, several of Peggy's bank accounts had been in the name of Margaret Mitchell. As long as she was alive, John had power of attorney and could transfer those funds to one of the Marshes' joint accounts, so that the bulk of Peggy's estate would not be tied up in probate after her death. With Margaret Baugh's help, John left the hospital on the fifth morning to make these transactions.

Meanwhile, Stephens hurried down to the offices of the *Atlanta Journal* to speak with Medora. Knowing that an obituary must already have been drafted, Stephens wanted to make sure that no mention of Peggy's marriage to Red Upshaw was printed. Just as the *Journal* clock struck noon, while Stephens was in putting his request to Medora, Frank Daniel received the news that, at 11:50 A.M., with three doctors in attendance, Margaret Mitchell had died. Daniel then had the difficult task of telling Stephens as he came out of Angus's office. Someone asked over the loud speaker for a minute of silence in Peggy Mitchell's memory, but many of the staff were not able to contain their sobs. People cried as they walked down Peachtree Street, and many Atlanta motorists who heard the news over their car radios pulled over to the nearest curb to absorb the news. Margaret Mitchell of Atlanta was dead. It was as though a member of their own family had died.

Bessie had been the first to be told of Peggy's death, for the hospital had called hoping to reach John. He walked in fifteen minutes later, but Bessie, concerned about how weary he appeared, decided he should not be told until after he had eaten his lunch. By then, Stephens had arrived and, with Bessie supporting John's arm, Stephens told him that Peggy was dead. John took the news stoically. "It was something that didn't have to happen," he said softly.

🏵

Tickets had to be issued to the funeral because the requests to attend were so overwhelming. The funeral cortege followed the route that the parade had taken on the night *Gone With the Wind* premiered in Atlanta. Peggy was buried beside Maybelle and Eugene and a brother who had died in infancy, in a plot surrounded by the graves of dozens of Confederate soldiers. Children stood on their parents' shoulders to see Margaret Mitchell being lowered into the red Georgia dirt, and police had to hold back the lines of the grieving and the curious, as well as the throngs of press photographers and reporters.

Though he had held up well throughout the crisis, after the funeral John became too ill to leave his bed. For several days he appeared troubled about something, and finally he called Margaret Baugh into his room. "Margaret," he said, "I promised Peggy I would burn all her papers. It was a trust. I can't do it. Can you?"

The shaken woman stood there unable to reply for a moment or two. "If Peggy really . . ."

"I have a list," he said. She nodded. "All manuscripts and notes, all the papers and correspondence that are left from *Gone With the Wind*. Original drafts, revisions, research, proofs — just keep out the papers marked on here." And he handed her a sheet that delineated certain pages from Peggy's work that were to survive the flames and, as he explained, were to be placed in a sealed envelope and deposited in a bank vault which would never be opened unless Peggy's authorship of *Gone With the Wind* was challenged. He then gave her the list of correspondence that he wanted her to burn, and he warned her "not to leave a single piece." Written in John Marsh's careful hand was a list that included the names Medora, Augusta, Lethea, Marjorie Kinnan Rawlings, Faith Baldwin, Clifford Dowdey, Edwin Granberry, Stark Young, Herschel Brickell, Lois Dwight Cole, Harold Latham, George Brett, and several others.

Carbon copies had been made of all of Peggy's correspondence since 1935. Margaret Baugh pulled those files specified by John. But, of course, she could only destroy carbons of Peggy's letters; and, though she could burn all the original letters Peggy had received from these people, they also might have carbons. She spoke to John about this and it was decided that letters would be written either by John or Stephens to Peggy's correspondents asking them to destroy the letters they had in their possession.

Then, with the old janitor's help, Margaret Baugh dragged all the material to be destroyed down two flights of stairs to the basement, where she stood by as the trusted black man fed Peggy's papers into the flames of the boiler. She remained until every shred was ash, unable to control her tears or to console the janitor, who was also crying. It seemed to both of them that here, on this spot, Margaret Mitchell was being consumed by flames. John had said it was a trust. And she had believed him. But once the papers were gone, Margaret Baugh was never sure that she had done the right thing.

Afterword

THE PRIVET HEDGES in front of John Marsh's house on Walker Terrace grew in tall, "sprangling" rows because he did not like to have them trimmed down into hard, compact walls. The shrubs were thick with blooms this spring of 1952, and their strong, sweet fragrance filled his rooms. Peggy had never seriously wanted a house, but it had been a long-held desire of his, and as soon as the estate had been settled, Margaret Baugh had gone house hunting for him.

She had helped him move into the charming one-story cottage on Walker Terrace just before Christmas, 1949. The house had an apartment attached to it, which Bessie Jordan occupied so that John need never be alone. In the three and a half years since Peggy's death, he had lived a quiet but fulfilling life. Stephens had taken over most of the "business of Margaret Mitchell," although John still kept his hand in on the foreign affairs. He had a number of friends who came by often to see him, and Margaret Baugh drove him wherever he wanted to go. His favorite entertainment was the opera and he looked forward to its arrival in Atlanta each spring, attending as many performances as he could.

In late April of 1952, he attended a performance by Dorothy Kirsten in *Carmen* with a young friend, Bill Corley. He was much enchanted with Miss Kirsten and, after leaving the theatre, told Corley, "That's my kind of woman!"

The following Monday, May 5, 1952, John felt weary, for there had been several visitors over the weekend and he had remained up long past his usual bedtime. Bessie served his dinner and, thinking he looked "peaked," told him he should go straight to bed. But he sat up reading rather late. Bessie heard him calling for help about 11:00 P.M. and instantly went to his aid. He had been stricken by a heart seizure. Bessie got him to the bed, called the doctor and an ambulance, and remained by his bedside until medical assistance arrived. But it was too late.

The "mama and papa" of *Gone With the Wind* were now both dead.

Margaret Mitchell had left all rights to *Gone With the Wind* to John Marsh. On his death, these rights passed to Stephens Mitchell. When asked once by an interviewer what *Gone With the Wind* was about, Stephens Mitchell replied, "Not change and survival or war or its aftermath. That's the background. It is the story of the inheritance of a certain characteristic, that characteristic being juvenile love for some man. [Scarlett O'Hara's] mother falls in love with her worthless cousin, who finally gets killed in a barroom. But she marries and is a faithful wife, builds up a big plantation for her husband, and dies with her worthless cousin's name on her lips.

"Her daughter inherits that characteristic. She loves her village beau, too, but she can't have him. And she will go through hell and everything else to get him. And then, after all these things have occurred — war, pestilence, and so on — she has her hands on him and all of a sudden finds out that it was just a juvenile fantasy.

"And that is the crux. It's a psychiatric novel."

But the millions of readers of Margaret Mitchell's *Gone With the Wind* would never accept Stephens Mitchell's explanation of his sister's book. Nor would they agree that he is the keeper of the Margaret Mitchell legacy. For *Gone With the Wind* has become a part of our culture and, therefore, its legacy belongs to the people. Atlanta and its environs will evermore be known as *Gone With the Wind* country, and the words of the title, *Gone With the Wind*, will always reverberate with the defiance of a people whom Margaret Mitchell refused to let die.

❦

In the vault of the Citizens and Southern National Bank, in a sealed envelope, are stored a few pages of the original manuscript of *Gone With the Wind*, preserved there as proof — should the need for it arise — of Margaret Mitchell's authorship.

Stephens Mitchell professes that he has not examined the contents of the safe-deposit box where John Marsh placed the envelope, which is supposed to contain samples of his wife's manuscript with corrections in her own hand and special research material that would prove without "a question of a doubt" that Margaret Mitchell and no one else wrote *Gone With the Wind*. Back in 1952, Stephens said he had no intention of ever breaking the seal on the envelope unless requested to do so by tax authorities. This was never asked of him, and so those remnants of the writing of *Gone With the Wind* remain in the vault, the seal unbroken.

Why John Marsh and Stephens Mitchell felt someone might challenge Margaret Mitchell's authorship of *Gone With the Wind* after her death is understandable, because Stephens, at least, had had to continue to contend with numerous lawsuits brought by unscrupulous people who wanted to trade in on the bonanza the book had made. But what is not so easy to understand is why they did not simply give the material to a university or library, so that scholars could have access to it and so that there would have been no question as to the book's authorship.

The answer Stephens Mitchell gives is that his sister had wanted all her papers destroyed and, in fact, had a passion for leaving nothing in the way of close personal possessions behind her. He further states that she had told him she even wanted the house on Peachtree Street destroyed once he no longer cared to live in it, as she did not want strange people wandering through rooms that had once been hers. And that deed was done — 1401 Peachtree Street was torn down in the 1950s shortly after Stephens Mitchell's first wife, Carrie Lou, died.

Whether or not *Gone With the Wind* is a masterpiece has always been a matter of controversy. It is, perhaps, the most compulsively readable novel in the English language, a book that, despite its length — it is as long as *War and Peace* — has been read by people over and over again, and each time with great suspense, as though, somehow, *this time* the story might end differently. The book has survived the passage of many decades of world change, changes that have made much of the work of Margaret Mitchell's contemporaries obsolete. But, ever since 1936, the South of the Civil War and Reconstruction periods has been viewed by Americans through Margaret Mitchell's eyes.

Excluding the Bible, *Gone With the Wind* has outsold, in hard cover, any other book, and its sales do not seem to be diminishing. To date, the book has sold six million hardcover copies in the United States; one million copies in England; and nine million copies in foreign translation. Worldwide, it continues to sell over 100,000 hardcover copies annually, and 250,000 paperback copies are sold every year in the United States.

Perhaps the sales of a novel do not determine its literary qualifications, but its lasting images do. And who can now think of the South before, during, and after the Civil War without images drawn from the pages of *Gone With the Wind*? Scarlett seated under the shade of a huge oak, surrounded by beaus at the Wilkeses' barbecue; Scarlett defying convention and dancing in her widow's weeds with the dashing scoundrel, Rhett Butler; the hundreds of wounded lying in the pitiless sun, "shoulder to shoulder, head to feet" by the railroad tracks at Atlanta's depot; the burning of Atlanta; Scarlett's journey on the road to Tara; the moment when Scarlett claws the earth to take from it a radish root to stave her hunger; Black Sam and Shantytown; Mammy and her red petticoat; Prissy during the birth of Melanie's baby; and — oh, yes — Scarlett O'Hara crying, "What shall I do?" when Rhett Butler finally decides to leave her and Atlanta, and Rhett's reply, "My dear, I don't give a damn."

To Edwin Granberry, Margaret Mitchell once wrote, "I didn't know being an author was like this, or I don't think I'd have been an author." Her life after the publication of *Gone With the Wind* certainly did become, as she said, "anxious and bedeviled," and it is perhaps the world's good fortune that Margaret Mitchell was not as prescient as she believed herself to be. Yet, it is my feeling that had she known that her novel was to become an enduring American classic, nothing could have stopped her from writing and publishing it.

Author's Note

All references to *Gone With the Wind* page numbers are to the original 1936 edition and are accurate only in printings with 1037 pages. There has been only one previous biography of Margaret Mitchell, Finis Farr's *Margaret Mitchell of Atlanta* (New York: William Morrow Company, Inc., 1965). For reference, I suggest *Margaret Mitchell's Gone With the Wind Letters, 1936–1949*, Richard Harwell, editor (New York: Macmillan, Inc., 1976); *GWTW: The Screenplay by Sidney Howard*, Richard Harwell, editor (New York: Macmillan, Inc., 1980); Roland Flamini, *Scarlett, Rhett & a Cast of Thousands* (New York: Macmillan, Inc., 1975); and *Technical Adviser: The Making of Gone With the Wind; The Letters of Wilbur Kurtz* (Atlanta Historical Society, vol. xxii, no. 2, 1978).

The two largest collections of Margaret Mitchell's letters and documents are in the Margaret Mitchell Marsh Archives, University of Georgia; and the Macmillan Archives, New York Public Library. Other collections repose at Smith College, Dalton Junior College, Emory University, the Atlanta Historical Society, the Atlanta Public Library, and the Margaret Mitchell Library in Fayetteville, Georgia.

The following abbreviations have been used to simplify the notes to this volume:

AHB	*Atlanta Historical Bulletin*, Richard Harwell, ed.
AHBMMM	*Atlanta Historical Bulletin*, Margaret Mitchell memorial issue, Richard Harwell, ed., May, 1950
AHSMMA	Atlanta Historical Society Margaret Mitchell Archives

AHSWKA	Atlanta Historical Society Wilbur Kurtz Archives
AJ	*Atlanta Journal*
AJ&C	*Atlanta Journal and Constitution*
AJMMM	*Atlanta Journal,* Margaret Mitchell memorial issue, Dec. 23, 1949
AJM	*Atlanta Journal Magazine*
AJMA	*Atlanta Journal Magazine* Archives
EM	Eugene Mitchell
FF	Finis Farr, *Margaret Mitchell of Atlanta* (New York: William Morrow Company, Inc., 1965)
FMZ	Frances Marsh Zane
GB	George Brett
HCC	Terry Bakken, *Historic Clayton County* (Jonesboro: Historical Jonesboro, Inc., 1975)
HSL	Harold Strong Latham
JM	John Marsh
LDC	Lois Dwight Cole
Letters, RH	*Margaret Mitchell's* Gone With the Wind *Letters, 1936–1949,* Richard Harwell, ed. (New York: Macmillan, Inc., 1976)
MANYPL	Macmillan Archives, New York Public Library
MSM	Maybelle Stephens Mitchell
MFPAJ&C	Medora Field Perkerson, *Atlanta Journal and Constitution*
MFPMc	Medora Field Perkerson, *McCall's*
MFPAUG	Medora Field Perkerson Archives, University of Georgia
MM	Margaret Mitchell
MMMAUG	Margaret Mitchell Marsh Archives, University of Georgia
NYTBR	*New York Times Book Review*
PI	Personal Interview
MMASC	Margaret Mitchell Archives, Smith College
SM	Stephens Mitchell
UG	University of Georgia
VM	Virginia Morris

Notes

EPIGRAPH

GWTW, p. 397.

CHAPTER ONE

page
4 Caroline Pafford Miller, *Lamb in His Bosom* (New York and London: Harper Brothers, 1933).
4 "the great houses": Mark Sullivan, Our Times — The United States, vol. 6, *The Twenties* (New York and London: Charles Scribner's Sons, 1936).
4–5 Erskine Caldwell, *Tobacco Road* (New York: Charles Scribner's Sons, 1932). Caldwell (b. 1903 in White Oaks, Georgia) worked with MM on the AJ.
5 "Peggy Mitchell Marsh": AJMMM.
6 "Peggy won't like it": AJMMM.
7 "a product of the Jazz Age": *Letters*, RH; MM to Gilbert Govan, July 8, 1936.
7 The three men immortalized on Stone Mountain are Robert E. Lee, Stonewall Jackson, and Jefferson Davis. They were not the men originally to be so honored. There were to have been five — Generals John Brown Gordon, Pierce M. Butler Young, Thomas R. R. Cobb, Henry Benning, and Ambrose Ransome Wright. Work had not been completed on the monument in 1935, and it was not finished until 1963.
7 "I have no novel": AJMMM.
8 "No sooner": AJM, May 6, 1923.
8 "I hate to press": AJMMM.
8 Which word in the text of GWTW MM considered dirty remains a mystery. There are numerous expletives in the text as printed, but none seem in bad taste.
9 "Jackassed": LDC, NYTBR, Dec. 12, 1962.

9 "Please don't talk": AJMMM.

9 "Why are *you* writing a book": LDC, NYTBR, Dec. 12, 1962.

9 "See!": Ibid.

10 "sixty first chapters": MM to FM(Z), undated.

10 "excerpts": Ibid.

10 "hatless, hair flying": Ibid.

11 "tiny woman": AJMMM.

11 "The book is about": Macmillan pamphlet, 1936, MANYPL.

CHAPTER TWO

15 General William Tecumseh Sherman (1820–1891). The Atlanta Campaign (July 22, 1864) and Sherman's subsequent March to the Sea led some historians to consider him the top federal officer of the war. After destroying Atlanta's military resources on Nov. 15, 1864, Sherman proceeded toward Savannah, successfully violating military convention by operating deep within hostile territory. GWTW pp. 313–392 deal with the Battle of Atlanta.

15 The founding of Atlanta is discussed in GWTW, pp. 141–143.

16 "vast sheets of flame": Captain George W. Pepper, *Sherman's Campaigns in Georgia*, pp. 239–240.

17 "go to the mayor": *Letters*, R.H.; MM to Mrs. Julia Collier Harris, April 28, 1936.

17 The house at 187 Jackson Street burned to the ground in 1916. Later, a Negro tenement occupied the spot. The area has recently been rebuilt.

17 "taught things": *Atlanta Constitution*, Oct. 1, 1979 (interview with SM).

21 "It was like an ancient": *Atlanta Constitution*, Oct. 1, 1979 (interview with SM).

22 "Somebody's Darling" is quoted in GWTW, p. 297.

22 "scooped up": AJMMM.

22 "on bony knees": Ibid.

22 "Cavalry knees": Ibid.

23 "pistol factories": Ibid. MM used this litany in GWTW, p. 146.

24 "terribly important": Ibid.

CHAPTER THREE

24 Description of afternoon rides: AJMMM.

25 "It would have taken": Ibid.

25 "Fine and wealthy people": Medora Field Perkerson, radio interview, July 1936.

26 Sarah (Sis) Fitzgerald (1838–1932) and Mary (Mamie) Fitzgerald (1840–1932) were MM's maternal great-aunts. Both were spinsters. Sis recorded her own oral history of the Fitzgerald family (MMMAUG).

26 "There was just": PI.

27 "Annie, visiting from": HCC.

27 "hangin' on": Ibid. This episode was the foundation of a scene between Rhett and Bonnie, GWTW, p. 915.

27–28 Stately Oaks, built in 1830, was moved in 1972 to MM Memorial Park, Clayton County; Johnson House (John-Blalock House), built in 1840, still standing; Warren House, built in 1840, visited often by MM, still standing; the Crawford House (The Crawford-Talmadge House), built in 1835, still standing. The latter could well have been the model for Twelve Oaks.

28 "hold against": HCC.

28 The stories of MM's maternal grandmother (Eleanor McGhan Fitzgerald) and her jewelry saved from the Yankees (Sarah Fitzgerald's recorded oral history, MMMAUG) were the basis of two important scenes in GWTW, pp. 464 and 545.

29 "blood-colored after rains": GWTW, p. 8.

30 "In the night": MMMAUG.

31 "contained depravities": JM to Edwin Granberry, Jan. 1937.

31 "the hide beat off of": a phrase often used by MM in letters and interviews. It appears three times in *Letters*, R.H.; and in two of Medora Field Perkerson's interview articles for the *Atlanta Constitution*.

31 "because none of the little boys": AHB, summer 1981.

32 "I would never forget": Ibid.

34 "Watch me turn": SM, AHBMMM. SM believes this accident was the basis of the death scenes of Gerald O'Hara (GWTW, p. 702) and Bonnie Butler (GWTW, p. 991).

CHAPTER FOUR

35 "Tolstoy and most of the Russian": *Letters*, R.H.; MM to Dr. Mark Allen Patton, July 11, 1936.

36 "Dream of Heaven Waltz": SM, AHBMMM.

38 "Locations": MMMAUG.

39 "fought for Georgia": Macmillan pamphlet, 1936, MANYPL.

40 "had not made a social": FF, p. 38.

40 "Margaret was only happy": PI.

40 "Nearly everybody": Ibid.

41 "Unity, Margaret": AHB, summer 1981.

41 "There are authors": FF, p. 34.

41 "Peggy lay": 1916–17 yearbook, Washington Seminary, MMMAUG.

42 This photograph of MM: MMMAUG.

43 "hideous red glow": AJ, May 22, 1917. MM used these exact words in GWTW, p. 383. MM drew images of Atlanta burning (GWTW, pp. 383–387) from this experience, and also from the AJ coverage of the disaster.

44 "Lost children here!": AHBMMM.

44 "to see that the soldiers": Ibid.

CHAPTER FIVE

46 "There was no girl": Ibid.

47 "insisted that I spend": Ibid.

47 Clifford West Henry (1895–1918), "so sadly handsome" and "most sincere": PI.

49 "I noticed that he was looking at us": MM to EM, Sept. 10, 1918.

49 "Funny meeting, wasn't it?": Ibid.

50 "Dear, you must have": MSM to EM, Sept. 10, 1918.

51 "crusty old place": MMMAUG, MM to SM, undated.

52 Letters from Clifford West Henry: similarities exist between the kinds of letters Ashley Wilkes wrote to Melanie (GWTW, p. 211) and those CWH wrote to MM.

52–53 "The rest of us were": VM, *Photoplay*, March 1938.

54 There is considerable evidence that the character Ashley Wilkes was based to some extent on Clifford West Henry.

55 "try to stump each other": AJ&C, May 16, 1961.

55 "One evening Peg and I": Ibid.

56 "a youthful genius": AHB, summer 1981.

57 "the air thick with screams": MM to VM, Dec. 23, 1918, MMMAUG.

57–58 "Dear Margaret": MSM to MM, Jan. 23, 1919, in FF, pp. 43–44.

58–59 Similarities between MM's experience on the death of MSM and Scarlett O'Hara's on the death of her mother, Ellen O'Hara: both real and fictional mothers died while their daughters were trying to reach their sides; each young woman took over her mother's tasks upon her death; and both had fathers crazed with grief and unable to function.

59 "Go back to Smith": FF, p. 45.

59 "I am beginning to miss": MM to EM, Feb. 17, 1919, in FF, p. 46.

60 "If I can't be first": MM to SM, April, 1919, in FF, p. 46.

61 "When I get through here": AJ&C, May 16, 1961.

CHAPTER SIX

65 Bessie Berry, later Bessie Jordan. She worked for EM from 1916 to 1926, and then for MM until her death in Aug. 1949, remaining to care for JM until his death.

65 Cammie's last name is unknown, but MM confessed several times in print that the character Prissy in GWTW was modeled after Cammie and was MM's favorite character.

66 Grandfather Mitchell's lumber business was to serve as a background during Scarlett O'Hara's marriage to Frank Kennedy in GWTW.

66 "all daring and put in its place": AHBMMM.

67 "stealing a young woman's youth": PI.

70 There could be a link between MM's experience at the dance — her

unconventional attire, and her dancing with the dashing but socially unacceptable Berrien K. Upshaw — and GWTW, pp. 191–192.

72 Grandmother Mitchell's evening prayers were probably a model for Ellen O'Hara's enforced evening prayers in GWTW, p. 68.

73 "When a girl is making": FF, p. 50.

73 "Terribly amusing": PI.

73–74 "a woman who doesn't": FF, p. 55.

75 Polly Peachtree: AJ, Oct. 17, 1918.

CHAPTER SEVEN

77 MM's fan letters to F. Scott Fitzgerald and Stephen Vincent Benét are lost. She mentioned having written them to both MFP and Frank Daniel, and later to LDC and to Benét himself.

77 "And to the piles of lingerie": Augusta Dearborn Edwards, *Reader's Digest*, March 1962.

78 "After the folks came back": SM, AJ&C.

78 "old fraternal order": AJ, April 16, 1921.

78 "to bring terror to the heart": Sullivan, Our Times, vol. 6, *The Twenties*.

80 "many a night": Augusta Dearborn Edwards, *Reader's Digest*, March 1962.

80 "exceptionally charming" through "razzle-dazzle": PIs.

82 "My new Sweetie": JM to FM(Z), March 1922.

82 "big cold house" through "I assumed": PI.

82 "rape became": MM to FM(Z), Nov. 1925.

83 "John never tried": MM to FM(Z), Aug. 1922.

84 "a fine American novel": PI.

85 "helping Red to get a trousseau": JM to FM(Z), Aug. 1922.

86 "heathenish bridegroom": PI. The wedding announcement in the AJ stated Upshaw had been to Annapolis and in the U.S. Navy during the war. In fact, Upshaw attended Annapolis *after* the war. It seems likely that both MM and JM thought Upshaw was older than he was until the time of the marriage, and that both did think he had served in the war.

88 "They attempted the impossible": JM to FM(Z), Dec. 1922.

CHAPTER EIGHT

92 MM replaced Mrs. Roy Flannagan on the AJ.

92 "swearing she was a speed-demon on a Remington": MFPAUG.

92 For four weeks MM was paid by chit. It was not until January 15, 1923, that her name was placed on the AJ payroll. She had abandoned the use of the name Upshaw and was listed as Peggy Mitchell.

92 "She had something of the look": MFPAUG.

93 "There's a man": AJM, Jan. 7, 1923.

94 The desk and chair that MM used at the AJM are on permanent exhibition at the offices of the AJ&C.

94 "stylish except": PI.

94 "She was perky": Ibid.

95 "As rugged as": William Howland, AHBMMM.

95 "an enthusiasm money": Ibid.

95 The galley proof of "Atlanta Sub Debs Pass up Tutankhamen" is in the MMMAUG.

96 MM was later to say she worked at the AJM six years. Payroll records show this to be incorrect. MM was employed at the AJM from Dec. 20, 1922, to Jan. 15, 1923, on chit, and she was on the payroll from Jan. 15, 1923, to May 3, 1926. She then free-lanced for them until Sept. 1, 1926 — a total of three years and nine months of employment on the AJM.

96 "due to any Chinese blood": MM, AP interview, July 1936.

96 "had the sweetest running movement": MFPAUG.

96 "Most of the things I asked": Ibid.

97 "taciturnity": AJ, June 4, 1923.

97 "Mrs. Maxim, tiny and sweet-faced": "Maxim Talks of Perfume, War, and Poetry," AJM, March 4, 1923.

98 "Writing always came hard": MFPAUG.

99 "about as large": "Hanging over Atlanta in Borglum's Swing," AJM, May 6, 1923.

99 Gutzon Borglum (John Gutzon de la Mothe Borglum 1867–1941), an American sculptor, began work on Stone Mountain in 1916, but it was interrupted by war. Work was resumed a few months after MM's article appeared, but Borglum had a controversy with the Stone Mountain Association and did not complete the sculpture. (See note to page 7.)

99 "In an enormous": AJM, May 6, 1923.

99 "Hey": Ibid. This is the story that MM retold to HSL in April 1935.

100 "Football Players Make the Best Husbands": AJM, June 24, 1923.

100 "How a Perfect Lady Refuses a Proposal": AJM, June 17, 1923.

100 "Georgia's Empress and Women Soldiers": AJM, May 20, 1923.

100 Rebecca Latimer Felton (1835–1930), born in Atlanta, worked for the AJ for nearly thirty years and served briefly (1922) as a U.S. senator, the first woman to hold that office.

100 "large masculine": AJM, May 20, 1923.

100 "despite her years": Ibid.

100 "who stood six feet tall": Ibid.

101 "I wasn't goin' to have": Ibid.

101 "writer's block": MFPAUG.

102 "Mr. Upshaw demanded" through "Yes sir": On file, Superior Court, Fulton County, Georgia, dated July 16, 1923 (presented as evidence on June 17, 1924).

CHAPTER NINE

107 "She walked straight": Robert Ruark, *Saturday Evening Post*, April 1950.

107 "His hair, still a thick shock": AJM, Jan. 27, 1923.

108 "romping hieroglyphics": "Spring Styles in Slang Reach Atlanta," AJM, April 22, 1923.

109 "little flirtations": MM to FM(Z), April 1923.

109 "Should Husbands Spank Their Wives?": AJM, Feb. 25, 1923.

109 "mirrored the flapper era": MFPAUG.

110 This second document is on file, Superior Court, Fulton County, dated Oct. 16, 1924.

110 In 1946, MM wrote a lengthy letter to the mayor of Atlanta nominating MFP for the Atlanta Woman of the Year Award, citing the work MFP had done on the "Marie Rose" advice column. MMMAUG.

110 "sympathetic but hard-headed": Ibid.

110 "Movie Stars Who Call Atlanta Home": AJM, Nov. 16, 1924.

110 "When he turned to bow": "The Sheik Visits Atlanta," AJM, March 9, 1924.

111 "What Causes Hiccoughs?": AJM, Dec. 28, 1924.

112 "I wish he had not picked": MM to FMZ, Jan. 7, 1925.

113 "clothes, stockings, hairpins" through "I'll have to do": PI.

113 "Good," "Inconsistent": MFPAUG.

114 "John and I are going to live poor": FF, p. 71.

114 *Open Door*, April 1925.

114 "brightened the occasion": MFPAUG.

114 "there was a flash": Ibid.

115 For the rest of her life MM was to claim she was two to four years younger than she was.

115 "Atlanta Boys Don't Want Rich Wives": AJM, July 12, 1925.

116 "sincerely glad": PI.

116 "good fortune at finding": Kitty Mitchell to JM, June 19, 1925. JM kept this letter for the rest of his life.

117 "with a touch of reality": PI.

118 "very Bebe Daniels": MFPAUG.

119 "might be misunderstood": FF, p. 72.

119 "a mighty tight squeeze": EM, AHB, 1931.

120 "maternal attitude": PI.

121 "Put Lee on": Ibid.

121 "Peggy would pretend": Ibid.

CHAPTER TEN

122 "short skirts": *Open Door*, April 1925.

122 "the only one" through "house full": MM to FMZ, 1926.

123 "a helluva lot of research": PI.

126 The thirty pages of MM's Jazz Age novel were destroyed by her secretary, Margaret Baugh, after MM's death, but Baugh made notes on the story line of what appeared to be the first two chapters of the book.

126 "Conjuring the Wood Out of Alcohol": AJM, Feb. 21, 1926.

126 MM's "Darktown" experience was the inspiration for the scene in Shantytown, GWTW, pp. 777–787.

128 "My wife used to be": "Tiger Flowers," AJM, March 14, 1926.

128 "Several hundred novels": HSL, MANYPL.

129 "bull-headed": PI.

129 "hated writing almost as much": MMM to GB, MANYPL.

129 " 'Ropa Carmagin" was given to HSL along with the ms. of GWTW. He returned it to MM in Aug. 1935, suggesting she hold on to it for a while as its short length made it more suitable for a magazine piece than a book. MM later showed it to Edwin Granberry (July 1936) and then destroyed it. Margaret Baugh had made notes about the story, but these were destroyed after MM's death.

131 "It looks to me, Peggy": MM phrased this sentence several ways in various letters and interviews. In all, the words "write a book" appear in the context of the quote.

133 "She had never understood either of the men": GWTW, p. 1036.

CHAPTER ELEVEN

134 MM made the statement "Indifference is worse than hate" to a reviewer, Mrs. Frances Zelnicker, in Feb. 1937.

136 No original ms. pages of GWTW are known to exist outside an envelope in an Atlanta bank vault, which has been sealed since MM's death. Correspondence in the MANYPL verifies that most notes and minor corrections *in the margins* of the first ms. submitted by MM were written in John Marsh's precise hand; and all other corrections in the context of the work, in MM's hand. MM had the habit of heavily inking out words, sentences, and even paragraphs that had been deleted or changed so that the original version could not be read.

137 "Something strange": *Atlanta Constitution*, Oct. 16, 1936.

139 "of her own generation": GWTW, p. 131.

140 "A master flaw-finder": JM to Edwin Granberry, Jan. 1937.

142 Upshaw did, in fact, fill out an application for reenrollment and registered with the UG Alumni Association on March 18, 1927, but did not return to UG. (UG Alumni Archives.)

CHAPTER TWELVE

144 "The greatest feat": AJ, May 21, 1927.

145 "for years": Frederick Lewis Allen, *Only Yesterday: An Informal History of the Nineteen Twenties* (New York: Harper & Row, 1931).

145 "Oh, it's just a new kind": PI.

146 The death of Gerald O'Hara, GWTW, p. 686.

146 Scarlett and Rhett are married on p. 845 of GWTW.

146 "in spite of the fact": *Letters*, RH; MM to Clifford Dowdey, July 29, 1937.

MM wrote Stephen Vincent Benét about this incident (July 9, 1936), claiming that Daniel read all afternoon and that she then purchased the book from him. Daniel is not identified in either of these letters. He identified himself in an article in the AJ (March 21, 1940), to MM's great irritation.

147 Gerald O'Hara's funeral: GWTW, pp. 687–720.

147 "Lula B. Tolbert": AJMMM.

147 "I remember": Ibid.

148 "I adore that type": MM to FMZ, Dec. 1927.

148 There was no resemblance between Bessie and Mammy in GWTW. There was, however, an elderly black woman in Jonesboro named Aunt Silla, who worked for the Camp family and upon whose knee MM sat to hear stories of the Yankee occupation of Jonesboro during the Civil War. She could well have been the model for Mammy.

150 Belle Breazing (1858–1940). Her whorehouse was famous for its influential patrons and for being the most luxuriant and orderly house in the South. The day after Belle Breazing's death, the *Lexington Herald* ran an obituary on the front page. All copies were sold by 10:00 A.M. and brought private speculators a dollar a piece. In rival papers the story provoked the caustic comment, "Is it true that to get on the front page of the *Herald* one must operate a house of ill repute?"

152 "given the world": PI.

152 "I never met": MANYPL.

152 "Isn't it a shame": FF, p. 93.

CHAPTER THIRTEEN

153–154 "Do you follow" through "with such fun": LDC, NYTBR, Dec. 12, 1962.

154 "What was the death rate": *Letters*, RH; MM to Gilbert Govan, July 8, 1936.

155 "It was especially interesting": JM to FMZ, Sept. 20, 1931.

156 "a good enough way": MM to LDC, Arpil 7, 1936, MANYPL.

156 "expect that she could be writing": Ibid.

159 "Tobacco Road district": MM to LDC, July 8, 1935, MANYPL.

160 "like a crotchety old woman": MM to HSL, July 9, 1935, MANYPL.

161–162 "I would not be at all" through "encouraging words": MM to HSL, Aug. 15, 1935, MANYPL.

CHAPTER FOURTEEN

163 "as tired as a hound": MM to LDC, July 7, 1935, MANYPL.

163 "hurtling out of a side street": Ibid.

164 "clumsy or unlucky": MM to HSL, July 9, 1935, MANYPL.

164 There was an oral agreement that Macmillan would pay MM a small fee

if they ever published an author she had found for them. This never occurred.

165 "Please hold off your request": HSL to MM, July 17, 1935, MANYPL.

165 "Macmillan terrible excited": LDC to MM, July 21, 1935, MANYPL.

165 "My enthusiasm": HSL to MM, July 21, 1935, MANYPL.

166 "necessitated a Luminal" through "Coming of a legal": MM to HSL, July 21, 1935, MANYPL.

167 "This book is really magnificent": C. W. Everett to HSL, July 2, 1935, MANYPL.

168 "so swell," "bearing up," and "Luminal and ice": MM to HSL, July 27, 1935, MANYPL.

168 "the author should": C. W. Everett to HSL, July 2, 1935, MANYPL.

168–169 "V, b and b in the book" through "to Pansies as Fairies": MM to HSL, July 27, 1935, MANYPL.

169 Both Wade Hampton, Pansy (Scarlett) O'Hara's son by Charles Hamilton, and Ella, her daughter by Frank Kennedy, were cut from the film version of GWTW, as was Will Benteen, one of the book's major characters, who married Suellen and ran Tara for his sister-in-law.

169 "The best way I can place these": MM to HSL, July 27, 1935, MANYPL.

169 "My dear Mrs. Marsh": HSL to MM, July 30, 1935, MANYPL.

170 "none of the elements": F. Scott Fitzgerald to Edmund Wilson, F. Scott Fitzgerald Papers, Princeton University Library.

171–172 "a lawyer of the old school" through "What if Macmillan": MM to HSL, Aug. 1, 1935, MANYPL.

172 "My dear child": LDC to MM, Aug. 5, 1935, MANYPL.

172 "of bad faith": MM to HSL, Aug. 6, 1935, MANYPL.

173 "After I asked": HSL to MM, Aug. 15, 1935, MANYPL.

CHAPTER FIFTEEN

175 "In the name of God": MM to C. W. Everett, Aug. 19, 1936, MANYPL.

175 "Tempo" story: Ibid.

177 "It's competent": MM to LDC, Sept. 15, 1935, MANYPL.

177 "the zip and bustle," "dare marriage," and "somehow got buried": Medora Field Perkerson to Carroll G. Bowen, Oxford University Press, May 21, 1954, MFPAUG.

178 "bright button" and "Peggy's energies": MFPAUG.

179 "fifty dollars from": MM to LDC, Sept. 22, 1935, MANYPL.

179 "I saw no reason": Ibid.

180 The Battle of New Hope Church: GWTW, p. 300.

180 Final fortifications of Atlanta were originally in GWTW, chapter 16, and were then moved to part 3, chapter 17.

180 "just been rescued from": MM to LDC, Oct. 16, 1935, MANYPL.

180 "poor photographer": Ibid.

180 "of all the characters": Ibid.

181 "amateurish": MM to HSL, Oct. 30, 1935, MANYPL.

181 "what on earth": Ibid.

181 "Really I don't know": HSL to LDC, Nov. 1, 1935, MANYPL.

181–182 "I at once": HSL to MM, Nov. 3, 1935, MANYPL.

182 Other titles known to be submitted by MM were: *Milestones, Jettison, Ba! Ba! Black Sheep, Not in Our Stars,* and *Bugles Sang True.*

182 "like the snows of yesteryear": MM to HSL, Oct. 30, 1935, MANYPL.

182 "somebody said": LDC to MM, Nov. 4, 1935, MANYPL.

183 "had fought with the Irish": GWTW, p. 421.

183 "Was Tara still standing": GWTW, p. 397.

184 "Can't see": an expression frequently used by MM in letters and interviews.

185 "Peggy collapsed": JM to LDC, Jan. 21, 1936, MANYPL.

185 "It may be that she will *never*": Ibid.

186 "I assure you my remarks": LDC to JM, Jan. 17, 1936, MANYPL.

187 LDC and her husband, Allan Taylor, wrote several juvenile books together under the pseudonym Allan Dwight. Macmillan published *Kentucky Cargo* (the contract for which LDC mentions to MM) in 1939.

188–189 "constant mystification" and "From the length": JM to LDC, Feb. 9, 1936, MANYPL.

189 "about as long as": HSL memo to staff, July 30, 1935, MANYPL.

190 "Miss Prink and I": MM to HSL, Aug. 1, 1941, MANYPL.

CHAPTER SIXTEEN

192 "Forget it Louie": Roland Flamini, *Scarlett, Rhett & a Cast of Thousands* (New York: Macmillan, Inc., 1975).

194 "It seems a very widespread rumor": *Letters,* RH; MM to VM, July 11, 1936.

195 "nothing in the world": MM to LDC, April 20, 1936, MANYPL.

195 "long and pointed" through "I have become": MM to LDC, April 24, 1936, MANYPL.

197 "blew up" and "when sick people": MM to LDC, April 30, 1936, MANYPL.

198 "and well, hundreds of others": MFPAJ&C.

198 "had to look through nearly a *million*": Ibid.

199 "I am very small" through "but while I was": Macmillan pamphlet, Sept. 1936, MANYPL.

200 "nearly threw up": MM to LDC, May 12, 1936, MANYPL.

200 "of the nightmare": Ibid.

200 "me laying me down": Ibid.

200 "I'd hate to land in New York": MM to HSL, May 23, 1936, MANYPL.

201 "like talking with" through "indelicate stories": MM to HSL, June 1, 1936, MANYPL.

201 One story MM told at the Atlanta Library Club luncheon was about

stopping to ask the date for planting cotton from an old farmer spreading manure by the side of a road in Clayton County one hot summer day. He told her, and then asked her what being a writer was like. She answered that it was hard work and made you scratch and sweat and smell. "Just like spreadin' manure!" the farmer exclaimed.

201–202 "I suppose you could call": *Letters*, RH; MM to Joseph Henry Jackson, June 1, 1936.

202 "I haven't any literary style": Ibid.

202 "My dear Mr. Edwards": *Letters*, RH; MM to Henry Stillwell Edwards, June 14, 1936.

202 "April, May and June of 1936": JM, AHBMMM.

203 "Wasn't her heroine a baggage": MFPAUG.

203 "very relieved" through "By the way": MM to HSL, May 25, 1936, MANYPL.

203 "Mrs. Marsh is to know": Memo dated May 24, 1936, MANYPL.

204 "What is it": Flamini: *Scarlett, Rhett & a Cast of Thousands*.

204 Telegram dated May 28, 1936, signed "Bette Davis" and sent from Burbank, California: MANYPL.

205 "I beg, urge, coax, and plead": Kay Brown to David O. Selznick. Richard Harwell, *GWTW: The Screenplay by Sidney Howard* (New York: Macmillan, Inc., 1980).

205 "Most sorry to have to say no": David O. Selznick to Kay Brown. Ibid.

205 "Translate dialect": MM to LDC, June 6, 1936, MANYPL.

205 "I shouldn't even think": Ibid.

206 "I wasn't suspecting it": MM to GB, June 6, 1936, MANYPL.

207 The comments from literary celebrities were made in letters and reviews and used by Macmillan in ads for the book.

207 "We are ready to stand or fall": Edwin Granberry, the *New York Sun*, June 30, 1936.

207 "striking piece of fiction": Herschel Brickell, the *New York Post*, June 30, 1936.

208 "a lather of apprehension": MFPAUG.

CHAPTER SEVENTEEN

211 "She's small-breasted": MM to LDC, July 5, 1936, MANYPL.

213 "the sole and innocent intention": *Newsweek*, Dec. 18, 1939.

213 "As God is my witness": GWTW, p. 428.

215 "decks of the Queen Mary": Frank Daniel to MM, Aug. 19, 1936, MMMAUG.

216 "why in Hell" through "just get in the car": MM to LDC, July 3, 1936, MANYPL.

216 "After reading your book": MFPAUG.

217 "hide out in the mountains": *Letters*, RH; MM to Herschel Brickell, July 7, 1936.

217 "a bundle of reviews": *Letters*, RH; MM to Gilbert Govan, July 8, 1936.

218–219 "As you may observe": *Letters*, RH; MM to Herschel Brickell, July 7, 1936.

219–221 "My dear Mr. Granberry": *Letters*, RH; MM to Edwin Granberry, July 7, 1936.

221 All of these letters are in the MMMAUG.

222 "I am not in the best condition": *Letters*, RH; MM to Stephen Vincent Benét, July 8, 1936.

223 "For all I know": *Letters*, RH; MM to Donald Adams, July 9, 1936.

223–224 "I never intended" and "I wouldn't go through": Ibid.

224 "Life has been": *Letters*, RH; MM to GB, July 8, 1936. The $5,000 check sent by GB to MM was the money from the chit requisitioned by HSL for MM. She had received the check six weeks prior to this letter. Gainesville is at most a two-hour drive from Atlanta under even the worst of road conditions. As MM started out on this trip by 1:00 P.M., it is hard to understand why she was afraid she might fall asleep. She could, however, have been suffering from the anxiety that she would crash — a fear she often had when driving a car. She never did go "back and beyond the mountains," but remained in the small city of Gainesville (pop. approx. 8,000 in 1936).

224–225 "We have a wonderful": Edwin Granberry to MM, July 9, 1936.

225 "pathetic note": PI.

CHAPTER EIGHTEEN

227 Baby Snooks was a radio and theatre character created by radio, stage, and film star Fanny Brice. The character was a devilish small girl of about six years of age.

228 "Not Janet Gaynor": MM to LDC, July 13, 1936, MANYPL.

228 "Miriam Hopkins": Ibid.

229 "a small, plain wren": PI.

229 "Would you please stop the car": PI.

231 "My idea is": JM to MM, July 16, 1936, MMMAUG.

231 "It occurred to me": JM to MM, July 17, 1936, MMMAUG.

232 "Is [sic] there any difficulties": James Putnam to MM, July 23, 1936, MANYPL.

232 "a lather of rage" through "the stupidest contract": *Letters*, RH; MM to HSL, Aug. 13, 1936.

233 "The pressures are worse than before": MM to LDC, July 25, 1936, MANYPL.

233 "no clothes": MM to LDC, July 27, 1936, MANYPL.

234 Television rights were being included in contracts of this period since the probability of commercial licensing in the near future had been shown at the Century of Progress Exposition in Chicago, 1933–1934.

234 "The Selznick lawyers": *Letters*, RH; MM to HSL, Aug. 13, 1936.

235 "Peggy has gone": JM to Edwin Granberry, July 29, 1936.

235 "stroke of blindness" and "in a bad way": Herschel Brickell to Edwin Granberry, Aug. 5, 1936.

236 "A dark room with": MM to LDC, Aug. 13 1936, MANYPL.

236 "Is this the same girl": VM to MM, undated.

236 "What a precocious smallfry": Ibid.

237 "I am not going blind": *Letters*, RH; MM to Louella Parsons, Oct. 29, 1936. This quote was reprinted by Louella Parsons in her newspaper column on Nov. 3, 1936.

237 "It isn't their fault": MM to Edwin Granberry, Sept. 7, 1936.

237 "the old eyes" and "habit of eating": Ibid.

238 "what a low blow": MM to HSL, Sept. 25, 1936, MANYPL.

238 "But my dear Child": LDC to MM, Sept. 29, 1936, MANYPL.

238 "God-knows-what-else": VM to MM, Oct. 6, 1936.

239 "Now there is an impasse": HSL to MM, Oct. 6, 1936, MANYPL.

239 "The film people" was a phrase that MM frequently used in referring to the Selznick company.

CHAPTER NINETEEN

240 "slanderous use": *Washington Post*, Sept. 29, 1936.

240 "Under Secretary Slattery threatened to sue": Ibid.

240–241 "I am so upset": *Letters*, RH; MM to Under Secretary Slattery, Oct. 3, 1936.

241 "Not all the financial rewards": Ibid. The *Washington Post* offered to print MM's letter to Under Secretary Slattery, but MM refused permission. On Oct. 17, 1936, an apology was published.

242 "tough criticism": MM to HSL, May 26, 1935.

244 "thieves and chiselers": MM to Edwin Granberry, Oct. 9, 1936.

245 "I never knew publishers": MM to GB, Oct. 9, 1936, MANYPL.

245 "this present business": *Letters*, RH; MM to Herschel Brickell, Oct. 9, 1936.

245 "Herschel, sometimes": Ibid.

247 Dr. Henry Link, *The Rediscovery of Man* (New York: Macmillan, Inc., 1938) pp. 23–24.

247 "No book need be that long": Joseph P. Lash, *Eleanor and Franklin* (New York: W. W. Norton & Co., Inc., 1971).

248 "Hollywood's historical inaccuracies": a phrase MM often used in criticizing films she had seen.

248 "Life has been awful": Harwell, *GWTW: The Screenplay*.

248–249 "I think the whole idea": *Letters*, RH; MM to Kay Brown, Nov. 18, 1936.

249 "When Miss Brown": *Letters*, RH; MM to Russell Birdwell, Nov. 24, 1936.

250 "If your story goes out": *Letters*, RH; MM to Russell Birdwell, Dec. 5, 1936.

250 "no intentions of doing anything": *Letters*, RH; MM to Sidney Howard, Nov. 21, 1936.

251 "as being in the path of Sherman's Cavalry": MM to Edwin Granberry, Nov. 28, 1937.

252 "John turns them down": *Letters*, RH; MM to LDC, March 5, 1937.

252 "Bessie answers": MM to Edwin Granberry, Nov. 28, 1936.

254–255 "embarrassing compromise" through "And if you can't get away": VM to MM, April 1937, MMMAUG.

CHAPTER TWENTY

258 "very hush-hush": PI.

259 "with the best intentions": *Letters*, RH; MM to Herschel Brickell, Jan. 7, 1937.

259 "not outgoing": PI.

260 "the word is too easily associated" through "here goes": JM to Edwin Granberry, Jan. 1937, MMMAUG.

261 "There is no secret" through "proud wives": Ibid, and reprinted in *Collier's*, March 17, 1937.

262 "the subject matter was self-promoting": Kenneth Littauer to Edwin Granberry, Feb. 13, 1937.

263 "If this is *true* I can't imagine": MM to LDC, Feb. 5, 1937, MANYPL.

263 "To tell the truth": *Letters*, RH; MM to LDC, March 5, 1937.

264 The Dutch piracy suit was eventually to become a landmark copyright case and did help to assure foreign copyright protection for U.S. authors abroad. George Brett traveled to the Netherlands as a witness in this case which, because of the war, lasted eight years. There is a vast correspondence, and all the depositions by MM and Macmillan employees are in the MANYPL.

264 "I feel pretty violently": *Letters*, RH; MM to Kay Brown, March 5, 1937.

264 "She looks prettier": JM to FMZ, March 24, 1937.

265–266 "those movies": MFPAUG.

266 "you could always locate": Ibid.

266 "I've even refused as much": *Letters*, RH; MM to Kay Brown, Feb. 14, 1937.

266 "out to the coast": Ibid.

266 "on the mercies": Ibid.

266 "please leave Tara ugly, sprawling and columnless": Ibid. The Selznick company did not do this.

267 "Honey Chile" story: PI.

268 "All over town": *Letters*, RH; MM to Herschel Brickell, May 9, 1937.

268 "Even a Pulitzer committee": Kenneth Littauer to Edwin Granberry, May 12, 1937.

268–269 "didn't dare intimate": *Letters*, RH; MM to Herschel Brickell, May 9, 1937.

269 "but didn't slop over": Ibid.

269 "slithering out of cracks in the floors" and "awfully dull": MM to Edwin Granberry, May 10, 1937.

269 "rang off the wall," "barrels of champagne," and "Kentucky Derby winner": Ibid. It was always said of MM that she never repeated a story. That may have been the case in conversation but, as she wrote so many letters in one day, often on the same subject, she frequently repeated the same phrases in numerous letters. Therefore, duplications of colorful descriptions appear quite frequently in her correspondence; ie, above phrases were used in letters to Edwin Granberry, GB, and LDC, all written on the same day, May 10, 1937.

CHAPTER TWENTY-ONE

272 "Reading them so close" through "I think it would": *Letters*, RH; MM to Herschel Brickell, April 14, 1938.

273 "a copyright on hoop skirts": MM to LDC, Sept. 9, 1938, MANYPL.

274 "Well, over the [drawing] boards": Wilbur Kurtz, AHSWKA.

274 "The revisions seem to be along the lines": *Letters*, RH; MM to Herschel Brickell, April 14, 1938.

275 "I was absolutely forbidden to use any word": F. Scott Fitzgerald to Maxwell Perkins, *Dear Scott/Dear Max: The Fitzgerald/Perkins Correspondence* (New York: Charles Scribner's Sons, 1973).

275 "ungentlemanly" and "not nice": Harwell, *GWTW: The Screenplay*.

277 On January 11, 1939, Sue Myrick wrote MM: "To your ears alone can I say the following. I have not written it to a soul and the studio is so secretive about it all I'm almost afraid to write it to y'all. But I have seen the girl who is to do Scarlett. . . . She is charming, very beautiful, black haired and magnolia petal skin and in the movie tests I have seen she moved me greatly. They did the paddock scene [Ashley chopping wood, GWTW, p. 518] for a test, and it is marvelous business the way she makes you cry when she is making Ashley. I understand she is not signed but as far as I can tell from George [Cukor] et al, she is the gal": Harwell, *GWTW: The Screenplay*.

278 "It is really and actually true": Sue Myrick to MM, Feb. 14, 1939.

278 "David, your fucking script": Flamini, *Scarlett, Rhett & a Cast of Thousands*.

279 "Groucho Marx, William Faulkner": MM to Wilbur Kurtz, April 9, 1939, Harwell, *GWTW: The Screenplay*.

279 "We have 60 pages": Sue Myrick to MM, March 12, 1939.

279 "God knows": Ibid.

279 "Sidney Howard is back on the script!": Sue Myrick to MM, April 9, 1939.

280 "I would not be surprised": MM to Sue Myrick, April 9, 1939. Harwell, *GWTW: The Screenplay*.

280 "They'd stone Christ": Flamini, *Scarlett, Rhett & a Cast of Thousands*.

280 "The street scenes are so fine": Sue Myrick to MM, June 2, 1939.

280 "I would like to keep": MM to VM, March 16, 1939, MMMAUG.

280 "ghoulish document": VM to MM, March 21, 1939.

280 "shocking attempt": Ibid.

281 "gigantic filmscript," through "ignored the mothball approach": *Photoplay*, May 1939.

281 MM's letter was printed in the July 1939 issue of *Photoplay*.

CHAPTER TWENTY-TWO

282 "steadily, harder, and higher": MM to LDC, Nov. 3, 1939, MANYPL.

283 "The whole of Atlanta": Ibid.

284 "I want you to be very careful": Howard Dietz, *Dancing in the Dark* (New York: Quadrangle, 1975).

284 "But you don't understand": Ibid.

286 "Above all": *Time*, Dec. 23, 1939.

288 "She is my Scarlett": MFPAUG.

288 "The sly, leather-lunged": *Time*, Dec. 23, 1939.

288 "The only big star": AJ, Dec. 16, 1939.

288 "It was an experience": Ibid.

289 "Oh, I do hope": MFPAUG.

290 "We did have a good Christmas, didn't we?": *Letters*, RH; MM to Herschel Brickell, Jan. 11, 1940.

290 "discussing every angle": MM to Clifford Dowdy, Jan. 1940, MMMAUG.

290 "Unqualifiedly marvelous" through "could have been": Ibid.

291 "It seems like a pleasant": *Letters*, RH; MM to Herschel Brickell, Jan. 11, 1940.

292 "The crowds on the street": MM to Mrs. Dorothy Hart, Jan. 5, 1939.

292 "Whatever else": JM to Clifford Dowdey, Jan. 9, 1939, MMMAUG.

CHAPTER TWENTY-THREE

293 "Have I written you": JM to Mary Toup Marsh, Aug. 1940.

294 "Trips are a pipe dream": MM to Edwin Granberry, Oct. 11, 1940.

294 Selznick did send Peggy an additional $50,000 in Dec. 1940, following the second premiere.

296 "that has no stuffiness": *Letters*, RH; MM to Ellen Glasgow, Nov. 11, 1940.

296 "I have a charming recollection": Ellen Glasgow to MM, *Letters of Ellen Glasgow* (New York: Harcourt Brace & Company, 1958).

297 "Of course I could have said": MM to LDC, Nov. 9, 1940, MANYPL.

298 "I think the war": *Letters*, RH; MM to Herschel Brickell, Nov. 11, 1940.

CHAPTER TWENTY-FOUR

299 "waking up in bed" through "My rustiness": MM to GB, July 1940, MANYPL.

300 "ever since the New Deal": FF, p. 206.

301 MM's letters to Herschel Brickell are the most revealing of this period, 1936–1939, and indicate her deep, warm regard for him. The few letters written to both of the Brickells have a different tone.

301 Frank Daniel revealed in the AJ that he was the young man who had once read Stephen Vincent Benet's *John Brown's Body* to MM. He also referred to the Marshes as "the mama and papa of GWTW." Daniel was the first to use the initials GWTW, in the AJ in May 1936.

302 Augusta Dearborn Edwards's copy of GWTW is in the Atlanta Historical Society's Augusta Dearborn Edwards Archives. The inscription reads: "To Augusta and Lee Edwards, old friends, this book: As the pledge of a nation that's passed away. Keep it, dear friends and save it. Show it to those who will lend an ear to the tale of this trifle will tell of Liberty born of patriots' dream of a storm-cradled nation that fell. Margaret." This verse appears in GWTW, p. 314 and is borrowed from an anonymous verse that was written on a piece of brown paper pasted on the back of a Confederate note. It was titled: "Lines on the Back of a Confederate Note."

302 "charming, funny self": PI.

303 "I am small" through "if you think": *Letters*, RH; MM to Lt. Commander E. John Long, Aug. 9, 1941.

304–306 "most probably doesn't know": publicity interview, Sept. 5, 1941. This interview was published in the *New York Times*, Sept. 6, 1941. The full transcript is in the MANYPL publicity file. The reporter's question about the second Dutch piracy suit illustrates the press's attitude toward suing a country at war.

306 "fight or stand cowards": GWTW, p. 5.

306 "varmints worth a damn": MM to Clifford Dowdey, Dec. 16, 1941, MMMAUG.

CHAPTER TWENTY-FIVE

308 "We had all the Atlanta Marines": Richard Harwell, AJ&C, March 17, 1974.

309 "I [want] you to know": MM to Leodel Coleman, reprinted AJ&C, March 17, 1974.

309 "normal and healthy sign": Ibid.

309 "must be having a return": Clifford Dowdey to MM, Feb. 21, 1943, MMMAUG.

310 "The gallantry, courage" through "several kinds of": *Letters*, RH; MM to Clifford Dowdey, May 13, 1943.

310 "improves my figure below": MM to Helen Dowdey, May 6, 1943, MMMAUG.

311 "I enjoyed that tacky party": RH, AJ&C, March 17, 1974.

311 "raised her stock": *Letters*, RH; MM to William Mauldin, May 14, 1945.

312 the Dowdeys' breakup: MMMAUG, Dowdey file.

314 "I hope the world is not too much": *Letters*, RH; MM to Betty Smith, June 9, 1945.
314 "trading with the" and "Has a policy or procedure": *Letters*, RH; MM to Dr. Charles A. Thomson, Oct. 14, 1944.
314 "GWTW was not sold in galley proof": *Letters*, RH; MM to Douglas Gilbert, Oct. 23, 1944.
315 "four closest boyfriends": AC, Sept. 23, 1945. (The identities of the four men were not revealed.)
316 "generally cheerful" and "glum": Margaret Baugh, MMMAUG, undated.
316 "I'm going to die": PI.

CHAPTER TWENTY-SIX

318 "Still no news from Poland": MM to LDC, Oct. 1945, MANYPL.
318 "He is always so fatigued": MM to Helen Dowdey, Dec. 11, 1945, MMMAUG.
319 "There is a faint hope": MM to LDC, Feb. 16, 1946, MANYPL.
319 "to stand the hospital" through "the patients wet": MM to Helen Dowdey, Feb. 17, 1946, MMMAUG.
320 "It seems wonderful to him": MM to Helen Dowdey, July 22, 1946, MMMAUG.
320 "to be frank" through "mad rush": MM to LDC, July 1946, MANYPL.
320 "the rights of every author": MM to GB, Aug. 14, 1946, MANYPL.
321 "bound to come down": MM to LDC, Dec. 15, 1946, MANYPL.
322 "As God is my witness": MM to Helen Dowdey, Aug. 14, 1946, MMMAUG.
323 "anxious to turn a penny" and "Even some of": MM to GB, Aug. 23, 1946, MANYPL.

CHAPTER TWENTY-SEVEN

329 "Are you all right?": Margaret Baugh, undated.
329 "The possibility": *Galveston Daily News*, Jan. 13, 1949.
330 "The theatre packed": *Letters*, RH; MM to Harold E. George, May 6, 1949.
331 "In Yugoslavia": *Letters*, RH; MM to Governor James M. Cox, July 28, 1949.
334 Hugh D. Gravitt, the taxi driver whose car hit MM, was convicted of involuntary manslaughter and sentenced to serve twelve to eighteen months. He was released after twelve months.
335 "It was something": AJMMM.
335 "I promised Peggy": Margaret Baugh, MMMAUG, undated.
340 Sales figures were supplied by Macmillan for 1980.

Index

ON LEAVING CHARLESTON

ALEXANDRA RIPLEY

Live this
magnificent
family saga
—from the
civilized,
ante-bellum South
through the wreckless,
razzle-dazzle Jazz Age

Southern heiress Garden Tradd sheds the traditions of her native Charleston to marry the rich, restless Yankee, Sky Harris. Deeply in love, the happy young couple crisscross the globe to hobnob with society in Paris, London, and New York. They live a fast-paced, fairy-tale existence, until the lovely Garden discovers that her innocence and wealth are no insulation against the magnitude of unexpected betrayal. In desperation the gentle woman seeks refuge in the city she had once abandoned, her own, her native land—Charleston.

$3.95   16610-1-17

Catch
SPRING
FEVER
with Dell

As advertised on TV

Dell

At your local bookstore or use this handy coupon for ordering:

DELL READERS SERVICE—DEPT. B1074A
P.O. BOX 1000, PINE BROOK, N.J. 07058

Please send me the above title(s). I am enclosing $_____ (please add 75c per copy to cover postage and handling). Send check or money order—no cash or CODs. Please allow 3-4 weeks for shipment.
CANADIAN ORDERS: please submit in U.S. dollars.

Ms./Mrs./Mr._____

Address_____

City/State_____ Zip _____